MW01232735

PORTRAIT OF A CHASSID

The Life and Legacy of Rabbi Zvi Hirsh Gansbourg

1928 – 2006

ISBN 1-886587-17-5
Printed in the United States

The GJCF preserves the legacies of institutions and individuals that have built and advanced Jewish life. For more info: E-mail mylegacy@gjcf.net.

This book has been graciously funded by the
Irving I. Stone Private Foundation.

Irving I. Stone

(1909-2000)

a noted philanthropist
transformed the landscape of Jewish life.
Growing up in a home where Torah
was precious and its study revered;
imbued with his parents' philosophy
that outstanding educators matter more
than bricks and mortar;
fired by the conviction that
Jewish education means Jewish survival –
he became one of the monumental
Torah pioneers and patrons of his time,
in his native Cleveland, in Israel,
and throughout America.

Irving Stone shares his own yahrtzeit, Yud Shvat,
with the Previous Lubavitcher Rebbe,
Rabbi Yosef Yitzchak Schneersohn.
Irving Stone is the father of
Hensha Gansbourg, the widow
of Rabbi Zvi Hirsh Gansbourg.

Dedicated

To the loving memory of
Rabbi Zvi Hirsh Gansbourg
Like a true Chassid of his Rebbe
R' Hirsh never left his post
Always remaining true to
his mission and purpose
Inspiring people wherever he went.

And to his beloved wife, Hensha
Who continues to be a true Chassid
Influencing everyone and everything
around her.
May she have many more
Healthy and happy days.

Table of Contents

Foreword

At the eruption of the Israel Independence War in 1948, Hirsh Gansbourg, a young man studying in New York, received a letter from his father back in Tel Aviv. His father's message was clear: "Come home and fight for your land and people, as are your two brothers. Is their blood any cheaper than yours?" Hirsh, the devout Chassid he was, wrote to the [Previous] Lubavitcher Rebbe, Rabbi Yosef Yitzchak Schneersohn, seeking his advice. The Rebbe replied, "In military terms, a deserter is not one who does not fight, but one who leaves his assigned post. Your post is here, stationed in the yeshiva." The War of Independence was fought on many fronts, both material and spiritual, equally crucial in victory. While some found their ammunition in arms and weaponry, others found it in the study of Torah.

What is a Chassid? A Chassid is a soldier who marches on the front lines, carrying out the commander-in-chief's orders without question or hesitation. A Chassid's life reflects the mission, vision and focus of his Rebbe.

"Ze sefer toldos adam" – every man's life is an entire book. Yet, some lives, due to historical circumstance and matters related, capture an entire era and reflect a broad stroke of the human story. Rabbi Hirsh Gansbourg was just such a man. Born in the throes of the rising Soviet menace to an illustrious family of Chabad Chassidim, his journey epitomizes the challenges, losses, joys and celebrations of life, unique to his generation.

As a genuine Chassid, a soldier in the fullest sense of the word, Hirsh loyally served his Rebbe. Despite personal challenges, he dedicated his heart and soul to the Rebbe's initiatives, always rising to the call of the hour. Rarely does one come across an individual whose thoughts, speech and actions mirror, and are so closely aligned with the goal and focus of his mentor. As such, Hirsh the soldier offers us a model of a Chassid – gentle, kind and committed; a beacon of light illuminating his family, friends and environment.

On the 23rd of Cheshvan 5766 – November 13, 2006, at the age of 78, R' Hirsh Gansbourg passed away. While reviewing his accumulated papers and documents, his family discovered his handwritten diaries, spanning the years 1945-1960, as well as letters from the Rebbe written to Hirsh's father and manuscripts of the Rebbe's edits on various publications he had prepared for print. Hirsh's elegant pen and beautiful prose on timeworn pages, revealed invaluable gems worthy of sharing. The timeless nature of these writings was immediately clear, not only for their sentimental value to family, but for the historic record. These diaries and documents capture, in intimate detail, the spice and spirit of a critical period in history: the formative years of post-war Chabad, as Jews replanted their roots and rebuilt their lives in Israel and the United States.

The diaries are a true Chassidic work of art, describing a Chassid's life revolving around his Rebbe. Their uniqueness lays in the fact, that in addition to depicting encounters, *farbrengens* and experiences in precise and fascinating detail, they also convey the electricity and the emotion – the delicate, between-the-lines nuances – which these events were charged with. They tell the story behind the story. Written with painstaking and defined detail, in a warm and personal tone, they capture a Chassidic student growing up in Israel and America, marrying, building a family, his involvement in community events, all imbued with the Rebbe's mission.

In light of the above, Hirsh's family felt compelled to publish this book in order to make its pearls of wisdom and precious insights available to the public.

~

The material in this book is comprised of: 1) R' Hirsh's Diaries; 2) Letters from the Previous Rebbe and the Rebbe to Rabbi

Dovber Gansbourg, Hirsh's father; 3) Facsimiles of the Rebbe's edits on various publications prepared by Hirsh for print; 4) Letters written to Hirsh by his friends; 5) Family pictures.

The documents presented here reveal fascinating details, **many never before publicized**, of the Rebbe's inner court and his Chassidim.

The original material was written primarily in Hebrew, with partial entries in Yiddish. For the benefit of the general public, we translated most of the material into English – expertly done by Rabbi and Mrs. Eliyahu Touger – and interspersed it with photos, facsimiles and supporting documents. The English section is followed by a section of the original writings in Hebrew.

A translation is always weaker than its original, even more acutely so when dealing with personal diaries in which the language and spirit are so unique. Upon translation, we attempted to keep our edits to the minimum while maintaining the authentic flavor of the original.

On his 22nd birthday the Rebbe blessed R' Hirsh (pg 84): "May a portion of the Rebbe's projects which he sought to accomplish be accomplished through you." R' Hirsh lived up to the Rebbe's promise and blessing. Like a true Chassid, he dedicated himself entirely to the Rebbe's projects. R' Hirsh never left his post – not in 1948 and not in 2006 – always remaining true to his mission and purpose, inspiring people wherever life took him. The aim of this book is to share a glimpse of the Chassidic world through the eyes and pen of one genuine Chassid and brave soldier – Zvi Hirsh Gansbourg.

It is our sincere hope and prayer that this collection of writings will inspire each individual reader to intensify his or her commitment to the study and dissemination of Chassidus and its Forebears.

Simon Jacobson

On A Personal Note

Our father, Rabbi Hirsh Gansbourg, had a beautiful voice. Gentle and soothing, it echoed from the depths of his soul. With great sensitivity it penetrated the hearts of the listeners. This was the voice that led the Chasidim in song as they stood before the Rebbe at the *farbrengen* gatherings where Chassidic melodies poured forth in between the Rebbe's talks. This was the voice that united and uplifted multitudes of guests at the Shabbos table, responded to questions, told stories, warmed and welcomed, and wove a tapestry of Jewish life for the newly acquainted with Judaism. And in indeed this was the voice that guided us, his very own children, and illuminated our lives' paths. For us it answered the unanswerable, removed the fear from the unknowable and disciplined with compassion, firmness and love. It was the voice of reason and truth and resonated securely with the wisdom of the ages.

Our father had many gifts; a fiery enthusiasm, a glorious sense of humor and sheer common sense. His keen intellect and love of Torah complemented an inherent curiosity and soldierly sense of mission that had him studying the holy texts every free moment and late into the night. His broad vision and ever expanding knowledge vitalized all he experienced, and colored all he undertook.

Our father was many things to many people – a husband, a father, a friend, a man who knew that action superseded words, that kindness was above philosophy. His hello was always genuine, his heartwarming smile, disarming., his concern for others, exquisite.

In essence our father was a Chassid, dedicated to his Rebbe with body and soul, personifying mind over matter, exuding compassion to fellow man and commitment to all things holy and good. His pen flowed, elegant and smooth, as he edited the Rebbe's talks for publication, wrote speeches, articles and personal diaries brimming with wisdom, memories and insight.

In the real drama of living what he believed, our father traveled to U.S. military bases, colleges and universities, prisons and outlying communities to share his passion for Judaism with others. Thus he spent the High Holy Days leading the prayers for Jewish prisoners for over thirty years, inspired countless students in their quest for meaning and ignited the Jewish spark in the hearts of families and individuals. In his own community he was from the earliest members of the Lubavitch Youth Organization and actively involved in the running of its affairs. With meticulous care for even the finest details he prepared and printed many Chassidic texts.

For decades he visited synagogues in surrounding neighborhoods, walking great distances on Shabbos to teach Torah with Chassidic dimension and to provide encouragement and inspiration wherever it was needed.

Our father's legacy is the legacy of his parents, his ancestors and the Jewish people. It is the legacy we wish to entrust to our children and the one which they, with G-d's help, will entrust to theirs. Certainly it is the legacy that will bring Moshiach.

May it be G-d's will that our father's endeavors live on with ever increasing vigor, in the lives of family, friends and fellow Chassidim everywhere. May we finally merit the realization of the lingering promise "*V'hakitzu v'ranenu shochnei afar...*" Arise and rejoice, those who dwell in the dust, speedily in our days.

Acknowledgements:

Thank you to the following individuals who have invested much time and effort in preparing this book:

Shlomo Boneh
Batsheva Buchman
Shaya Gansbourg
Yosef Yitzchak Kratz
Mendel Jacobson
Shaindy Jacobson
Yosef Y. Jacobson
Chaim Meir & Sara Lieberman
Rashi Marcus
Dovid Olidort
Avrohom Rainitz
Rabbi & Mrs. Eliyahu Touger

This book is being distributed in honor of the wedding of Rabbi Hirsh's grandchildren, Rashi and Benzion Marcus, 4 Adar I 5768, February 10, 2008

biography...

Rabbi Zvi Hirsh Gansbourg

A Biographical Sketch
1928-2006

Following the downfall of Russia's last czar, Nicholas II, and the end of World War I, the face of Russia – and the world – underwent drastic change. The Revolution of 1917 and the ensuing tumultuous years of war left Russia and Eastern Europe in turmoil. The USSR, or the Soviet Union as it came to be known, was established in 1922 and would last until its collapse in 1991.

Along with the shifts in Russia's political and social scene, the face of Russian Jewry began to change dramatically as well. While Jewish life under the czars was in no way easy, under the Soviet regime it became downright unbearable, threatening Russian Jewry to its very core.

With prophetic vision, the Chabad-Lubavitch leader at the time, Rabbi Yosef Yitzchak Schneersohn, the Frierdiker (previous) Rebbe, created an underground educational and social network to ensure the survival of Jewish life in the Soviet Union. Thousands lost their lives so that Yiddishkeit could survive. Yet, the Chassidim stood strong – despite the constant cloud of Stalinist fear and death that hung over them.

In Moscow, just a few blocks from the Kremlin, the headquarters of all things Soviet, Rabbi Moshe Dovber Gansbourg and his young wife, Doba, lived with their two sons, Leibel and Itchke. With little regard to their personal safety, their home was always open, a bastion for every Jew that entered. Religious, secular, Chassidim, Misnagdim – it made no difference; all were welcome with open arms and warm food.

In 1928, three days before the Jewish New Year, Doba gave birth to her third son, Zvi Hirsh. Despite the danger of arrest and execution, Hirsh and his two older brothers grew up in a profoundly devout and Chassidic home, infused with Torah and Mitzvos, and dedicated to helping others in every way possible.

After unceasingly visiting the Kremlin day after day, Doba miraculously received permission for herself and her family to leave the Soviet Union. In 1937, at the age of nine, Hirsh, his parents and two brothers moved to the holy Land of Israel, then called Palestine.

The family lived in Tel Aviv, where R' Moshe Dovber was one of the founders of the Chabad Yeshiva in Tel Aviv and was involved as well in other public institutions. R' Moshe Dovber also owned a bookstore at 25 Montefiore Street, where Hirsh cultivated his love for the written word.

In 1947, after ten years of living and studying in Tel Aviv, Hirsh traveled to New York, USA, to be near the Frierdiker Rebbe (who had settled in New York in March 1940), and to study in the central Chabad Yeshiva, Tomchei Temimim.

While in yeshiva, Hirsh began to work for the Frierdiker Rebbe's son-in-law, Rabbi Menachem Mendel Schneerson (known then as the Ramash), who headed the Chabad publishing arm. Hirsh worked at the Balshon Printing Co. where he helped the Ramash produce the Frierdiker Rebbe's publications – Sichos, Maamorim and Kuntresim. His passion for publishing and disseminating Chassidic texts and teachings would become a lifelong endeavor.

On Yud Shevat, 1950, the Frierdiker Rebbe passed away and exactly one year later, his son-in-law, Rabbi Menachem Mendel Schneerson, the Rebbe, became the seventh leader of Chabad-Lubavitch. Hirsh continued working closely with the Rebbe assisting him in preparing the various publications for print.

In 1952 Hirsh married Rasha Denburg in Montreal, Canada. Six years later, with the arrival of a daughter and a son (Sarah and Shaya), the young family moved to Brooklyn, New York, where they were blessed with three more children (Rychel, Berel and Shaindy).

Hirsh resumed working in the printing houses of Balshon and Shulsinger Brothers, and years later, along with R' Mottel Chein, he founded his own printing business – Empire Press. He became involved in many of Chabad's communal affairs and educational systems, particularly The Associated Beth Rivka School for Girls. He was one of the founding members of Tzeirei Agudas Chabad (Tzach), the Lubavitch Youth Organization in New York, and would remain dedicated to its growth for the rest of his life.

In the late 1950's, Hirsh, whose father was a violinist in the Russian army during WWI, began leading the Niggunim (Chassidic songs) at the Rebbes's *farbrengens* (gatherings). He was also a founding member of NiCHoaCH, the organization for preserving and recording Chabad Niggunim. To this day, many of the NiCHoaCH recordings feature Hirsh's soulful voice.

On the 19th of Nissan, Chol Hamoed Pesach 1960, Hirsh's father, R' Moshe Dovber, passed away in the holy Land of Israel. He was buried in Tzfas, next to the Rebbe's brother, HaRav HaChossid, R' Yisrael Aryeh Leib Schneerson. Four years later, Hirsh's mother, Doba, passed away on the 3rd of Shevat, 1964.

Directly prior to the Six-Day War, the Rebbe initiated the well known Tefillin campaign, declaring the power this mitzvah holds in fortifying the Holy Land. Hirsh took this to heart and, for the rest of his life he would encourage a myriad of Jews to don Tefillin.

Following the Chassidic teachings that were imbued in him as a child in Soviet Russia, that a Jew is always obligated to help his fellow no matter how dire the circumstance, Hirsh would visit Jewish Army and Air Force personnel, to share and bring them the joy of the Holidays. For over thirty years, on the holiest days of the year, Hirsh would forgo his personal needs, would leave his wife and children, his Rebbe and community, to spend Yom Kippur, Purim, Chanukah in various prisons, bringing a ray of light to the Jewish prisoners.

On the second day of Sukkos, 1969, the Gansbourg family was dealt the unthinkable: at the age of 37, Rasha, Hirsh's wife, was returned to her Creator, leaving him to raise his five young children.

On Lag B'Omer, 1975, Hirsh married Hensha Stone of Cleveland, Ohio. Just like his parents' home in Moscow, Hirsh and Hensha's home at 1295 President Street, in Crown Heights, Brooklyn, directly across from the home of the Rebbe and Rebbetzin, was always open, and thousands of guests, from all different backgrounds and walks of life, walked through their doors. For many, this marked the beginning of a new stage in their spiritual journey.

One such guest, Lis Harris, a writer for New Yorker magazine, spent five years in the Gansbourg home, and her classic book, *Holy Days*, is based on her experiences there.

In 1984, Hirsh, along with his wife Hensha, returned to Soviet Russia for the first time since his childhood, on a mission for Ezras Achim, a Jewish organization dedicated to helping Jews behind the Iron Curtain.

In the summer of 2000, Hirsh and Hensha moved to Boca Raton, Florida, where they became prominent members of the Jewish community and were deeply involved in the Chabad outreach and educational activities.

On the 23rd of Cheshvan 2006, at the age of 78 years old, Hirsh passed away. Through his family, friends and good deeds, Rabbi Zvi Hirsh Gansbourg lives on.

Gansbourg-Denburg Family Ancestry[1]

Rasha Denburg-Gansbourg

Rasha Gansbourg was the daughter of R' Yeshayahu and Mrs. Henya Chyena Denburg. R' Yeshayahu had studied in Lubavitch and was a remarkable scholar. He knew the entire Talmud by heart. For some time, he worked as a farmer and while tilling the land, he would recite passages of the Talmud by heart.

R' Yeshayahu was the son of R' Yehudah Leib and Sarah Denburg. R' Yehudah Leib owned a farm in the town of Schedrin in the province of Minsk in White Russia. Schedrin was founded by the Tzemach Tzedek in 5604 (1844). He purchased a tract of land from the gentile count Schedrinov and settled many Jewish families on it to work the land. Later, the village hosted a division of Yeshivas Tomchei Temimim.

As mentioned, R' Yehudah Leib was a farmer. From time to time, he would sell the produce of his farm in the larger cities. At that time, there were no cars in Russia and R' Yehudah Leib would bring his produce to the cities via horse and wagon. On the way, he would review the Medrash Rabba which he knew by heart.

The Denburg family originated in the town of Dinaburg in Latvia from which they moved to Schedrin. In Schedrin, there lived the Gaon, R' Leibel Batlan who was one of the famous chassidim of the Tzemach Tzedek.

Dinaburg was later referred to as Dvinsk. The Rav of the chassidic community there was the famous Gaon, R' Yosef Rosen, renowned as the Rogatchover Gaon. In his childhood, he received a blessing from the Tzemach Tzedek.

[1] Written by Hirsh for a school project of his oldest granddaughter, Rashi Minkowitz.

The Denburg family were – and are at present – generous supporters of the Lubavitcher yeshiva in Montreal and in New York.

R' Nachum Dov Denburg was R' Yehudah Leib's brother. He was a chassid of the Rebbe Rayatz. In his merit, his children printed the holy text entitled Yahel Or that includes Tehillim Ohel Yosef Yitzchak together with maamorim from the Tzemach Tzedek. Several letters from the Rebbe Rayatz to R' Nachum Dov are printed in all texts bearing the name Tehillim Ohel Yosef Yitzchak.

Sarah Denburg came from the Okun family from Schedrin and from which too stemmed many scholars and chassidim. (Among them is the Gaon, R' Yisrael Zuber whom the Rebbe Rashab sent to Stockholm, Sweden, and who later became the head of the Lubavitcher Yeshiva in Boston.)

Henya Denburg was the daughter of R' Yitzchak and Shaina Chaya Nemenov from Bobroisk. R' Yitzchak was extremely G-dfearing. He was a merchant, esteemed by everyone. In the last years of his life, he was arrested by the Communists. He contracted an illness in prison and passed away shortly thereafter. He is buried next to the Tzemach Tzedek's grandson, the Rebbe, R' Shmaryahu Nachum of Bobroisk. Henya Denburg's brother was the esteemed *mashpia*, R' Nissan Nemenov whom the Rebbe Rayatz charged with guiding the chassidim after the Rebbe left Russia in 5687 (1927). Later, he became the head of the Lubavitcher Yeshiva in France.

R' Nissan was arrested many times in Russia and was forced to bear much suffering, but he never lost his trust in G-d. He would continually recite Tehillim and Tanya by heart.

During WWII, when Hitler's army conquered Schedrin, they murdered all the Jews in the village. The Denburg family, however, had left the village beforehand. Fleeing from the Germans, they continued looking for a sanctuary until they settled in Central Asia. There, in Tashkent, Uzbekistan, R' Yeshayahu passed away in 5703 (1943).

After the war, Henya, her daughter Rasha and son Yehudah Leib, left Russia together with many chassidim when permission was granted for Polish Jews, who had fled to Russia during the war, to leave that country. They proceeded to a displaced person's camp near the city of Poking in Germany.

The Rebbe's mother, Rebbetzin Chana was in the same camp. Both Henya and Yehudah Leib helped her in many ways and she remained a close friend of the family. Later, when she settled in New York, she would give sweets to the Gansbourg children.

With the help of relatives in the U.S. and Canada, Henya and her daughter Rasha, and later, her son, Yehudah Leib were able to settle in Montreal, Canada.

Zvi Hirsh Gansbourg

R' Zvi Hirsh Gansbourg was the son of R' Moshe Dovber and Doba Gansbourg. Doba Gansbourg was the daughter of R' Yehudah Leib Dotlibov and Nechamah Dotlibov. R' Yehudah Leib was a Rav in the village of Verchnedneiporovsk in the Ukraine. Their children studied in Lubavitch and many of them were martyred in sanctification of G-d's name.

Nechamah Dotlibov came from the Shapiro family in Slavita who were descendants of the *tzadik*, R' Pinchas of Koritz.

Rav Pinchas' sons, R' Shmuel Aba and R' Moshe were the esteemed printers of the renowned Slavita edition of the Talmud. Because they were framed in a blood libel, they were sentenced to pass through two rows of Cossacks who rained heavy blows upon them with their bludgeons. The *yarmulka* from one of the brothers fell off. Rather than proceed bare-headed, he went back to pick it up, even though by doing so, he subjected himself to further blows.

After WWI, there were terrible pogroms against the Jews in the Ukraine and White Russia. There were several marauding groups led by Petliura, Denikin, and others who murdered Jews and pillaged their homes throughout that region.

These marauders came to the village were R' Yehudah Leib and Nechamah lived. When they entered their home, one of the Cossacks raised his rifle to shoot R' Yehudah Leib. His daughter Doba, however, jumped in front of him, shouting "shoot me instead." This show of bravery embarrassed the Cossack and caused him to retreat.

Doba's fine character traits and self-sacrifice defy description. She lived in Moscow, not far from the Kremlin, the seat of Communist power. Even there, she was renowned for her hospitality. She was able to raise chassidic children while Russia was under Communist rule. Moreover, their home offered food and shelter for many Jews who passed through the city. Their home was open to everyone, chassidim and misnagdim, religious and non-religious, despite the danger this involved.

R' Simcha Gansbourg was the father of R' Moshe Dovber Gansbourg. He was a student of the *mashpia*, R' Moshe Dovber Lechvitzer, who was a student of R' Yisrael Ber Vellizer, one of the renowned students of the Tzemach Tzedek and the Mitteler Rebbe. R' Simcha had unique abilities, as reflected in the fact that he was granted Semichah on all four components of the Shulchan Aruch at age 18.

His father, R' Mordechai Yitzchak was the son of R' Menachem Gansbourg, who in turn was the son of R' Shneur Zalman Gansbourg whose father was one of the Alter Rebbe's chassidim. He descended from one of the hidden *tzadikim* who were disciples of the Baal Shemtov. The family traces its lineage to Shimon Ginsburg who is mentioned in Seder Hadoros.

In his youth, R' Simcha Gansbourg worked as a smith, but afterwards, he became a Rabbi in the town of Verchnednieprovsk (where R' Yehudah Leib Dotlibov lived and whose daughter his son would later marry). In addition to his great knowledge in Nigleh and Chassidic thought, he was an energetic, vibrant chassid in the full sense of the term. Several times, Rebbitzen Chana mentioned him in a positive light. During WWII, he and the entire community were martyred in sanctification of G-d's name by the Germans.

R' Moshe Dovber Gansbourg had a brother, R' Menachem, who was six years older than him. He studied in Lubavitch during the first years of the yeshiva's establishment. At times, when the Rebbe Rashab would go for long walks, he would take R' Menachem with him. R' Menachem was a student of R' Levi Yitzchak Schneerson, the Rebbe's father, the Rav of the city of Dnieprapetrovsk. In 5699 (1939), when the Soviet authorities arrested the Rebbe's father, Rebbetzin Chana, the Rebbe's mother, had no means of support. Despite the danger, R' Menachem would see to it that she was given whatever help possible. The Rebbetzin mentions him in her diary, Eim HaMelech.

R' Moshe Dovber Gansbourg studied in Lubavitch from 5670 (1900) to 5603 (1903) when he was drafted into the Czarist army. He served in the army for many years. In WWI, he was captured by the Germans. When he was released, he returned home and organized the Jewish self defense program that protected Jews against the pogroms that ravaged the Ukraine after WWI. In 5638 (1937), R' Moshe Dovber and his wife Doba made *aliyah* to Eretz Yisrael. He was the primary founder of the Lubavitcher yeshiva in Tel Aviv. He also helped found the Reshet Oholei Yosef Yitzchak organization of primary schools.

He passed away 19 Nissan, 5720 (1960) and is buried in Tsfas, near the grave of the Rebbe's brother, R' Yisrael Aryeh Leib.

Hirsh's parents, R' Moshe Dovber and Doba

Gansbourg children left to right: Leibel, Hirsh, Basya (cousin), Itchke

Hirsh and his middle brother, Itchke

Hirsh's maternal grandmother Nechama Dotlibov

Hirsh's father Moshe Dovber during his service in the Russian army

Hirsh's parents, R' Moshe Dovber and Doba

Hirsh's oldest brother, Leibel

Hirsh's brother, Itchke

Hirsh's passport picture

Hirsh as a young man

Left to right: Sholom Chaskind, Mottel Dubinsky and Hirsh Gansbourg

Left to right: top: Leibel Zisman, Berel Alenick, Mottel Dubinsky, Shlomo Baum; middle: Leibel Posner, S. B. Goldshmidt, Hirsh; bottom: Ezriel Chaikin

R' Zvi Hirsh reading the Megillah at Fort Sill, an army base in Oklahoma.
Purim 1967

Hirsh presiding over a Tzach event

Purim 1967: *Mivtzoim* at Fort Sill, an army base in Oklahoma. Left to right: R' Yankel Getz, Hirsh and R' Itche Meir Kagan

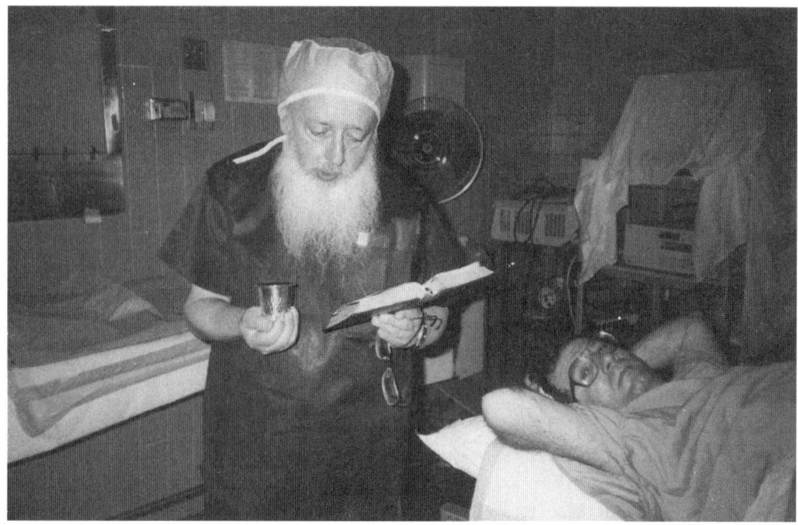

Hirsh as *Sandek* at the *bris* of a Russian immigrant

Rasha Gansbourg and her mother Henya Denburg

The Gansbourg family in 1970. Clockwise,
Sarah (in yellow), Shaindy, Rychel, Berel, Shaya
and Hirsh in the center

Hirsh donning Tefillin with a young Jewish man

The burial place of Hirsh's father, R' Moshe Dovber, in the old cemetery in Tzfas, Israel

Hirsh and Hensha at the wedding of their first grandchild

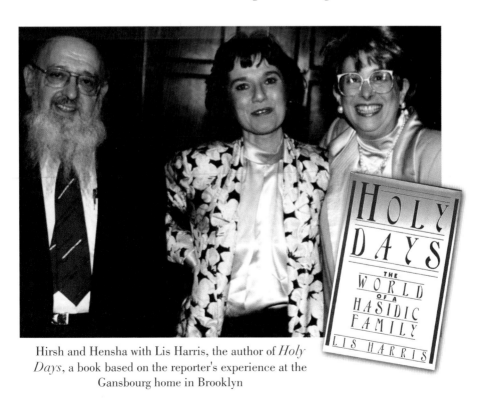

Hirsh and Hensha with Lis Harris, the author of *Holy Days*, a book based on the reporter's experience at the Gansbourg home in Brooklyn

Hirsh in front of the Hermitage Museum in Petersburg, Russia

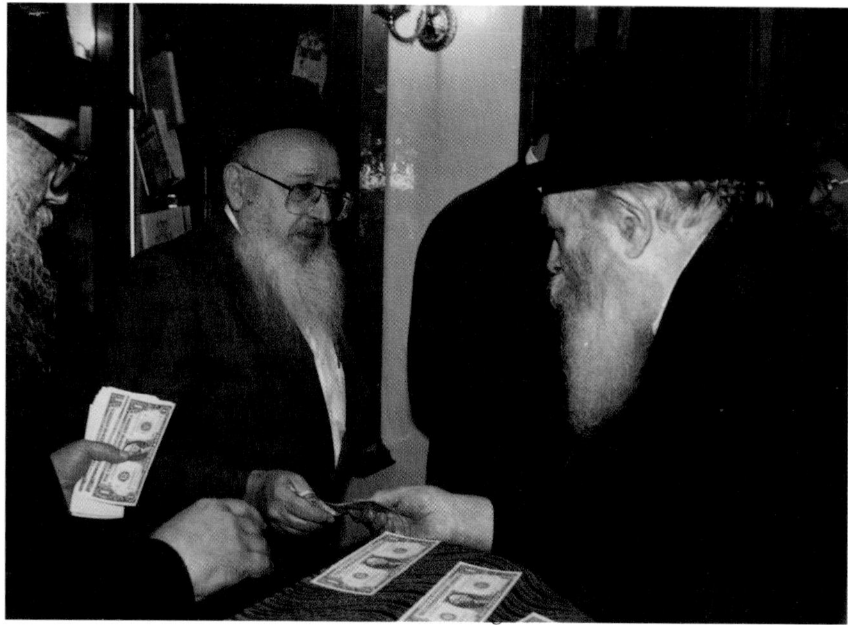

Hirsh receiving a dollar from the Lubavitcher Rebbe

ס"ד. שיחת ש"פ וארא, מבה"ח שבט ה'תשמ"א.

. מ'האט גערעדט אין דער התוועדות פון כ"ד טבת, אז די ששת ימי ה
ו כ"ד טבת, אזוי ווי די ששת ימים דכל שבוע ושבוע. זיינען עולה אי
לאח"ז, ביז אז זיי קומען דעמולט צו צו א מעלה ודרגא פון שלימות.

בידוע אז ביום השבת איז דער "ויכולו" פון די ששת ימי השבוע
וואס אין "ויכולו" זיינען דא פאראן צוויי הפכיות'דיקע פירושים: "ו
לשון כליון, אז די ששת ימים ווערן דעמולט אויס מציאות. און "ויכו
ענוג, וואס דאס איז שלימות און תכלית המציאות, אז די ששה ימים שט
עמודט בתכלית המציאות ושלימות,

און ווי מ'זעט עס בפשטות ביי א מענטשן א אידן וואס "אתם קרוי
אדם ע"ש אדמה לעליון (4) - אז בשעת ער שטייט בתענוג. שטי (3),
תכלית המציאות שלו, ווארום תענוג איז תכלית ההתרחבות והתפשטות.

וואס די צוויי ענינים אין ("ויכולו" וואס איז דא אין) שבת,
אין פשטות הענינים,

וואס דאס איז גאר דער עיקר פון אלץ, ווארום א המעשה הוא העי
וואס דאס איז אויך כולל אין עולם העשי' איז דער עיקר, און אין עולם
גופא איז דער "עקב", סיי דער "עקב" אין זמן, עקבתא דמשיחא, סיי
אין עבודת האדם נפש, אין עבודת האדם. דער ענין המעשה,
סיי דער "עקב" אין מקום, אין עולם - דער העיקר".

ובידוע דער המשל (6), אז בשעת מ'איז מגביה א בנין מתחתיתו
הויבט מען אויף דעם גאנצן בנין, משא"כ בשעת מ'איז מגביה דעם בנין
ווערט ניט אויפגעהויבן דעם גאנצן בנין. עס ווערט נאר אויפגעהויבן
פון וואנעט מ'האט עס אנגעכאפט און העכער, אבער דער חלק נידעריק
דערפון בלייבט במקומו.

און דאס (וואס דער חלק התחתון איז ניט אויפגעהויבן געווארן)
נאר נוגע צו שלימות פון דעם חלק התחתון (אז
במקומו, ניט אויפגעהויבן געווארן) - נאר ווייבאלד אז דאס איז איך
איז בשעת איין חלק פון אים ווערט ניט אויפגעהויבן, איז דאס נוגע א

Much work went into preparing the Rebbe's talks for print. The edits on this draft, from a 5741 talk, were made by Hirsh's pen.

Marina Roscha Shul in Moscow, Russia, where Hirsh's family prayed

The corner of the Marina Roscha Shul where Hirsh's father, R' Moshe Dovber, prayed

The Moscow apartment where Hirsh grew up

Hirsh at the entrance to the Marina Roscha Shul

Hirsh and his older son, Shaya

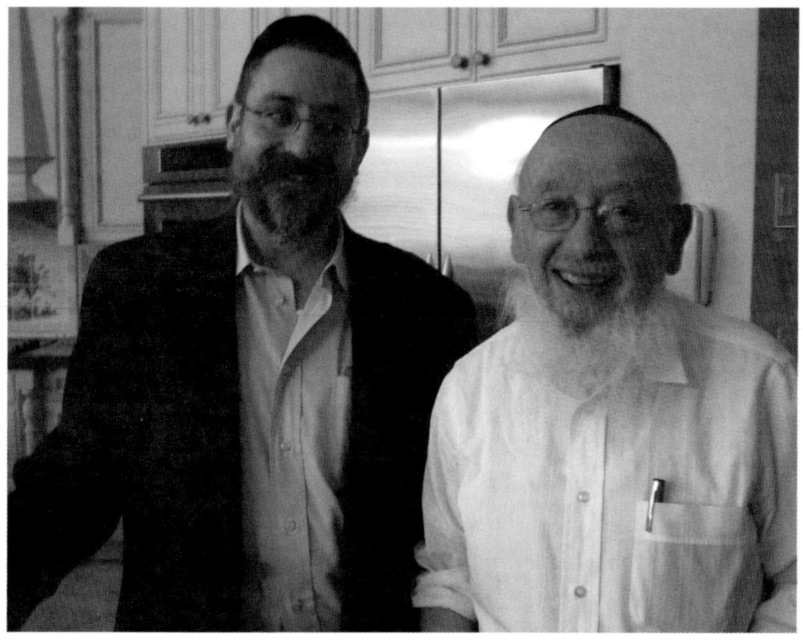

Hirsh and his younger son, Berel

Hirsh at his home in Boca Raton, Florida

from the diaries...

Diaries

Part 1
5705, 5707 (1945, 1947)
Tel Aviv

Part 2
5711, 5712 (1950, 1952)
New York

Part 3
5718 (1957-58)
New York

Part 4
5720 (1960)
New York

Part 1 – Israel 5705, 5707

19 Kislev, 5705

At the *farbrengen* last Saturday night held at the home of R' Rafael Nachman Kahn, R' Michoel Dworkin was also present. R' Michoel described this *farbrengen* with an analogy: Just as a girl and her friends hold a celebration on the Saturday night before her wedding, so too, on the Saturday night before Yud-Tes Kislev, a *farbrengen* should be held.

R' Rafael Kahn related that when he was traveling by train to Jerusalem, he met a Jew from Vienna, R' Nosson Shimon, who lived close to R' Baruch Paris. He told him that when he was in Vienna, he met many Rebbeim, including the Rebbe. He related one particular occurrence that he witnessed. Among the Jews living in Vienna was R' Yisrael Mordechai Teitlebaum, the gabbai of the Rebbe, R' Moshe Dovid of Tchortkov, the son of the holy Rebbe, R' Yisrael of Ruzhin. When the Rebbe [Rayatz] was staying at the Pukersdorf sanatorium near Vienna, R' Nosson Shimon told R' Yisrael Mordechai that the Lubavitcher Rebbe was nearby. R' Yisrael Mordechai was older and it was difficult for him to travel alone. He therefore suggested that R' Nosson Shimon accompany him. R' Nosson Shimon happily agreed.

R' Yisrael Mordechai spent an hour and a half with the Rebbe. R' Nosson Shimon heard the stories related below and then

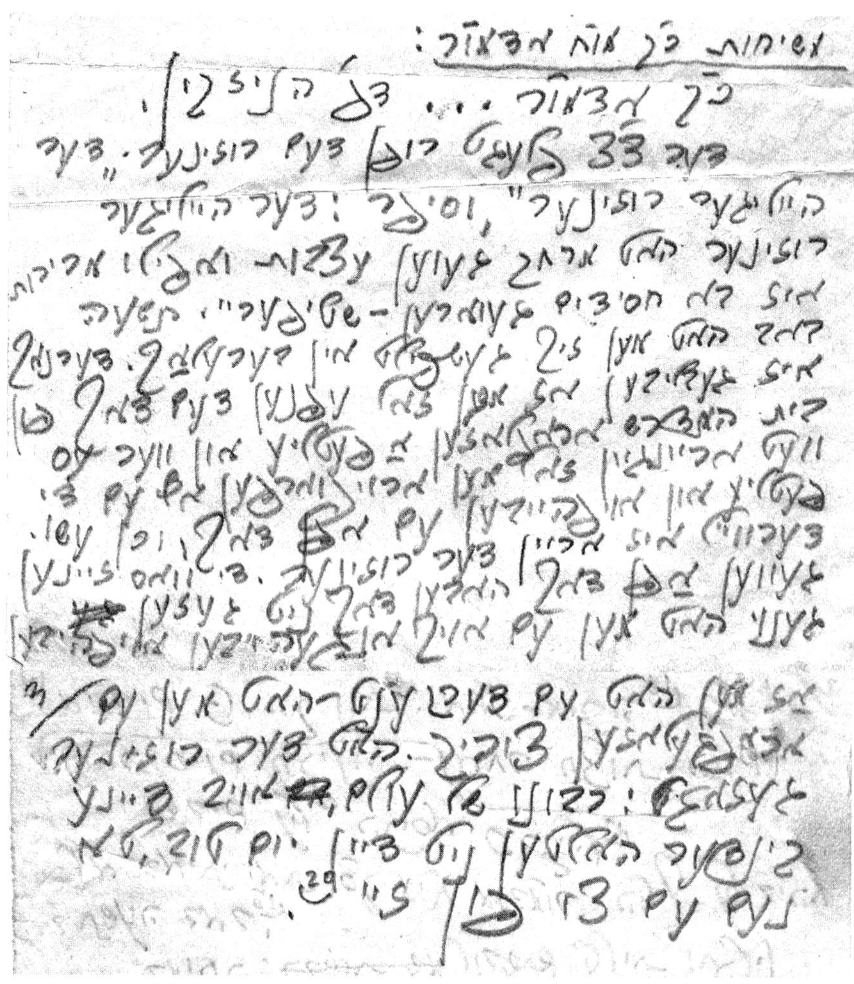

Rebbe's manuscript about "the Holy Ruzhiner" (from the Minhogim (customs) of Tisha b'Av)

was asked to leave the room. The stories he did hear, however, remained imprinted on his memory.

R' Yisrael Mordechai told a story about the Alter Rebbe which he had apparently heard from the Tchortkover Rebbe: During the prayer services, each of the disciples of the Maggid of Mezritch had a place, with a lectern, near the eastern wall of the Shul, except for the Alter Rebbe. He did not stand near the eastern wall, nor did he have a lectern.

On Rosh Hashanah, the Maggid and all the other students had already finished their prayers, but the Alter Rebbe was still engrossed in his. The other disciples looked askance at the Alter Rebbe's prolonged supplications, but the Maggid told them: "Don't bother my Zalman. When he says: 'And everything that You have wrought will know that You wrought it,' he does not move from his place until the ground itself comes to the awareness that G-d brought it into being."

In the course of their conversation, the Rebbe told R' Yisrael Mordechai: "I had a teacher, R' Shmuel Betzalel, whom we call Rashbatz, who studied under the Tzemach Tzedek. Once when the Tzemach Tzedek was standing with his sons, Rashbatz was nearby and heard the Tzemach Tzedek say: "I must rend my garments, for at this moment, the holy Ruzhiner Rebbe passed away."

The Seventh Day of Pesach, 5705

Today, we held a *farbrengen* at the home of R' Chaim Yosef Rosenbloom. The chassid, R' Michoel Dworkin was present. Afterwards, R' Pinchas Althaus, R' Moshe Gurary, and several others arrived. R' Michoel Dworkin began singing a melody known as Zavil, the chazan's *niggun*. R' Pinchas Althaus explained that Zavil, the *chazzan*, was from Nikolaev and would sing this *niggun* in the presence of the Rebbe Rashab.

Before R' Pinchas Althaus came, R' Michoel Dworkin related the following stories:

a) "On the Seventh Day of Pesach, 5676, the first year the Rebbe [Rashab] was living in Rostov, the Rebbe [Rashab] sat and delivered a *maamar*. The Rebbe [Rayatz] stood opposite him. I stood to his right. Behind him, at the end of the hall was the door through which people entered and there was a table there.

"The *maamar* was wondrous. Even the souls of the tzadikim[1] came to hear the *maamar*. Now the souls of the *tzadikim* always come to hear a *maamar*, but this time, I actually saw them.

"The *maamar* was very deep; it focused on the concept of the 'non-existential' nature of G-d's Being, totally different than any other existence. As I was standing, I thought I fell asleep and I saw the Rebbe of Kapust, dressed in his Shabbos clothes and shtreimel, descend onto the table at the end of the hall. I was shocked. I awoke and continued listening to the *maamar*.

"On the following day, in the morning, I went to have a hot drink with the Rebbe [Rayatz], because he told me to take meals at his home. I shared with him all of the above. Afterwards, when the Rebbe [Rashab] was partaking of the meal – I sat at the end of the table – the Rebbe [Rayatz] told him what I had related. The Rebbe [Rashab] turned to me and asked: 'When did he pass away? Wasn't it before Shavuos?'

"I answered him: '*Malchus ShebiYesod*.'[2]

"He responded: 'Nu, that's before Shavuos.'"

[1] I.e., the souls of the righteous from the Afterworld.

[2] According to the Kabbalah, there are seven emotional qualities. Now each interacts with each other, resulting in combinations. Seven times seven equals 49, the number of days counted while Counting the Omer. Thus every one of those days is identified with one of these compounded emotional qualities. Malchus ShebiYesod thus represents the day which is eight days before the conclusion of the counting and hence it is close to the holiday of Shavuos.

b) "Once I brought two chairs as a present to the Rebbe [Rashab] before Pesach. They were luxurious seats like those used by the gentry. I brought them to the room outside the Rebbe's private chamber. I thought I would tell the attendant and he would arrange them. When I opened the door, I saw the Rebbe sitting with his Rebbetzin, eating breakfast (rolls with milk). The Rebbe was obviously pleased with the gift and blessed me that I become a graf (a term used to describe nobility in Germany and Eastern Europe). He then explained that גרף (*gr'f*) is an acronym for the Yiddish words גיזונט (*gezunt*, health), רייך (*reich*, rich), and פרום (*frum*, observant)."

R' Michoel Dworkin continued: "Thank G-d, I am healthy and I am rich. And with regard to being frum, there, no upper limit exists."

R' Moshe Gurary related: "When I went to the Belzer Rebbe to deliver a copy of the Rebbe's annual letter, he said that although most people think that the second version of the first four sections of the Alter Rebbe's Shulchan Aruch is a later revision, that is a misconception. Instead, when the Maggid instructed him to compose a Shulchan Aruch, the Alter Rebbe wrote these sections and showed them to the Maggid. The Maggid commented: 'It's good, it's fine, it's choice, but it's not for the world at large.'"

B"H, Monday, Parshas Vaeira, 21 Teves, 5707. Tel Aviv, 4 PM (My father's Judaica store, 25 Montefiore Street)

In my last letter to the Rebbe[3], I asked for permission to go to the Rebbe and for his advice how that goal could be achieved.[4] Mordechai Dubinsky and my brother Yitzchak sent similar letters together with mine on Sunday, 23 Cheshvan of this year.

[3] The Rebbe Rayatz.

[4] At that time, receiving a visa to the U.S. was a detailed and involved process.

We all received the Rebbe's consent on 15 Kislev with the advice to speak to the directorate of the yeshiva regarding the necessary papers. The Rebbe also gave each of us a blessing to "succeed in the study of Nigleh and Chassidus, to be a Chassid, G-d-fearing, and a scholar." Another student, Sholom Ber Goldshmidt, sent his request by telegram on 2 Kislev and received a similar answer. All of the answers were signed by the secretary, R' Chaim Lieberman.

On Saturday night, the eve of 29 Kislev, we drew up a request to the directorate of the yeshiva in Brooklyn to act on our behalf and to send us the necessary papers as soon as possible. We sent this request with R' Meir Ashkenazi, the Rav of Shanghai, who left Eretz Yisrael to America by plane via Cairo. On that same day, Rebbetzin Goldshmidt, the daughter of the Chassid, R' Yechiel Zvi Gurary, and the wife of the *mashpia* (chassidic mentor), R' Nachum Goldshmidt, also set out for America.

The American Consulate requires from each of us: a passport, a birth certificate (this we were able to obtain in Jerusalem), a certificate of upright character from the police, medical records of our health, an affidavit and a bank guarantee from America. The pictures for the visa must be on a white background.

On Monday, the first day of Rosh Chodesh Shvat, we made our request for citizenship papers to the local authorities on 138 Allenby Street in Tel Aviv. We filed our request for a certificate of upright character on Monday, 3 Shvat, at the police station in the Machaneh Yehuda market in Jerusalem.

On Sunday, 6 Shvat, we again wrote to the yeshiva in Brooklyn, sending this request by airmail.

We have received information that both Rav Ashkenazi and Mrs. Gurary reached the U.S., but we have not received detailed letters from there as of yet.

R' Shmaryahu, the son of R' Nosson Gurary, arrived in Haifa on Friday of the week of Parshas Shmos, returning from a visit to the Rebbe. R' Shmaryahu brought a letter from the Rebbe for the Chassid R' Michoel Dworkin, saying that the Rebbe wishes to see him and that he should come to America in the summer.

For a long time, over a year, R' Michoel Dworkin has wanted to go to the Rebbe, and he has received almost all the necessary papers from the American Consulate.

Unfortunately, however, he contracted pneumonia and another illness that weakened him tremendously. Nevertheless, when he recovered from his sickness, he asked the Rebbe whether to come, but the Rebbe replied that it was unnecessary. When R' Shmaryahu Gurary went to the Rebbe, R' Michoel Dworkin asked him (I heard that he spoke with heartfelt tears) to bring a letter from him to the Rebbe, submitting his request again.

R' Shmaryahu Gurary fulfilled this request when he visited the Rebbe at *yechidus*. The Rebbe told him that he would speak further about the matter. Upon leaving Eretz Yisrael, the Rebbe told R' Shmaryahu Gurary to send a telegram to R' Michoel Dworkin informing him that he was bringing a letter from the Rebbe. When he arrived, he gave him the above letter.

By the way, R' Rafael Nachman Kahn received a reply from the Rebbe: "Your son Yoel need not journey here."

R' Baruch Paris, R' Avraham Paris' recently married son, also received a letter from the Rebbe to come in the summer. It is also known that R' Zalman Levin, Avraham Paris' future son-in-law, received an answer from the Rebbe that his wedding should be held at the designated time and then he should make his way to the U.S.

The student, Nosson Gurary, R' Shmaryahu's son, also received an answer to study in Yeshivas Tomchei Temimim in Brooklyn.

~

The wedding of the student, Menachem Yisrael Malov, R' Shmuel's son, was held – in a good and auspicious hour – on the 17th of Kislev in the hall of HaPoel HaMizrachi on Achad HaAm Street.

On the suggestion of his father, Menachem Malov and Yaakov Flask from Talnesht established a small spool factory. May it be G-d's will that their work prove successful.

Last Friday, Dovber Shilansky from Yekatrinislav died in the Belinson Hospital near Petach Tikvah. Last Shabbos, R' Pesachya Menken died in the same hospital. He served as a Rabbi in several chassidic villages. The first time I saw R' Menken was in Adar 5700, at the wedding of Yosef Sherman and the daughter of the director of the yeshiva, R' Moshe Axelrod. He brought happiness to the congregation with many clever remarks and gematrios and with his graceful dancing even though it was only a month after he recovered from an illness that affected his legs. A short while ago, the same illness returned, and this time it overcame him.

~

R' Moshe Gurary said that tonight, study sessions will be held at 7:30 PM in the Shul of the Gerer chassidim, Achad HaAm Street 55. The first time we studied with him was 11 Teves 5706 (1945), and since then, we are studying with him on an average of twice a week.

The students studying with him are Yoel, Rafael Nachman Kahn's son, Nosson, R' Mordechai Gurary's son, my brother Yitzchak, and myself. Avraham Yitzchak Shaulzon studied with us for a short while as well. Avraham Yitzchak is from Jerusalem and entered the yeshiva in the last semester. He also wrote to the Rebbe of his desire to visit him and is awaiting an answer.

R' Meir Blizinsky also wrote the Rebbe that he wants his son, Shmuel, to visit the Rebbe, and is awaiting a reply.

~

A vintage Chassid received a letter from his grandson from Brooklyn, who was at *yechidus* with the Rebbe. The Rebbe told him (I am not quoting exactly): "I heard that you have good abilities to study, but your study is not yet complete; your davening (prayer) is also not complete; and your [commitment to] do a favor for another Jew is not complete.

"One must study and labor in the task of prayer, and do a Jew a favor from time to time. You should study Yoreh Deah[5]. In about half a year, no more than three quarters of a year, you should come to me having completed your studies for Rabbinic Ordination. One should be a Jew and a Rav. Being a Jew is not the same as being a Rav.

"One should not speak in the middle of study, not even about matters of Chassidus. There is a special time to speak about subjects in Chassidus: Thursday night and Shabbos at night, both Friday night and Saturday night. It is necessary to review chassidic teachings, not merely to tell someone else to review these teachings."

B"H, Tuesday, 22 Teves, Tel Aviv, 11 AM (in our home, Har Sinai Street 1)

This morning, we were visited by Reuven Gesheid of Kfar Atah (a village near Haifa), the future father-in-law of the notable student, Shlomo Kuptshik, the son of R' Alter Betzalel Kupt-

[5] The section of the Shulchan Aruch that includes the laws of kashrus, which are studied to receive ordination as a Rabbi.

shik. He visited us to speak to my father about matters concerning his future son-in-law.

I wrote my first letter to the Rebbe – together with my brother Yitzchak – about going to Brooklyn, on 12 Sivan, 5705. On Rosh Chodesh Elul, the Rebbe wrote an answer and that answer was received in the middle of the month of Tishrei, 5706. That answer was sent to the address of R' Moshe Gurary – in contrast to the last answer that was sent to my address.

All the others also received their answers sent to their homes with the exception of Sholom Ber Goldshmidt whose answer was sent to R' Moshe Gurary.

With regard to the student Nosson Gurary, I heard the following from Sholom Ber Goldshmidt when we visited the vintage Chassid, R' Shabbatai Berman, who was living with his daughter in Jerusalem: When Nosson's father, R' Shmaryahu, entered *yechidus* with the Rebbe, he suggested that his son come to the Rebbe for several months, the Rebbe told him: "We will yet speak of the matter."

The same interchange was repeated once or twice more.

On the last occasion, he spoke to the Rebbe before returning to Eretz Yisrael, he told the Rebbe that he wanted his son to come to Brooklyn, because it is not quiet in Eretz Yisrael at this time. The Rebbe answered that there is no reason to be afraid, but if his son wants to come to study, he may come.

8 PM, the eve of 24 Teves, the *yahrtzeit* of the Alter Rebbe

Today, it is a year since the young man, Menachem Dov Mustovitz, came to our house. He is the son of R' Yitzchak Mustovitz, a Gerer Chassid who was one of the prominent wealthy men in the resort town of Otwock in Poland. He owned vast properties which extended over several streets in that town. He also owned other buildings and a manufacturing plant for wine and liquor in the city of Radom. Shortly before WWII, he opened one of his estates and made it the home of the Lubavitcher Yeshiva. His firstborn son, Menachem Dov, studied in the yeshiva for a while. During the war, Menachem and his sister Devorah lived with Polish gentiles. His mother, his younger brother and another sister died martyr's deaths in Otwock and his father, R' Yitzchak, was sent by the Nazis to the gas chambers in Treblinka. He and his sister were the only ones who remained alive from his entire family.

He has been living in our home. He works in the knitting business. The Rebbe wrote to him that certainly the members of the Lubavitch community will draw him close. His sister is living in the dormitory of Beis Yaakov in Jerusalem and is studying in the Seminary there.

The Saturday night following Shabbos Parshas Vaera, the eve of 27 Teves, Tel Aviv, 7 PM

On Thursday evening, my mother told me that right before she underwent surgery in Moscow, she had a vision of her father, R' Leib of Verchnedneiporovsk who told her: "My daughter, say 'In Your hand I entrust my spirit.'"[6]

That evening she remembered that the same evening a year be-

[6] Tehillim 31:6, the verse recited at the conclusion of the prayers before sleep at night.

fore was a Friday night. Outside, there was a severe curfew. At the Shabbos meal, we had a guest, the student Chaim Lipshitz. In the middle of the meal, someone knocked on the door. Without waiting for an answer, a student Yonatan Balter opened the door and entered. He told us that during the afternoon, he had gone with the young man Hillel Levinson to the Rabbanit Ziskind to get bread for the Shabbos meals. A British soldier saw them and they fled. Hillel was able to hide in the courtyard of one of the homes. (Later, I heard that he was able to hide in the home of Rav Brandvein.) They took Yonatan in an army vehicle to Beit Hadar. In the evening, after the Shabbos commenced, he was taken to a tribunal. The judgment was to pay a fine of 200 lire. Since the Shabbos had already commenced, he was not able to pay. One of the policemen offered to pay for him and, as a result, he was released and allowed to go home. On his way, he passed our home and decided to enter.

On Friday morning, Zerach Verhaftig, the son of our neighbor, R' Yerucham Verhaftig, a member of the international executive board of Mizrachi arrived in Haifa. Just before candle lighting, he was able to reach his parents' home.

Before WWII, he was a little-known lawyer in Poland. During the war, he worked to save Jews from the Holocaust. He fled to Shanghai, together with many refugees, and from there he reached the United States In America, he labored with great self-sacrifice to save his brethren in Eastern Europe, to the extent that he became recognized throughout the world. A year ago, he traveled to Europe to save Jewish children who had survived the war and were found in Christian monasteries and convents. He was elected to the World Zionist Council in Basel and from there journeyed to visit his parents.

He relates, that in Otwock, they found papers belonging to R' Yechezkel Feigin, the Rebbe's secretary, as well as some letters of the Rebbe that he had not been able to take when fleeing

Poland, and several other writings from other Lubavitcher Chassidim. All of these manuscripts were given to Rav Kahanah. He also brought greetings from the Lubavitcher Yeshiva in New York, which, in his words "is leaving an impression that is not bad at all."

During Shelosh Seudos,[7] the conversation in Shul focused on Rav Shimon Menashe who served as a Rav in Chevron during the lifetime of the Tzemach Tzedek. R' Menachem Mendel Slonim related that his father, Shneur Zalman Slonim, once went to receive a blessing from Rav Shimon Menashe. Rav Shimon Menashe demurred, saying: "I should bless you?!" When, however, R' Shneur Zalman pressed him, he said: "For a Jew, it is necessary that 'All the wellsprings are in you.' 'All the wellsprings are in you.'"[8]

R' Shimon Menashe would loan money to the Jews he knew. The total of the outstanding loans he had given reached 20,000 rubles. When this was related to the Tzemach Tzedek, the Tzemach Tzedek said: "About my Shimon Menashe, about my *tzadik*, don't talk." He was utterly removed from worldly matters.

~

Today, I heard that a telegram was received from the young man, Yonason B. The telegram was received by his uncle, Mr. Tzafariri (Morgenstern), and related that he was now in Paris.

Yonason B. left Vilna together with the other students of the Lubavitcher Yeshiva. He was able to flee to Kobe, Japan. From there, he came to Eretz Yisrael and entered the Yeshiva Achei Temimim here. In Av, 5706 (1946), he left Eretz Yisrael to return to Europe to search for his mother. In the interim, almost no in-

[7] The third Shabbos meal which is often eaten communally in the synagogue.
[8] Tehillim 87:7.

formation was forthcoming about him.

Yitzchak Yudason, who is also in Europe on a mission from Agudas Yisrael, wrote to his father, R' Alexander Sender Yudason is a Rav for several neighborhoods in Jaffa, that he heard that Yonason B. has already passed through the following countries: Egypt, Italy, Switzerland, France, Holland, Belgium, and Germany, and that he is still thinking of visiting other lands.

I heard that R' Moshe Gurary desires to visit the Rebbe for Shavuot this year and that he is already planning his trip.

B"H, Wednesday, 8 Shvat, Tel Aviv

Last Shabbos, during the second meal, a discussion ensued about the concept that Shabbos food does not cause harm. R' Chaim Ber Lerman related: he heard that R' Yitzchak Yoel Rafaelovitch once came to Lubavitch for Shabbos and the Tzemach Tzedek invited him to his table for the Shabbos meals. Now, R' Yitzchak Yoel had serious digestive disorders. Therefore when certain foods were brought to the table, he refrained from eating them. The Tzemach Tzedek assured him that he could eat, because as stated above, "Shabbos food does not cause harm." R' Yitzchak Yoel ate heartily and did not suffer any consequences.

After he returned home, he told his family what had happened and asked them to prepare all sorts of delicacies for the Shabbos meal. After partaking of them, his gastric disorders erupted and he felt that even his life was in danger.

R' Chaim Ber also related that R' Baruch Mordechai, the Rav of Bobroisk, once said about himself – he spoke in an accent similar to that of Galician Jews: "I do not have to study, because I already know. I don't have to know, because I already have a reputation."

~

The *tenaim*[9] between the oldest daughter of R' Moshe Gurary and the student Heshel Broida, one of the foremost students of the Chevron Yeshiva were supposed to have been held on Monday evening, but were postponed because of the curfew. Yesterday, they were held at the home of R' Moshe Gurary.

~

My brother, Yitzchak, received a letter from the Rebbe via R' Moshe Gurary on Saturday night. This was sent in reply to the letter my brother sent on the advice of the vintage chassid, R' Shabbatai Berman, on 10 Kislev. The Rebbe's letter is dated 3 Teves and states (I am not quoting exactly): "*You have undoubtedly received my letter of 15 Kislev. I just received your letter of 10 Kislev, mentioning your father's suggestion which is proper. Although you desire that we meet, at present, you must postpone your journey, establish yourself with a good* shidduch, *and assist your father in earning a livelihood. May G-d send you a fitting* shidduch *and may you enjoy ample sustenance.*" It was signed in the Rebbe's name by his secretary, R' Chaim Lieberman.

Last Friday, my father sent an airmail letter to R' Moshe Dovber Rivkin to undertake endeavors on our behalf and to obtain an affidavit for us.

Saturday night following Shabbos Parshas Yisro, 18 Shvat

Last Saturday night, R' Moshe Dubinsky wrote a letter to R' Berl Chaskind regarding our journey to America. The letter was sent on Sunday. A similar letter was sent on Monday to R' Meir Ashkenazi.

Last Monday, *tenaim* were held between the oldest daughter of

[9] Celebration accompanying a prenuptial agreement.

R' Shmaryahu Gurary and R' Nosson Eichenshtein, the son of the Zhiditochover Rebbe. Many Rebbeim were present.

On Shabbos Parshas Bo, a son was born to our Rosh Yeshiva, R' David Chanzin. The *bris* was held on the following Shabbos in Petach Tikvah.

Last Shabbos, there was a *farbrengen* in the central Chabad Shul. The attendant, R' Tzvi Hirsh Ginsburg, the son of the Rav of Yakobshtot was slightly intoxicated and related that once when he came home from yeshiva – he had studied in several Lithuanian yeshivos including the yeshiva of Radin – his father and his grandfather were sitting at the table saying L'Chaim. His grandfather related that after the Tzemach Tzedek passed away, the Chassidim cut up some of his clothing and divided it among themselves. "I merited," he said, "to acquire one of his pockets."

He also related that it was popular knowledge that those who visit the Tzemach Tzedek at *yechidus* would naturally shudder in awe. Once, an "enlightened" Jew boasted that he could enter *yechidus* without shuddering.

When he entered, the Tzemach Tzedek asked him: "Where does a Jew come from?"

He answered brazenly: "From a couple." (The Yiddish term, "*fun a por folk*," could also be rendered "from several nations," or, "from several peoples.")

The Tzemach Tzedek commented: "The Jews are 'one nation.' Since he said "*fun a por folk*," it is apparent that he is illegitimate." The Chassidim heard, investigated the matter, and discovered that the Rebbe was correct.

B"H, Wednesday, Parshas Terumah, the eve of Rosh Chodesh Adar, 5707, 11 PM

Today, at 4 PM, the long-awaited affidavit from Yeshivas Tomchei Temimim in Brooklyn arrived at our yeshiva, 16 HaRav Kook Street. The envelope was addressed to R' Sholem Ber Goldshmidt. When it was received, R' Chaim Shaul Brook sent the student Shlomo Kuptshik to notify Sholom Ber Goldshmidt, who was studying with a group of students in the *shtiebel* of the Rebbe of Lutsk on 9 HaAri Street. The student, Mottel Dubinsky came to notify me. The affidavit came as a surprise. We had already sent another request with the Chassid, R' Michoel Dworkin, who is leaving tomorrow to the U.S. via Alexandria and Cairo.

Together with the affidavit was also a letter from the Rebbe's son-in-law, Rashag, the director of the yeshiva, instructing us to go to the American Consulate where we will certainly receive the necessary visas. He concluded with wishes that in the near future he would be able to see us diligently applying ourselves to Torah study and Divine service. He also asked that we notify him about the progress of our plans. (The affidavits were sent for my brother Yitzchak, Sholom Ber Goldshmidt, and Mordechai Dubinsky and myself.)

Today, the wedding of R' Shmuel Zalmanov's daughter and Mr. Kaposta was held in Heichal HaMelacha.

At 11 o'clock this morning, a telegram arrived from the Rebbe. It read: "To Gansbourg, Montefiore 25. May it be successful in both material and spiritual things. Rabbi Schneersohn." At its top was written "Brooklyn NY 18, 1334."

This telegram was sent in response to a telegram that my parents had sent to the Rebbe concerning a suggested *shidduch* between my brother, R' Sholom Yudah Leib and the daughter of Mr. Menachem Zaev Butchan Chasida from 24 Jeka Street in Warsaw who is now living in Jerusalem. Our telegram was sent the Sunday night of Parshas Yisro and two weeks had passed without an answer being received. On Sunday night of this week we sent a telegram to R' Dovber Chaskind, asking him to inquire about the matter, and today we received this answer. R' Reuven Gesheid from Kfar Atah was the shadchan.

Sunday, Parshas Sissa, 10 Adar, 4 PM

Last Wednesday, 4 Adar, the *tenaim* were held between my brother, R' Sholom Yudah Leib, and the daughter of Menachem Zaev Butchan Chasida. The celebration was held in the home of the bride's family, 8 Beer Sheva Street, in the Beis Yisrael neighborhood of Jerusalem. Besides the families of the bride and groom, there were scores of guests. A definite date for the wedding was not set, but it was agreed that it would not be any later than Elul and that it could be even earlier.

On Saturday night, *tenaim* were held between Yaakov, R' Tuvia Polusk's son, and the daughter of R' Shmuel Malov. Last Tuesday was the wedding between R' Zalman Levin and the daughter of R' Avraham Paris. The wedding was held in the Bris Yitzchak Synagogue of Ramat Gan Bet. After the wedding, he is planning to go to America as the Rebbe advised him.

~

The student Yoel, the son of R' Rafael Nachman Kahn, received the following letter from the Rebbe on Thursday. (I am quoting from memory.)

B"H, 26 Shvat, 5707, Brooklyn

My friend, the prominent student, R' Yoel Kahn,

My friend, your father wrote to me (or "I received your father's letter") saying that you are applying yourself to your studies. I derived great satisfaction. Continue strengthening your studies.

At fixed times occupy yourself with the Divine service of prayer, G-d-fearing conduct, and the acquisition of good character traits. May G-d help you and bring you success in your studies and in your Divine service. May you become a Chassid, G-d-fearing, and a scholar.

(The Rebbe's signature)

~

R' Chaim Shaul Brook told the following story: In Zhitomer, Ukraine, there was a G-d-fearing Jew who worked as a tailor and who employed a Jewish attendant and a non-Jewish maid. The employer thought that the attendant had a relationship with the maid. He shared his suspicions with the heads of the community and they ruled that the attendant should be tied together with the maid, placed in a wagon, and driven through the entire town.

The young man was not guilty of this sin. When he was being taken past the holy Rebbe, R' Zaev of Zhitomer, he protested his innocence. R' Zaev told him that if in fact he was innocent, he would merit that his descendants would marry into the family of one of the leading sages of the generation.

After receiving the above punishment, the community let him be. He invested in several business enterprises and prospered. He left that city and settled in another community. There he married and success continued to shine upon him. Soon he became one of the wealthiest members of the community.

In the beginning, he sought involvement in communal matters, but since his lineage was undistinguished, the communal leaders would argue with him. They would refer to him as the chassidishe goy ("the chassidic gentile"). Needless to say, he did not appreciate their attitude and to the extent that they distanced themselves from him, he distanced himself from them.

Several years passed. During that time, his wife gave birth to a son who was recognized as uniquely gifted. As he grew older, the boy became known as a prodigious genius.

Once the saintly Rebbe, R' Baruch of Mezhibuz, passed close to this city and there was a report that he wished to stay overnight. All the city's leading citizens drove their carriages to the cross-roads of the city where R' Baruch would pass, hoping that they would merit to offer R' Baruch a ride and hospitality.

The attendant turned magnate did not go out with the others, for he was used to being distanced by the Jewish community. Nevertheless, his wife asked him to present himself before the *tzadik* with the others. Although he initially refused, after she continually pressed him, he consented. He drove his carriage to the meeting place and waited in the back.

When R' Baruch arrived, he surveyed all the wagons that were there and, to everyone's surprise, motioned that the ex-attendant should approach him. Upon entering his carriage he was asked if he could enjoy the hospitality of his home.

The attendant turned magnate obviously agreed and sent a messenger to hurry to his home and inform his wife. When the good woman was informed, she fainted in shock.

As R' Baruch was riding with his host, he asked him about his family and his business. The man related that G-d had blessed him with ample financial success and that he had a son who was renowned as a genius. R' Baruch asked his host if he would be willing for his son to marry into R' Baruch's family. (R' Baruch had a daughter of marriageable age.) The magnate thought R' Baruch was joking with him, but soon his guest's serious tone convinced him that the offer was genuine and he readily agreed.

While they were speaking, the messenger returned and told the magnate that his wife had fainted. R' Baruch instructed him to

Selection of letters from the Previous Rebbe to R' Moshe Dovber Gansbourg, R' Hirsh's father (from the years 5698 and 5707).

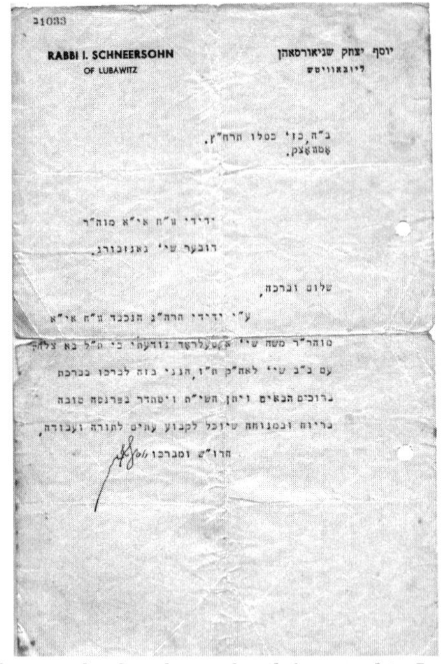

21033

RABBI I. SCHNEERSOHN
OF LUBAWITZ

יוסף יצחק שניאורסאהן
ליובאוויטש

ב"ה, כז' כסלו תרח"ץ.
אטוואצק.

ידידי וו"ח אי"א מוה"ר
דובער שי' גאנזבורג.

שלום וברכה,

ע"י ידידי הרה"ג הנכבד וו"ח אי"א
מוהר"ר משה שי' אקסעלרעד נודעתי כי ה"ל בא צלחה
עם ב"ב שי' לאה"ק ת"ו, הנני בזה לברכו בברכת
ברוכים הבאים ויתן השי"ת ויטהדר בפרנסה טובה
בריוח ובמנוחה שיוכל לקבוע עתים לתורה ועבודה,
הדו"ש ומברכו

Blessing the Gansbourg family's arrival in Israel

מזכיר כ"ק אדמו"ר שליט"א מליובאוויטש
הרב יחזקאל פייגין
SECRETARY OF RABBI OF LUBAVITZ RABBI H. FEIGIN
ADRESS: RABBI I. SCHNEERSOHN, OTWOCK - POLAND, PRUSA 6

ב"ה ב' דר"ח אייר תרח"ץ.
אטוואצק.

כבוד ידידי הנכבד והנעלה וו"ח אי"א
מוהר"ר דובער שי' האנזבורג.

שלום וברכה,

הנה יש ענין נחוץ לשלוח לרמ"ל אברמסאן מכתב,
אמנם זה איזה זמן אשר אין לנו מהם מכתבים ואחרים כתבו
שלא לכתוב להם, אמנם הנה מחמת נחיצות הענין שלחתי מכתב
על שם ידידנו ר' יונה שי' כהן למוסקוע, אמנם כ"ק אדמו"ר
שליט"א אמר לי כי העתקה מהמכתב אשלח עוד ע"י כבודו
ולבקש את כבודו אולי יש לכבודו אדרעס למי לשלוח המכתב
באופן שיגיע לאברמסאן, והנני שולח המכתב לכבודו חתום כפי
שאמר לי כ"ק לשלוח, אם אין לו האפשריות לשלוח בטח יבין
לשלוח לי המכתב חזרה.
בכלל אין חדשות כ"ק אדמו"ר שליט"א בא צלחה
לביתו ביום י"ב ניסן בחג הפסח בימים הראשונים לא אמר
חסידות אבל חיינו נכנסים כעת ב התועדות לשמוע שיחות קדש
וביום שביעי של פסח לעת ערב אמר מאמר חסידות ע"פ וירם משה
את ידו ובאחרון של פסח בסעודה הי' מאמר יתחיל והניף
ידו כו', גם כש"קהעבר אמר מאמר ע"פ רפאני ה' וארפא.
ידידו הדו"ש ומברכו
בכל אופן יודיע מקבלת המכתב ומהנעשה אתו.

Letter from R' Yechezkel Feigin, secretary of the Previous Rebbe

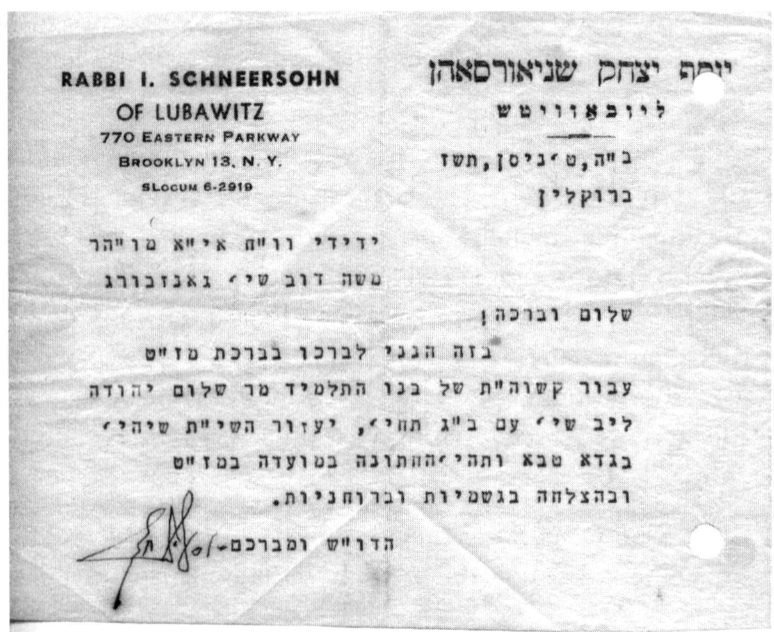

RABBI I. SCHNEERSOHN
OF LUBAWITZ
770 EASTERN PARKWAY
BROOKLYN 13, N. Y.
SLOCUM 6-2919

יוסף יצחק שניאורסאהן
ליובאוויטש

ב"ה, ט' ניסן, תשז
ברוקלין

ידידי וו"ח אי"א מוה"ר
משה דוב שי' גאנזבורג

שלום וברכה!

בזה הנני לברכו בברכת מז"ט
עבור קשוה"ת של בנו התלמיד מר שלום יהודה
ליב שי' עם ב"ג תחי', יעזור השי"ת שיהי'
בנדא טבא ותהי' התונה בשעטה בשעה טובה ומוצלחת בגשמיות וברוחניות.
הדו"ש ומברכם

Engagement blessing for Leibel, Hirsh's oldest brother

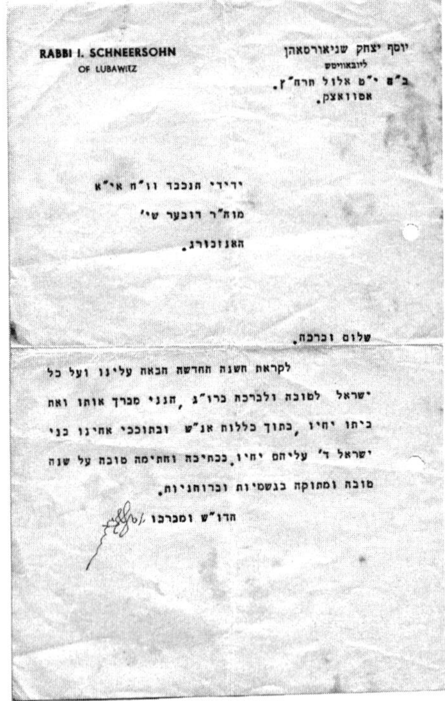

RABBI I. SCHNEERSOHN
OF LUBAWITZ

יוסף יצחק שניאורסאהן
ליובאוויטש

ב"ה י"ט אלול תרח"ץ.
אטוואצק.

ידידי הנכבד וו"ח אי"א
מוה"ר דובער שי'
האנזבורג.

שלום וברכה.

לקראת השנה החדשה הבאה עלינו ועל כל ישראל לטובה ולברכה ברו"ג, הנני מברך אותו ואת ביתו יחיו, בתוך כללות אנ"ש ובתוככי אחינו בני ישראל ד' עליהם יחיו, בכתיבה וחתימה טובה על שנה טובה ומתוקה בגשמיות וברוחניות.

הדו"ש ומברכו

5699 Rosh Hashanah greeting

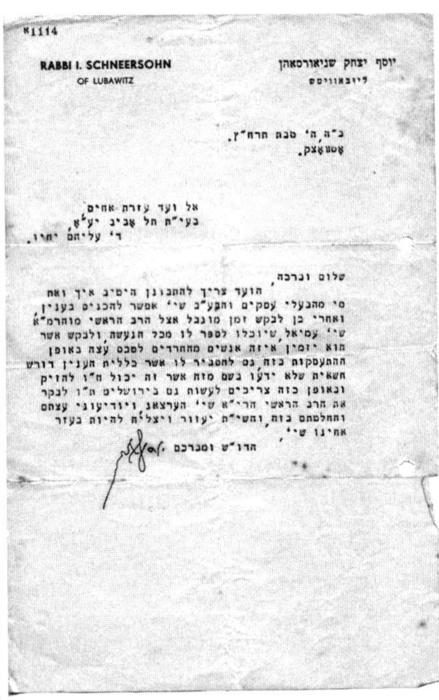

א1114

RABBI I. SCHNEERSOHN
OF LUBAWITZ

יוסף יצחק שניאורסאהן
ליובאוויטש

ב"ה, ה' טבת תרח"ץ.
אטוואצק.

אל ועד עזרת אחים
בעי"ת תל אביב יע"א,
ד' עליהם יחיו.

שלום וברכה,

הועד צריך להתבונן היטב איך ואת מי מהבעלי עסקים והבע"ב שי' אפשר להכניס בענין, ואחרי כן לבקש זמן מוגבל אצל הרב הראשי מוהרמ"א שי' עמיאל, שיוכלו לספר לו מכל הנעשה, ולבקש אשר הוא יזמין איזה אנשים מחחרדים לטכס עצה באופן ההתעסקות בזה, גם להסביר לו אשר כללית הענין דורש תשאית שלא ידעו בשם מזה אשר זה יכול ח"ו להזיק ובאופן כזה צריכים לעשות גם בירושלים ת"ו לבקר את הרב הראשי הרי"א שי' הערצאג ויודיעוני עצתם והחלטתם בזה, והשי"ת יעזור ויצליח להיות בעזר אחינו שי'.

הדו"ש ומברכם

To the board of Ezras Achim in Tel Aviv

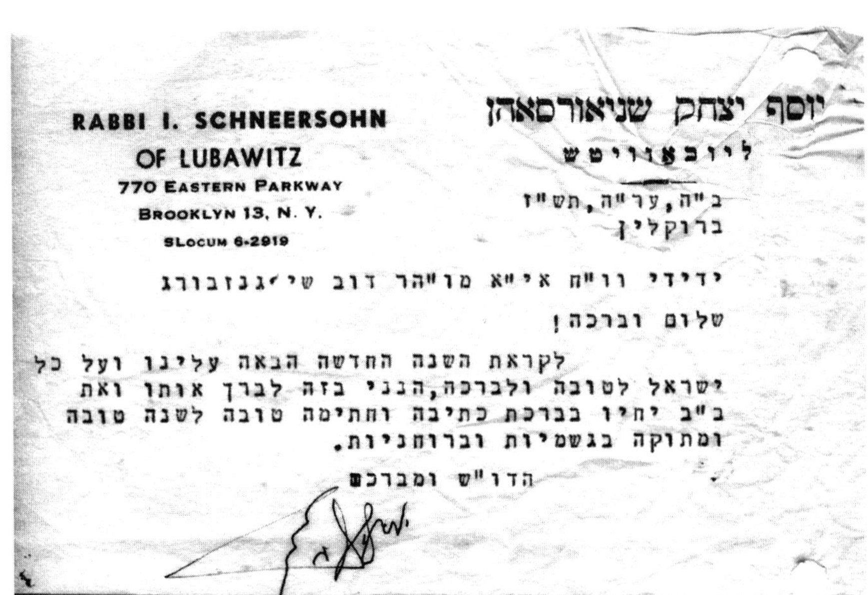

RABBI I. SCHNEERSOHN
OF LUBAWITZ
770 EASTERN PARKWAY
BROOKLYN 13, N. Y.
SLocum 6-2919

יוסף יצחק שניאורסאהן
ליובאוויטש

ב"ה, ער"ה, תש"ז
ברוקלין

ידידי וו"ח אי"א מוה"ר דוב שי' גנזבורג

שלום וברכה!

לקראת השנה החדשה הבאה עלינו ועל כל ישראל לטובה ולברכה, הנני בזה לברך אותו ואת ב"ב יחיו בברכת כתיבה וחתימה טובה לשנה טובה ומתוקה בגשמיות וברוחניות.

הדו"ש ומברכם

5707 Rosh Hashanah greeting

tell her that his granddaughter would marry her son. That, he said, would rouse her. The messenger conveyed the message and the woman happily came to.

When they arrived at the magnate's home, R' Baruch retired to rest. Shortly afterwards, *tenaim* were written up, and a date for the wedding was set.

When the day of the wedding arrived, R' Baruch, the wedding party, and their guests arrived. R' Baruch approached the groom's father and began berating him: "You are a boor! Unlearned! A commoner!" Shocked, the magnate retreated, waited some time, and then appeared again. This time as well, R' Baruch greeted him with harsh insults. The pattern was repeated several times until R' Baruch indicated that the chupah ceremony could be held.

After the chupah, he asked R' Baruch to explain his outburst. "After all," he asked, "I did not suggest the *shidduch*, the Rebbe did. Didn't you know that I was simple and unlearned? Why then did you embarrass me?"

R' Baruch replied: "To every chupah come the forebears of the bride and groom from the other world. When the time of the chupah arrived, my ancestors had arrived, but yours had not. Not only that, I could not locate them in heaven. So I began to shout at you. Ultimately, they took notice. Once I was able to see where they were, I brought them to the chupah."

~

At midnight, it was announced on the radio that a complete curfew would take effect. At 11 AM, martial law was announced. Exactly what this means is still unclear. I will not write, because it will certainly be written about in the newspapers.

B"H, Wednesday, Parshas Tzav, 5 Nissan, 5707; our new apartment, 10 Tiomakin Street, the corner of Ibn Gabirol Street.

On Monday, 18 Adar, the declaration of martial law was rescinded, and today, 20 Adar, we entered our new apartment; may it bring us success and good fortune. The reason we moved was that our previous landlord desired to destroy the entire building and construct a new one in its place. Our previous neighbors also had to leave. Our new apartment is located in the midst of Tel Aviv, on the ground floor of 10 Tiomakin St., at the corner of Ibn Gabirol St. It is the first apartment to the right of the entrance.

The building in which our new apartment is located is new and has four stories. Mr. Kahana, the owner of the lot, built it to sell to the owners of the individual apartments. It is known as a condominium.

Yissacher Dov Friedman (who deserves a chapter of his own) told us that his uncle said that even in his home town of Chiyust in Hungary, Mr. Kahana constructed many buildings and it was said about him: "*Vos es falt ein boyt er un vos er boyt falt ein*," loosely translated: Whatever "falls" (arises in someone's mind), he builds, and whatever he builds, falls.

Like any apartment, ours has advantages and disadvantages. The primary disadvantage, however, is that it is located opposite the station of the British soldiers. If the terrorists attack this station – or even if the soldiers just think that they are being attacked – they begin to shoot with handguns and automatic weapons to any and all sides, as happened on the Saturday night following Shabbos Parshas Tetzaveh. Even today, it is possible to find many holes in our building – though mostly in the upper stories – that were created by such bullets.

On the Saturday night following Shabbos Parshas Vayikra, the eve of 2 Nissan, the *yahrtzeit* of the Rebbe Rashab, there was a *farbrengen* in the yeshiva. Menachem Mendel Slonim related that when his father, R' Schneur Zalman Slonim, the Rav of Jaffa, visited the Rebbe Rashab in Yalte, in 5647, the Rebbe Rashab would walk for 6 hours each day, three hours one way and three hours back. He took R' Schneur Zalman with him.

For the first six weeks, the Rebbe Rashab did not say anything. Apparently, he was thinking about the subjects that he wanted to discuss with him. Afterwards, he spoke to him for the entire time that they would walk together. Each day, when R' Shneur Zalman returned home, he would write down what the Rebbe had told him.

Two or three days before R' Shneur Zalman was to leave the Rebbe, he brought these notes to him. It was winter and the house was warmed by a furnace. The Rebbe took the papers from R' Shneur Zalman, leafed through them for a certain amount of time, and then threw them into the furnace.

R' Shneur Zalman protested: "Why did the Rebbe do this? I have labored over these pages for many months. Moreover, since I wrote down everything I heard, I did not commit the concepts to memory. Why did the Rebbe destroy them?"

The Rebbe answered: "I do not desire to be publicized as a Rebbe."[10]

R' Rafael Nachman Kahn related that he remembered R' Shneur Zalman Slonim well: "Once – from 5695 to 5696 (1945 to 1946) - R' Shneur Zalman was not home because he had gone for a therapeutic vacation. Since he was the Rav in Jaffa and would teach Chassidus publicly, he asked me to substitute for him. I did, teaching Torah Ohr, Likkutei Torah, and occa-

[10] In 5643 (1882), soon after the passing of his father and predecessor, the Rebbe Maharash, the Rebbe Rashab began guiding the chassidim. However, his acceptance of the position of Rebbe was reluctant and gradual. It was not until Rosh Hashanah 5654 (1893), that he fully and formally undertook the *nesius*.

sionally, the Rebbe's maamorim.

"On Friday, after he returned from his journey, I was sitting in the synagogue, teaching as usual. In the middle of the lesson, R' Shneur Zalman entered the synagogue. Obviously, the entire congregation stood up in his honor. I halted the lesson, but he said that I should continue."

R' Rafael Nachman also related: "The gravesite of the Rebbe Rashab in Rostov on the River Don, is located in the cemetery.[11] Opposite his grave – though outside the cemetery – are the graves of Karaites,[12] because it was not desired that they be buried among the Jewish people.

"The Rebbe[13] commented that this is similar to the gravesite of Moshe who is buried 'across from the House of Peor.'[14]

"Once I merited to observe the Rebbe while he visited the gravesite. The gravesite is roofless. When other chassidim and I saw that the Rebbe was going to visit the gravesite, we climbed on the fence where we could watch. When the Rebbe approached the gravesite he opened a book of Tehillim, said something, walked around the gravesite, and then said something else. He followed this pattern several times.

"Afterwards, he was obviously preparing himself for something. He prepared himself in exactly the same way he used to prepare himself before listening to the Rebbe Rashab deliver a *maamar*. He then stood opposite the gravesite in exactly the same manner as he would when listening to a *maamar*.

"He stood this way for a long time. He then opened the Tehillim

[11] At the time this diary was written, the gravesite of the Rebbe Rashab had already been moved. Chassidim, risking their very lives, had exhumed his body just before the old cemetery was bulldozed to make way for a Soviet housing project.
[12] Jews who accepted only the Written Law and not the Oral Law.
[13] I.e., the Rebbe Rayatz.
[14] Devarim 34:6.

again and said something. We saw that he was preparing to depart the gravesite so we hurried down from the fence and hid."

At the above-mentioned *farbrengen*, R' Chaim Shaul Brook related: "When the saintly Rebbe, R' Baruch of Mezibuzh conducted audiences with people, he did not allow anyone to sit. The Rebbe's was the only chair in the room. Once one of the other Rebbes (he gave his name, but I did not hear it clearly) came to him with his attendant and the attendant brought a chair for him. Thus when he entered *yechidus* with R' Baruch, he sat.

This other Rebbe was renowned for his wisdom. R' Baruch told him: "I am unique in this generation."

The other Rebbe countered: "I am also unique in this generation."

R' Baruch questioned: "How can there be two who are both unique?"

"You are unique in your righteousness. And I am unique in wisdom."

"If you are unique in wisdom, identify the accusing spiritual force which challenged the Jewish people this Rosh Hashanah."

"The accusing force was focused on the fact that the Jews keep the Torah and its mitzvos for their own sake and not for G-d's sake."

"So how did you respond?"

"I said: G-d, act the same way: 'Do for Your sake and not for ours.'"[15]

[15] One of the phrases in the Avinu Malkeinu prayer.

11 PM

A son was born to R' Yisrael Zvi Heber on 5 Adar. He was named Shmuel. His first son was named Avraham Alter, the name Alter having been given for the renowned *mashpia* (spiritual mentor), R' Alter Potzaper. Rabbi Fleishman was the mohel.

A son was also born to R' Shlomoh Potshein. Two or three years ago, his wife gave birth to a girl. He telegrammed the news to the Rebbe and the Rebbe answered him with a mazel tov for the birth of a son. At that time, R' Pinchas Althaus said that a son would certainly be born to him. The mohel was Rabbi Shechter.

~

R' Chaim Chanovitz is leaving for America. A. Kaplan returned from a trip to Europe. He had visited his sister who is living there now and had much to say about what he saw and heard about the Chassidim in the refugee camps. He related: "I saw the *mashpia* R' Nissan der geller (the red-head) from Zlobin (R' Nissan Nemenov) teaching Tanya. I pictured myself in Lubavitch hearing a *mashpia* teach Tanya; the only thing missing was the large hall auditorium. They are worthy to be placed in a museum" (i.e. priceless), A. Kaplan said about the Chassidim he met on his trip. "They all want to go to the Rebbe."

He was also in Paris. He said that since R' Zalman Schneerson went to the Rebbe, his place was taken by R' Elya Par. All of the Chassidim are working with great energy and their warmth is wondrous.

A. Kaplan studied in Lubavitch. He has, however, strayed far from the Chassidic path. He is related to R' Chaim Shaul Brook.

R' Shmuel Dovber Ziskind received an entry visa for his grandson who is located in Poking and his granddaughter who is located in Linz.[16] He hopes that soon he will be able to bring them to Eretz Yisrael. A while ago, he received a letter from the Rebbe with a blessing that he be successful in bringing his grandchildren to Eretz Yisrael.

~

On Monday, 3 Nissan, we baked shemurah matzos. Today, almost all the yeshiva students are baking, as is R' Shmuel Dovber Ziskind. R' Tzvi Ginsburg is the supervisor. We baked the matzos in the storage of R' Moshe Yeruslavski, the son of R' Ahrale Habishitz in Kiryat Yosef, in Givataim.

Monday, Parshas Tazria, 24 Nissan, 9 PM

On March 12, the American Consulate sent us a letter saying that we must prove that we will return to Eretz Yisrael and that the proof should be the existence of a family, commercial activity, or property [in Eretz Yisrael]. R' Yosef Citon told us that we need verification of the above from a recognized institution. Sholom Ber Goldshmidt and Mordechai Dubinsky received verification from the Communal Board of Jerusalem based on the testimony of Mr. Segal and I received verification from the Chief Rabbinate of Tel Aviv based on the testimony of R' Menachem Mendel Slonim and R' Avraham Paris. The verification was signed by R' Yaakov Moshe Toledano and Rabbi Isser Yuda Unterman.

R' Menachem Mendel Slonim undertook efforts on my behalf and went with me to the secretary, R' Shlomo Rohld and asked that such verification be drawn up on my behalf. He also went to Rabbi Toledano and asked for him to sign it. Without his help, several days would have passed before the document

[16] Two of the camps for displaced persons in Europe for WWII refugees.

would have been arranged, because there is a heavy overload and much pressure on the Chief Rabbinate.

Yesterday, we received a letter from the consulate saying that apparently we did not understand the intent of the letter of March 26. We must provide a guarantee in a financial institution that we have the funds to return and other similar information.

~

On Thursday, my father and my brother, R' Sholom Yudah Leib, received letters from the Rebbe from 9 Nissan with blessings of mazel tov. To my brother, the Rebbe wrote that he should establish himself financially and that he should work as a shochet, a ritual slaughterer. This came in addition to the telegram he received from the Rebbe several months previously in which the Rebbe wrote: "I agree that you should establish yourself in the profession of a shochet." The letters were signed by the Rebbe himself.

R' Hendel Havlin, the director of Yeshivas Toras Emes in Jerusalem, received a letter from the Chassid R' Nachum Zalman Horowitz, the son-in-law of Dovber Levertov (Berl Kabaliaker, as he was called), from one of the refugee camps in Austria. In his letter, he recalls my father, R' Rafael Nachman Kahn, and R' Nissan Eber. He also writes that the nephews of his mother, Mina Horowitz, were found. Their names are Shlomo and Simcha Chein from Ovruch, Ukraine. When my brother Yitzchak and I visited Mr. Zalman Leibowitz (Arieli) who is also from Ovruch, at his home, 8 Ben Ami Street in Tel Aviv, he told us that he knows both of them. One of them is very poor. His wife died recently and he comes to him to receive help. He does not know his address. The other changed his name to S. ben Israel and lives in Tiberius where he works as a teacher in the public school.

Mr. Zalman Leibowitz studied in Lubavitch for three years from about 5663. After he left Lubavitch, he "pastured in foreign fields"[17] and later worked as a teacher in the schools of "the Spreaders of the Enlightenment" in Moscow. There, as he told us when we visited him, he would occasionally meet his friend, the Chassid R' Eizik, the son of R' Gronem Esterman.

He remembers several of the friends who studied with him in Horoditz, including Shlomo Leib Paritcher and his teacher, R' Zalman Havlin, who was the *mashpia*. Now he is entirely distant from all Jewish life. He serves as the principal at the Bialik School on Levinsky Street in Tel Aviv. He also mentioned that one of his relatives, R' Moshe Avraham Greenspan – he is also a relative of R' Shlomo Fiatshein – who lives in Paris now, is moving with his family to America to be close to the Rebbe.

~

On Chol HaMoed Pesach, Mr. Levin, the brother-in-law of Moshe Diamond, who is the brother-in-law of Naftuli, the son of R' Shmuel Aba Dolitsky, who left Moscow eight or nine weeks ago, came here from Paris. His son is still in Paris and is thinking of moving to Eretz Yisrael.

B"H, 26 Nissan, 10 AM

Today, at 4 AM, before daybreak, four of the Jews who were condemned to death by the tribunal in Acre were hung. At that time, a curfew was declared throughout Eretz Yisrael to remain in effect until further notice.

Since we were unable to daven with a *minyan* because of the curfew, we davened communally in the apartment of Mr. Shlomo on the second floor of our building. Rav Yochat lives on that floor, as does his son-in-law, Moshe Sepoklina.

[17] I.e., became involved in a secular lifestyle.

B"H, Monday, 24 Iyar, 5707, 9 PM

It has been two hours since I returned from Jerusalem. At 5 PM, I left on the last bus, because there are restrictions on travel that take effect at 7 PM. I went to Jerusalem to undergo the medical examinations required by the American Consulate at almost the last moment.

Two weeks ago, I received a letter from the consulate telling me to come on May 20th at 10 AM with a passport and three photos, with no one from my family accompanying me. (I had received my passport on April 27th, two months after I had submitted my request on Feb. 27th.) Mordechai Dubinsky also received a letter to come at 9:30 AM that day. To his letter were attached two medical forms and a letter from the consul that he should undergo an examination by doctors, D'Giani from Mamila Street, and M. Neuman from Betzalel Street, near the Eden Hotel – these were general practitioners – and an eye examination at the St. John's clinic, near the railroad station.

Mordechai Dubinsky went to the doctors immediately. I did not go, because I did not have the forms and the consul did not instruct me to do so, even though I understood that an error must have been made. Several days ago, Sholom Ber Goldshmidt received a similar letter concerning the medical examinations with instructions for him to come on May 28th (without a specific time being stated).

Sholom Ber also went to the doctors and while being examined by Dr. Neuman told him about me. Dr. Neuman explained that the examinations are required, he has copies of the forms and I should come to him on Thursday. He said that he would make the connection to the consulate.

I visited him today and when I came, he spoke to Mrs. Solomon, a clerk at the American Consulate. She told him to give me the forms.

Dr. Neuman comes from a religious background. His father was from Grodno. He was born in Jerusalem and studied in Yeshivas Toras Chaim. "From there, I departed to *tarbus raah*,"[18] he concluded with a smile.

He is approximately seventy years old and speaks many languages. While I was there, he spoke Hebrew, English, Yiddish, and German. From his office, I went to the British eye clinic. (There they spoke only in English.) Afterwards, I sent the forms to the consulate.

The financial guarantees from the bank, as well as my letter and the letter from my parents, we already sent to the consulate. My father received the bank guarantee from Bank LeMalacha. Mordechai Dubinsky received his bank guarantee from the Israeli branch of Bank Britannia. Sholom Ber Goldshmidt received his guarantee from the Joint and from the Anglo-Palestine Bank.

I heard that R' Elazar Karasik and R' Moshe Gurary are also preparing to go to the Rebbe. It appears that they are seeking to enter America as merchants. R' Moshe Gurary will travel as an agent for the Lieber brand of chocolates; he is presently their agent here in Eretz Yisrael. His brother, who is the agent for the Dubek tobacco factory here, traveled to America as an agent for them.

B"H, Wednesday, Parshas Bahaaloscha

On Tuesday, Rosh Chodesh Sivan, I went with Mordechai Dubinsky to the American Consulate. The entrance to the office for entry visas is through the courtyard. The office itself is

[18] Lit. "a bad cultural environment," a Talmudic term for a secular lifestyle.

a circular brick hut, plated with metal.

When we knocked on the door, an Arab guard dressed in a consulate uniform opened the door for us and we entered. The office for entry visas is a rather large room, separated into two portions by cabinets. The first portion near the door was a small waiting room and the second, larger portion was the sitting room of the assistant consul who issued visas, in which several clerks worked as well.

After we gave our invitations to the guard, he gave them to the head clerk and then took our fingerprints. He began with the right thumb and then took the print of each finger individually. This same pattern was followed for the left hand and then repeated for each hand. Afterwards, he fingerprinted the right thumb and then all the fingers of the right hand together. Then he fingerprinted the left thumb and all the fingers of the left hand together. He then gave the fingerprints to the clerk. After some time passed, they called Mordechai Dubinsky. When he approached the clerk, she said that since it is likely that we do not speak English, she will speak in Hebrew and then proceed to investigate all the particulars of his application. After about half an hour, she called me and did the same.

After answering the questions, we had to take an "oath" in the presence of the assistant consulate, G. Cattal. The oath involved the following. The clerk said: "I swear that all the above is true and that after my studies, I will return to Israel." We raised our hands in affirmation. Afterwards, we were told to come again at 1 PM the following day to receive our visas. Mordechai Dubinsky received visa number 363 and I, number 364. The visa was for four years and permission was granted to delay our entry into the U.S. for four months. The cost of the visa was 2500 lire which is equivalent to $10.

A week later, Sholom Ber Goldshmidt received his visa. We

submitted a request that we be given places on the ship, Marine Carp, which was scheduled to leave on June 13, 1947. Although we brought a letter from the yeshiva, they refused our request and, instead, gave us places on that same ship but scheduled to leave around Rosh Chodesh Av.

~

Last Thursday, R' Nosson Gurary left Eretz Yisrael by plane and reached his destination on Sunday of this week. Rav Takatz left Eretz Yisrael to work on behalf of the yeshiva in America on the ship Russi that left several weeks ago from Haifa. In the papers, it was stated that the ship already reached New York. After he left Eretz Yisrael, a telegram from the Rebbe was received that the representative of the yeshiva should leave in the month of Elul and not before then. It was thought that the reason was because of the summer vacation which has already begun in America.

~

In the coming weeks, R' Shmaryahu Gurary, the Rebbe's son-in-law is scheduled to visit Eretz Yisrael. Rav Chenoch Havlin worked on procuring the visa for him.

~

R' Yeshaya Ginzburg received a telegram that Rav Nisan Telushkin, one of the active members of Aggudas Chassidei Chabad in America, set out on a trip to Eretz Yisrael.

~

On the evening of Lag B'Omer, the marriage between the student Shlomo Kuptshik and the daughter of R' Reuven Gesheid, a Piaseczna Chassid, was held in Kfar Atah. Many of the students of the yeshiva came for the wedding and some of the students remained for the following Shabbos. On Shavuos,

Shlomo Kuptshik had been our guest in Tel Aviv.

~

R' Shaul Dov related: "The *mashpia*, R' Shmuel Gronem Esterman, had a son named Meir. When he was called for army duty, the Rebbe Rashab was asked what to do to obtain his release and he answered that it was necessary to offer a bribe.

"He had to go to the conscription office in Borisov. There he stayed in the home of my father-in-law, R' Chaim Yair. One of the high-ranking officials on the conscription board in Borisov was named Ferdinand. He had a relationship with the Rebbe Rashab and understood to some extent who the Rebbe Rashab was.

"When Meir arrived in Borisov, he went with my father-in-law to this Ferdinand. They wanted to give him 150 rubles. Ferdinand answered that he did not desire to take the money, because they were lacking many conscripts and he was certain that Meir would be conscripted. Therefore he did not want to take money for no reason. They pushed the money into his hand, but he absolutely refused to take it.

"They returned home and Meir wrote a letter to his father, describing the situation and telling him that Ferdinand refused to take the money.

"R' Shmuel Gronem went to the Rebbe Rashab – I was standing in the room before the Rebbe's chamber – and showed him his son's letter. He asked: 'Since they do not want to take money, what should be done now?'

"The Rebbe Rashab leaned his head on his arms. He remained in that position for a few moments, thinking. He then lifted his head and said: 'You're asking what to do. I don't have *ruach hakodesh*.[19] I said that a bribe should be given. One must make a receptacle and then G-d's blessing will rest within it.

"When R' Shmuel Gronem left the Rebbe's chamber, he told me what the Rebbe told him.

"He immediately wrote a letter to his son, telling him what the Rebbe said. His son then went to Ferdinand again with my father-in-law. When they told him what the Rebbe said, he took the money.

"Shortly thereafter, there was a report in Borisov that the conscription committee had been dismissed. Severe charges were leveled against them and they were fired. In their place, a committee from Leiple was brought in.

"One evening, while Meir was waiting in my father-in-law's home, two young men came in. They asked if a young man named Meir Esterman was staying there. They called him into a private room and told him that they were working with the conscription committee from Lieple. The committee had told them that it would be difficult for them to free the prospective conscripts, but that if the prospective conscripts would all pay a collective sum of 2000 rubles, they could be freed. These two had accepted the task of collecting the money. They apportioned 50 rubles of that sum to Meir. He paid the money and was released from army service."

The Saturday night following Parshas Shelach, 26 Sivan

On Friday morning, R' Nissan Telushkin from New York arrived in Haifa. R' Nissan is one of the leading Chassidim working with Rebbe. He is staying with his former townsman, R' Yeshaya Ginzburg. Today, a large Kiddush was held at R' Yeshaya's home in honor of the distinguished guest. R' Nissan related several points, including the following:

[19] The spirit of Divine inspiration.

a) At the reception made for the Rebbe when he came to America, the Rebbe said: "When Moshe returned from Yisro's home to Egypt, G-d told him that Aharon will 'see you and be glad within his heart[20].' Now why was Aharon only happy "within his heart" to see his brother, but he did not show any outward signs of happiness? Because he was broken and crushed by the suffering undergone by the Jews in exile.

"Although I am happy to see my brethren here in America. I am broken and crushed by the suffering of the Jews in Europe."

b) At *yechidus*, the Rebbe compared the difference between the spiritual situation of the Jews in America to those in Europe to R' Nissan: "They both have fire within them. Yet there is a difference between fire that uses wood as fuel and fire that uses oil as fuel. When wood is used as fuel, after the fire burns out, coals will remain, but if oil is used as fuel, when the fire burns out, nothing will remain. What must be done then is to keep the fire burning continually.

~

The Rebbe sent a letter in connection with R' Nissan's arrival to the members of the Chassidic community in Tel Aviv. In the letter, he asked that the study sessions in Nigleh [the Torah's revealed, legal dimension], and Chassidus be strengthened and that new study sessions be established in those places where study sessions were not yet held. The Rebbe's letter mentioned that R' Nissan would be coming and that he should be greeted with the proper respect, for he would be bringing greetings from the Rebbe and from the institutions in America. This would certainly inspire the listeners. The letter was signed by the Rebbe. In response to the letter, R' Shmuel Zalmanov and the director of our yeshiva, R' Moshe Axelrod, went to Haifa to greet the guest.

[20] Shmos 4:14.

The Previous Lubavitcher Rebbe, Rabbi Yosef Yitzchak Schneersohn

The Rebbe, Rabbi Menachem Mendel Schneerson

Rebbe's Footnotes to the Sukkos *kuntres*, printed in Sefer Hamaamorim 5711 p.102

Part 2 – America 5711, 5712

B"H, Thursday, 3 Tishrei, Tzom Gedaliah, 5711, Brooklyn, 11 AM

On Shabbos, Parshas Nitzavim, the 27th of Elul, I reached my twenty-second birthday. In connection with this event and in accordance with Chassidic custom, I entered *yechidus* on Thursday, 25 Elul, at approximately 10:30 PM.

Recitation of Selichos

The Selichos prayers were recited in the Shul. Reb Shmuel Zalmanov who had served as the chazan for the Rebbe Rayatz, led the services. The Rebbe did not stand at his regular place in the southeast portion of the Shul (near the door leading to the adjoining room). Instead, he stood next to the table in the northeast corner of the Shul.

The Rebbe's usual place of prayer was two or three cubits to the right of the Rebbe Rayatz's lectern, which stood in the southeast corner of the Shul. The Rebbe Rayatz prayed at the lecturn on the High Holidays in the first years after his arrival in America.[1] [After his passing, the lectern was broken into pieces and the center board used for the part of his coffin placed under his head. I also have a small piece of that lectern.]

~

The recitation of Selichos began a few minutes after midnight according to standard time.[2]

After Selichos, the Rebbe motioned for me to approach him. When the Rebbe finished speaking, I told him that on Shabbos, I will be 22 years old and I would like to know when I could enter *yechidus*. The Rebbe answered that I could come on Friday during the day or on Thursday night.

When I entered, the Rebbe was sitting at his desk, facing east. He was wearing a short jacket and a black hat. When I entered, the door was open and the Rebbe told me to close it. I closed the door and approached the Rebbe with the *pan*[3] which stated that I reached the age of 22 and was asking for the Rebbe's blessing.

When he took the *pan* from me, his face was very earnest. He read it with careful attention. His reading took a long time, considering that I had written only one line. He then raised his holy eyes and looked at me and said: "May you grow to be a Chassid, G-d-fearing, and a scholar. May the Rebbe's[4] blessings be fulfilled. May a portion of the Rebbe's projects which he sought to accomplish be accomplished through you. In the course of this year, a good suggestion with regard to a *shidduch* should be made to you and may you establish yourself in a fitting manner.

"You will probably use the day to study the Rebbe's *maamar*

[1] In later years, a separate *minyan* was arranged for him in his apartment.
[2] I.e., the prayers began shortly after 1 AM Daylight Savings Time, which is actually a few minutes after midnight.
[3] An acronym for the words *pidyon* nefesh, literally, "the redemption of the soul," a note given by a Chassid to his Rebbe.
[4] I.e., the Rebbe Rayatz's.

from the third day of Selichos. It can be assumed that you will travel to the gravesite."

I told the Rebbe that if one must go the gravesite, I will go. The Rebbe answered: "You should go and you should tell the Rebbe everything, just like here."

I asked whether to write a *pan* and the Rebbe answered: "Certainly." I asked whether to leave the *pan* at the gravesite and he said to do so. He also said: "When you are at the gravesite, tell the Rebbe that you prepared a portion of the Rosh Hashanah *maamar* for printing."[5]

When the Rebbe instructed me to study the *maamar* of the third day of Selichos, I was not certain whether he meant that *maamar* or the *maamar* of Rosh Hashanah. I asked him and he replied emphatically: "The *maamar* of the third day of Selichos."

Friday, 4 Tishrei, 5711, Brooklyn, a continuation of the above entry

On the following day, in the afternoon, I went to the gravesite and carried out all the Rebbe's instructions.

The Kabbalas Shabbos service and the evening prayers were recited in the room of the Rebbe Rayatz, the Rebbe's place was on the southern side of the table for Shemoneh Esreh. The chazan stood near the small table, the place where the Rebbe Rayatz would sit when he would lead the services. There were five candles burning on the table in three candelabra, three in the middle candelabrum, and one in each of the side candelabra.

[5] See facsimile of the preface to the *maamar* in the Hebrew text.

After I wished the Rebbe "good Shabbos" and he wished me "good Shabbos," the Rebbe took out his Siddur, the Siddur Torah Ohr published by Aggudas Chassidei Chabad in New York. I heard that this was the Siddur of the Rebbe Rayatz. In the Siddur were placed several of the *maamorim* and *kuntresim* that were published after the passing of the Rebbe Rayatz.

The Rebbe gave me a letter typed on the stationery of Merkos L'Inyonei Chinuch in which he blesses me to be a fit medium through which the blessings of the Rebbe Rayatz will be realized in a complete manner. He also mentioned that I surely saw the entry for 11 Nissan in HaYom Yom regarding the conduct on a birthday. He also instructed me to study the statement in Kiddushin 30a concerning the age of 22.[6] He concluded with a blessing for a *kesivah vechasimah tovah* and added in his handwriting: "And to establish yourself successfully in a fitting manner, materially and spiritual." He signed it: M. Schneerson. The letter was dated 26 Elul.

~

On the night preceding Rosh Hashanah, at 11 PM, I went to 770 to see if the Rebbe had anything to give me in connection with the printing of the *kuntres* to be published for the night following Yom Kippur.[7] I stood in the corridor. When the Rebbe passed, he turned to me and asked: "Did you see Leibel Groner?" for the Rebbe had given him material for me.

With regard to my question about the editing of the proofs, the Rebbe responded: "What? I haven't even started yet."

[6] According to one of the opinions mentioned there, the period in which one is educated by his parents' continues until the age of 22.
[7] The Rebbe had prepared a *maamar* and talks of the Rebbe Rayatz to be published in connection with that date. Rabbi Gansbourg worked in the printshop that published these works and had already given the Rebbe proofs for review.

At 6 AM, during the recitation of the Selichos prayers, Leibel Groner gave me the package which the Rebbe gave him for me to give to my partner R' Mordechai Shusterman. It included a book owned by R' Avraham Yehoshua Heschel, the Kopishnitzer Rebbe, the father-in-law of R' Zalman Gurary in which were bound several works of Mussar and Chassidus, including Tzavaas HaRivosh.[8] The Rebbe desired that the first passage of the text be typeset together with some notes he had prepared.

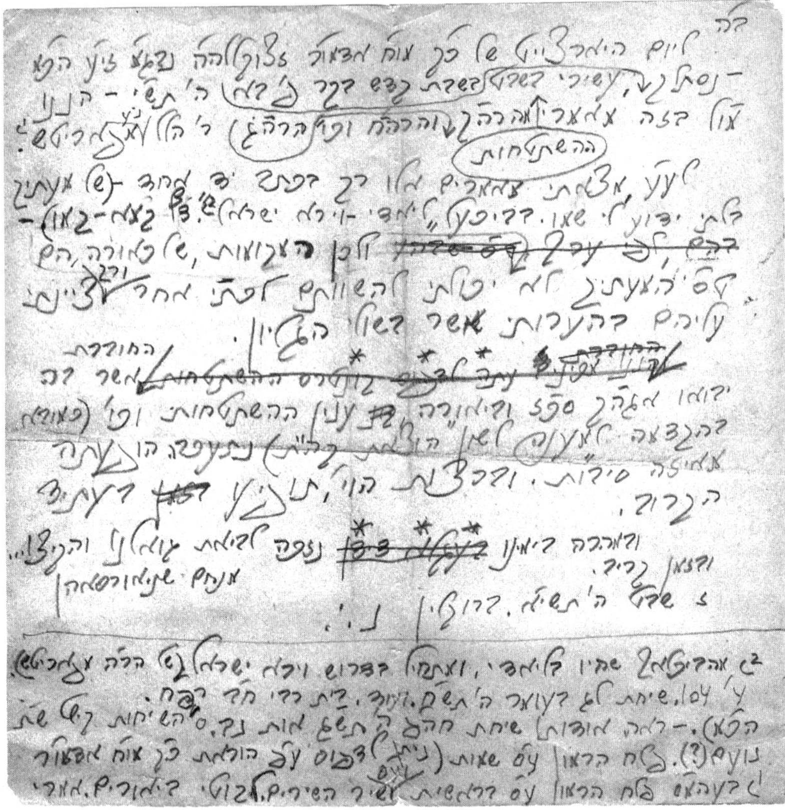

Rebbe's preface to the publication of Maamorei HaHishtatchus from R' Hillel Paritcher in honor of Yud Shvat 5711

[8] "The Testimony of the Baal Shem Tov," a collection of his teachings, recorded by his students.

He also gave me Kuntres HaHishtatchus[9] by the Mitteler Rebbe and asked that the first passage, that which continues until 'והב be set. He told me to tell my partner that he should continue to typeset the work Ohr Torah by the Maggid of Mezritch and that these should all be brought to him before candle lighting.

At 2 PM, the Rebbe traveled to the gravesite. A large number of the Chassidim and the yeshiva students traveled with him. There were two busloads. The Rebbe traveled in the second bus, sitting on the first bench to the right. Rabbi Chodakov, the director of Merkos L'Inyonei Chinuch, sat next to him as was his practice whenever they traveled to the gravesite.

The Rebbe read the *pannim* that were sent to him. This took an hour and half. When we returned it was already ten minutes after seven.

The rain was pouring. The Rebbe stood without shoes[10] opposite the gravesite. The student Moshe Kazarnofsky stood at the Rebbe's left and held an umbrella over the Rebbe to protect him from the rain, as he was instructed to do. Before making the journey, the Rebbe told Leibel Groner to take many envelopes with him. After the Rebbe read even a small portion of one of the *pannim*, Leibel would open one of the envelopes and the Rebbe would insert it.

The Rebbe would separate the *pannim* into groups and organize them in the following manner: Each group would contain around ten to fifty *pannim* and would be secured together with a stapler. Several small bundles would be put together and then they would be placed in an envelope. This was a new pattern that the Rebbe began the day before Rosh Hashanah, in contrast to the way he would do it previously, when he would

[9] A text describing the virtues of visiting the graves of *tzadikim*.

[10] It is customary to remove one's shoes when standing on the sacred ground of a holy gravesite.

return the *pannim* to the envelopes from which he took them. In eartlier times, he would place the *pannim* on the earth of the gravesite beforehand. But this happened only several times.

Afterwards, he would place the *pannim* in the pocket of his coat and then he would place them in an envelope as described above.

Before leaving, the entire community gave the Rebbe *pannim*, as well as money for the *pannim*. I gave four *pannim*: a) one for my parents and myself; b) one for my older brother and his wife; c) one for my brother Yitzchak and his wife; and d) one for my cousin Leah and her children. With each note, I gave a dollar.

When I entered the Rebbe's room and gave him the *pannim*, he asked me if I wrote my father's name, and the names of all the others. He said: "Possibly – or probably – they also wrote *pannim*."

Selection of the Rebbe's edits to publications prepared for print by R' Hirsh in 5711.

Edits on *Chabad Lubavitch (Askanus Tziboris)*, a publication printed in 5711, chronicling the communal work of Chabad

— 34 —

פרק ג.

איך שיטת חב"ד דאגה
להטבת המצב הרוחני של היהודים.

בפרקים הקודמים הוכחנו איך שהטבת המצב החומרי של היהודים לקחה חלק גדול כל כך בעסקנות הציבורית של נשיאי חב"ד. אולם עיקר תשומת לב של נשיאי חב"ד בכל דור ודור, שהשקיעו בזה כל כחותיהם במסירת נפש ממש הי' בעד הרמת והטבת המצב הרוחני של היהודים ברוסיא וביחוד בענין החינוך. וזהו הדבר שנטפל בו בפרק יה ובפרקים הבאים, אף כי בסקירה קצרה בלבד.

ונתחיל בפעולותיו של כ"ק אדמו"ר הזקן בשעתו. שהניח בזה יסוד נאמן לשיטת עבודה הציבורית של חב"ד.

הי' זה בתחלת הזמן שמלכות רוסיא היתה כובשת את מדינת פולני', ויהודים מפולני' באו לרוסיא ולקחו בה מקום בראש במסחר ובמלאכות מקצוע שונות. ומסופר אדות הזמן הזה באחת מרשימותיו של כ"ק אדמו"ר מוהריי"צ נ"ע:

„אף שהגבול בין רוסיא ופולין הי' שמור היטב, מ"מ היו משפחות יהודים עוברות את הגבול ברשיון הפקידים. שומרי הגבול, בעד מתנה מועטת או חנם אין כסף, כי הרוסים היו טובי לב ומתיחסים ברחמים לעני וקשי יום, ובאופן כזה הנה כמה וכמה משפחות יהודים העתיקו מושבם מערי פולין לערי רוסיא בפלכי סמאלענסק, אריאל וטולא. רובם אומנים סנדלרים, חייטים וחרשי פח (בלעכער), ובמשך זמן

— 35 —

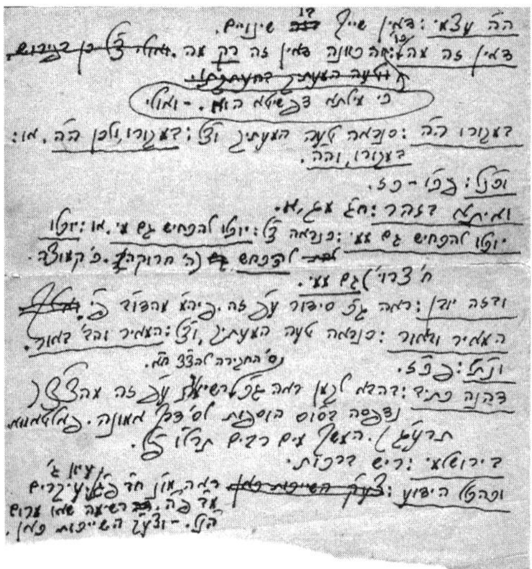

Footnotes to the Maamar, *Ayn Aroch 5694*, printed in Sefer Haim 5711 p.137-144

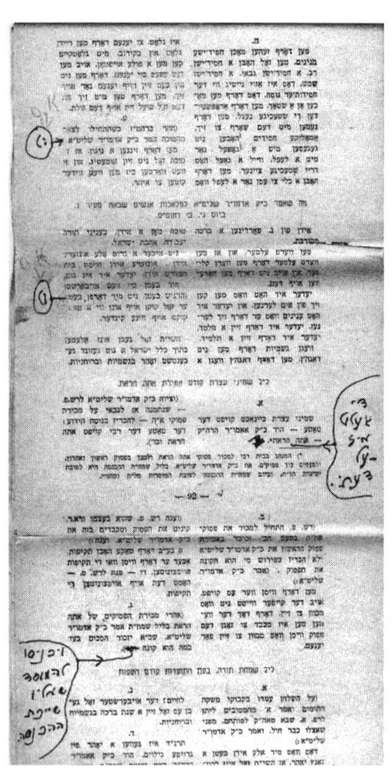

Edits to a Shemini Atzeres *sicha*. Printed in Sefer Hamaamorim 5711 p. 89

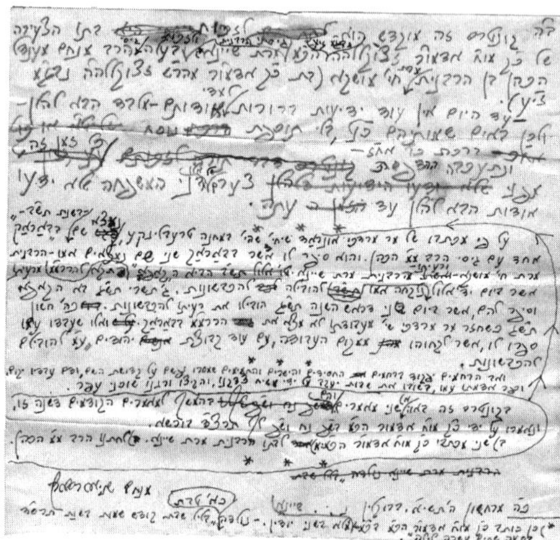

A deeply moving preface, dedicated to Rebbetzin Sheina (the Previous Rebbe's youngest daughter), and her husband, Harav Menachem Mendel Hakohen Horenstein, who were murdered in Treblinka. Printed in Sefer Hamaamorim 5711 p.106

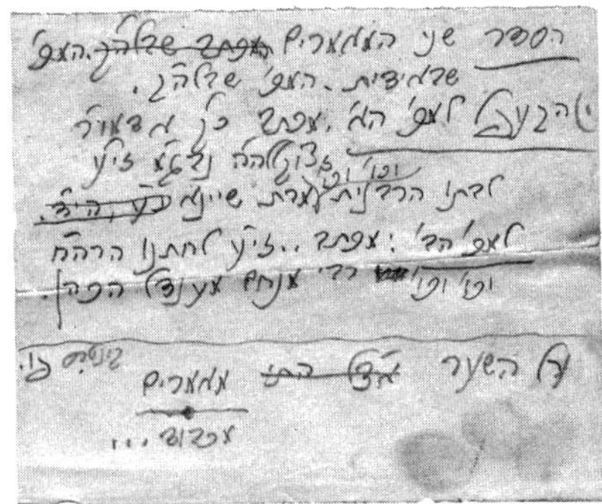

Instructions to the printer, how to typeset the *kuntres*

B"H, the Thursday of the week of the passage "*And you shall make Me a Sanctuary*,"[1] 2 Adar, 5712, Brooklyn, the apartment of R' Moshe Dubinsky, 767 Eastern Parkway

Last Shabbos, Shabbos Mevorchim Adar, Shabbos Parshas Mishpatim, the Rebbe left his room at 12:35 PM and entered the study hall through the back door (i.e., passing through the cheder sheni, adjoining room), taking his place at the head of the table which is positioned in the south-west portion of the room. (This is where the Rebbe sits every Shabbos Mevorchim. In contrast, when a *farbrengen* is held on other occasions, a special platform is set up and his table positioned on it.)

Upon his entrance, a special chair was brought for him (a blue, padded chair). In response, he made a motion with his hand as if to express surprise at something new, but he still sat at his place. After several moments, he began delivering the Maamar, *Lo Sihiyeh Mishakeilah ViAkarah*.[2] (As on occasions before delivering a *maamar*, the Rebbe's deep and intense feeling was noticeable and his face was white. From the last *yahrtzeit* of the Rebbe Rayatz onward, the Rebbe began a new practice. From Yud Shvat of last year until Shabbos Mevorchim Shvat of this year, when he delivered the Maamar, *VaEra El Avraham*, he would say a few words before delivering the *maamar*. On Yud Shvat, this year, he ceased doing that.)

The *maamar* lasted 55 minutes. While delivering the *maamar*, he cried very much. On several occasions, he could not hold himself back and cried loudly. At one point, he explained as follows: "It is written:[3] 'I shall fulfill the number of your days.' G-d grants every person a fixed amount of days to complete his Divine service. The amount of days granted a person is defined.

[1] Shmos 25: 8.
[2] Shmos 23:26. "There shall be no women who loses her young or who is barren."
[3] Ibid.

This applies not only to the days; even the hours and minutes are accounted for and a person must perform the Divine service necessary to use every moment to the fullest. This point should constantly be gnawing at a person; he should feel under strain and under pressure, contemplating what he could be doing to use this moment fully."

When he said these words, we could see that he was living them. He spoke them from the depths of his heart and could not continue speaking. He placed his head on his right hand and cried for several moments.

It is impossible for a pen to capture those moments. I ask G-d to allow that picture to remain in my mind for my entire life.

When he completed the *maamar*, those present said L'Chaim to the Rebbe as is customary and the Rebbe answered each one, L'Chaim Ul'verachah, as is his custom.

The vintage Chassid, R' Yisrael Gottesman, who is called Yisrael Baal Shem, said several words to the Rebbe with his L'Chaim. The Rebbe answered him: "The promise 'I shall fulfill the number of your days' will be fulfilled. It is necessary that the charge 'And you shall serve G-d your Lord' be fulfilled."

The Rebbe asked if the student, Sholom Morozov, had already davened. When he was answered in the negative, he said: "If so, he is before the morning service and can say L'Chaim."

Afterwards, he delivered a *sicha* on the same subjects, completing with a blessing (the quote is not exact): "May G-d help that those who still have not had children will this year be blessed with healthy children. May those who are lacking health be blessed with good health. May G-d help that those who are lacking sustenance be granted abundant sustenance as can be granted from G-d's 'full, open, holy, and generous hand.' And may we merit the coming of Mashiach here on this earthly plane, speedily in our days. Amen."

Part 3 – America 5718

Motzei Shabbos Tetzaveh, Parshas Zachor, 9 Adar, 5718, Brooklyn, 8:00 PM

Our home, 763 Eastern Parkway apt. 21 E

As I entered 770 this morning at 8:50 AM, I saw R' Dovid Raskin hurrying over to the yeshiva students. After a short exchange, all the students jumped up and, almost frantically, rushed toward the stairway outside the Rebbe's room. Someone informed me that a few minutes earlier, the Rebbe had come into the study hall and the adjoining room and then summoned R' Dovid Raskin. The Rebbe had said: "Those who want to hear Chassidus should enter [my] room." When I saw the commotion, without further thought, I quickly took off my coat and tallis and joined the students.

One or two minutes later, the door opened, enabling the thirty some people – of them only five young married men – who were crowded at the door to enter. Other students had been in the building, but were not able to reach the Rebbe's study before the door closed. Later, I heard that Gershon Mendel Gorelick was heartbroken and cried bitterly that he had missed this opportunity.

I placed myself by the window right next to the desk. The Rebbe sat on his chair, wearing his hat, looking in front of him, but slightly to the left. Later, in middle of reciting the *maamar*, he turned further leftward, towards the wall. There was an empty chair before him. This continued throughout the recitation of the *maamar*.

He seemed very taut, almost to the point of breaking into tears. He instructed that the door be closed. A moment later, he inquired if indeed the door had been closed. Only when he was assured that it was did he begin reciting the *maamar*.

The *maamar* was entitled *Zachor Asher Asah Lecha Amalek* and focused on the concept that we are given two commandments: to remember Amalek and to destroy that nation. He also explained the verse: "*The first of the nations is Amalek...*"[1] and highlighted the difference between Amalek and the seven Canaanite nations, as explained in the *maamorim* entitled *Zachor Asher Asah Lecha Amalek* from 5665 and 5687, except that the Rebbe altered the order of the concepts. When he referred to the phrase "*the wall of the daughter of Zion*"[2] his voice broke and he was near tears. Upon concluding the *maamar*, the Rebbe wiped his eyes.

The delivery of the *maamar* took about fifty minutes. When we had all left the room, R' Dovid Raskin approached the Rebbe and informed him that the young people were arranging a *farbrengen* after davening to mark the date, the ninth of Adar, the

[1] Bamidbar 24:20.
[2] Eicha 2:18.

The Previous Rebbe's Maamar, *V'Kibel Hayehudim* 5687, with the Rebbe's preface, edits, and footnotes. Printed in Sefer Hamaamorim 5711 p. 178-193.

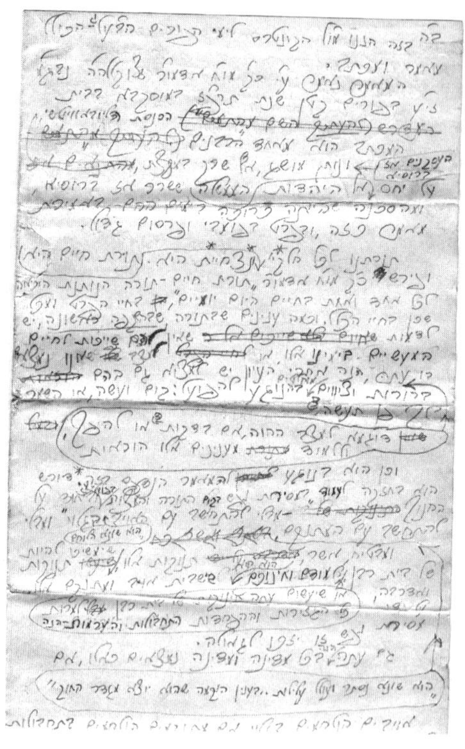

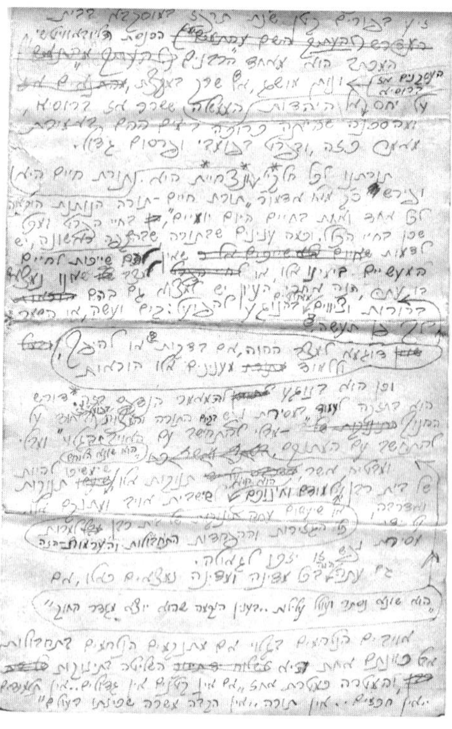

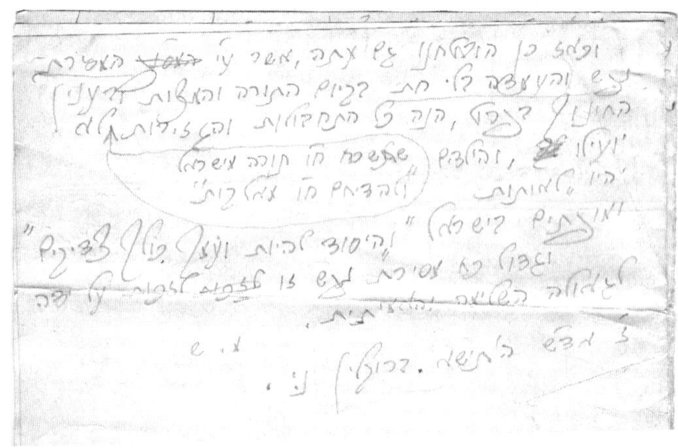

וקבל היהודים את אשר החלו לעשות. דעתה בזמן הגלות הם קבלו
מה שהחלו כבר בזמן דמתן תורה, וכאמרם ז"ל (שבת פ"ח)
ע"פ קימו וקבלו היהודים וכו', דקיימו עתה מה שקבלו כבר בזמן דמ"ת.
דלכאורה הוא דבר נפלא, דבמ"ת היו ישראל בתכלית העילוי דגאולה,
והיו במעמד ומצב משובח ביותר בענין החירות והחופש, וראו כמה
אותות ומופתים ביציאת מצרים, שהוא מה שבהטבע ממש הי' ניכר
ונראה בו הכח והחיות האלקי שלמעלה מהטבע, ובפרט בקריעת ים סוף,
עד כי בבואם להר סיני היו בתכלית העילוי, והי' גילוי אלקות במוחש
ממש, ובזמן הגלות הוא ההיפך מזה ממש, דאותותנו לא ראינו, כי האור
והחיות האלקי אינו נראה כלל בגילוי, ואדרבא החשך יכסה ארץ בריבוי
צמצומים והעלמות והסתרים. אשר כל גלות הוא בדוגמת גלות מצרים,
דכשם שבגלות מצרים כתיב ולא שמעו אל משה מקוצר רוח ומעבודה
קשה בעבודת פרך, כן הוא בכל גלות וגלות. אשר כל אחד בנפשו יביא
לחמו, בכמה נסיונות בקיום התורה ומצוות, ובזעת אפו בעבודה קשה
מאז קומו בבקר עד שעה מאוחרת בלילה, באופן אשר אין לו זמן לא
על תפלה ולא על תורה, וכל היום הלך ילך בטרדה עצומה, דבבקר
יאמר מי יתן ערב ובערב יאמר מי יתן בקר, ומבולבל כל היום וכל
הלילה, ובפרט בזמן המן אשר עמד עלינו לכלותינו, להשמיד להרג
ולאבד את כל היהודים מנער ועד זקן טף ונשים מבלי להשאיר ח"ו
שריד ופליט. וכדאיתא במדרש במקומו (פרשה ז') אמר (המן)
אין אני שולח ידי תחלה אלא באלו התינוקות של בית רבן, דזהו דכתיב
ויהי בימי אחשורוש, וארז"ל (במד"ר במקומו) דבכל מקום שנאמר ויהי

eighteenth anniversary of the arrival of the Rebbe Rayatz in America. The Rebbe responded: "It is very appropriate. As for my participation, the *maamar* is the best form of participating."

Two weeks ago, one of the *maamorim* mentioned above, *Zachor Asher Asah Lecha Amalek*, 5665, was given to us to typeset using the Simpson manuscripts as the source. R' Leibel Groner informed me that the end of the *maamar* was compiled by someone who had heard it. Last Thursday, he handed me a copy of the end of the *maamar* which was the Rebbe Rashab's original manuscript. We hope to have the *maamar* printed by the upcoming holiday of Purim.

The student Avraham Shemtov reviewed the *maamar* publicly. He was assisted by Yaakov Yitzchak Kadaner, Ephraim Rosenbloom and others. I was also able to help a bit as I was familiar with its content because I had typeset the *maamar* of 5665.

R' Yoel Kahn was not present when the *maamar* was delivered. When he arrived, he told me that he had studied the *maamar* from 5665, assuming that the Rebbe would refer to its contents in a *farbrengen* after davening. No one knew that today's schedule would be different and a *maamar* would be recited before davening. After the review, R' Yoel, of course, knew the *maamar* far better than I did.

~

After davenning, the *farbrengen* was held and Avraham Shemtov reviewed the *maamar* once again. R' Shmuel Levitin spoke a few words. R' Elya Chaim Roitblatt had taken L'chaim liberally and harangued R' Zalman Duchman somewhat.

~

Last Saturday night, a community-wide melaveh malkah-*farbrengen* organized by Tzach was attended by about one hundred people, eighty of whom were young married men. It was held in Rabbi Novak's Shul on Troy Avenue. R' Dovid Raskin gave a general overview of Tzach's activities. A guest from overseas, Rabbi Shneur Gorelick, read the letter which the Rebbe had written on Rosh Chodesh Shevat to the branches of Tzach. (As is known, this letter was addressed mainly to the branch in Rio De Janeiro, Brazil.) The contents of the letter include an explanation of the verse: "*And on the first day of the eleventh month, on the first of the month, Moshe began explaining the Torah*."[3]

Rabbi Mordechai Mentlik delivered an inspiring speech that focused on the importance of dedicating oneself to the Rebbe's activities. He suggested that a few young married men should undertake to devote themselves wholly to these activities. He spoke like a genuine Chassid, and even Reb..., the great critic, was impressed.

~

On Sunday there was a women's event, including a play performed by the students of Bais Rivkah, as a fundraiser on behalf of Yeshivas Oholei Torah whose principal is R' Michoel Teitelbaum. The program also included a showing of a film of last year's Lag B'omer parade.

I spoke for the women, expounding upon the story cited in the *maamar* entitled *V'Kibel Hayehudim*, 5687, and the *sicha* of Purim of last year, where the Rebbe elaborated on the story from the Medrash about the twenty two thousand children whom Mordecai gathered and taught.

~

On Monday, we held a meeting in R' Yoel's house to discuss the issue of singing at the upcoming Purim *farbrengen*. Rabbi

[3] Devarim 1:1.

Chodakov had again urged that something be done about it. We decided that a specific area would be designated and fifteen people would be assigned with leading the singing together. Perhaps something will come of this. We also compiled a list of twenty niggunim and signals when they should be sung at the *farbrengen*.

~

On Tuesday, a shiur attended by friends was held in our home. We studied the laws of Pesach from the Shulchan Aruch and the series of *maamorim* entitled Kimei Tzeitzcha, 5708. After the study session, R' M. Goldman, R' Yoel and myself remained. We discussed the role and future of Tzach well into the night.

~

On Wednesday, R' Yoel came over to visit me again. I am busy editing Rabbi Yisrael Y. Pikarski's book on the Alter Rebbe's Shulchan Aruch, laws of *nidah*. We spoke for a few hours on various topics; it is quite interesting to farbreng with him.

~

On Thursday, we held a rehearsal of the niggunim we plan to sing at the Purim *farbrengen*. Most of the young married men who promised to participate didn't show up but a few did, as did about ten yeshiva students. We practiced the niggunim until 11:30 PM. May G-d help that it should work out well. Honestly, I don't have great expectations. Still, if we put in some effort, some good will result.

~

I must stop writing because I still have to speak for a group of women at the home of Mrs. Popack and then there is a Tzach meeting which will be held at R' Chaim Asher Garfinkel's house.

B"H, Monday, 11 Adar, 5718, 9:15 PM

On Saturday night, I spoke for Neshei Chabad and told the story of the Rebbe Rayatz from his diary of 5653 that is printed in the *kuntres* published for 12 Tammuz, 5711.[4]

At 10:15, I arrived at the Garfinkel–Kahanov home. Those assembled included: R' Moshe Pesach Goldman, the secretary of Tzach, R' Chaim Asher Kahanov, R' Yudah Krinsky, and R' Dovber Alenik. Later, R' Dovid Raskin and R' Moshe Kazarnovsky also joined the meeting. We discussed the planned visits to the Rabbis of Igud HaRabonim, the evening study classes that were recently established, the publication of various materials and *sichos*, and other subjects.

We concluded at 1:00 AM. I hope that the outcome of this meeting will be positive.

Last night as I was busy editing the Rosh Yeshiva, Rabbi Pikarski's book, R' Yoel came over to borrow the book of *maamorim* from 5660-5665. We spent a few hours discussing several Torah subjects, among them, a situation of compounded doubt (*s'fek s'feikah*). He reminded me of the Rebbe's talk delivered on 24 Teves, 5711 (1951), at the *farbrengen* held to mark the conclusion of the study of the Talmud. The Rebbe delivered a siyum of the tractate of Nidah. At that time, he showed how the rulings of the School of Shammai and the School of Hillel on various, seemingly discrete Torah subjects, e.g., a woman's status of ritual purity, the categorization of honeycombs as food or liquids, and the order of kindling the Chanukah lights, are all interrelated.

R' Yoel has a depth of understanding and a sharp memory.

[4] Sefer Hamaamorim 5711 pp 304.

After he left, I finished the editing of the book. It will be called Chikrei Halachos, Vol. II. As we agreed, he will pay me 50 cents per page and there are over 100 pages.

~

Yesterday the Rebbe gave back the edited proofs of the *maamar* entitled Zachor, 5665, and today its printing was completed.

R' Leibel Groner told me that the Rebbe had intended to print – or select merely an excerpt from – the conclusion of the *maamar* that was originally prepared based on a listener's record contained in a book of manuscripts compiled by Rabbi Simpson. Eventually, however, the *maamar* was printed with the conclusion taken from the Rebbe Rashab's manuscript substituted for that in the listener's record.

I interrupted my writing due to a visit from R' Sholom Ber Butman who lives on the fourth floor of our building. We went down to his apartment and joined R' Yoel and Eizik Shwei who were there. We read a few of the vast collection of copies of the Rebbe's letters that he amassed. I also confirmed that he would accompany me tomorrow at 7:30 on a visit to Rabbi Shlomo Goldman, as we planned in our last meeting. R' Yudah Krinsky had already arranged the appointment. I also called R' Moshe Pinchus Goldman about this, but he was not home. He had gone to the wedding of R' Yosef Waldman. I called R' Dovid Raskin and it was agreed that R' Yudel Krinsky would give the publications, *Kovetz Lubavitch*, *Bitaon Chabad*, and a copy of the Tanya to R' Sholom Ber Butman for Rabbi Goldman.

At 7 PM after work this evening, as I walked into 770, I noticed that the Rebbe had not davened the evening service with the yeshiva students at 6:45 as was his routine. He had been in his room in *yechidus* with Rabbi Binyamin Gorodetzky, who had arrived that day. He davened after the *yechidus*, at 7:30 PM.

Tuesday, 12 Adar, 12 AM

This evening, at 8 PM, R' Sholom Ber Butman and I went to visit Rabbi Shlomo Goldman on Pennsylvania Ave. We spoke to him for about half an hour about Tzach activities and urged him to organize evening classes for students who had studied in Talmudei Torah, but who had since left all formal Jewish education. He promised to act upon this. He shared with us that he had visited the Rebbe Rayatz – and also the Rebbe – on a number of occasions. Together with his wife, he had sought the Rebbe's blessing before their marriage.

We left some Chabad publications with him including a copy of *Kovetz Lubavitch, Bitaon Chabad*, a digest of some of the Rebbe's *sichos*, and a few other items.

Later, over ten of us gathered at R' Moshe Pesach Goldman and studied, as usual, until 10:30 PM. We lingered on to discuss Tzach activities. We spoke about the need to revive the campaign of house-to-house visits, which had been neglected lately. There are many activities in which effort should be invested. However, special effort should be made regarding those that Rabbi Chodakov insists upon, for presumably this is based on the Rebbe's directives.

Leib Motchkin related: One of the people who was close to the Rebbe told me that the Rebbe was concerned that not enough was being done about the activities he promoted. That person commented to the Rebbe that the Rebbe Rayatz would himself urge people to be active in his projects. The Rebbe responded: "My way of doing things is different." The Rebbe wants people to take the initiative on their own.

R' Kehos Wiess, son in law of Moshe Dubinsky, related: "I heard that before the dinner for the benefit of Yeshivas Tomchei Temimim[5] held in the winter, Rashag[6] had spent 20 minutes,

[5] The Central Lubavitcher Yeshiva.
[6] The Rebbe's brother-in-law, R' Shemaryahu Gurary, the director of the yeshiva.

right before candle lighting, in *yechidus*. He had invited the State Attorney General, Mr. Lefkowitz, to the dinner and was notified that he would attend. Rashag was contemplating as to whom to assign to be the personal host and companion for the distinguished guest at the dinner.

"Whom did you have in mind?" the Rebbe had asked.

"Judge Klienfeld or Mr. Yekutiel Kramer," Rashag replied. Mr. Kramer was one of the people actively involved in assisting with the Rebbe Rayatz's emigration to America. He and his brother were of the main supporters of the yeshiva from the day of its establishment. "However," Rashag continued, "The judge will probably not be present and Mr. Kramer is away on vacation in Florida."

The Rebbe instructed Rashag to call Mr. Kramer and request that he make the effort and return for the dinner. Evidently, Rashag seemed hesitant, apparently, he was afraid that this might irritate Mr. Kramer. The Rebbe added that Rashag was welcome to speak in the Rebbe's name.

Throughout the Shabbos, Rashag contemplated the matter. On Saturday night, he made the call without intending to directly request that Mr. Kramer cut short his vacation. To his surprise, it was Mr. Kramer himself who informed him that he made plans to attend the dinner and had already arranged his flight. Indeed, he came back to New York and attended the dinner.

Wednesday, Ta'anis Esther, 12 AM

Today, twelve students from Pittsburgh arrived to celebrate the Purim holiday and Tzach arranged host families for them. Other guests included the Litvin family from Boston whom we invited for the Purim feast.

The evening service began at 6:30 PM. The Megillah was read by R' Mordechai Shusterman.

Certainly there are *farbrengens* being held in various places tonight. I believe that R' Yoel is farbrenging with the Sephardic students from Argentina. Since they do not understand Yiddish, a special *farbrengen* was arranged for them.

I feel that it will be too much of a strain for me to go out tonight. Apparently, I have caught a cold in addition to feeling weak from the fast.

Motzei Shabbos Parshas Ki Sissa, 12 AM

On Purim day, the Rebbe davened with the *minyan* and was called up to the Torah. R' Dovid Raskin read the Torah. As on the previous night, R' Mordechai Shusterman read the Megillah.

The Litvin family is staying at our home and will probably leave tomorrow. The Rebbe shows them much warm attention. They are now Torah observant and support the yeshiva in Boston. Recently, they helped in the purchase of a new building. Previously, it housed a conservative synagogue. It is large enough to contain both a yeshiva and a center for prayer and study. The Rebbe had given many blessing for this purchase.

The Purim *farbrengen* began at 8:30 PM and continued until 5:30 AM. There were many wondrous and unique revelations from the Rebbe.

I do not remember the bulk of the content of the *sichos*. On many occasions, the Rebbe spoke in a low voice and at times, he spoke to individuals. All of this, I was not able to hear very well, because I was standing somewhat far away.

Moshe Levertov promised to lend me his notes of the *sichos*, and selections from them, and I will copy them *bli neder*, with

G-d's help.

In the beginning of the *farbrengen*, the Rebbe was extremely joyous and instructed the congregation to sing happy niggunim. We, the group of people leading the singing, gathered near the platform and did the best we could. We think that the singing was better than in the past, though there is still room for much more improvement.

After a few *sichos*, the hall was getting quite noisy due to the large number of people assembled. It was very hard to keep them quiet and in addition, the microphone did not work well. It seems to me that all this affected the Rebbe's mood and as he had previously stated, "Everything is a directive from Above...." He instructed that the *niggun* Hei Tzomah be sung. (It appears to me that he instructs this *niggun* to be sung when things are not flowing as they should.) He also began the *niggun* Darkecha. Our attempts to lead a joyous song were of no avail.

At some point, something had a positive affect. When we concluded singing one vintage, heartfelt *niggun*, the Rebbe smiled and said: "That's a Fast of Esther *niggun*. Now a Purim *niggun* should be sung." The crowd burst out enthusiastically in a joyous *niggun* and the Rebbe was very happy. When that *niggun* concluded, the Rebbe began singing a Simchas Torah *niggun*, clapping his hands in great joy.

The Rebbe delivered a *maamar* entitled *Chayav Inish Livisumei* which lasted over an hour. The *maamar* was very deep, including an explanation about Haman building a gallows fifty cubits high and many classic Chassidic subjects.

In the middle of the *farbrengen*, the Rebbe singled out the Chassidim who had been of the original group of students in Yeshivas Tomchei Temimim when it was established in America on Shushan Purim eighteen years ago. Among them were: Ze'ev Shildkraut, Avrohom Barnetzky, Mendel Feldman,

Mordechai Altein, Yitzchok Kolodny, Yehoshua Goodman and others. Some who were called were not present. The Rebbe noted the significance of the anniversary and praised the yeshiva extensively. He personally gave each of those summoned *mashkeh* and instructed them to sing a joyous *niggun* and dance. He also signaled to Rabbi Mentlik to join the dancing. When Rabbi Mentlik thrust himself into the dance, the Rebbe too, stood up and danced in place. Rabbis Yisrael Jacobson and Shneur Garelick joined the dancing which continued quite some time. Afterwards, the Rebbe began speaking about the *sicha*: "All who go out to wage the wars of the house of David."[7]

The Rebbe continued speaking extensively about the yeshiva and seemed to direct some of his statements to those at its head, probably Rabbi Simpson in particular. Perhaps later I will have notes of at least some portions of the *sichos*.

The Rebbe drank a lot of *mashkeh*. He poured a full cup of Benedictine and drank it entirely in two mouthfuls. He requested more, but there was none. R' Binyamin Levitin drove home to fetch another bottle. However, out of concern for the Rebbe's health, Rashag would not allow him to pass it to the Rebbe. The Rebbe requested of Rabbi Mentlik to fill his glass, but Rashag prevented him from doing so. One of the younger men insisted and handed the bottle to R' Mentlik, but some of the elders intervened and instead filled the Rebbe's cup with soda. The Rebbe was less than pleased and emptied the cup on the floor instead of drinking it.

Rabbi Dovber Rivkin slipped his hand under the Rebbe's fist while he was pounding on the table. The Rebbe said: "People want to protect my health. They should simply invest them-

[7] A *sicha* originally delivered by the Rebbe Rashab in 5661 (1900), shortly after the establishment of the yeshiva in which he spells out his goals for that institution.

selves in Tomchei Temimim."

Leib Motchkin approached the table and requested a blessing for his mother's health. The Rebbe then turned to Rabbi Chodakov saying: "Perhaps you could announce that the hospitals have been closed and that the economic issues have been resolved..." A while later, the Rebbe filled Leib's cup with *mashkeh*. (I am not necessarily writing in the exact order of events, as I do not remember clearly.)

The hall was very noisy and the organizers were not able to do their job. R' Zalman Duchman wanted to get up and make a public request for quiet and order, but the Rebbe restrained him, saying: "This should have been thought about and planned yesterday. Now sit down."

In a low tone, the Rebbe gave an inclusive blessing for children, health and sustenance. It was an elongated blessing and detailed: "The children should be healthy and those who do not have children should be blessed with offspring. Those who have daughters should be blessed with sons. With regard to health, everyone should be blessed with vigorous health. And with regard to earning a livelihood, not only should everyone be able to make ends meet, but they should receive abundant financial blessings." All of these requests were elaborated upon in great detail. May G-d fulfill his blessings.

The Rebbe told Reb A. B. to send his children to Tomchei Temimim and elaborated on the matter. He gave the same directive to S. F. adding: "Though I had agreed to taking him out, nevertheless, he should send him to Tomchei Temimim. He also spoke a long *sicha* to Reb A.'s son, urging him to desire to go to the yeshiva.

Some of the *sichos* were based on the *maamar* of the Alter Rebbe entitled, *LaYehudim Hoyisah Orah*, explaining that the term orah employs a feminine form. Several *sichos* began with this quote. At one point, the Rebbe instructed that the *niggun* Ani Maamin be sung.

While speaking on the subject of Tomchei Temimim, the Rebbe said: "Everyone should participate in efforts on behalf of the yeshiva with his body and soul... and he should not neglect to participate with his money."

At the end of the *farbrengen*, at about 5:00 AM, the Rebbe made a Purim appeal on behalf of Kupas Rabeinu. He instructed that the Baal Shem Tov's *niggun* be sung and then the Alter Rebbe's *niggun* of four stanzas. The last stanza was sung only once.

A few minutes later, the first rays of dawn shined.

Thursday, Adar 21, 12:30 AM

Unfortunately, I could not write extensively on Saturday night, because while I was writing, Mr. and Mrs. Litvin came in and I had to speak to them. At 8 PM, they had entered *yechidus* with the Rebbe. The *yechidus* lasted 45 minutes.

During the Purim *farbrengen*, Mr. Litvin had approached the Rebbe with his four-year-old daughter and requested a blessing. The Rebbe had handed her a piece of cake and instructed her to recite a blessing. She did so and the Rebbe answered Amen.

On Shabbos day, a *farbrengen* was held at 1:30 PM in the structure in the courtyard of 770. It lasted for about two hours. There were a few *sichos* and the Rebbe instructed us to sing the *niggun* Ani Maamin. The Rebbe spoke about the Chassid, R' Pinchas Raizes, whose last name derives from the name of his mother-in-law, Raize, and not his father, the Gaon of Shklov.

R' Pinchas' mother-in-law was a wealthy woman from Shklov who had three married daughters. When the Alter Rebbe had visited her city, he had made a powerful impact upon her. She marveled at how an unknown Maggid from Vitebsk had impressively answered all the questions posed to him by the Gaonim of this city known for its scholarship, while they could only answer one out the three questions that the visitor posed to them. She duly declared that she would bequeath her wealth to any of her sons-in-law who would spend time with the Alter Rebbe in Liozna.

R' Pinchas traveled to Liozna and stayed there for about three months. He returned with a signed letter confirming that he had studied there, which he presented to his mother-in-law. She in return granted him all her wealth, quite a large sum. R' Pinchas returned to Liozna and handed all the money to the Alter Rebbe who blessed R' Pinchas with both Torah knowledge and material success. R' Pinchas asked for an additional blessing (evidently, children) but the Alter Rebbe did not respond.

Often the Alter Rebbe – and the Rebbeim of subsequent generations – would deliver a Chassidic discourse, a *maamar*, without a prepared text. There were certain Chassidim, called *chozrim*,[8] gifted with the ability to commit a discourse to memory while hearing it and then repeat it to others. Among the chozrim of the Alter Rebbe's discourses were: the Mitteler Rebbe; his brothers, R' Chaim Avraham and R' Moshe; their uncle, R' Yehuda Leib (or Leibele as he was affectionately called); and others.

R' Pinchas was the most proficient of all. He would be able to meticulously transcribe the exact wording used by the Alter Rebbe. At times, in the midst of the delivery of a *maamar*, the Alter Rebbe would roll on the ground in *dveikus*, an intense state of attachment to G-d. R' Pinchas would bend down and

[8] Literally, "repeaters."

extend himself, listening attentively to catch the words. If he missed a phrase, he would leave a blank space in his transcript. The text Torah Ohr, a collection of the Alter Rebbe's discourses, was to a large extent compiled from R' Pinchas' transcripts. Therefore in certain places, there are lapses in the flow. R' Pinchas had missed several words or lines and had left a blank space. The Tzemach Tzedek had filled in the missing connections, but in some instances, the conceptual flow is still somewhat choppy.

The Rebbe was obviously joyous throughout the *farbrengen*. He explained that though the obligation to perform the mitzvos of Purim applies only until the 15th day of Adar, the entire month is permeated by joy and celebration.

After the davenning on Shabbos, the Rebbe (via Rabbi Chodakov) summoned R' Yoel and Avraham Shemtov (one of the talented students who reviews the Rebbe's teaching by heart). They remained in the Rebbe's room for about twenty minutes. The Rebbe asked them if they knew all the *sichos* from the Purim *farbrengen*... [and what] transpired during the *farbrengen* after the first two *sichos* and the *maamar* which followed.

(Evidently, this was a matter of "the Divine spirit speaks through his throat." I heard that this phenomenon also occurred with previous Rebbes.)

The two reviewed a portion of the *sichos* and related the proceedings that took place at the *farbrengen*. The Rebbe expressed surprise at some of the things accounted, including the singing of the last stanza of the Alter Rebbe's *niggun*.

"Why only once?" the Rebbe asked.

"This is what the Rebbe had instructed."

"I requested that? Nu..." the Rebbe said, implying that he

accepted their reply. He requested an outline of the *sichos*. Today, it was presented to him.

R' Yoel called me, informing me that the Rebbe had returned the outline that had been prepared, editing some of its content, and erasing the comments directed to individuals. R' Yoel was not certain whether the intent was to publicize the *sichos*. I suggested that Dovid Raskin should ask, via Rabbi Chodakov, about including these notes in the digest of the Rebbe's talks published by Tzach.

On Sunday and Monday night, I stayed late at 770 to listen to R' Yoel review the *maamar* and the *sichos*. He explained that there is a new insight in the *maamar* regarding the concept of the inner and external dimensions of Will which helps clarify a number of passages in the Chassidic classic, the series of *maamorim* entitled, *Yom Tov Shel Rosh Hashanah*, 5666.

On Monday, I also assisted R' Dovid Raskin in arranging a list of classes organized through Tzach, which will be advertised in a newspaper on Friday.

On Tuesday, we attended the marriage of the student, Baruch Brikman, to the daughter of Rabbi Chaiken from Montreal. The Rebbe officiated at the chupah. We stayed late, returning home after 1 AM.

Yesterday, R' Yoel came over and we worked for over three hours preparing the digest of the Purim *sichos*. We hope they will be approved by the Rebbe and printed in the near future.

~

This week, Mrs. Pruss, mother in law of Sholom Ber Levertov (Kabiliaker) and Mordechai Dubinsky, visited us. She related a wondrous incident about the Rebbe. One of the members of the Shul where Sholom serves as the attendant had an eleven-year-old daughter with an agonizing condition. Her hair was falling out at a rapid pace. She was so distraught and embarrassed that she refused to leave her home. Though she was taken to many doctors and also to Rebbes for blessings, her condition did not improve. Upon Sholom's advice, they went to consult the Rebbe.

The Rebbe told them that if the child would make a commitment to wear a wig after her marriage, G-d will help and her hair would grow back. The young girl gave her word and shortly thereafter her hair began to grow. She now has a head full of long, lush hair.

B"H, Saturday night following Shabbos Parshas Parah, Vayakhel-Pekudei, Adar 23 (Addenda to the description of the Purim holiday)

R' Yaakov Holtzman told me that the Rebbe read the Megillah for the Rebbetzin. He read very quickly and she listened without following in a text.

During the Purim *farbrengen*, the Rebbe turned to Reb... and said: "He should make a commitment to follow my instructions, even if, according to his understanding, this is not what is stated in the Shulchan Aruch. He can rely on me that the instructions are indeed compatible with the Shulchan Aruch." (The quote is only approximate.) At today's *farbrengen*, the Rebbe commented: "He has begun following my instructions, may it be a good beginning."

Evidently, the Rebbe noticed puzzled looks on some people's faces and he responded smiling: "There was an Armenian in Rostov who would say, 'Mine, yours, mister.'"

~

At the end on the *farbrengen*, the Rebbe spoke about the importance of studying Chassidus on Shabbos morning before davening. With a smile, he stated that they should arrive in the early morning, at 9 AM. R' Shmuel Levitin said: "This most probably does not refer to the yeshiva students." To which the Rebbe announced that he was not addressing the students, for they have a fixed study schedule.

~

A terrible tragedy struck this week. The seven year-old son of R' Yehoshua Goodman (R' Yehudah Krinsky's brother-in-law) passed away. This is doubly tragic, because last year the family suffered the sudden loss of another child of the same age. Tomorrow, some of our friends are planning a Shiva call to their home in New Haven. May G-d comfort them among all the mourners of Zion and Jerusalem.

Today's *farbrengen* lasted for about two hours. There were three *sichos* and a *maamar* based on the verse Zos Chukas HaTorah. The Rebbe did not appear particularly high-spirited, but he did speak about the joy during the month of Adar. He also instructed that a Purim *niggun* be sung. By the end of the *farbrengen*, "the clouds had scattered" and he appeared joyous.

~

When the Rebbe was given the digest of the *sichos* prepared by Tzach, he responded: "I already gave back [*sichos*] for Tzach." (His intent was the outline of the *sichos* originally prepared by R' Yoel and R' Avraham Shemtov.)

When R' Leibel Groner told him that those were merely an outline, he replied: "This is the same." He did say to include the digest of the first two *sichos* from Purim which were not included in the original outline.

Much editing is necessary to prepare the outline for publication, because, originally, it was not written to be disseminated to a wide audience. Today, R' Yoel and R' Avraham visited me and we worked on that. Afterwards, R' Yoel reviewed the *sichos* and the *maamar* in 770. Later, there was a melaveh malkah at the home of R' Mordechai Groner for the sake of *maamad*.[9] The Rebbe released two letters of the Rebbe Rayatz for this purpose: one to R' Zalman Duchman concerning the study of the Tanya and one to R' Yosef Flier from Chicago, from 5703, where he complains that he is not being helped in his work. It is an interesting letter, filled with much substance. It will probably be publicized over the course of time.

Mendel Baumgarten relates that of one his female cousins gave birth to a child shortly after marriage and then did not have children for many years. She and her husband went to the Rebbe to ask his advice and blessing. He told them that if they keep *taharas hamispachah* (family purity), they will have a child. At first, the woman did not desire to heed the Rebbe's suggestion, but after others persisted in convincing her, she agreed to try. On the very first occasion afterwards, she conceived.

A person from Detroit did not have children for a long time. He asked the Rebbe for a blessing and the Rebbe instructed that he check his Tefillin. It was discovered that the word, *beneichem*, "your children," was written in an invalid manner. When the Tefillin were corrected, his wife conceived and gave birth to a healthy child.

Wednesday, 27 Adar

On Sunday evening, I went to New Haven with Sholom Ber Goldshmidt to pay a condolence call to R' Yehoshua Goodman because of the passing of his son. It was a two-hour drive and we arrived before the evening service.

[9] Money given to the Rebbe by his followers to use at his discretion.

We stayed there for about an hour. There were others there including his wife's parents, R' Shmaya Krinsky and his wife, their children, Velvel, Yosef Dovber, and Shmuel Pinchas, his brother-in-law, R' Moshe Hecht (principal of the local yeshiva), R' Zaev Shildkraut and R' Hershel Fogelman.

We told some stories about the Rebbe. It was a good thing we came, because it gave him an opportunity to temporarily divert his attention from his deep pain.

R' Yehoshua related: "When the Rebbe Rayatz had visited America in 1929, an observant man approached him telling him about his son who (like many young people at the time) followed the communist ideology. The young man was soon to be married and the father was anxious to bring him closer to a Torah lifestyle. The Rebbe suggested that he should broach the topic of *taharas hahishpachah* with him and explained that this would be aligned with their perspective that the youth should be allowed free choice. A child who is not born in *taharah* would lack the full opportunity to choose freely. This approach proved effective and the young man agreed to adhere to the guidelines of *taharas hamishpachah*.

We returned to New York at about 10 PM.

~

On Monday, R' Yoel came over and we worked for a few hours on the outline of the Purim *sichos*. We had to correlate this outline with the digest of the *sichos* which we had worked on the previous week. There was much work and we still had not concluded by the time he left. Nachman Sudak and Baruch Sholom Kahn are assisting with the copying.

Yesterday, Tuesday, a shiur in halachah was held at R' Yoel's home and he reviewed the *sichos* from Shabbos. We concluded studying at 10:30, but I stayed for two hours longer to continue work on the *sichos*.

Yesterday, we received a letter from our uncle, R' Nissan Nemanov, in which he writes about the need to inspire oneself in the service of the heart. He is simply a Chassid of yesteryear. He takes everything to heart; nothing is superficial.

~

On Shabbos Parshas Ki Sissa, I reviewed the Rebbe's *sichos* of Purim, 5717 in the Shul where R' Michoel Teitelbaum serves as an attendant. This last Shabbos, I reviewed the Rebbe's *sichos* on the topic of the eighteen blessings in the Shemoneh Esreh paralleling the eighteen commandments given to Moshe regarding the erection of the mishkan, and the obligation of committing oneself to love a fellow Jew before one begins davening.

Today I completed putting together the schedule for daily lesson in Tanya in Yiddish for an ordinary year that was compiled by Leibel Groner. I believe that the Rebbe will take it with him when he goes to the ohel tomorrow.

Lately, the Rebbe is being driven to the ohel in his private car by R' Yehuda Krinsky. In contrast to the practice in the past, no one else accompanies him.

~

I had forgotten to add a point concerning the *farbrengen* on the Shabbos following Purim: In the middle of the *farbrengen*, the Rebbe instructed an individual to say L'Chaim and told him: "The Divine image should be revealed." (He was implying that he should grow a beard).

At the *farbrengen*, the *sheva brachos* were recited for Baruch Brikman. The Rebbe instructed that a wedding *niggun* be sung and we sang the *niggun* Od Yishoma to the tune it is sung in Jerusalem, as is customary.

The Rebbe instructed those who were traveling to Eretz Yisrael to say L'Chaim. He singled out Minski and, of course, Rabbi Shneur Gorelick. Later, Rabbi Baruch Naeh said L'Chaim, stating that he was traveling that week. The Rebbe inquired which ship he was sailing on and he responded: "The Queen Elizabeth." The Rebbe was visibly pleased and announced that it should be publicized that traveling on Jewish ships is a public desecration of Shabbos.

~

Tonight there is a N'Shei Chabad event where the *sicha* that the Rebbe delivered on Purim that relates specifically to women will be reviewed.

~

Sunday was the engagement of Yaakov Winter of Pittsburgh to Chasiah Polner.

~

This Shabbos, Parshas Parah, during the reading of the Haftorah, the Rebbe recited the words: "When I will be made holy through you, before your eyes" (לעיניכם) as well as "before their eyes" (לעיניהם), following the opinion of the commentary, Minchas Shai.[10]

Sunday, Nissan 2, the Yarhzeit of the Rebbe Rashab, 11:30 PM

R' David Raskin told me that the yeshiva students typed up the synopsis of the *sichos* and there was some blank space left on the pages. They had asked if that space should be used to include the letter that the Rebbe had sent to Tzach on Rosh

[10] I.e., the standard text of Yechezkel 36:23 reads לעיניהם. Minchas Shai, a classic commentary that deals with textual questions and grammar, maintains that the text should read לעיניכם. The Rebbe recited both versions.

Chodesh Shvat with the *sichos*. The Rebbe responded that he would compose a special letter. A while later, when the new letter was requested, the Rebbe said that it would be forthcoming after he edits the digest of the *sichos*. (On the one hand, it is very pleasing to know that the Rebbe will edit the synopsis. Hopefully, this will not delay the printing.) We are looking forward to printing the *sichos* and the new letter in the very near future.

When Yaakov Winter (the fiancé of Chasia Polner) was at *yechidus* this week, he inquired whether there would be a *farbrengen* on Shabbos. The Rebbe replied that he is undecided as of yet.

The congregation was actually anticipating a *farbrengen* and therefore prepared the structure in the courtyard, cleaning the snow that had accumulated heavily on Thursday and Friday. However, after the davening, the Rebbe informed Rabbi Chodakov that there would not be a *farbrengen*.

That Shabbos, Eizik Shwei, the future son in law of R' Chaikel Chanin of France, was called to the Torah before his upcoming wedding. (His future in-laws arrived this past week.) The Chassidim held a *farbrengen* and *mashkeh* flowed freely. Afterwards, I took the groom to our home where we were joined by about forty yeshiva students. Here, too, the spirit was very lively, but also uncontrolled. This vigor – and also the lack of decorum – continued at a further gathering held in the home of the groom's eldest future brother-in-law, Zelig Katzman.

On Saturday night, the monthly Tzach *farbrengen* was held in the home of R' Yaakov Lipsker. Among those gathered were R' Zalman Duchman and R' Shlomo Aharon Kazarnovsky who told many interesting stories.

R' Zalman Duchman related that at a *farbrengen*, he had heard directly from the Rebbe Rayatz: "When something [troublesome] occurs, one should picture in one's mind my father's face. If one had not known him, one should bear in mind my face. I bear a stark resemblance to my father." The Rebbe Rayatz repeated: "I look very much like my father."

R' Shlomo Aharon Kazarnovsky spoke at length about the instructions he was given when he was called for army service in Russia. He also shared some wondrous details about the Rebbe Rayatz, but it is hard for me to recount them, since I do not remember the names of the towns in Russia and the like. He also shared some details about his own marriage. (His wife is the daughter of R' Asher, a shochet from Nikolaev) When he had brought word about the *shidduch* to the Rebbe Rayatz, requesting his approval, he noticed a slight change in the Rebbe's facial expression and what seemed to be an uncomfortable shifting in his chair. R' Shlomo Aharon did not wait for a verbal response and immediately left the room.

He related what had transpired to one of the Chassidim. The Chassid responded: "A similar incident had once occurred and the Rebbe Rayatz gave instructions to go to the ohel." (This was in the year 5680 [1920] in Rostov.)[11]

R' Shlomo Aharon went to the ohel and wrote a *pan*, mentioning the *shidduch* and requesting that the Rebbe relay his response through his son, the Rebbe Rayatz.

Afterwards, he went back to the Rebbe Rayatz. When he entered his room, the Rebbe appeared very pleased and gave his hearty approval to the *shidduch*. Then he added: "My father has left a dowry for you," and handed him the sum of one thou-

[11] The year of the Rebbe Rashab's passing.

sand rubles.

There were numerous other stories told but many lacked precise detail. It is also very late and I am tired from today's work.

R' Mordechai Dubinsky's wife gave birth to a daughter.

Monday, Nissan 3

R' Yoel called me last night and informed me of the outcome of the meeting that was called by Rashag to further efforts on behalf of the yeshiva. Unfortunately, only a handful of people showed up. This is upsetting, for the yeshiva lies at the core of our souls and the Rebbe had addressed this issue on Purim. I was not able to attend, since the meeting was called for 3:00 PM while I was at work at the print shop. R' Yoel told me that it was decided to establish a committee that would act to benefit the yeshiva and that I was put on that list. I don't know how I will be able to participate, as my time is very limited.

I received a letter from my friend, Zvi Zahler from Zurich, Switzerland. He relates that when he received the synopsis of the Yud Shvat *sicha*, he relayed their contents in a number of *farbrengens*, specifically in the city of Basel where he has influenced a group of young people in the spirit of Chassidus. He also sent the originals to be copied and distributed in a number of other Swiss cities. He is the only person in Switzerland who is totally devoted to the Rebbe. He is an extremely G-d-fearing man, a genuine tamim and scholar, well versed in Shulchan Aruch, Orach Chaim and Yoreh Deah. I have just concluded writing him back.

We are getting ready to go to Eizik Schwei's wedding. His future father-in-law mentioned that he remembers my father from days back in Moscow. The Rebbe will be officiating at the wedding.

~

On Thursday, *yechidus* was over at 6:30 AM. Dr. Yaakov Grifel headed a delegation of people involved in activities in Europe who entered *yechidus* and remained for over two and a half hours. There was also a group of people who spoke to the Rebbe regarding the demonstration that was held yesterday regarding the swimming pool in Jerusalem. I do not have details as of yet.

B"H, Tuesday, Nissan 4, 5718, Brooklyn. 11:30 PM

Yesterday was the wedding of Eizik Shwei. The chupah took place at about 10 PM. The Rebbe officiated. As we were riding the bus to the Milrose Chateau Hall, I spoke with R' Yoel about R' Chaim Naeh's work concerning the different halachic measurements. R' Yoel related that, during the year of mourning, the Rebbe was accustomed to pray in the room of the Rebbe Rayatz. After davening, he would converse with the people who were assembled.

Once he was asked about the minimum halachic requirements for the size of a *tallis katan*. The Rebbe said; "There is a *tallis katan* that belonged to the Rebbe Rayatz. It should be measured, because it is smaller than some of the sizes required by certain halachic authorities (e.g., the Chasam Sofer and others). In general, one can rely on the halachic rulings regarding measurements issued by R' Chaim Naeh. My father-in-law esteemed his scholarship."

R' Yoel had commented: "There is a measure suggested by someone – the Chazon Ish."

The Rebbe responded with a smile: "'Someone – the Chazon Ish...' People give him *pidyonos* and he says – just someone?!"

Afterwards the Rebbe added with a gesture of dismissal: "This is all insignificant, merely intended to differ in opinion with chassidim."

I told R' Yoel that the Gaon, R' Chaim Zimmerman showed me a letter that the Rebbe had written to Rabbi Chaim Uri Lifshitz (the Director of Igud HaRabbonim) in response to an article that he wrote in the scholarly journal HaKerem about crossing the international dateline during Sefiras HaOmer. Rabbi Lifshutz had written derisively about Rabbi Menachem Kasher (author of the classic work Torah Shleimah) using strongly derogative language. The Rebbe had responded stating that it was inappropriate for a scholar to employ such language. Since the other person has a following that considers him a Torah scholar, writing in this manner could be considered as shaming a Torah scholar. And if the intent was to show that the other person is not fit to be considered as a scholar, why choose a topic that is understood only by select few? It would have been more appropriate to write against that person's ruling to drink a fifth cup of wine at the Seder, for this is clearly against Halacha. And he maintains that his understanding supersedes the Shulchan Aruch, the Rama, and all the later sages.

~

On Shabbos, the Rebbe read the *Haftorah*, beginning with the verses: "All the people in the land…" (Yechezkel 45:16-17) and concluding with: "Thus said G-d…" (ibid. 46:16-18) which are only recited by the Rebbeim.[12]

~

Today, a study class was held at the home of R' Sholom Ber Butman. R' Dovid Raskin called me there and informed me of a

[12] Ashkenazic custom is to recite these verses, while Sephardic and Lubavitch custom is to omit them. The Rebbeim, however, would customarily recite them. Chassidim explain that the rationale is that the verses speak about the Nassi, the leader of the Jewish people.

Tzach meeting scheduled for tomorrow. He also told me that the Rebbe had edited a portion of the digest of the *sichos*, adding many comments, and that it was ready to be typed.

R' Leibel Groner told me that the Rebbe had invested much time in editing the digest of the Purim *sichos*. He had asked: "Who wrote this up?" R' Leibel had remained silent and the Rebbe continued: "Why does [the quality of the work] diminish?"

R' Yoel and I had decided not to change the outline that he and Avrohom Shemtov had written originally, because it had been edited by the Rebbe already (as I stated earlier). Evidently, this was not desirable and the Rebbe was very dissatisfied. We should have started anew and written up all of the material again. This is a directive for the future.

~

I heard that the Rebbe had instructed some students to participate in the meeting about the demonstration regarding the swimming pool in Jerusalem. I do not have further details. R' Yudel Krinsky related that a few years earlier, when there were meetings and demonstrations concerning the subject of drafting women in Eretz Yisrael, a delegation of three men requested a meeting with the Rebbe. Among them were the Rav of Krasne; presumably, they were sent by the Satmar Rebbe. Rabbi Chodakov did not grant them access and upon their insistence, he stated: "Where were you when you planned and decided to hold the demonstration?"

On Sunday, Rabbi Chodakov spoke at a meeting arranged by Tzach for the educators. I did not attend.

Today, Rabbi Stern, an esteemed scholar and the head of the Debretziner Beth Din, told me that when his brother traveled to Australia, he had refrained on Sunday from doing any labors that would be forbidden on Shabbos, but that he did put on Teffilin. Rabbi Stern had visited the Rebbe at that time and he mentioned this point. The Rebbe differed, maintaining that there was no basis for such conduct, even though in one traveler's hometown, the day he was observing as Shabbos would be Sunday and in another's hometown, the day he is observing would be Friday. Although Rabbi Stern sought to substantiate his opinion with Rabbinic logic, the Rebbe persisted in his own approach. Rabbi Stern spent an hour and a quarter in the Rebbe's room.

Thursday, Nissan 6, 10 PM

Last night there was a Tzach meeting. The participants included: R' Dovid Raskin, R' Moshe Pesach Goldman, R' Mendel Baumgarten, R' Chaim Asher Garfinkel, R' Yoel Kahn, R' Yudel Krinsky and myself. We discussed the preparation of the speeches for the *tahaluchah* to be held on the upcoming holiday, plans to visit Rabbonim during Chol HaMoed, and the organization of a *farbrengen* for the students from other yeshivos who study Chassidus. Chaim and I were charged with organizing the visits to the Rabbonim.

Today a group of friends drove to Detroit, where Berel Shemtov is organizing a *farbrengen* and other activities. R' Yoel, myself and others are planning to go to Monsey, a two-hour drive, on Saturday night.

I have to cut short my writing as Pesach is approaching and there is much work to be done.

Sunday, Nissan 9, 12 AM

On Shabbos, the Rebbe read the Haftorah, according to our custom, beginning Yirmeyahu 7:21, continuing to 7:28, and then skipping to 9:22-23.[13] A few verses before the phrase: "Their faith has been lost and has been cut off," his voice broke and he recited the words in a low and tearful tone.

Last Shabbos, Mr. Reinin related that he had once visited the Rebbe in Paris. (I believe this was in ח"צרת, 1938). Upon entering the Rebbe's room, he saw the Rebbe engrossed in the study of a small volume. He requested that Mr. Reinin wait until he concluded his study. When he finished, the Rebbe showed him that he had been studying a text that had been authored by R' Aharon of Strashelye. He related that in their youth, R' Dovber (later to become the Mitteler Rebbe) and R' Aharon were friends and study-partners. Once the Alter Rebbe was standing by a window and saw the two walking together. The Alter Rebbe cited the verse: "Beloved and pleasant in their lifetime,"[14] and rephrased its conclusion to read: "May it be that in their death, they will not be parted." (Among Chassidim, there is an alternate version. He cited the phrase of the Tikkunei Zohar, "Two friends that never separate" and rephrased it, "May they never separate.")

When Rabbi Reinin concluded his story, I saw his eyes tearing. He is an interesting man, this Rabbi Reinin. The Rebbe Rayatz had shown him much warmth and closeness, as does the Rebbe. It would be good if I would be able to hear more from him, he must have much that is worth hearing.

On Saturday night, those who went to Monsey included: R' Mendel Baumgarten, R' Yoel Kahn, R' Yisrael Freidman, Elazar (the grandson of the Rav, Rabbi Shneur Gorelick, who had arrived on Thursday from Eretz Yisrael), R' Zalman Lipsker, and myself.

The *farbrengen* was held in the home of R' Gershon Helman.

[13] The Ashkenazic custom for reading this Haftorah is different.
[14] Shmuel II 1:23.

There were only a few participants, (because everyone was busy with preparations for Pesach). R' Yoel reviewed a few *sichos* and I told some stories.

Avi Helman showed us a portrait of the Rebbe Rayatz painted by the Tamim, Tanchum Levin. I recalled that when Tanchum had completed the portrait, he brought it to the Rebbe. The Rebbe summoned the yeshiva student Avraham Rosenfeld, myself and a few other students to his room. The portrait was positioned upright on his desk. The Rebbe asked whether, in our opinion, the picture resembled the Rebbe Rayatz. This occurred during the first year after the passing of the Rebbe Rayatz.

Mr. Helman feels deeply bonded to the Rebbe. Every Shabbos Mevorchim, he comes to Crown Heights to be present at the Rebbe's *farbrengen*.

Thursday, Nissan 13, 12 AM

On Saturday night, I merited to stand to the left of the Rebbe during the sanctification of the new moon. I believe that I saw him place two fingers on his lips when he uttered the words "As I dance...." When he recited the words "Sholom Aleichem", he turned to R' Zalman Duchman, then to myself and then to Sholom Yisrael Chodakov (Rabbi Chodakov's son who was not yet of Bar Mitzvah age).

On the afternoon of Tuesday, Yud-Alef (11) Nissan, his birthday, the Rebbe visited the ohel (gravesite) of the Rebbe Rayatz and stayed there for about five hours.

Yesterday evening, the eve of the thirteenth of Nissan, the *yahrtzeit* of the Tzemach Tzedek, R' Shmuel Levitin held a *farbrengen*.[15] (In contrast to his practice in previous years, the

[15] An informal brotherly gathering – with introspective melodies, refreshments and L'Chayim – at which chassidim exchange insightful teachings and recollections of Rebbes and of memorable chassidim.

Rebbe did not provide money for refreshments.) Several of the Chassidim told stories. R' Zalman Duchman related: "Once, R' Chaim Ber, the attendant of the Tzemach Tzedek, brought out a loaf of bread immediately after Havdalah on the final day of Pesach, saying that it was part of the *chametz* sold before Pesach. He explained that the Rebbe was obviously weak and the bread was necessary for his health."

R' Yitzchak Groner (Leibel's brother) related: "Before the passing of the Rebbe Rayatz, he had mentioned to the Rebbe that he had heard that the Rebbe Rayatz made Havdalah on beer after Pesach and that the beer had been sold together with the *chametz*. The Rebbe replied that he knows that the Rebbe Rayatz would make Havdalah on beer, but thought that the beer had been purchased from a non-Jew after the conclusion of the holiday."

R' Yitzchak questioned: "How it is possible to purchase products that are *chametz* directly after Pesach, since the contract of sale generally used does not contain the halachic conventions the Alter Rebbe requires in the contract of sale he suggests. ?"[16]

R' Shmuel Levitin answered, "the Alter Rebbe's rulings were directed to avoid possession of *chametz* when forbidden by Scriptural law. The prohibition against *chametz* after Pesach is of Rabbinic origin. Hence, even other contracts of sale are effective in such a context."

R' Zalman Duchman related that once a Sephardic Jew visited the Rebbe Rayatz in Leningrad and complained that the Communists do not allow them to pray. Several times, the Rebbe Rayatz repeated the words: "They do not let us pray, we pray underground."

After a while, he advised him to go to R' Shmuel Betzalel Al-

[16] The Alter Rebbe requires that the *chametz* be sold using the convention of an *erev kablan*. Other authorities do not require this measure.

thaus to learn a specific *niggun*[17]. "If you sing this *niggun* in their presence," he told him, "they will let you pray."

On the eve of Yud-Alef Nissan, the yeshiva students farbrenged at the home of R' Baruch Sholom Shwei. R' Cheikel Chanin and R' Michoel Teitelbaum were also present and I spent several hours there. Afterwards, they went to 770 to continue the *farbrengen*. R' Michoel related that his father-in-law, R' Leizer Tchitzshersker once told the Rebbe that if another Jew enters the Shul when he is davening, he davens better. The Rebbe replied that a Jewish soul is a candle and when another candle enters, the first candle burns more powerfully.

My daughter Sarale caught measles, but it does not appear serious. May G-d grant her a speedy recovery. On Yud-Alef Nissan, I asked R' Leibel Groner to convey word of her condition to the Rebbe.

Yesterday, R' Leibel Groner called, saying that a telegram came to 770 for me. I asked him to read it. It contained news that my brother Leibel's[18] wife gave birth to a boy. I asked him to convey the news to the Rebbe immediately. Afterwards, R' Yudl Krinsky told me that a similar telegram was sent to the Rebbe.

The night following the second day of Chol HaMoed Pesach, 11 PM

On Friday, the day before Pesach, the Rebbe burnt his *chametz* in the incinerator in the basement of 770. Before burning the *chametz*, he gave R' Leibel Groner all the newspapers that had

[17] Chassidic melody.
[18] R' Gansbourg's oldest brother, who lived in Israel.

collected in his office throughout the year to burn. He brought with him all of the *pidyonos*[19] that had been sent to him throughout the year. He threw them into the incinerator himself and mixed the *pidyonos* together with the *chametz* until they caught fire. Afterwards, he recited the *Y'hi Ratzon* prayer.

At 3 PM, he recited the afternoon service with a *minyan*. Afterwards, he began distributing the matzos that were baked that afternoon in R' Sheya Korf's matzah bakery. When I approached, he gave me matzah. I asked for some also for my father, my brothers, and uncles in Israel. The Rebbe gave me several pieces and said: "A kosher and happy Pesach." Afterwards, I asked for my brother-in-law, and the Rebbe gave me a piece for him and again wished me: "A kosher and happy Pesach."

R' Zalman Duchman related that when R' Shmuel Levitin and R' Binyamin Gorodetzki arranged the sale of the Rebbe's *chametz*, the Rebbe told them that a year in which Parshas Shemini is read eight times[20] is a year of blessing.

The Pesach sederim were held in the dining room of Rebbetzin Nechamah Dinah[21], like every year. The Rebbe sat at his fixed place to the left of the chair where the Rebbe Rayatz had sat. A silver plate with folded matzah clothes was positioned before the place of the Rebbe Rayatz. At the Rebbe's left, there was an empty chair with pillows on which the Rebbe would recline. To its left, sat R' Shmuel Levitin, at his side, R' Mendel Cunin, and then the students Leib Raskin, Hirsh Leib Begun (who, last week, became engaged to Moshe Herson's sister; they are both from Brazil), Kalman Brikman, and Yaakov Zvi Holtz-

[19] Notes requesting blessings.

[20] I.e., three times on Shabbos afternoon, twice on Monday, twice on Thursday, and once, on Shabbos morning. The Torah reading was read according to this pattern that year.

[21] The wife of the Rebbe Rayatz.

man, who waited on the Rebbe.

Rashag[22] sat opposite the Rebbe. At his left, there was also an empty chair with pillows. Out of respect, he did not recline. To his right, sat his son, Sholom Ber, to his right, R' Yaakov Katz (who had been appointed by the Rebbe Rayatz to read the Haggadah), and then, R' Hendel Lieberman, and R' Yitzchak Churgin. On the first night, I came in the midst of the recitation of Hallel and on the second night, before the eating of the Afikoman.

The Rebbe recited the Hallel until the conclusion of the Haggadah in a slightly upraised voice, in a chant somewhat reminiscent of that which he uses when chanting the verses before the sounding of the shofar on Rosh Hashanah. He recited the words in a state of potent *dveikus*[23], with a pronounced adherence to the melody. In certain places, it appeared that he would soon break out in tears.

It appears to me that while reciting the passage, *Min Hametzar*, he said ה' לי **ולא** אירא, adding a *vav*. Also, I heard him say יהללוך[24]...**על** כל מעשיך and in the blessing ובכן ישתבח, I heard him say: ומעולם **ועד** עולם, adding a *vav*.

At the second Seder, I saw the Rebbe put the matzah in his mouth, small pieces at a time instead of all at once as his practice was rumored to be. He ate half a matzah as the afikoman. (This is somewhat surprising, because R' Chaim Naeh writes that a *k'zayis* – an olive size portion – is an ounce, which is a little more than half a matzah, and preferably, two such portions should be eaten for the afikoman.) R' Nachman Sudak told me that the Rebbe also did not put all the maror in his mouth at the same time, but rather ate it bit by bit. He took some of the

[22] The Rebbe's brother-in-law, R' Shemaryahu Gurarie.
[23] Clinging to G-d.
[24] Hayom Yom, entry 1 Teves, states that Lubavitch custom is to omit the word על.

charoset that was placed on the table and put it in the plate of his wine cup in which there was some wine. Afterwards, he dipped the maror into the wine and dripped it on the charoset. Then he dipped the maror into the charoset. For maror, he used horseradish wrapped in Romaine lettuce. After each time he bit it, he wrapped the open portion with Romaine lettuce.

On the second night, the Cup of Eliyahu was filled following the Grace After Meals. (I don't know what was done the first night.)

On both nights, several times during the recitation of the Haggadah, the Rebbe looked at R' Yaakov Katz and motioned for him to read louder.

After pronouncing Leshanah Habaah BiYerushalayim, the Rebbe poured the wine from the Cup of Eliyahu back into the bottle, which was held by Yaakov Holtzman. (He also had given the bottle of wine to the Rebbe to fill his cup during the Seder. The filling of the cup was performed by the Rebbe himself.) The manner in which the Rebbe poured the wine of the Cup of Eliyahu back into its bottle was wondrous; none of us followed exactly what he did. He poured wine from the bottle to his cup and then from the Cup of Eliyahu to his cup and from his cup to the bottle, repeating this pattern several times. He also poured from the tray into the cup. It is hard to know how many times he poured. Nachman Sudak says that on the first night, he poured seven times and on the second night, nine, but I am not certain that this is correct.

While the wine was being poured, the Chassidim present sang the *niggun* Keili Atah. As the Rebbe departed, he motioned that they should sing with even greater joy.

(The only one other than the Rebbe who reclined during the Seder was Rashag's son, Sholom Ber. He also had a unique wine cup that was different from the others and also wine of his own.)

On the first night after the Seder, the Rebbe went down to his room and stayed there until 2 in the morning. (The Seder concluded at about 12.) On the second night, the Seder concluded at about 1 AM. He then went to his room and from there went to the study hall to explain the Haggadah, as is his practice every year.

The *farbrengen* lasted from 1:15 AM to 4 AM. In the first two *sichos*,[25] the Rebbe explained the connection between the heading Maggid and the passage Hei Lachma and also the passage Amar Rabbi Elazar ben Azariah. In the latter two *sichos*, he explained the passages Echad Chacham, Vayeimar LiAvraham, Ilu Kara Lanu es HaYam, Kamah Maalos Tovos. He then delivered the *maamar*[26] entitled Kamah Maalos Tovos and then explained the passage Tzafon.

After completing one of the *sichos* at the beginning of the *farbrengen*, he asked that a happy *niggun* be sung. R' Mordechai Dubinsky began singing the *niggun* ViHi SheAmda. When the *niggun* was completed, the Rebbe said: "In the Torah, sequence is also a significant lesson. This *niggun* relates to a later portion [of the Haggadah]." Mendel Baumgarten and I began singing the *niggun* Mi Mitzrayim Gealtanu and the Rebbe commented: "That relates to an even later portion." (For it is part of the Nishmas prayer.)

After concluding one of the *sichos*, he said: "There is a person whom my father-in-law chose to read the Haggadah. The writings of the Arizal state that the Haggadah should be recited with happiness and in a loud voice. He, however, read neither with happiness, nor in a loud voice. He probably is here. Let him at least sing a happy *niggun* now.

[25] Talks, an informal Torah address delivered by a Rebbe.
[26] A formal Chassidic discourse delivered by a Rebbe.

The individual was not at the *farbrengen*. It appeared that the Rebbe was vexed by that; he continued: "So let those here sing a happy *niggun*."

After some time passed, he looked for him again and then said: "The Rebbe Rashab once held a *farbrengen* in Petersburg – at the time when the city was still called Petersburg. In that city, there was a wealthy and distinguished Chassid who was not at the *farbrengen*. The Rebbe Rashab said that the Chassidim should go to him, tell him... and bring him to the *farbrengen*. And they did in fact do so."

Somebody apparently went and brought the individual to the *farbrengen*. When he saw him, the Rebbe was happy.

When he began to explain the passage *Ilu Kara Lanu es HaYam*, he said: "Before Pesach, someone brought me a Haggadah that contained an approbation from my father. I would like to repeat a teaching from there." (A student, Shabsi Alperin, brought the Haggadah to the Rebbe. He had found it among the sheimos.)

{By the way, Moshe Groner, Leibel's younger brother, told me that Rabbi Weitzman (who was a Rabbi in Brownsville in the synagogue where I review Chassidic teachings) once came to visit the Rebbe and brought him a postcard written by the Rebbe's father. When the Rebbe saw it, he rose.}

Wednesday, the third day of Chol HaMoed, 9 PM

On the night following the second day of Pesach, the students held a *farbrengen* in the study hall of 770. I also sat with them until 4 in the morning. We reviewed the Rebbe's talks and spoke among ourselves. Nevertheless, when I saw that it was getting a little wild, I left. I drank a lot of wine. Understandably, on the following day, I did not feel so well.

I related what I had heard from the student, Yeshaya Trietel of Montreal, that once when his father, R' Menashe, was at *yechidus*, he told the Rebbe that his family lineage stems from Reb Avraham Yehoshua Heschel of Apt. He asked the Rebbe if he had heard of him. The Rebbe replied: "Who didn't hear of the great Ohaiv Yisrael?"[27]

The students commented that once (I think during one of the meals) the Rebbe gave justification for one of the customs that Reb Avraham Yehoshua Heschel had followed, prefacing his words by saying: "In general, it is not my responsibility to explain his conduct."

Yitzchak Meir Gurary related some of the details of the Rebbe's visit to his grandfather, the Kopitshnitzer Rebbe, several years ago, when he comforted him after the passing of his sister, the wife of R' Leizer, the Vizhnitzer Rebbe. I must ask him more particulars about the matter.

~

On the first day of Chol HaMoed, Rabbi Simpson called together the students and conveyed to them the Rebbe's words of rebuke regarding their *farbrengen*, saying that it was very wild and that he had asked that the students be gathered together and reprimanded.

~

Yesterday, after the morning prayers, Rabbi Yollis from Philadelphia approached the Rebbe as is his custom every year. All those present in the synagogue gathered around to hear their conversation. I was fortunate enough to stand next to the Rebbe. Rabbi Yollis spoke of the *maamar* entitled BeEtzem HaYom Hazeh that the Rebbe Rayatz delivered in 5701 to a quorum (The Rebbe Rayatz was the tenth person there). Rabbi

[27] Literally, "Lover of Israel," the title of the book of chassidic teachings authored by R' Avraham Yehoshua Heschel.

Yollis mentioned that it was seventeen years after the delivery of that *maamar*. He told the Rebbe that it was his custom every year to bring a present to the Rebbe Rayatz and then he gave the Rebbe five dollars, saying that it was for the redemption of a firstborn son, born in purity. The Rebbe then replied:

May G-d help that this be "the redemption of the son." In the tractate Pesachim, the Talmud states that the father recites two blessings. In general, Pesach is connected to circumcision. The only mitzvah (aside from Terumah) which circumcision prevents one from fulfilling, is the Paschal offering. Indeed, even the failure to circumcise one's servants prevents one from partaking of that offering. After circumcision, comes the redemption of the son and the father recites two blessings.

Rabbi Yollis: What is the difference whether the father recites the blessing or not?

The Rebbe answered: "The difference is that a priest may not touch impurity and a father may." (The implication appeared to be that G-d, our Father, cares for His children even when they are impure.)

The Rebbe continued: "May G-d help that there be the redemption of the son and that the father of the son recite two blessings: the blessing of the redemption and the blessing Shehechiyanu. For the blessing Shehechiyanu to be recited, there must be revealed happiness. There are opinions that the blessing Shehechiyanu should be recited only for mitzvos that bring bodily satisfaction and not for mitzvos that do not bring such satisfaction. (Implied is that the redemption will also bring satisfaction to the body, that the body will be redeemed from the matters that are disturbing it.) In Tanya, the Alter Rebbe rules that the redemption is dependent on our Divine service during the era of exile. Now the Holy One, blessed be He, Himself performs what He demands of the Jewish people. Accordingly, at present, there must already be a foretaste of the redemption. May there be a complete redemption, a complete beginning of the redemption already, and then the complete and ultimate redemption in the near future."

Rabbi Yollis told the Rebbe that he wanted to see him at *yechidus* and the Rebbe agreed. Shortly afterwards, R' Shlomo Hornstein entered *yechidus* and then Rabbi Yollis entered *yechidus*.

~

Yesterday evening, R' Yoel visited to write up a summary of the *sichos* from the second night of Pesach. We sat until 1 AM. He has now arrived to complete the task, so I must interrupt this journal.

~

12 AM, the day following Pesach

Some further details regarding the episode related to me by Yitzchak Meir Gurary concerning the Rebbe's visit to his grandfather, the Kopitshnitzer Rebbe, several years ago, when he comforted him after the passing of his sister, the wife of the Vizhnitzer Rebbe: They spoke about the Vizhnitzer Rebbe. The Kopitshnitzer Rebbe said that the Vizhnitzer Rebbe brought additional happiness to Eretz Yisrael.

When the Rebbe entered the Kopitshnitzer Rebbe's library, he saw a copy of the Alter Rebbe's Shulchan Aruch. He commented that a new edition of that text had recently been published which contains a photocopy of a page from the Alter Rebbe's manuscript. From that page, it appears that the Alter Rebbe wrote, erased, and rewrote his text several times.

R' Sholom Ber Butman told me – apparently, the matter was known among the yeshiva students – that a short time before Pesach, the Rebbe asked Rav Chodakov if he knew anything concerning the health of the Vizhnitzer Rebbe. Afterwards, Rav Chodakov made inquiries of R' Uriel Zimmer, some Vizhnitzer Chassidim, and the Squarer Rebbe, and no one was aware of any difficulties. Later, it was discovered that the Vizhnitzer Rebbe had suffered severe digestive problems and had been forced to hold the Pesach Seder alone.

On Wednesday, the third day of Chol HaMoed, my mother-in-law traveled to Montreal for the last days of the holiday. Yesterday, at 4 AM, when I came home after the conclusion of the *farbrengen* of the last day of Pesach, Rasha[28] told me that her brother, Laiba, called from Montreal and told her that his wife gave birth to a boy on Shabbos in the morning. I immediately called Rabbi Chodakov to inform the Rebbe.

My brother-in-law begged me to come for the *bris*, but I am not sure that I will go, because on that day, there will be a *farbrengen* on Shabbos. It is the Rebbe's custom to hold a *farbrengen* after making Kiddush on the Shabbosos that follow Pesach and Sukkos and these *farbrengens* are simply beyond description.

As is the custom every year, on the seventh day of Pesach in the evening, the *tahaluchah*[29] to Williamsburg organized by Tzach[30]

[28] R' Gansbourg's wife.
[29] Lit. "parade." The chassidim would walk en masse from Crown Heights to Williamsburg where they would fan out to various shuls to share the Rebbe's thoughts and encourage holiday celebration.
[30] Tze'irei Agudas Chabad, the Lubavitch Youth Organization, the umbrella organization responsible for outreach activities in New York City and its surroundings. Rabbi Gansbourg was one of the members of its steering committee.

was held. This year there were many more participants than in previous years despite the rains and stormy weather. When we came to Williamsburg, we split off into small groups, each going to another Shul where one of the Chassidim would speak. Chassidim spoke in approximately 100 shuls. In many places, the Chassidim were received with warm affection. Afterwards, all the participants gathered in the Shul led by R' Avraham Ziskind (the brother-in-law of R' Mordechai Mentlik, and R' Moshe Pinchas Katz). There we made Kiddush and then danced in the street in joyous spirits.

After their prayers, Jews who had davened in other shuls came out to watch the dancing. We proceeded to the large square in front of the Shul of the Satmar Rebbe. (At that time, I did not know that his Shul was located there.) After much joyous dancing, my friends lifted me up on their shoulders and I spoke before the crowd that had gathered together. My talk was based on the Rebbe's *sicha* that focuses on the advantage of Moshe our teacher, that he highlighted the positive qualities of all Jews, even those who had willfully sinned by worshiping the Golden Calf. He was willing to sacrifice his own life for them, as he prayed: "Forgive their sin, if not, erase me now from Your book.[31]" I concluded by underscoring the parallel to the Rebbe, the Moshe of our generation, and his self-sacrifice on behalf of all Jews, his ability to motivate them to Teshuvah and, in that way, hasten the coming of the redemption.

Here and there, there were snickering calls: "There blood is flowing and he is speaking of their merits," but, by and large, those assembled listened attentively.

We returned to 770 with joyous dancing. Those in charge conveyed a report to Rabbi Chodakov to inform the Rebbe, who was partaking of the festive meal in the apartment of Rebbet-

[31] Shmos 32:32.

zin Nechamah Dinah at that time.

The *farbrengen* of the last day of Pesach, the feast of Moshiach,[32] was held in the courtyard adjoining 770. It began about 6:30 PM, close to sunset, and continued until 3 in the morning. Afterwards, the evening service was recited, the Rebbe himself made Havdalah, and then he distributed wine from "the cup of blessing" to all those assembled.

There were many *sichos*, most of them concerning Moshiach. The Rebbe also told several stories. He asked that the niggunim associated with all the Rebbeim be sung as well as the *niggun* of the Baal Shem Tov of three stanzas, one from the Baal Shem Tov, one from the Maggid, and one from the Alter Rebbe.

Many attended the *farbrengen*. A large number of others drove in from distant places after reciting the evening service in their respective synagogues.

One of the *sichos* concerned the *tahaluchah* to Williamsburg. The Rebbe cited the verse: "He will lead [the people in dry] shoes"[33] and asked all those who had participated to say L'Chaim and sing a happy *niggun*.

He told Rashag to provide wine for the four cups and told Rabbi Simpson to make an announcement regarding drinking four cups of wine. He made such an announcement, but it was not very clear. The Rebbe then asked Rabbi Mentlik to repeat the announcement and he announced that the Rebbe Rashab

[32] As reflected by the Haftorah read on that day, the eighth day of Pesach is associated with Moshiach's coming. To enable this spiritual concept to be internalized, the Baal Shem Tov instituted the practice of partaking of "the feast of Moshiach" at the conclusion of that day. The Rebbe Rashab, the fifth Lubavitcher Rebbe, augmented this custom by ordaining that the participants drink four cups of wine reminiscent of the four cups drunk at the Pesach seder. Shem Tov instituted the practice of partaking of "the feast of Moshiach" at the con-clusion of that day. The Rebbe Rashab, the fifth Lubavitcher Rebbe, augmented this custom by ordaining that the participants drink four cups of wine reminiscent of the four cups drunk at the Pesach seder.

[33] Yeshayahu 11:15; from the Haftorah recited on the last day of Pesach.

had instructed the students to drink four cups of wine. The Rebbe then asked that an announcement be made in accordance to his statements in previous years and pointed to R' Yoel. R' Yoel announced that in the previous years, the Rebbe had asked that not only the students of the yeshiva, but also all those assembled should drink four cups of wine. It appeared that the Rebbe was satisfied with this announcement. The Rebbe himself also drank all four cups of wine. After drinking the first cup, he announced: "It's already after the first cup of wine. We can sing the *niggun* Vihi SheAmda." All those assembled then sang the *niggun*.

(This journal does not follow the exact order of the *farbrengen*, because I have not heard the review of the *farbrengen* yet and am writing from memory.) The Sephardic yeshiva student, Aharon Tawihl from Argentina, began singing the *niggun* Azreini Kel Chai. The Rebbe motioned to Rabbi Mentlick that the student, Yehoshua Chadad, should also join in the singing, which he did. When that *niggun* was concluded, the Rebbe asked that the *niggun* Ein Adir KiBorei should be sung. Yehoshua Chadad sang the different stanzas and the entire congregation joined in the chorus: MiPi Kel Yivorach Yisrael. When all the stanzas were completed, the chorus was repeated many times. The Rebbe rapped on the table with his fist to encourage the singing and the Chassidim increased the pace of their singing according to the tempo he set. The Rebbe began to clap his hands very rapidly, heightening the joy and the singing of the congregation. The Rebbe then stood up and began to dance in his place and the entire congregation followed him with overwhelming rejoicing.

The Rebbe saw that R' Avraham Holderman came from Newark. R' Avraham was also called Avraham Kalisker and R' Avraham *der baal ha'galah*, because he was the driver of the Rebbe Rayatz when he visited America in 5690 (1920). There is much to tell about him. The Rebbe motioned for him to drink the four cups of wine. He walked on the tables and sat down at the table of the Rebbe. After drinking the third cup, he asked to partake of the Rebbe's matzah. The Rebbe told him: "Between the third and fourth cups of wine, it is forbidden to eat." He then told him to drink another cup. When he finished the fourth cup, the Rebbe told him to begin drinking the four cups all over again and added that thus he would be before Kiddush and before Kiddush, it is also forbidden to eat. He instructed several of those who came at night to wash and partake of matzah.

He called a young yeshiva student, almost Bar Mitzvah age, who was related to Yisrael Shmuel Engel. The boy was an orphan who came from Detroit, who had difficulties with both his left hand and left leg. The Rebbe asked that he approach him. Since it was difficult for him to walk, he asked Yisrael Shmuel to help him. When he approached, the Rebbe gave him three pieces of matzah, one after the other. Each time, he made sure that the boy took it with his left hand.

The Rebbe asked several of the participants if they drank all four cups of wine. As is his custom every year, he distributed wine to those traveling abroad and those living in outlying cities. This year, there were small bottles with labels from the Kedem winery. After distributing the bottles to those in distant places, he told them to boil the wine.

Towards the end of the *farbrengen*, he filled a cup with his own special wine and gave it to Rabbi Gorodetsky and did the same for Rabbi Ziskind. There was enough wine for one more cup and he looked around him to see to whom else he could give it. R' Yaakov Zvi Holtzman was standing not far from his right. He asked him: "Will you be driving?" (R' Yaakov was a truck driver). R' Yaakov indicated that he could be given the wine and the Rebbe filled his cup. R' Zalman Duchman wanted to receive a cup of wine as well, but the Rebbe did not give any to him, waving him away with his hand.

Several of the participants were slightly intoxicated, including R' Mordechai D. Teleshevski. When the Rebbe distributed wine to the Chassidim traveling to distant places, he also approached the Rebbe, but he could not stand up. The Rebbe smiled at him and gave him wine with a gentle laugh, saying, "...ופרצת 'And you should spread out westward and eastward, northward and southward,'[34] 'an inheritance without boundaries..'"[35]

When he distributed the wine, he gave first to Rabbi Gorodetsky and afterwards, to R' Yaakov Katz for Chicago.

Throughout the *farbrengen*, only happy *niggunim* were sung. The Rebbe clapped frequently and his face beamed forth great joy. He delivered one *sicha*, especially for women. In the middle of the *farbrengen*, the Schlesinger brothers, Rabbi David Hollander of Histadrut HaRabbonim, and the composer Nechemiah Winover came. The Rebbe showed them much warm attention.

During the *farbrengen*, he delivered the *maamar* entitled ViHechrim. In the middle, he explained the verse: "For the conductor, [a plea] not to be destroyed, a michtam of David's," the beginning of Psalm 57, the psalm corresponding to his age, as is his custom.

Wednesday, 26 Nissan, 5718, 8 PM

R' Chaim Serebranyski came from Australia in the middle of Chol HaMoed. He asked the Rebbe how he should conduct

[34] Bereishis 28:14.
[35] Berachos 51a.

himself with regard to counting the Omer since Australia is a day ahead of New York. (For example, now it is already the 27 of Nissan in Australia.) He began counting the Omer there according to the local practice. When he arrived here, he changed and counted according to the practice here. The Rebbe answered as follows:

The tenth day of the Omer, the 24th of Nissan, the eve of the 25th of Nissan, 5718:

I wrote that you should come for the Pesach holiday (i.e., not during Chol HaMoed).

1) With regard to a blessing, listen to it recited by another person;

2) [With regard to the counting itself,] count as you began; (for, according to my understanding, this is what is fundamentally required of you. As an additional measure,) also count as is counted here. Make an interruption between the two counts; i.e., one should not be counted directly after the other. (In such an instance, the counting would appear false. It is also directly opposite to the concept of counting, i.e., making a definitive determination, without a doubt. Accordingly, it is questionable if a blessing could be recited even if one would count in this manner through the Counting of the Omer.)

Ask Rabbis for a halachic ruling with regard to the observance of the holiday of Shavuos (which is dependent on the counting of every individual and not on the counting of the court).[36] *For, according to the above, you should celebrate the holiday of Shavuos one day earlier (on Shabbos and Sunday). This would produce a great halachic novelty.*

On Monday, R'Yoel reviewed the *maamar* (after we sat together

[36] See Likkutei Sichos (Vol. VII of the English translation), Parshas Emor, where this concept is discussed.

writing down the *sichos*). Yesterday, he reviewed a further portion of the *sichos*. He left me some notes regarding their content and I went over them. Today, I went over other notes. The text of the *sichos* for the second night of Pesach was given to the Rebbe during Chol HaMoed.

~

When we were at *yechidus* during the month of Shvat last year and the Rebbe asked about our financial situation, he told me to learn the profession of offset printing. I asked whether it was proper to open such a printing shop myself. The Rebbe answered: "Why is it necessary to open a new business, and then continue to have to invest money? It is better to expand the existing business."

From the stories told by the Rebbe at the *farbrengen* on the last day of Pesach: The Rebbe Rayatz once related that one of the "enlightened"[37] Jews came to his father, the Rebbe Rashab in Lubavitch and asked him if there was any proof that the angels existed. Since they cannot be touched or seen, how is it possible to know and prove their existence?

The Rebbe Rashab saw that intellectual arguments would not affect him, he told him a parable: "The way from Krasnia to Lubavitch is made by horse and buggy..."

At this point, the Rebbe paused and said: "As long as we are speaking about traveling from Krasnia to Lubavitch, I would like to tell another story.

"When the Russians began to develop a system of highways and roads across Russia, the czar Nicholas ordered that a railway line run through Lubavitch. The Tzemach Tzedek objected saying: 'In my town, I am in charge.' The Tzemach Tzedek

[37] I.e., one of those who had cast off Torah practice in favor of a secular lifestyle.

did not desire that a railway line run through Lubavitch because that would turn it into a major city and 'living in a city is trying.'[38]

"A Jewish contractor who had been offered the rights to build the railway in the area asked the Tzemach Tzedek whether he should accept the proposition. The Tzemach Tzedek told him to accept the proposition partially, taking the rights to the route shortly before Lubavitch and those for the route shortly after Lubavitch, but not the rights for the area in proximity to the town itself. He was able to arrange such a deal and he made a substantial profit. The rights to the railroad in Lubavitch were acquired by a gentile. When he began to build the rails, he saw that the ties sank into the ground. He replaced them several times at a great expense until he abandoned the project entirely. As the Tzemach Tzedek said: 'In my town, I am in charge.' A railway was not built in Lubavitch until the time of the Rebbe Rashab."

The Rebbe then returned to his original story. The Rebbe Rashab said: "In the wagon traveling from Krasnia to Lubavitch are sitting two scholars, contemplating the angels. Now the wagon-driver is thinking about the wages he will receive at the end of the journey. And the horses are thinking about the fodder they will receive when they reach their destination.

"But," the Rebbe concluded, "does the fact that the horses think about their fodder detract from the existence of the angels?"

Sunday, the first day of Rosh Chodesh Iyar, 11 PM

I just now came from a meeting of Vaad HaMesader concerning renovating the 770 structure in the courtyard. Approxi-

[38] Kesubos 110b.

mately $2000 will be necessary for this. The city's regulations prevent building a permanent structure in the courtyard. Therefore it will be necessary to cover the existing structure every Friday and remove the covering on Sunday. There were only 20-30 people who attended the meeting. It was decided that every member of the community should donate $25 for this purpose and $2 per month for the salary of a person to maintain the upkeep of the Shul. A search had been made for a suitable building, but nothing appropriate had been found as of yet.

~

Yesterday, the Rebbe held a *farbrengen*. It began at 1:30 PM. As I mentioned, the Rebbe had said that from now on, the *farbrengens* would begin at 1:30 and not at 1, as was the previous practice. The *farbrengen* continued until 4:15 PM, relatively short in comparison to other *farbrengens* that follow holidays. There were three *sichos* and a *maamar*, entitled, Kimei Tzeischem, that lasted approximately an hour.

The content of the *sichos*: To be totally given-over to the Rebbe without questioning or making personal considerations. The Rebbe told the story found in Shivchei Arizal,[39] that once, on Friday, the Arizal went out with his students to receive the Shabbos queen in the fields outside the city, because according to Kabbalah, one should receive the Shabbos at the outskirts of the city. The Arizal asked his students if they wanted to receive the Shabbos in the outskirts of Jerusalem. Several of the students replied that they had to go home and ask their wives. This answer lowered the Arizal's spirits. Afterwards, he told his students that if they had agreed to spend the Shabbos in Jerusalem, they would have brought about the redemption.

[39] Literally, "the praises of the Arizal," a book of stories concerning this Kabbalistic sage.

The Rebbe explained that the idea to consult with one's wife is based on the Shulchan Aruch and is particularly relevant with regard to the Shabbos, where an emphasis is placed on Shalom Bayis, "peace in the home." Indeed, that is the motivating factor for lighting Shabbos candles. Nevertheless, because of their *hiskashrus* (bonding) to the Arizal, the students should have realized that his suggestion was in line with Shulchan Aruch. For, as Rav Chaim Vital writes in Taamei HaMitzvos, the Arizal was a great Gaon even in *nigleh*, the Torah's external legal dimension, and by requesting to consult with their wives, the students delayed the coming of Mashiach.

The Rebbe explained that the Arizal's example was emulated by the Rebbe Rayatz who (in the first years) would send out students – and would do this after the holidays of Tishrei, at which time the students particularly appreciated being in the Rebbe's presence, and yet he sent them to the outlying cities, and they obeyed and were successful – and were also successful with regard to their personal matters. (The Rebbe instructed the students who journeyed on such missions – among them, R' Yitzchak Groner and R' Sholom Ber Popack – to say L'Chaim.)

(It appears that this talk was associated with Reb.... whom the Rebbe desired to send to Morocco on shlichus and, for various reasons, did not accept the mission.)

The Rebbe instructed R' Yitzchak Groner to gather together the students who came from New Haven and for them to say L'Chaim and sing a *niggun* that they knew. They sang the *niggun* MiMitzrayim Gialtanu. Everyone joined in and the Rebbe encouraged the singing, motioning with his hands with great happiness.

He instructed the student Gedaliah Tzinamus, who was going to study in Eretz Yisrael, to say L'Chaim and gave him cake. He told him that he should conduct himself in a way that is fitting for a tomim,[40] and he should serve as a role model.

He called a Bar Mitzvah boy, Chaim Aryeh, and gave him cake, instructing him to take it with his left hand. Similarly, he gave cake to the boy's two brothers and instructed them to sing a happy *niggun* in their brother's honor. He also joined in the singing with great joy.

He instructed R' Michal Raskin to say L'chaim over a full cup of wine so that he "will have a full store." (He opened a fruit and vegetable store before the holidays.)

He instructed R' Shlomo Zalman Hecht to drink four cups of wine, saying: "Anyway, it is in the afternoon which is a time when people become intoxicated, as stated in Shulchan Aruch."[41]

I said L'Chaim for my brother-in-law who made a *bris* for his son that Shabbos. The Rebbe answered L'Chaim Ulivrachah. While they were arranging the students from New Haven, the Rebbe said: "In the meantime, let the students from Montreal, Canada, say L'Chaim. It's up north, the source of the cold. Let them spread warmth there too."

~

On Motzei Shabbos, there was a melaveh malkah at R' Mordechai Dubinsky's home. R' Yoel reviewed the *sichos* the Rebbe delivered on Shabbos. R' Zalman Duchman told the following story: After R' Shalom DovBer, the Rebbe of Retzitza, passed away, his son, R' Chaim Schneerson, thought of accepting his position. He consulted with the Rebbe Rashab, telling him that he knows certain qualities necessary for the position and some advice to give, but if someone asked him whether he

[40] A student of the Lubavitcher Yeshiva; the title derives from the yeshiva's name Tomchei Temimim.
[41] See Shulchan Aruch, Orach Chayim 129:1.

should undergo an operation, he would not know what to answer. The Rebbe Rashab replied: "When one does not know, it is not appropriate."

R' Mordechai Dubinsky related that after the passing of the Tzemach Tzedek, his son, Maharil, wanted to journey to Kopost, where he became Rebbe. His brother, the Rebbe Maharash, asked him if his father had taught him to write a *pidyon*, he answered: "Yes." He asked him if he taught him how to write *pidyonos* while on the road, he answered: "No." Afterwards, the Rebbe Maharash said that he had regrets, because he should have delayed Maharil's journey.

~

Today, the student Sholom Ber Drizin, traveled to Eretz Yisrael. I gave him saccharin for my father. It is several weeks that I have not received a letter from home. I hope everything is fine.

11 Iyar, 5718, 11 PM

During the last weeks, there were no special events and I was slightly busy. Hence, I did not write anything.

On Tuesday, there was a women's meeting in the house of R' Nosson Gurary. Rav David Hollander, who traveled to Eastern Europe last year, spoke and showed a film of pictures that he had taken. He also showed pictures of the structure built over the gravesite of the Rebbe Rashab in Rostov.

I thought that I would be able to study or write some, but R' Yoel came to visit me, and afterwards R' Mordechai Dubinsky came, and we sat for several hours.

Last week, there was a meeting of those involved in Tzach and we spoke about purchasing a building for Tzach, because Rabbi Chodakov conveyed a directive to that effect before Pesach. The intent was a small building where people could gather together to study, daven, and hold gatherings. There is no practical suggestion. Someone spoke of purchasing the building previously owner by the Sphinker Rebbe, because he moved to a different building. Unfortunately, however, the suggestion came too late, because the building had already been sold.

Similarly, at the meeting, we spoke of visiting New Brighton, where the yeshiva student Nelson lives and has influence; to visit South Fallsburg where Mr. Naftuli Ross lives; and to arrange a *farbrengen* in Bayonne.

The students' trip to Detroit for Shabbos HaGadol was a great success. Besides visiting several shuls, they arranged a melaveh malkah, with several of the city's Rabbis attending, at which the students spoke. Among the highlights was the speech of R' Avraham Shemtov, who also spoke about Halachic issues, and this made a great impression on the listeners. R' Berl Shemtov has much influence in the city. He knows many people and has brought several people to the Rebbe already.

Yesterday, a study session was held in the home of R' Yisrael Duchman; last week, it was held at the home of R' Chaim Hersh Moskowitz. They began studying the Alter Rebbe's Shulchan Aruch again from the beginning and are studying the *maamar* entitled Zachor, 5665.

Today, the study guide for the Tanya[42] in Yiddish prepared by R' Leibel Groner was completed. I heard from R' Yechezkel Langsam (R' Mordechai Shusterman's brother-in-law) that one of the members of the Shul, in which he serves as a caretaker, was sick and the Rebbe told him to study the Tanya and told him that if it was difficult, he could study the daily portion in Yiddish.

[42] The fundamental text of Chabad Chassidus.

~

There is a proposal that R' Leibel Raskin should work for several hours a day as a secretary for Tzach, because there is much work to do and without a person in charge, it is difficult to organize matters.

~

Last Tuesday, Mordechai Dubinsky was at *yechidus*. He related that he asked the Rebbe whether to go to the country for the summer and the Rebbe advised him against it (apparently, out of fear of the effect the change in the atmosphere would have on his children). Leibel Groner related that last year, he also asked whether to go away on vacation and the Rebbe advised him against doing so (for the above reason). He then asked whether to go to Far Rockaway (which is not far away, but located on the ocean shore). The Rebbe answered: "What difference does it make? The point is the change in the atmosphere. What difference does it make, Far Rockaway or another place?" He concluded: "It's possible to have a very happy summer here." Leibel said that his entire family enjoyed a healthy summer that year.

~

On Monday, I was treated by Dr. Shapiro, a dentist in Crown Heights, and he pulled a wisdom tooth that had bothered me for several weeks. He told me that he had also treated the Rebbe Rayatz and the Rebbe and all the members of the family. Once, when he came to the Rebbe Rayatz, he was unable to understand his speech[43], Chana, the Rebbe Rayatz's daughter, was telling him what the Rebbe said. He told the Rebbe that he

[43] Due to the effects of the stroke the Rebbe Rayatz had suffered.

came from a family of Misnagdim. The Rebbe answered: "There are no Misnagdim. There are Jews." On another occasion, Chana said about him: "He is a good Jew," and the Rebbe answered: "There are no bad Jews. There are Jews."

Sunday, 14 Iyar, 12 PM

On Shabbos (13 Iyar), the Rebbe recited the Mourners' Kaddish during all three prayer services, because it was the *yahrtzeit* of his brother, R' Leib. During the evening and morning services, I did not stand far from the Rebbe and I observed his conduct. R' Shmuel the Tailor led the evening service and R' Avraham Popack, the morning service.

During the Kabbalas Shabbos service, the Rebbe stood for Mizmor L'David. During the hymn Lecha Dodi, he stood facing north. At the stanza beginning Vihayu LiMshisa, he turned and faced east until the words Bo'i LiShalom when he turned to his right and faced the west. Afterwards, he continued turning to his right and faced east.

After Mizmor Shir LiYom HaShabbos, he recited Kaddish. While reciting Kaddish, he bowed his head at the words: Yisgadel, Viyikareiv Meshichei, Bichayeihon, Yehei Shmei, Shmei DiKudsha Brich Hu, Damiran Bialmah.

The Rebbe would recite the Kaddish alone. When he concluded, the others who were obligated to recite it did so. After the Mourners' Kaddish following Mizmor Shir LiYom HaShabbos, the Rebbe sat while the others recited Kaddish. He stood for the recitation of the blessing Hashkiveinu. When the *chazzan* recited the blessing Hashkiveinu, he wiped his eyes. It appeared that he had been crying. In general, he appeared anxious.

~

Leibel Groner relates that the Rebbe's mother, Rebbitzen Chana, does not know of the passing of her son, for she receives letters which the Rebbe writes in his handwriting. She sends packages to her son and is under the impression that he receives them. It is obvious that this causes the Rebbe great sorrow. May G-d send him joy.

~

During the reading of the Torah, the Rebbe stood facing north, looking into a Chumash (the Chumash Torah Temimah; the Rebbe Rayatz would also use such a Chumash).

During the Torah reading – as well as during the *chazzan*'s repetition of the Shemoneh Esreh – he would, from time to time, hold the four *tzitzios* of his *tallis*.

At the recitation of Borchu, he would bend his head during the *chazzan*'s recitation, lower it further while the congregation responds, and then raise is at the conclusion of their response.

When he took three steps back before the recitation of Shemoneh Esreh, he would begin with the left foot. After the third step back, he would lift his right foot. He would not place it together with his left, but instead would step forward, beginning the three steps before the Shemoneh Esreh.

B"H, Thursday, Lag B'Omer, 11 PM

On Shabbos, several Chassidim held a *farbrengen* at the home of R' Yosef Reizes. More exactly, it was a meeting more than a convivial gathering. Everyone had felt motivated by the Rebbe's words at the *farbrengen* last Shabbos Mevorchim. We decided that every one of us should inform the Rebbe that we are prepared to accept any and all positions and responsibilities with which he would charge us whether in New York, outside of it, and even outside the U.S.

On Sunday, Rasha and I gave in a note with such a message to the Rebbe. On the following day, Rabbi Chodakov returned the note to me with the Rebbe's answer written upon it so that I could copy it. (The note itself was to be given back to the Rebbe as was the common practice.) The Rebbe answered as follows: "[I assume that] the above was, of course, written with the full consent of your wife. You are conscripted to work here, each one of you in your framework (Tzach, N'Shei Chabad[44])."

Mendel Baumgarten submitted a similar note and received almost the same answer except that a blessing was added. If I'm not mistaken, this is what the Rebbe wrote to him: "[I assume that] the above was, of course, written with the full consent of your wife. You are conscripted to work here, spreading the wellsprings outward, each one of you in your framework (Tzach, Neshei Chabad). May it be G-d's will that this be in a good and auspicious hour."

Berl Alenik relates that he wrote a similar note several months ago after the Rebbe spoke at a *farbrengen* in praise of Berl Shemtov and Yosef Rosenfeld who set out on shlichus to other cities. At that time, the Rebbe had said: "They should be looked upon as models. Their example should be noticed and emulated." The Rebbe blessed them with great and ample blessings for great success.

The Rebbe answered Berl Alenik that his mission and that of his wife is spreading the wellsprings of Chassidus in the city and from time to time, to travel to the surrounding areas.

Someone else submitted a similar note after the *farbrengen* of

[44] The Lubavitch Women's Organization.

Shabbos Mevorchim. The Rebbe answered with a question: "Did you pay off all your debts?" He replied that he expected to pay off his debts within a few months. He then asked about an offer proposed to him by the owner of the print shop in which I work, that he enter into partnership with them in the offset business. The Rebbe answered him: "Why do you need this? (A while ago, the Rebbe wanted such a partnership very much and they were not interested. Apparently, something changed.)

~

Yesterday, I went with R' Moshe Goldman to a large Shul on the East Side to publicize the books of Merkos L'Inyonei Chinuch. I spoke for about twenty minutes. After the evening service, we held a short *farbrengen* with the congregants.

~

We are preparing to travel to New Haven on shlichus for Tzach to speak in shuls. May G-d enable us to be successful.

~

On Sunday, there was a Tzach meeting in Berl Alenik's house. We spoke about spreading the books of Merkos in synagogues on Lag B'Omer and about journeying to other cities. Thank G-d, there are students who want to go.

By the way, R' Yoel was very active in encouraging people to write the notes described above.

~

B"H Motzei Shabbos Parshas Acharei-Kedoshim

I am very sorry that I am unable to continue writing in a consistent manner, because I am very busy in these last weeks to the extent that I am cutting back everything, even sleep. Hopefully, the readers will forgive me.

Last Shabbos, we held a Shabbaton in New Haven. Our group included Moshe Pesach Goldman, Chaim Serebranyski, Dovber Alenik, myself, Sholom Ber Kievman, and the driver, Yosef Riezes. Before we left on Friday, R' Dovid Raskin asked the Rebbe for a blessing for those who made the journey, submitting their names and the names of their mothers.[45] The Rebbe wrote that it was very good that Chaim Serebranyski was going. He also added that the potentials of Elazar Gorelik should also be used. (Certainly, you understand that these are internal matters. I know, however, that "stolen waters are sweet."[46])

On Shabbos, we spoke in the synagogues in that city, both in the morning and in the afternoon. We also arranged a *farbrengen* at the home of R' Moshe Hecht, the principal of the local yeshiva. There we read the recently printed letter of the Rebbe Rayatz about establishing fixed times for the study of Torah. Sholom Ber Kievman reviewed a *maamar*. All of the young members of the city's Torah community and many of the important members of the community attended. On Saturday night, there was a melaveh malkah at the home of R' Zaev Shildkraut. It is clear that the trip there brought about a very positive effect, inspiring the yeshiva students there as well as those who attended the synagogues.

This city has 250,000 inhabitants and 25,000 are Jewish. There is a yeshiva, a branch of Achei Temimim[47] with 300 students. It appears to have a firm foundation, because the principal R' Moshe Hecht works very energetically and he is a very strong-willed person.

I remember that when the Rebbe farbrenged on Yud-Tes (19)

[45] As is customary when asking the Rebbe for a blessing.
[46] Mishlei 9:17.
[47] One of the satellite branches of the Lubavitcher Yeshiva.

Kislev last year, R' Moshe Hecht was standing somewhat removed from him. The Rebbe instructed him to say L'Chaim and told him: "Not two hundred, not three hundred – a thousand!"

To explain: When he was working to purchase the new building for the yeshiva (which he did with great speed, because of his influence with one of the members of the community who owned the building), Rabbi Hecht asked the Rebbe for a blessing that it house at least 200 students. At the *farbrengen*, he received his answer.

R' Dovid Deitsch, the son of the seasoned Chassid, R, Menachem Mendel Deitsch, moved there, apparently due to the Rebbe's instructions. He runs a plastics business and is very successful. He is devoted to the Rebbe with every fiber of his being. His influence is apparent in the city, because he is a communal activist, far from a fool, and yet characterized by simple faith. He is serious, though not to a fault. He also had a positive effect on the principal, increasing his bond with the Rebbe. He conducts his household in an appropriate manner. It appears that the Rebbe is very happy with him.

I was in his house before the melaveh malkah with R' Chaim Serabranyski and we spoke, sharing warm Chassidic talk. He told us that a year and a half ago, he came to the Rebbe at *yechidus*. He did not tell us what the Rebbe spoke to him about, but it is obvious that the Rebbe asked something of him. The Rebbe asked him if he would obey. He answered straightforwardly: "Of course. We're soldiers. What the Rebbe orders, we will carry out." The Rebbe was very moved by the simple faith manifested in his answer and cried with great joy. He also cried with him.

The Rebbe has true soldiers. When compared to them, our achievements pale.

His wife also related several miracles the Rebbe worked for them and for others, but I do not have the time to write them up now. Maybe I will do so at a later occasion.

Sunday, the day preceding Rosh Chodesh Sivan, 11 PM Monday was the day preceding R"Ch

On Shabbos Mevorchim (the Shabbos when the new month is blessed), the Rebbe held a *farbrengen* in the structure in the courtyard. He came out at approximately 1:30 PM and the *farbrengen* continued until about 3:15 PM. He delivered two *sichos* concerning the commandment of Shmitah[48] and its connection to Mt. Sinai. Afterwards, he delivered the *maamar* entitled *Lehavin Inyan Sefiras HaOmer* in which he explained how all the other sefiros are included within the sefirah of Chessed. It was a relatively short *maamar*. He then delivered two *sichos* concerning Sivan being the third month and the Torah reading of the coming week, Parshas Bamidbar.

A group of students from Yeshivas Achei Temimim in the Bronx came with Rabbi Futterman and R' Moshe Levertov. The Rebbe instructed them to say L'Chaim and to sing a *niggun*. They sang MiMitzrayim Gealtanu. The Rebbe encouraged them and the entire congregation sang with them. The Rebbe also asked that the *niggun* Ani Maamin be sung. He also mentioned the convention of Neshei Chabad to be held tomorrow and gave his blessings for its success.

[48] The observance of the Sabbatical year.

From the digest of the *sichos* of Pesach that were written up, the Rebbe edited[49] only the first *sicha* from the second night of Pesach. He told Rabbi Chodakov and also R' Leibel Groner that the style of the writing is not desirable and that if the talks will continue to be written up in this manner, he will cease editing them. When R' Leibel Groner told him that the writers did not know how to improve the style, he replied that they should study the additions he made and use them as a guide in writing up the *sichos* in the future.

We studied his additions and saw that he barely changed the style at all, adding only a few chosen words. In certain places, however, he added to the development of the concepts. What he added, however, did not correspond to the way the *sichos* were repeated when reviewed and, in certain places, it did not correspond to the way they were delivered. Obviously, we could not make such additions ourselves. Afterwards, R' Yoel told me that the Rebbe said that this was his intent: not necessarily to improve the style, but to develop the content itself. The material was, nevertheless, also given to R' Shmuel Zalmanov to work over. He made some additions, but they also were merely stylistic.

Apparently, no *sichos* from this holiday that are *mugah* will be released other than the digest of the second night, which was already sent to the printer.

Rabbi Chodakov suggested that Tzach publish a monthly journal with a digest of the *sichos* of the month, together with a list of activities, various articles, and other matters. It is possible

[49] The Rebbe would deliver *sichos* and *maamorim* without a prepared text. Since most of the *farbrengens* were held on Shabbos and festivals, as Rabbi Gansbourg has described, the talks would be transcribed from memory. Afterwards, the text would be submitted to the Rebbe for editing. If its final wording was approved, it would be categorized as mugah (lit., "checked" or "edited"). By contrast, a teaching that is recorded only in a listener's unauthenticated notes is described as bilti mugah ("not checked"). Obviously, the *sichos* and *maamorim* that are mugah have more authority.

that the Rebbe made this suggestion to him. We have not, however, found the person capable of carrying out such an undertaking. We hope that in the near future, however, this will be accomplished.

There was a suggestion to publish the digest as a printed work like other *kuntresim*. The Rebbe, however, said that it should not stand out that this is a letter from Tzach. For the present, at least, we have decided to continue using the present format of printing (mimeograph) until we begin publishing the monthly journal.

~

Last Tuesday, Mr. Porat, the Israeli Consul General in New York, visited the Rebbe. Rabbi Hollander came with him. (It has been rumored that Rabbi Hollander has begun seeking the Rebbe's advice on personal matters. He visits the Rebbe very frequently.) They were in *yechidus* with the Rebbe for approximately two hours. It is not known what they spoke about. Afterwards, he spoke with the yeshiva students. They showed him the digest of the Rebbe's *sichos* and the monthly journal published in Eretz Yisrael. He asked to be given a subscription to these publications and that they be sent to him when published.

~

Yesterday, there was a major assembly organized by Tzach. Many members of the community were present. The focus of the meeting was the coming *tahaluchah* for the Shavuos holiday in which the Chassidim will march to East New York and to Boro Park, some of the places being a two hour walk from 770. Similarly, Chassidim signed up to travel to various outlying cities, including Cleveland and Albany, and perhaps Philadelphia, for Shabbatonim on the Shabbos following Shavuos. R' Elazar Gorelik also gave an overview of the activities of Tzach in Eretz Yisrael and R' Chaim Serebranyski gave an overview of the activities in Australia.

I was not present at the assembly; when I came at 11 PM, it already had concluded. I had been busy checking the bulletin that will be published tomorrow for the convention of Neshei Chabad. This bulletin contains a *sicha* from Yud (10) Shvat of last year, which the Rebbe edited, and several of his letters. Tonight, we are also working overtime in the print shop to complete the printing before the convention. The bulletin also contains an article written by Mrs. Leah Kahn. The Rebbe looked the article over and made some corrections. The essay focuses on the concept of the Counting of the Omer. Recently, Mrs. Kahn has been working very energetically in organizing the convention and she has a position on the executive committee of Neshei Chabad.

~

Merkos L'Inyonei Chinuch is preparing to present a series of courses on electrical engineering. R' Moshe Kazarnofsky who works for the electric company in New York is involved in this effort.

We are surprised that we have not received a letter from home in almost two months. Why don't our parents write? We are certain that everything is okay, with G-d's help, but still it's been almost two months.

~

Last Sunday, there was a meeting of the steering committee of Tzach at our home that focused on the ongoing matters. Thank G-d, the activities have expanded lately and the list of those involved has grown. There has also been an arousal with regard to reviewing Chassidus in the synagogues in the surrounding communities on Shabbos. Leibel Raskin was hired as a part-time secretary for Tzach. This matter, however, has not been publicized and, as of yet, is unknown to people at large.

~

Last Tuesday, the study session was held in the home of R' Yechezkel Levanthal and, the week before, in the home of R' Yaakov Simon. The number of participants is increasing.

~

Chaim Asher Garfinkel and Elimelech Shpalter received answers similar to those given to us when they wrote to the Rebbe volunteering to accept any mission with which he would charge them.

Sholom Ber Butman was at *yechidus* and told the Rebbe that he is prepared to go on shlichus to any and every place. The Rebbe told him that he should remain here and be involved in an endeavor that enables him to use his potentials.

B"H, the Friday preceding Shabbos Bamidbar, 5 PM

Rav Yollis did not come to visit the Rebbe yesterday, as is his practice every year. Consequently, we did not hear the *siyyum*[50] of the tractate of Sotah that the Rebbe delivers to him each year. Rumor is that the Rebbe promised Rav Yollis that he would write out the *siyyum* for him.

~

The digest of the *sichos* of the second night of Pesach were already printed. Similarly, a *sicha* of the Rebbe to be delivered

[50] Conclusion of a Talmudic tractate.

on the *tahaluchah* for Shavuos was edited by the Rebbe and printed by mimeograph. My brother-in-law came in from Montreal yesterday morning. We are preparing for the holiday when we receive the Torah with joy and inner feeling.

B"H, Thursday, 9 Sivan, 12 AM

On Shabbos, the Rebbe held a *farbrengen*. He came out at 1:30 PM and farbrenged for about an hour and a quarter. There were several *sichos* including a *siyyum* of the tractate of Sotah. (As mentioned, every year, the Rebbe would deliver such a *siyyum* in honor of Rabbi Yollis.) It appears that among the subjects that he spoke about was a *maamar* of the Alter Rebbe. The Rebbe cried slightly when reciting the verses at the conclusion of the Haftorah.

On the first night of Shavuos after the recitation of Tikkun, at 3 AM he delivered the *maamar* entitled *Mashkeini*.

During the festive meal, some of the vintage Chassidim, including Rabbi Simpson, asked Rashag the source for the *maamar* delivered by the Rebbe.[51] Rabbi Simpson wanted to say that it was based on a *maamar* from 5666. The Rebbe answered that these concepts are not found in the *maamorim* that he studied from 5666. Others said that it was based on *maamorim* from 5668 where the concept of the interrelation of the emotional qualities is discussed. The Rebbe said that the subject of the interrelation of the emotional qualities is mentioned in the *maamorim* 5668, but that was not the focus of the *maamar* he delivered. It appeared that he was not at all happy with this discussion. He said: "All of the Rebbeim, including my father-in-law, delivered *maamorim* without mentioning their source. Although a person who relates a teaching in the name of its

[51] Following the tradition of his forebears, many of the *maamorim* delivered by the Rebbe developed and elucidated similar discourses delivered by the Rebbeim of previous generations.

author brings redemption to the world,[52] this concept does not apply with regard to delivering a *maamar* of Chassidic teachings." (Afterwards, at the *farbrengen* on the second day of Shavuos, he delivered a *sicha* explaining this concept.)

~

Following the afternoon service, a *tahaluchah* organized by Tzach was held. About ninety Chassidim went to Boro Park and about sixty to East New York. Although it was pouring, the rain did not deter the younger Chassidim from carrying out their mission.

One of the participants in the festive meal told me that a report of the *tahaluchah* was given to the Rebbe at the meal and Rashag exclaimed: "This only the Lubavitchers can do." The Rebbe was also very happy. It appeared that he even dried tears of happiness from his eyes.

~

On the second day of Shavuos, at approximately 8 PM, the Rebbe came out for a *farbrengen*. He washed from a cup brought to him by Berl Junik and made the blessing HaMotzi on two challos. He said L'Chaim and asked that the entire congregation say L'Chaim. He then announced that all those who had not yet washed to partake of bread should do so at this time. He asked that a *niggun* be sung and R' Shmuel Zalmanov began singing and the entire congregation joined in. The Rebbe encouraged the singing, motioning and clapping with his hands to heighten the rejoicing.

There were about twelve or thirteen *sichos* during the *farbrengen*. Among them was a special *sicha* about the *tahaluchah*. He explained at length how the Divine service of our generation involves the feet, particularly acting without reservation, fol-

[52] Avos 6:6.

lowing the motif: "Spread out your feet,"[53] particularly with regard to giving to the poor and performing mitzvos. He gave blessings to those who participated in the *tahaluchah*, citing the verse: "Blessed are you in your coming…"[54] He asked that they all say L'chaim and sing a happy *niggun*. They sang Napoleon's March.[55]

He asked that the children who were present at the *farbrengen* say L'chaim and sing a *niggun*. They sang MiMitzrayim Gealtanu. The Rebbe joined in the singing and also motioned to the entire congregation to sing. He also delivered a *sicha* to them.

Additionally, the Rebbe delivered a *sicha* on the theme mentioned above, that the Rebbeim did not mention the sources for their *maamorim*. He delivered a *maamar* entitled Karov Adonai Lichol Korav which continued the themes mentioned in the previous *maamar*. In the midst of the *maamar*, while mentioning the adage of the Alter Rebbe: "I don't want your Gan Eden… I want You alone,"[56] his voice broke and he had to wipe his eyes. This also happened during the delivery of the previous *maamar*.

He delivered a special *sicha* for women, emphasizing the concept that the scroll of Ruth bears her name and not that of Boaz.

He was extremely happy during the *farbrengen*. It appeared that this *farbrengen* was a continuation of the *farbrengen* of Simchas Torah and Shabbos Bereishis, for the Rebbe cut short, somewhat, the Simchas Torah *farbrengen* this year. Many of the Simchas Torah niggunim were indeed sung. In the midst of the

[53] Bava Kama 60b.
[54] Devarim 28:6.
[55] A French march that illustrated physical victory. The Rebbe taught that when the march is sung in Chassidic settings, it illustrates spiritual victory.
[56] Shoresh Mitzvas Hatefilah of the Tzemach Tzedek, chapter 40.

33⅓ RPM
12p. H.
28p.
18p. L.F.

CHABAD NIGUNIM

PERFORMED BY U&L.
CHABAD CHOIR — Cap
ACCOMPANIED BY ORCHESTRA U&L
CANTOR MOSHE TELESHEVSKY C.
DIRECTOR
MUSICAL SETTINGS U&L.

12p. Metromed.

P. SOKOLOW C.
~~Music Director~~
~~CHOIR CONDUCTOR~~ U&L.
SEYMOR SILBERMINTZ C.

PRODUCED BY: "COMMITTEE FOR ESTABLISHMENT OF SEVENTY ONE INSTITUTIONS"
14p Bernard

18p. H.

A draft of a Nichoach record jacket, prepared by Hirsh and edited by the Rebbe

farbrengen, the Rebbe asked that the *niggun* Ani Maamin be sung and it was repeated several times.

He asked that the *niggun* entitled the Benoni, a *niggun* which the Rebbe Rayatz regarded with special favor, be sung. When the congregation completed singing it, R' Shamshon Charotonov stood on a bench at the end of the Rebbe's table and began to sing the *niggun* again. (He had a slightly different version which his father had taught him.) The entire congregation remained silent. The Rebbe listened to him attentively. When he finished, the Rebbe smiled and said: "If Charitonov agrees to sing, it is only because it is the season of the Giving of Our Torah. May G-d help that this be a good beginning for all the years to come."

Afterwards, he asked that a *niggun* of the Rebbe Rashab be sung. They sung the Rostover *niggun*. He then asked that a *niggun* of the Rebbe Maharash be sung, then one by the Tzemach Tzedek, one associated with the Mitteler Rebbe, and the *niggun* of three stanzas, one from the Baal Shem, one from the Maggid, and one from the Alter Rebbe. Then they sang the *niggun* Tzama Lecha Nafshi, the *niggun* Avinu Malkeinu, and then the Alter Rebbe's *niggun* of four stanzas. The last stanza was sung once.

Several of the guests, Berl Baumgarten from Argentina, Zvi Chitrik from Brazil, and several from New York, provided bottles of *mashkeh* for the Rebbe to distribute. Similarly, Nachman Kubalsky who brings "first fruits" to the Rebbe every year for Shavuos[57] brought a large cake, a basket of fruit, and a bottle of *mashkeh*. The Rebbe instructed that all the bottles be opened. He then poured a little from each bottle into his cup and then drank from the cup. He then instructed that the *mashkeh* be distributed among the entire congregation.

[57] For Shavuos is "the holiday of the first fruits." Kesubos 105b equates bringing a present to a Torah scholar with bringing the first fruit.

The Rebbe spoke specifically regarding Chassidim who were sent to distant places to spread the teachings of Chassidus, but now desire to leave. He emphasized that they should remain in their places and continue their activities, making these places "places of Torah," and correcting the lack in Jewish practices that are there. In the middle of the *farbrengen*, he asked that the *niggun* Ein Adir KiBorei be sung.

R' Berl Baumgarten had caught a severe cold during the *tahaluchah* and had a high fever. When this was told to the Rebbe, he instructed that he come to the *farbrengen* and he gave him from his own challah. Rav Yollis from Philadelphia came and the Rebbe gave him some of the cake brought as "first fruits."

After the *niggun* of the four stanzas, the Rebbe asked that the *niggun* Nye Zshuritzi Chloptzi be sung. He was in very high spirits, to the extent that he stood up and danced in his place for a long time. Needless to say, the entire congregation also stood and danced.

The Rebbe took one grape from the basket brought by Nachman Kubalsky, recited the blessing over it and ate it. He asked that the congregation refrain from grabbing the remainder of the basket, but his words did not help. The elder Chassidim began to grab the fruit and they also grabbed from the cake from which the Rebbe had eaten. It looked like the Rebbe was not at all happy with this. Last year, when a similar thing happened, the Rebbe asked that the *niggun* Essen Esst Zich[58] be sung afterwards.

The *farbrengen* concluded at approximately 3 AM. The Rebbe recited Grace over a cup of wine, and the evening service was recited. The Rebbe then recited Havdalah himself and then dis-

[58] A song whose (Yiddish) lyrics loosely translate as: Eat it eats, sleep it sleeps; but what should we do that it does not pray?

tributed wine from "the cup of blessing" to all the assembled amidst joyous singing. The distribution of the wine took several hours.

~

Berl Baumgarten came from Argentina where he serves as the Rebbe's *shliach*. He has already brought several Sephardic students from there to study in the yeshiva here. He told me a wondrous story that happened to him last Yud-Beis (12) Tammuz.

On that day, he had to cross the border between Brazil and Argentina. In this place, the two countries were divided by a large and powerfully flowing river. The river would be crossed by ferry. In the morning, while waiting for the ferry, he sat and shared some *mashkeh* with a middle-aged Jew who was originally born in Poland and had studied in Yeshivas Chachmei Lublin in his youth. Nevertheless, over the course of time, he had drifted away from Jewish practice and no longer kept Shabbos, kashrus, or the like, nor did he put on Tefillin. Berl spoke to him about the observance of the mitzvos, but the man was not interested. On the contrary, he responded with silly, brazen remarks, blaming G-d for the deaths of the six million and the like. When Berl saw that he was unable to influence him, he ceased speaking to him.

In the evening, Berl went into his car on the ferry. With him was a suitcase containing his wardrobe, other articles, and two thousand dollars in cash. After journeying on the ferry for a while, a banana boat hit it and its cargo and many of the cars cascaded into the river's depths. Many cars and people were cast beneath the water. Berl's car was also among those that sank. He remembers preparing to say the confessional prayers, but then refraining from doing so, because those prayers are not recited on Yud-Beis Tammuz.

With super-human powers, he was able to push one of the doors open. He felt himself being lifted upward from above. Though he did not know how to swim, somehow he managed to stay above water until he could be pulled to the opposite shore. Eighty people drowned in the accident.

Earlier that morning, he had felt something of a strange intuition and therefore sent a telegram to the Rebbe. The Rebbe visited the ohel that day and, according to his reckoning, the accident occurred at the same time that he was there.

After being pulled to the shore, the relief agencies wanted to take him to the hospital. He, however, refused, because his Tefillin were in the car that had sunk and he desired to hurry to a town with an orthodox community so that he could fulfill the mitzvah the next day.

He was taken to a local police office to report the accident. The Polish Jew whom he had met earlier in the day also came there to inquire about his health and to offer him assistance. At that time, he still had difficulty speaking in Spanish and was unable to communicate with the police in this distant outpost. He went to a separate corner of the police station and began reciting the evening service. And did he pray. On one hand, he felt very bitter because of his losses. But as he prayed, he began to realize the miracle G-d had wrought for him. As he recited the words, "Who led His children through the splitting of the Red Sea," he was aroused and began to cry. His prayers lasted a long time.

Afterwards, he returned to the police counter to see if there was anything else he should do. The Polish Jew greeted him with tears in his eyes: "I just recited the evening service. And I can't remember how long ago it was that I prayed like this." He promised Berl that from that day on, he would put on Tefillin every day.

Berl relates that he met him a few months later and while he still does not keep Shabbos or kashrus, he puts on Tefillin every day. He even showed him the Tefillin which he carries with him at all times.

There are several other points which perhaps I will add at a later date.

Sunday, 13 Sivan, 7 PM

Nisan Mangel, a yeshiva student from Montreal, stayed with us for Shavuos. Today, he is returning there. He is one of the students who were saved from the gas chambers in Germany. For more than seven years, he has been studying in the Lubavitcher Yeshiva in Montreal. He is a Chassidic student, with special abilities and character traits. I heard that the Rebbe instructed him to study in a university, but that he himself does not desire to attend such an institution. He has influence on others. I know of people whom the Rebbe sent to speak to him and to study with him. Now he is serving as a part time instructor in the yeshiva.

Monday, 14 Sivan, 12 AM

Last week, on Thursday, the study session was held in the home of R' Moshe Kazarnofsky. They began studying the *kuntres* released for Yud-Beis Tammuz, 5709. Today, it is being held in the home of Chaim Asher Garfinkel.

For Shabbos, Tzach arranged for a Shabbaton in Cleveland. Mendel Baumgarten, Yehoshua Dubravsky, Leibel Motzkin, Berl Alenik, Nachman Sudak, and Shmaryahu Pruss journeyed there. On Friday, they visited the Telshe Yeshiva. On Shabbos, they visited synagogues and spoke there. In one synagogue, they were able to arrange a communal recitation of Tehillim. In another, a study session was established. There was also a *far-brengen* during the afternoon on Shabbos.

Nissan Mangel told me that Moshe Sklar (Eli Nachum Sklar's son) was at *yechidus* and inquired of the Rebbe what to do if one comes to a synagogue at the time the congregation is reciting Hallel. Should one recite it with them or should one wait and recite it in the order of one's own prayers?

The Rebbe answered him: "The Rebbeim would recite Hallel in the order of one's own prayers."

Moshe asked again: "What happens if one prays after the congregation does?"

"One should not be late for prayers."

"But what if, after all, someone is late?"

"If the full Hallel must be recited, one should say it alone after the Shemoneh Esreh. If half-Hallel must be recited, since one must fulfill his obligation by listening to the chazan's blessing,[59] one should say it with the congregation."

~

Yesterday, Yoel visited to write a digest of the *sichos* of Shavuos. We were able to transcribe only a portion. With G-d's help, we hope to complete it tomorrow.

~

On Thursday, the Rebbe edited a portion of a *sicha* from Yud Shvat, 5713, so that it could be reviewed in different synagogues on Shabbos. This is the second *sicha* that has been printed by Tzach to serve as the basis for speeches in synagogues. When Rabbi Chodakov gave the *sicha* to the Rebbe, the Rebbe sought to demur, saying: "There are already several *sichos*

[59] See the instructions in the Alter Rebbe's Siddur.

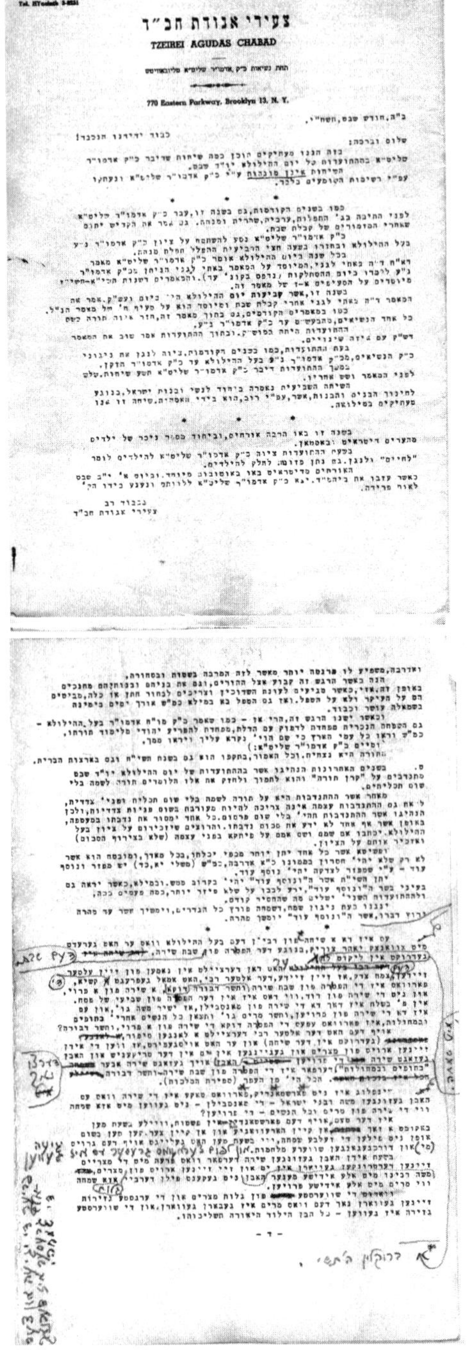

ב"ה

Tel. HYacinth 3-9551

צעירי אגודת חב"ד

TZEIREI AGUDAS CHABAD

תחת נשיאות כ"ק אדמו"ר שליט"א מליובאוויטש

770 Eastern Parkway, Brooklyn 13, N. Y.

ב"ה, חודש שבט, תשח"י.

כבוד ידידנו הנכבד!

שלום וברכה:

בזה הננו מעתיקים הוכן כמה שיחות שדיבר כ"ק אדמו"ר שליט"א בההתועדות של יום ההילולא יו"ד שבט.

השיחות אינן מוגהות ע"י כ"ק אדמו"ר שליט"א ונעתקו עפ"י רשימות השומעים בלבד.

* * *

כמו בשנים הקודמות, גם בשנה זו, עבר כ"ק אדמו"ר שליט"א לפני התיבה בג' התפלות, ערבית, שחרית ומנחה. גם גמר את הקדיש יתום שאחרי המזמורים של קבלת שבת.

כ"ק אדמו"ר שליט"א נסע להשתטח על ציון כ"ק אדמו"ר נ"ע בעל ההילולא ובחזרו בשעה חצי הרביעית התפלל תחלת מנחה.

בכל שנה ביום ההילולא אומר כ"ק אדמו"ר שליט"א מאמר ד"ה באתי לגני, המיוסד על המאמר באתי לגני הניתן מכ"ק אדמו"ר נ"ע ליום ההסתלקות (נדפס בקונ' עד). והמאמרים דשנות תשי"א-תשי"ז מיוסדים על הסעיפים א-ז של מאמר זה.

בשנה זו, אשר קביעות יום ההילולא הי' ביום ועש"ק, אמר את המאמר ד"ה באתי לגני אחרי קבלת שבת ומיוסד הוא על סעיף ח' של מאמר הנ"ל.

כמו במאמרים הקודמים, גם בתוך מאמר זה, חזר איזה תורה בשם כל אחד הנשיאים, מהבעש"ט עד כ"ק אדמו"ר נ"ע.

ההתועדות היתה במוש"ק, ובתוך ההתועדות אמר שוב את המאמר דש"ק עם איזה שינויים.

בעת ההתועדות, כמו בשנים הקודמות, ציוה לנגן את ניגוני כ"ק הנשיאים, מכ"ק אדמו"ר נ"ע בעל ההילולא עד כ"ק אדמו"ר הזקן.

במשך ההתועדות דיבר כ"ק אדמו"ר שליט"א תשע שיחות. שלש לפני המאמר ושש אחריו.

השיחה השביעית נאמרה ביחוד לנשי ובנות ישראל, בנוגע לחינוך הבנים והבנות, אשר, עפ"י רוב, הוא בידי האמהות. שיחה זו אנו מעתיקים במילואה.

* * *

בשנה זו באו הרבה אורחים, וביחוד במס' ניכר של ילדים מהערים דיטראיט ובאסטאן.

בעת ההתועדות ציוה כ"ק אדמו"ר שליט"א להילדים לומר "לחיים" ולנגן. גם נתן מזונות לחלק להילדים.

האורחים מדיטראיט באו באוטובוס מיוחד. וביום א' י"ב שבט כאשר עזבו את ביהמ"ד, יצא כ"ק אדמו"ר שליט"א ללוותם ונענע בידו הק' לאות פרידה.

בכבוד רב
צעירי אגודת חב"ד

ואדרבה, משפיע לו פרנסה יותר מאשר לזה המרבה בשעות ובסחורה.

הנה כאשר הרגש זה קבוע אצל ההורים, וגם את בניהם ובנותיהם מחנכים באופן זה, אזי, כאשר מגיעים לעונת השדוכין וצריכים לבחור חתן או כלה, מביטים הם על העיקר ולא על הטפל. ואז גם הטפל בא במילא כמ"ש אורך ימים בימינה בשמאלה עושר וכבוד.

וכאשר ישנו הרגש זה, הרי אז - כמו שאמר כ"ק מו"ח אדמו"ר בעל ההילולא - גם המשפחה הנכרית מפחדת לדפוק עם הדלת, מפחדת להפריע יהודי מלימוד תורתו, כמ"ש וראו כל עמי הארץ כי שם הוי' נקרא עליך ויראו ממך.

וסיים כ"ק אדמו"ר שליט"א:)

התורה היא נצחית. וכל האמור, בתקפו הוא גם בשנת תשי"ח וגם בארצות הברית.

ס. בשנים האחרונות הנהיגו אשר בההתועדות של יום ההילולא יו"ד שבט מתנדבים על "קרן תורה" והוא לתמוך ולחזק את אלו הלומדים תורה לשמה בלי שום תכליתים.

מאחר אשר ההתנדבות היא על תורה לשמה בלי שום תכלית ופני' צדדית, לכן גם ההתנדבות עצמה אינה צריכה להיות מעורבת בשום פניות צדדיות, ולכן הנהיגו אשר ההתנדבות תהי' בלי שום פרסום. כל אחד ימסור את נדבתו במעטפה, באופן אשר אף אחד לא ידע את סכום נדבתו. והרוצים שיזכירום על ציון בעל ההילולא, יכתבו את שמם ושם אמם על פיתקא בפני עצמה (שלא בצירוף הסכום) ואזכיר אותם על הציון.

ופשיטא אשר כל אחד יתן יותר מכפי יכלתו, בכל מאדך, ומובטח הוא אשר לא רק שלא יהי' חסרון בממונו כ"א אדרבה, כמ"ש (משלי יא, כד) יש מפזר ונוסף עוד - ע"י שמפזר לצדקה יהי' נוסף עוד.

יתן השי"ת אשר ה"ונוסף עוד" יהי' בקרוב ממש. ובמילא, כאשר יראה גם בעיני בשר ה"ונוסף עוד", ירע לבבו על שלא מיזר יותר, כמה פעמים ככה, ולההתועדות השני' ישלים מה שהחסיר קודם.

ינגנו כעת ניגון שמח, דשמחה פורץ כל הגדרים, וימשיך אשר עד מהרה ירוץ דברו, אשר ה"ונוסף עוד" יומשך מהרה.

* * *

עס איז דא א שיחה פון רבי'ן דעם בעל ההילולא וואס ער האט גערעדט מיט צוואנציג יאהר צוריק, בנוגע דער הפטרה פון שבת שירה, [illegible] בעדרוקט אין ליקוט [illegible]

[illegible] האט דאן דערציילט אין נאמען פון זיין עלטער זיידעז צמח צדק, אז זיין זיידע, דער אלטער רבי, האט אמאל געפרעגט א קשיא, פארוואס איז די הפטרה פון שבת שירה (וחשר דבורה) דוקא, א שירה פון א פרוי, און נים די שירה פון דוד. ווי דאס איז אין דער הפטרה פון שביעי של פסח. אין פ' בשלח איז דאך דא די שירה פון מאנסבילן, אז ישיר משה גו', און עס איז דא די שירה פון פרויען, ותשר מרים גו' ותצאן כל הנשים אחרי' בתופים ובמחולות, איז פארוואס עפעס די הפטרה דוקא די שירה פון א פרוי, ותשר דבורה?

אויף דעם האט דער אלטער רבי דערציילט א לאנגען סיפור, [illegible] (בעדרוקט אין דער שיחה) און ער האט אויסגעפירט, אז ווען די אידן זיינען ארויס פון מצרים און געגאנגען אין ים אין דער טריקעניש און האבן געזאגט שירה [illegible] די פרויען [illegible] האבן) אויך געזאגט שירה אבער [illegible] "בתופים ובמחולות") דערפאר איז די הפטרה פון שבת שירה - ותשר דבורה [illegible]. הכל הי' מן העפר (ספירת המלכות).

[illegible] איז נים פארשטאנדיק, פארוואס מאקע איז די שירה וואס עס האבן געזונגען משה ובני ישראל - די מאנסבילן - נים געווען מיט אזא שמחה ווי די שירה פון מרים ובל הנשים - די פרויען?

איז דער טעם, אויף דעם פארשטאנדיק [illegible] פשוט, ווייל געשת מען באקומט א זאך [illegible] אן קיין הארעוואניע און אן קיין צער, קען מען בשום אופן נים פילען די דעלבע שמחה, ווי בשעת מען האט געליטן אויף דעם גרויס (מי') און דורכגעגאנגען שווערע מלחמות. [illegible]

בשעת אידן האבן געזונגען שירה דערפאר וואס פרעה מיט די מצריים זיינען דערטרונקען געווארן אין ים און זיי זיינען ארויס פון מצרים, [illegible] משה רבינו מיט אלע אידישע מענער האבן נים געקענט פילן דערביי אזא שמחה ווי מרים מיט אלע אידישע פרויען.

וויבאלד די שווערסטע [illegible] פון גלות מצרים און די ערגסטע גזירות זיינען געווארן נאך דעם וואס מרים איז געבארן געווארן, און די שווערסטע גזירה איז געווען - כל הבן הילוד היאורה תשליכוהו.

- ד -

A talk from Yud Shvat 5718, edited by the Rebbe and published by Tzach. Printed later in Likkutei Sichos vol. 1 p. 139.

printed in Kovetz Lubavitch." Rabbi Chodakov persisted, saying that this *sicha* was designated specifically to be used for this Shabbos, and then the Rebbe agreed to edit it. It was printed in mimeograph.

The number of Chassidim reviewing Chassidic teachings in other synagogues keeps growing. There must be more than 100 already.

In response to a request from the editor, Rabbi Elberg, yesterday, the Rebbe submitted his letters concerning traveling on Israeli ships to be printed in the halachic journal HaPardes. This journal is printed in our print shop.

B"H, Thursday, 17 Sivan, 7 PM

(A continuation of the journal of the Shavuos holiday.)

In the midst of the *farbrengen*, the Rebbe delivered a special *sicha* in connection with Kinus Torah (the assembly for Torah study) to be held on the following day. He invited everyone to attend the assembly: those who were already invited and those who were not invited, adding with a smile: "Whether they were not invited unintentionally and even if they were intentionally not invited."

In connection with this *sicha*, the Rebbe asked that the halachic version of the *niggun* Echad Mi Yodeia be sung, i.e., the one that continues: "I know 'one.' 'One who digs a cistern[60].'" R' Yoel began to sing the song with a strange Misnagdeshe melody. The Rebbe commented that this was not his intent. Reb Avraham Mahyor began to sing the melody from its beginning, but apparently did not know all of the words. He also seemed somewhat embarrassed. The Rebbe asked that the singing continue

[60] Bava Kama 5:5.

and the congregation did in fact help, but they also did not know all the words. In some cases, the Rebbe himself supplied the correct words, including the final bar, "There were thirteen gates in the Beis HaMikdash."[61] After the *niggun* was completed, the Rebbe said: "May G-d help that those who study Chassidus with the yeshiva students should study better themselves."

R' Yoel has not completed writing up the digest. I do not know when it will be possible to go over it, for almost two weeks have passed since Shavuos.

Today, there is a meeting of the steering committee of Tzach in the home of R' Moshe Goldman.

Yesterday, I visited R' Yoel with the hope of doing something with regard to the digest of the *sichos*. He, however, is busy writing up the Torah insights that were delivered at the Kinus Torah, because the Rebbe wants them to be published.

The Kinus Torah was held on Tuesday, the day following Shavuos. I was not present, because this was a workday for me. I came, however, in the evening, for the *farbrengen* led by R' Shmuel Levitin and, primarily, for the review of the *maamar* delivered on Shavuos.

As it was told to me, this was an assembly of several Lubavitch Rabbis, for the Rebbe told Rabbi Mentlick that he desired that only they be invited and that they deliver new Torah insights. Among those who spoke were: Rav Meir Greenberg, a Rabbi in Paterson, New Jersey, Rabbi Menachem Mendel Feldman, Rabbi Zvi Chitrik from Brazil, Rabbi Berl Shemtov from Detroit, Rabbi Chaim Serabranyski from Australia, Rabbi Avraham Osdaba from Toronto, and others. At the conclusion of the Kinus, a *farbrengen* was held and the *maamar* delivered by the Rebbe was reviewed. I do not know the details, but it appears

[61] See Middos 2:6.

that Rabbi Mentlick suggested that the insights delivered by the Rabbis be published and the Rebbe not only accepted the suggestion but explicitly stated that he desired that there be such a printing.

~

Yitzchak Koren, the head of the moshavim of Poalei Agudas Yisrael in Eretz Yisrael visited the Rebbe last Tuesday. He entered *yechidus* at 8:10 PM and departed at 11:50. Only then did the Rebbe come out and recite the evening service. Usually, he recites that service at 9:30.

B"H, Sunday, 27 Sivan

After taking a break, I will try to inform you of what is happening here. Forgive me for the interruption.

Yesterday, Shabbos Mevorchim, Parshas Shelach, the Rebbe held a *farbrengen*, as is his custom. There were several *sichos* concerning the spies sent by Moshe to Eretz Yisrael and then he delivered a *maamar* entitled Shlach Lecha Anashim. It highlighted the positive quality of the attribute of yesod which is identified with Yosef, the source of sustenance, who provided bread for the poor. The *maamar* continued the theme of the *maamorim* of Shavuos. It is apparently connected with the month of Tammuz (when the redemption of the Rebbe Rayatz[62] occurred). When the Rebbe spoke of the virtues of Yosef, he trembled and cried some.

He delivered a *sicha* concerning the mitzvah of challah and a special *sicha* about Yosef. When delivering this *sicha*, his voice also trembled. He asked that the *niggun* Ani Maamin be sung. In the last *sicha*, he gave blessings to the institutions educating Jewish boys and girls. It appeared to be connected to the ban-

[62] Whose first name was Yosef.

quet being held by the Beis Rivkah Schools.

With regard to the question asked by Tzach concerning the niggunim sung at the *farbrengens*, it appeared that the Rebbe desired that the niggunim be sung by the entire congregation, but several of the yeshiva students and young married men should prepare themselves beforehand, planning which niggunim would be sung. It also appeared that there should be a choir, led by a professional in the field. On Thursday, we prepared several niggunim to be sung on Shabbos. During the *farbrengen*, the singing was better than beforehand, but still not as it should be.

The Rebbe's uncle [Rabbi Ben Zion Schneersohn], who is also the brother-in-law of the Rebbe Rashab, is here at present. He arrived on Monday morning, two weeks ago. After concluding *yechidus* Sunday night, the Rebbe went to the airport to greet him. He gave me greetings from my father. During the *farbrengen*, a special place was arranged for him at the Rebbe's right, opposite Rashag.

As mentioned, the Rebbe submitted his letters concerning traveling on Israeli ships to be printed in the journal entitled HaPardes. They will be printed in this month's edition. These letters are selections from his letters to Rabbi Zevin[63] and Mr. Wilhelm in Jerusalem regarding this matter.

Monday, 5 Tammuz, 11 PM

The Rebbe held a *farbrengen* on Shabbos, 3 Tammuz.[64] He came

[63] Rabbi Shlomo Yosef Zevin (1890-1978).

[64] The day on which the Rebbe Rayatz was released from prison and his sentence commuted to exile.

out at 1:30 PM and farbrenged for about an hour and a half.

On Shabbos, three bridegrooms were given aliyos: Gershon Mendel Garelik (he is marrying the daughter of R' Sholom Posner of Pittsburgh), Shmuel Dovid Gurkov, and Shmuel Heber (his father is the uncle of R' Chaim Eliezer Heber and the brother-in-law of R' Mordechai Dovid Rivkin). It was also the Bar Mitzvah of Zalman Morozov, Mendel Morozov's son.

The Rebbe was very happy. He delivered five *sichos* and the *maamar* entitled *HaSam Nafsheinu BeChayim*.[65] The *maamar* explains the interpretation offered in the text Noam Elimelech of the Targum's rendition of the phrase "*And Korach took*."[66] The Rebbe elaborated on the concept of the division of the upper waters from the lower waters and cited the Tzemach Tzedek's explanation of this concept. The *maamar* was not delivered in the chant in which *maamorim* are usually delivered and the congregation did not rise[67] during its delivery.

The *sichos* underscored how, for Chassidim, the holiday of Gimmel Tammuz surpasses the holiday of Yud-Beis Tammuz, for on Gimmel Tammuz, the life of the Rebbe Rayatz was saved. He also cited the statement of Seder Olam: that the miracle G-d wrought for Yehoshua in which the sun stood still over Givon occurred on Gimmel Tammuz. He explained how the miracle of Gimmel Tammuz is intrinsically related to the Rebbe Rayatz.

He asked that happy niggunim be sung. In one of the *sichos*, he asked that a wedding *niggun* be sung. The parents of the grooms gave *mashkeh* which the Rebbe returned to them and told them to distribute it among the congregation.

[65] Printed in Sefer Maamorim Melukat, Vol. III, p. 201.
[66] Bamidbar 16:1.
[67] As is normally done for a *maamar*.

Yesterday was the wedding of Gershon Mendel Gorelik. The Rebbe conducted the wedding ceremony. Afterwards, the bride and groom and their parents flew by plane to Pittsburgh for the wedding feast. Several yeshiva students also went to the celebration. Zalman Morozov's Bar Mitzvah took place in the evening.

~

The student Yehoshua Wilansky from Bridgeport brought the sister of Mrs. Golda Meir to *yechidus* with the Rebbe. She is one of the active members of the Jewish community, particularly, in the area of Jewish education. During part of the *yechidus*, Yehoshua was with her. In the middle, the Rebbe motioned for him to depart. He spoke with her primarily about Jewish education.

~

B"H, Wednesday, 14 Tammuz, 12 AM

The farbengen of Yud-Beis Tammuz, the holiday of Redemption, was held on Monday night after the evening service. It began at 9:30 and continued until almost 3 AM. The *farbrengen* was held in the structure in the courtyard. In preparation for Yud-Beis Tammuz, the students raised its roof and built it on a slant so that the water would flow down it. The one who planned the building was the student Mendel Futerfass. In this way, more air enters the structure and it appears roomier.

When the Rebbe entered and sat down at his place, he appeared very happy. He said: "It's a beginning; may it be a good beginning for an expansion." His facial expression clearly reflected his satisfaction.

R' Shmuel Zalmanov began the Yud-Beis Tammuz *niggun*. The

Rebbe sang along with noticeable happiness. Afterwards, the Rebbe began another happy *niggun* that he liked (one of the niggunim that used to be sung by R' Michoel Dworkin). The congregation joined in with exuberant joy.

He delivered a *sicha* concerning Yud-Beis Tammuz, explaining how it is a continuation of the redemption from Egypt. He explained the difference between all the various redemptions, including the ultimate redemption that will be led by Moshiach. Afterwards, I began the *niggun* MiMitzrayim Gealtanu. Following that, there were several *sichos* and between them, happy niggunim. The Rebbe himself began a Simchas Torah *niggun*. (First, he leaned toward R' Yoel and then he began the *niggun*.) The congregation sang happily and powerfully, as the Rebbe motioned with his hands in encouragement.

He delivered the *maamar* entitled *Mi Manah Efar Yaakov*, explaining the difference in Divine service between Yaakov and Yisrael. In that context, he offered an interpretation of the verse: "And Yaakov departed from Beersheba and went to Charan,"[68] explaining that Charan is identified with the throat, which represents a state of contraction between the head (the intellect) and the heart (the emotions). He also explained the differences in implication when writing Beersheba with the vowel *kamatz* or the vowel *segol*.

In one of the *sichos* after the *maamar*, he explained the phrase from Psalm 79: "And repay our neighbors sevenfold."[69] On Tuesday, he called R' Yoel and gave him several instructions, among them, to include the latter concepts in the *maamar* when writing it up.

In the *maamar*, he spoke about the concept of ופרצת, that

[68] Bereishis 28:10.
[69] Tehillim 79:12. The psalm connected with the years of the Rebbe Rayatz's life.

Chassidus should be spread "to the west, east, north, and south." He concluded: "'May the one who breaks through (הפורץ) go before them.'[70] This refers to Moshiach who will be from the descendants of Peretz. May he come, speedily, in our days."

After the *maamar*, he spoke about the building to be constructed in Kfar Chabad that will serve as a synagogue and house of study and gave great blessings for it. Following this *sicha*, he instructed all those who purchased or who are purchasing buildings to say L'Chaim. He specifically mentioned Boston (where the purchase of a building for the yeshiva was completed on that day), Beis Rivkah in Montreal (where a building was recently purchased), the Educational Institute Ohelei Torah (headed by R' Michoel Teitlebaum which just purchased a building on Eastern Parkway), and Gan Yisrael. He also instructed that L'Chaim be said for Gan Yisrael in Kfar Chabad and other institutions.

R' Zalman Duchman was somewhat intoxicated. He asked for a blessing for the Vaad HaMesader for a building for the Shul. The Rebbe asked in wonderment: "Do they already have a building?"

In one of the *sichos*, the Rebbe related how when the Rebbe Rayatz was fifteen, he was vacationing with his father, the Rebbe Rashab. On the night of Yud-Beis Tammuz, his father told him to come to him early in the morning. He came at 4 AM. His father told him that they were going to go to Lubavitch. (They would usually come into Lubavitch from the country on Monday and this was a Wednesday.) Their trip took several hours. During the journey, the Rebbe Rayatz mentioned to his father that his grandmother (i.e., the Rebbe Rashab's mother) did not know of their journey and that she would become worried if they came suddenly. The Rebbe answered him:

[70] Micha 2:13.

"Your grandmother already knows."

When they came to Lubavitch, they visited his grandmother. First, the Rebbe Rashab entered and spoke to her, spending some time with her. When he left, she accompanied him with a beaming face and heartfelt blessings. Then they went to the ohel.[71]

Among the matters that transpired at the ohel was that the Rebbe Rashab conveyed the leadership of the Chassidic movement to the Rebbe Rayatz. He placed his two hands upon him and blessed him. He spoke about the concept of the Akeidah[72] and the concept of mesirus nefesh (self-sacrifice). (There were many details. I don't remember them now. I am writing only in brief.) The Rebbe Rashab concluded, summarizing the approach he desired to impart to the Rebbe Rayatz with a short, but rich Yiddish phrase: *Azoy un nit andersh* ("This is the way it is. There is no alternative.") He delivered the *maamar* entitled *Poschin BeBerachah* for the Rebbe Rayatz. The *maamar*, like its source in Tanya, Iggeres HaKodesh, Epistle 1, focuses on the concept of mesirus nefesh, using the analogy of the loins which support the body. The Rebbe explained how these concepts are relevant to every person and explained how "*Azoy un nit andersh*" can serve as a guideline for all of us.

In the midst of the *farbrengen*, the Rebbe instructed that the niggunim of all the Rebbeim beginning from the Baal Shem Tov be sung. For the Rebbe Rayatz, they sang the *niggun* he cherished, the *beinoni*.

I am certain you are aware of the demonstration held outside the White House in Washington by Neturei Karta. Last Thursday, a delegation of seven or eight Rabbis, apparently Satmar Chassidim, visited the Rebbe. Rabbi Chodakov entered the Rebbe's room with them. It is not known what was spoken

[71] The gravesite of the Tzemach Tzedek and the Rebbe Maharash.
[72] Avraham's binding of Yitzchak.

about, but it appears that they desired that the Rebbe make public statements supporting their approach with regard to Eretz Yisrael and the Rebbe demurred.

The Rebbe delivered a special *sicha* concerning this matter. It is difficult for me to write up even a summary of this *sicha*, but I will try to write what I understood. The Rebbe related that the Rebbe Rayatz would keep several old manuscripts and papers on his desk so that if someone would look for those letters and papers that had to be hidden, he would not be able to find them, because they would be mixed with the older papers. When the Rebbe Rayatz was arrested (before his liberation on Yud-Beis Tammuz), this ruse was successful. The Russians were unable to find the papers they were looking for, because they were mixed together with the older papers.

Jokingly, he told a story of how a Jew in a small village became very frightened when he saw a policeman. The policeman asked why he was frightened. He explained that he had written a letter to a friend and, by accident, had placed the stamp on it upside down. Now the stamp had a picture of the Czar on it, so placing it upside down could be considered an act of rebellion against him. The villager was afraid that the Czar had become aware of this and had sent the policeman to arrest him.

The Rebbe continued, stating that the matter is something that everybody has read about and everybody has written about. There is an accusation involved. But everybody is shouting merely about turning the stamp upside down; and it's the essence of the matter that requires clarification. If the accusation is untrue, then it is a lot worse than placing a stamp upside down or sending the letter to the wrong address. And if the accusation is true, what does it matter that the stamp was turned upside down. What is necessary is to clarify the essence of the matter. But they do not want to focus on the essence at all. Instead, they beat around the bush with superficial matters.

He spoke extensively about the point that the opinions of the Rabbis are not heeded at all, only the opinions of the lay leadership. Even those who are Torah observant are not fit to sit together with the Rabbis. What is necessary is that two or three Rabbis be charged with clarifying the matter.

The Rebbe stated that with regard to this, we can learn from the positive qualities found in the Conservative and the Reform movements. He said: "The laws regarding them are stated in the Shulchan Aruch, their positive qualities, however, should be emulated." Among the positive qualities he mentioned were: a) not to speak during the reading of the Torah or the *chazzan*'s repetition of the prayers, b) not to raise money through projects that are not becoming to the synagogue, e.g., bingo, ping-pong, or cards, c) that in all religious matters, the Rabbi's ruling is the determining factor; the lay leaders do not become involved.

With regard to the previous matter, he spoke about the fact that Torah scholars who should devote themselves solely to study and prayer are torn from their books, on the pretense that this is an important matter, that the sanctification of G-d's name is involved.

(What I wrote above is not exact. I wrote down what I understood. When the Rebbe called R' Yoel, he told him to write up the *maamar* and the *sichos* as soon as possible, because everyone is writing about it in the papers....)

When the Rebbe spoke about Kfar Chabad, R' Benyamin Althaus said L'Chaim. It appeared that he wanted the Rebbe to tell him something, but the Rebbe merely responded: L'Chaim ULiverachah. The Rebbe's uncle who was sitting to his left said: "His father is involved in these activities." The Rebbe said: "Yes, he has 'to the west and to the east,' but he lacks the Ufarartza, the breakthrough potential".

Rashag drank a lot of *mashkeh*. There was a discussion between him and the Rebbe. I do not know what they discussed, but I did hear the Rebbe say out loud: "The students from Tomchei Temimim are here. The directorate of the yeshiva should see to it that all of the students shout *Uforatzta Yamah*... and sing a happy *niggun*."

The students together with the entire congregation shouted in a loud voice: *Uforatzta Yamah Vikeidmah Tzafonah Vinegbah*. I began a very happy *niggun*.[73] The Rebbe stood up and sang the *niggun* out loud with great exuberance. In the middle of the *niggun*, he said: Everyone should shout out: *Uforatzta*... The entire congregation shouted *Uforatzta*... again and the Rebbe himself shouted in a loud voice and with emphasis: *Uforatzta Yamah Vikeidmah Tzafonah Vinegbah*. Everyone then continued singing the *niggun* with great joy until the Rebbe sat down.

There was a special *sicha* about the directorate of the yeshiva. The Rebbe said: "When it comes to their own children and grandchildren, they look for all possible ways. When it comes to the yeshiva, they always complain about obstacles."

There was also a special *sicha* directed to women. When the Alter Rebbe's *niggun* was sung, the Rebbe directed that the last stanza be sung three times.

It's already late and I must get up for work tomorrow. People are saying that the Rebbe will go to Gan Yisrael tomorrow. I asked Rabbi Chodakov about the matter, but he said that he does not know anything about it. The same thing happened two years ago. No one knew of the Rebbe's trip until two hours beforehand.

[73] At that time, the melody for the words Uforatzta had not yet been composed.

Sunday, 18 Tammuz, the night following the fast of 17 Tanmnuz, may it be transformed into a day of celebration, 12 AM

I am very sorry that I am not writing this journal in an orderly manner, but my free time has become very limited recently. I accepted the job of checking a portion of the novellae of Rabbenu Nissim on the tractate of Niddah to be published by Rav Stern. He will pay me with books. (Understandably, I do not have money to buy books yet.) Yesterday, together with R' Yoel, I prepared the digest of the *sichos* of Yud-Beis Tammuz. We sat until 3 in the morning.

Last Shabbos, the Rebbe entered the study hall of the yeshiva at 7:05 AM. There were only about ten students there. He told R' David Raskin: "Prepare the students. I want to review a *maamar*."

At 8 AM exactly, the students entered the Rebbe's room. He delivered the *maamar* entitled *Vehayah Shearis Yaakov* which lasted approximately 40 minutes. In the midst of the *maamar*, he also repeated the portion associated with the phrase: "*And repay our neighbors sevenfold*" from psalm 79. The students said that his face was shining (in contrast to the parallel situation of Shabbos Zachor when he was very serious, as I mentioned in my notes above).

R' Yoel and R' Avraham Shemtov, the ones who usually repeat the *maamorim* by heart, were not present. The student Yisrael Friedman reviewed the *maamar* by heart. It appears that he grasped it well.

Mrs. G. (R' Moshe Aharon's wife) told me that a while ago, while she was pregnant, the doctors told her that it was necessary to abort the pregnancy. She relayed the information to the Rebbe in writing. In the evening, Rabbi Chodakov called her and told her: "You and your husband will live to bring your children to the wedding canopy."

After several days passed without any improvement in her condition and after the doctors told her again that an abortion was necessary, she entered *yechidus* and poured her heart out to the Rebbe. The Rebbe interrupted her free-flowing outpouring of feelings, telling her simply: "I have nothing to add beyond what I had Rabbi Chodakov communicate."

With G-d's help, everything worked out well and she gave birth to a healthy girl.

~

Next Tuesday, my mother-in-law is planning to go on vacation and visit my brother-in-law in Canada for several weeks. With G-d's help, Saraleh will also go with her. I asked the Rebbe if it is a good idea and he answered: "It should be in a good and auspicious hour."

~

For Shabbos Parshas Chukas, I went to the Bronx for a Shabbaton organized by Tzach together with Shmerayahu Pruss. We stayed by his brother-in-law R' Mordechai Dubinsky. Berl Junik and Chaim Serabranyski came with us and stayed by R' Moshe Levertov. We spoke in many shuls and held a *farbrengen* in the home of R' Mordechai Dubinsky. That Shabbos, a significant number of students were in Brighton Beach (it is also a part of New York City). They also spoke in many shuls and held a *farbrengen*.

On Sunday, 11 Tammuz, R' Avraham Elya Lis and Mendel Baumgarten traveled to Albany and held a beautiful *farbrengen*. The concept of traveling to other cities has already become part of the routine work of Tzach and quite a number of Chassidim participate.

Similarly, the review of the teachings of Chassidus in various synagogues has grown stronger. In particular, this is true now that each week portions of the Rebbe's *sichos* are published, for they are excellent material to teach.

In addition to the study of the Shulchan Aruch and Chassidus on either Monday or Tuesday each week, we have also begun studying Gemara, the tractate Niddah, each Thursday. Berl Junik, the organizer of the group, notified the Rebbe of this and received the reply: "I will mention you at the gravesite [of the Rebbe Rayatz] for success in all the above. May it also lead to success in all your matters."

Rebbe's letters to R' Moshe Dovber Gansbourg, Hirsh's father, from 5715 and 5720.

גנזבורג= ת"א

RABBI MENACHEM M. SCHNEERSON
Lubavitch
770 Eastern Parkway
Brooklyn 13, N. Y.
HYacinth 3-9250

מנחם מענדל שניאורסאהן
ליובאוויטש
770 איסטערן פארקוויי
ברוקלין, נ. י.

ב"ה. א' מ"ח תשט"ו
ברוקלין

הרה"ח הוו"ח אי"א נו"נ כו'
מוה"ר משה דובער שי'

שלום וברכה!

מאשר הנני קבלת מכתבו מז' תשרי, והכיתי לבשו"ט נוספות. ולפלא שבכלל אין מכתבים מהם, וגם לא ע"ד קביעות חתונת מרת רבקה תחי' שרייבער, שלפי השערתי הי' צ"ל בתחלת חדש מ"ח,

מ"ש שהדפיס מעדני שמואל על הלכות פסח, בטח ידוע לו שהדפיסוהו ג"כ זה מזמן במחנות ההסגר בפערנוואלד. כן מזכיר במכ' שהשלים הקופיר של תרס"ו ותר"ס, אבל אינו כותב אם הגיהו את הנ"ל.

בודאי למותר לעורר על ההכרח הכי גדול בהשתתפותם בעניני הרשת, כאו"א באופן המתאים ויכולתו, אבל בכל יכולתו, ומ"ש אודות הסדר החדש שההנהלה בפועל ע"י הרה"ג והר"ד שי' כו' הרי אין זה ממעט האחריות של אנ"ש בכלל, והקרובים להרשת ואלי בפרט, בזה.

בברכה - המחכה לבשו"ט

גנזבורג= ח״א

RABBI MENACHEM M. SCHNEERSON
Lubavitch
770 Eastern Parkway
Brooklyn 13, N. Y.

HYacinth 3-9250

מנחם מענדל שניאורסאהן
ליובאוויטש

770 איסטערן פארקוויי
ברוקלין, נ. י.

ב״ה. ב׳ סיון תשט״ו
ברוקלין

הוו״ח אי״א נו״נ עוסק בצ״צ
מוה״ר דוב שי׳

שלום וברכה!

מאשר הנני קבלת מכתבו מלפני חג הפסח עם המוסגר בו, ובשאלתו בהנוגע להמכתב שקבל ממדינתנו לפנים שפירושו בקשה הגשת דרישה לעלות לאה״ק ת״ו. הרי בהתאם עם גיל המבקש-נכון הדבר בכלל. ומובן שצריך להתייעץ עם המומחים בזה באיזה אופן יותר טוב להגיש, אם בתור קרוב כו׳.

מ״ש אודות לעשות פאטאסטאט מסידור תהלת ד׳. הנה מובן שזהו שייך לקה״ת, אשר הביאו גם הסידורים לאה״ק ת״ו ע״פ החוזה. ואין ענין להתחרות עם קה״ת.

מ״ש אודות המיבה שיצא מהנהלת הרשת בתור אחד הגזברים, אף שממשיך בקבוץ סכומים וגם זה-סכומים קטנים לפי מכתבו. הנה כבר נלאיתי לכתוב בכגון דא לכאו״א מאנ״ש, שלא רק שאין מועיל לאחד מה שכותבים לחשני, אלא שאין מועיל גם מה שכותבים להאיש עצמו. וכבר ידוע מרז״ל אשר מצוה לזכות לכאו״א מבני ישראל וזכין לאדם אפילו שלא בפניו-אבל בע״כ אין זכין לאדם, וכמה פעמים כתבתי לחברי הנהלת הרשת, שאין הענין שהם עושים טובה להקב״ה או אפילו לנשיאנו הק׳ זצוקללה״ה נבג״מ זי״ע, אלא שזהו זכות גדול ונעלה בשבילם מה שכ״ק מו״ח אדמו״ר עורר ר״ר וסיבב כמה סיבות והעמידם על חלק היפה לעשות בהתפתחות מוסדות חינוך הנקראים על שמו, שמזה מובן, שאם מי שהוא יפגע בכבודו או אפילו ימעט ח״ו את דמותו-הנה לא זו היא הדרך אויף אויס-פאטשן זיך אליין מפני שפב״פ אינו נוהג כבוד כדבעי. ואין לי מה להוסיף על הנ״ל. וגם שורותי הנ״ל הם לכאורה מיותרות, כיון שכהנ״ל כתבתי את כל זה כ״פ ולא הועיל. ויה״ר שעכ״פ יתאמץ בכל מו לקחת חבל בעניני הרשת ע״י קבוץ סכומים הנ״ל. ובלי האי ואולי יזכהו השי״ת להרבות בהם. מובן שאין הנ״ל מכוון אליו בלבד, אלא לכל אלו שהיו בהנהלת הרשת ומטעמים שונים ומשונים נשתמטו מזה, ואומרים שהם בעלי מחשבות ועלה הדבר בידם לרפות את שאר חברי ההנהלה, בה בשעה שאין בזה אלא אבוד זכות של עצמו. וכבר ידוע פתגם כ״ק אדמו״ר מוהר״ש נ״ע ששמענו כ״פ מבו״ק מו״ח אדמו״ר, שבענינים דקדושה ברור הדבר שריוח והצלה יעמוד ליהודים, אלא שאם זוכים-הוא ע״י את ובית אביך. ובא״ל-הרי מאבדים זכות זה, והריוח והצלה הוא ממקום אחר. מובן ופשוט שאין כאן כל ענין של קפידא וכו׳, אלא שכאב הלב לראות אז מען מאטערט זיך לבוא לענינים רוחנים וגשמים אויף קרומע וועגן, ובלבד שלא ללכת בדרך הישרה המובילה לסיפוק צרכי האדם ובי״ב, הן בגשמיות והן ברוחניות, ובלי העלמות והסתרים יותר מן המדה.

בברכה לקבלת התורה בשמחה
ובפנימיות ולבשו״ט

נ.ב.

עיינתי בהדו״ח של חברת גמ״ח. ולכאורה צ״ע שבמשך השנה לא ניתנו אלא לג׳ הלואות.

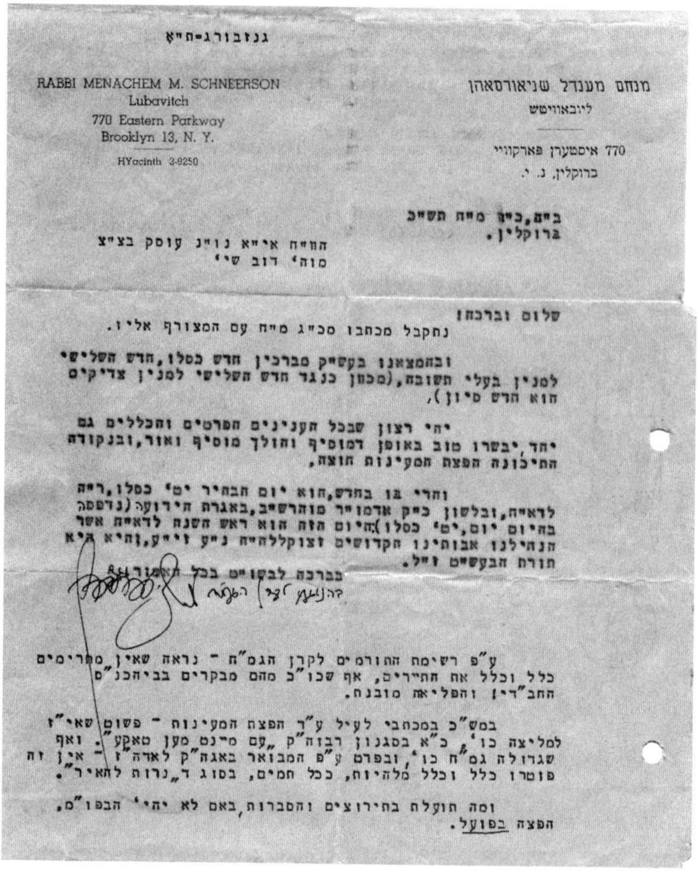

גנזבורג=ח"א

RABBI MENACHEM M. SCHNEERSON
Lubavitch
770 Eastern Parkway
Brooklyn 13, N. Y.
HYacinth 3-9250

מנחם מענדל שניאורסאהן
ליובאוויטש
770 איסטערן פארקוויי
ברוקלין, נ. י.

ב"ה, כ"ז מ"ח תש"ב
ברוקלין.

הוו"ח אי"א נו"נ עוסק בצ"צ
מוה' דוב שי'

שלום וברכה!
נתקבל מכתבו מכ"ג מ"ח עם המצורף אליו.

ובהמצאנו בעש"ק מברכין חדש כסלו, חדש השלישי למנין בעלי תשובה, (מכוון כנגד חדש השלישי למנין צדיקים הוא חדש סיון),

יהי רצון שבכל הענינים הפרטים והכללים גם יחד, יבשרו טוב באופן דמוסיף והולך מוסיף ואור, ובנקודה התיכונה הפצת המעינות חוצה.

והרי בו בחדש, הוא יום הבהיר יט' כסלו, ר"ה לדא"ח, ובלשון כ"ק אדמו"ר מוהרש"ב, באגרת הידועה (נדפסה בהיום יום, יט' כסלו): היום הזה הוא ראש השנה לדא"ח אשר הנחילנו אבותינו הקדושים זצוקללה"ה נ"ע זי"ע, והיא היא תורת הבעש"ט ז"ל.

בברכה לבשו"ט בכל האמור
דהנ"ל [handwritten]

ע"פ רשימת התורמים לקרן הגמ"ח - נראה שאין מתרימים כלל וכלל את התיירים, אף שכו"כ מהם מבקרים בביהכנ"ס החב"דין והפליאה מובנת.

במש"כ במכתבי לעיל ע"ד הפצת המעינות - פשוט שאי"ז למליצה כו', כ"א בסגנון רבזה"ק „עם מינט מען מאכע". ואף שגדולה גמ"ח כו', ובפרט ע"פ המבואר באגה"ק לאדה"ז - אין זה פוטרו כלל וכלל מלהיות, ככל חמים, בסוג ד„נרות להאיר".

ומה תועלת בהירוצים והסברות, באם לא יהי' הבפו"מ, הפצה בפועל.

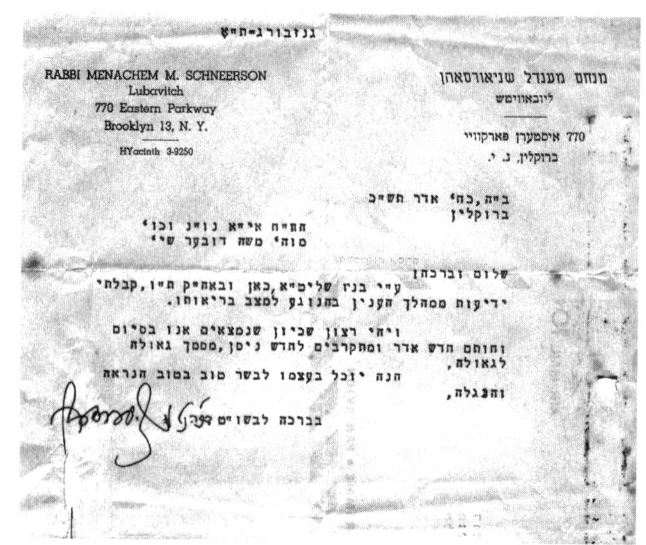

גנזבורג=ח"א

RABBI MENACHEM M. SCHNEERSON
Lubavitch
770 Eastern Parkway
Brooklyn 13, N. Y.
HYacinth 3-9250

מנחם מענדל שניאורסאהן
ליובאוויטש
770 איסטערן פארקוויי
ברוקלין, נ. י.

ב"ה, כה' אדר תש"ב
ברוקלין

הוו"ח אי"א נו"נ וכו'
מוה' משה דובער שי'

שלום וברכה!
ע"י בנו שליט"א, כאן ובאה"ק ת"ו, קבלתי ידיעות ממהלך הענין בהנוגע למצב בריאותו.

ויהי רצון שכיון שנמצאים אנו בסיום וחותם חדש אדר ומתקרבים לחדש ניסן, מסמך גאולה לגאולה,
הנה יזכל בעצמו לבשר טוב בטוב הנראה והנגלה,

בברכה לבשו"ט

Part 4 – America 5720

On Monday, 27 Elul, I will reach the age of 32. Since there is no formal *yechidus* during the entire month of Elul, nor in the month of Tishrei, I asked Rabbi Chodakov to arrange that if there will be others entering *yechidus* on Sunday, I would also be allowed to enter. Rabbi Chodakov agreed.

On Sunday, 19 Elul, he told me that I would be able to enter *yechidus* sometime between the hours of 8-10 PM. When I arrived at 770 a little before eight, the entire corridor was filled with women from the Ladies Auxiliary of Beis Rivkah and Yeshivas Tomchei Temimim, who, as is the custom every year, would enter the Rebbe's room to receive his blessing before Rosh Hashanah. They entered at nine accompanied by R' Yitzchak Goldin and R' A.Y. Kornblit who wrote down their names and their mothers' names. My mother-in-law [Rebbetzin Henya Denburg] entered with them.

They all entered together. Since there were very many women, they were not all able to fit into the Rebbe's room and many remained in the stairwell outside. However, the setting was not well coordinated. When the Rebbe finished delivering a *sicha* and his blessings, many of the women approached him with notes asking for individual blessings. Try as he did, R' Leibel Groner found it very difficult to usher them out of the Rebbe's room.

When they finally left, others came, including R' Shlomo Aharon Kazarnovsky with a delegation from his Shul in Brighton Beach. Among them, R' Meir Yashar, R' Shmuel Shulsinger, the owner of the print shop, the president of the synagogue, and other members. They had collected 2500 dollars for the Trade School in Kfar Chabad. After they entered the Rebbe's room and departed, R' Shmuel Shulsinger remained. As he afterwards related, the Rebbe insisted that he publish the Jerusalem Talmud. (For a long time, the Rebbe has been asking the Shulsinger brothers to publish the Jerusalem Talmud. On Purim [5718 (1958)], he delivered a special *sicha* concerning printing that appeared to be directed to them.)

R' Shlomo Aharon Kazarnovsky told him – he himself does not remember – that while the congregants were in the Rebbe's room, the president of the congregation asked the Rebbe: "What is a Lubavitcher Chassid?" The Rebbe took R' Shmuel Shulsinger by the hand and said: "This is a Lubavitcher Chassid."

Several others entered *yechidus* including the son of the Gaon, R' Isser Zalman Meltzer.

The Rebbe interrupted *yechidus* to attend the evening service and then resumed seeing people. I entered *yechidus* about 11 PM. I gave the Rebbe a note which said the following: "On Monday, 27 Elul, with G-d's help, I will reach the age of 32. I ask the Rebbe to bless me, Zvi Hirsh ben Doba."

The Rebbe's face was beaming. He asked: "How is your daughter doing?" (Several days previously, I had written the Rebbe a note that hives had appeared all over my daughter Sarah's body. With G-d's help, after a few days, they disappeared.) I replied that her situation has improved, but in general, her health is fragile and that she vomited Saturday night.

The Rebbe asked: "What is it like in your home? Hot or cold?"

I answered: "Normal."

He replied: "It's probably the result of the heat," and continued: "I assume you received an *aliyah* on Shabbos...."[1] With concluding his words, he began reading my note. "It's 27 Elul. Nu, on Shabbos ask for an *aliyah*. On your birthday, give *tzedakah* before *davening* in the morning and also before the afternoon service. You should have a year of success. G-d should grant you, together with your wife, and your children, a *kesivah vechasimah tovah* for a good and sweet year in both material and spiritual matters."

He asked: "On the day before Rosh Hashanah, will you be going to the gravesite?"[2]

I replied: "With G-d's help."

He continued: "Nu, leave a note there and mention your birthday as well. It is only two days afterwards. May G-d fulfill his holy blessing for our good."

On Thursday, 23 Elul,[3] the Rebbe recited all of the *kaddeishim* in all the prayer services. For Shacharis, I served as the *chazzan*.

[1] It is Lubavitch custom to receive an aliyah on the Shabbos before one's birthday. Apparently, the Rebbe originally thought that Rabbi Gansbourg's birthday was to be celebrated in the coming week.

[2] I.e., of the Rebbe Rayatz.

[3] The *yahrtzeit* of R' Shlomo Yanovsky, the Rebbe's maternal grandfather.

When the Rebbe received an *aliyah*, he took his Torah Ohr Siddur with him and recited the Kaddish after the Torah reading from it. He held the staves of the Torah scroll while reciting the blessings, lifting the scroll slightly when reciting the word Borchu and at the conclusion of the first and last blessings.

When reciting Kaddish..., he would raise his head slightly while reciting the words *vayatzmach porkanei, baagalah, yehei shmei rabbah*. When reciting the words, *yisbareich, viyishtabach, viyispaar, viyisrommam*, and *viyisnasei*, he would progressively lower his head, inclining it downward with each word. He would raise it when reciting the words *viyishader, shmei dikudsha brich hu*, and *diamiran bialma*. When he said: *vichayim tovim aleinu*, he nodded his head. When reciting the stanza, *oseh shalom*, he took three full steps backwards. When he said *oseh*, he bowed to his right, *shalom*, he bowed to his left, *bimromav*, in front of him, and when he said *hu*, he lifted his head up. When he said *viimru amen*, he raised his heels. (When he would lead the prayers, when saying *tiskabel*, he would incline his head forward very slightly. He said the following prayers together with the congregation:[4] *L'David HaShem Ori*, I think also *Amar Rabbi Eliezar amar Rabbi Chanina* and T*anna d'bei Eliyahu*, and *Aleinu*.)

The individuals obligated to recite Kaddish did so after the Rebbe completed saying Kaddish. After the morning service, he said the chapters of *mishnayos* customarily recited, concluding in a loud voice: *machat shehi nesunah al maaras hamaarah... Rabbi Chananya ben Akasha omar...* When reciting the lines of *Tanya* following the *mishnayos* in a hushed tone, he passed his left hand over his eyes.

[4] In those years, the Rebbe would rarely recite the entire morning service together with the congregation. He would come to listen to the Torah readings and depart after the Torah was brought back to the ark. On those days when he would recite Kaddish, he would remain until the conclusion of the service and recite the Kaddeishim.

Similarly, he recited Kaddish on Shabbos, 25 Elul, (I think it is the *yahrtzeit* of his cousin, Rebbitzen Chayah Mushka,) including the kaddeishim after each of the books of Tehillim.[5] After the recitation of the entire Book of Tehillim, I saw that he opened to the page on which the *Yehi Ratzon* recited after Tehillim is printed. When we recited the *kaddeishim*,[6] he stood, but he sat after the recitation of the phrase *diamiran bialma, vi-imru Amen*. He recited Tehillim from the text Yahel Ohr, also known as Tehilim Ohel Yosef Yitzchak HaShaleim.

At 1:30 PM, he held a *farbrengen*. He delivered three *sichos* before the *maamar* and one afterwards. The *sichos* focused on the verse: "*You are all standing together, your heads...*"[7] The *maamar* also began with that verse. In the last *sicha*, he cried extensively and spoke in a low voice, elaborating on the topic of Teshuvah, how it has the potential to transform the entire year. He mentioned our Sages words[8] that in the ultimate future, even trees that do not usually bear fruit will do so. He explained that such trees can be understood as an analogy for Jews who do not observe the Torah and its mitzvos. Through performing Teshuvah, they will "bear fruit" and their Divine service will bring about such a change in the world as well.

He spoke about having success in business and making profits, associating that with Teshuvah and making a transformation from one extreme to another. Mitzvos, by contrast, relate to the ordinary pattern of the spiritual cosmos; they are confined to the natural pattern, e.g., taking nine months for a child to be born. This is the implication of Moshe's declaration: "Heavens, give ear," in contrast to Yeshayahu, who said "Earth, give ear."

[5] That Shabbos was Shabbos Mevorchim, the Shabbos when the coming month is blessed. It is Chabad custom to recite the entire book of Tehillim before the morning prayers on such a Shabbos.
[6] During that year, Rabbi Gansbourg was reciting Kaddish for his father.
[7] Devarim 29:9.
[8] Kesubos 112b.

Moshe was on a level above the world, and on that level, it is possible for a woman to give birth every day, as will take place in the era of Resurrection. Similarly, in business, there is the ordinary, natural order, and then, it is difficult to succeed; and then there is the possibility to rise above the limits of nature and become awesomely wealthy. For this, however, Teshuvah is necessary. During the *sicha*, he also gave many blessings for a kesivah vechasimah tovah for the coming new year.

I began the *niggun* of R' Asher of Nikolaiev (which is associated with the Rebbe Rashab) and the congregation sang with much inspiration. The Rebbe instructed that it be sung twice. When he spoke about the spreading of Chassidus and how that will lead to the coming of Mashiach, I started the *niggun* which communicates that theme.

On Shabbos, the Rebbe made Kiddush on wine and also said L'Chaim. After the *farbrengen*, he recited the blessing *al hamichyeh vial hagefen* and himself began the *niggun* Ki B'Simchah Tzeitzeiu.

The student Meshulam Rosenfeld who was married last week desired to arrange for the seven marriage blessings to be recited, but the Rebbe was in a state of *dveikus* and Rabbi Chodakov was unable to get his attention.

Motzaei Shabbos, 2:30 AM, after Selichos

The recitation of Selichos began after midnight, at approximately 1:10 AM, and concluded at 1:50. R' Shmuel Zalmanov served as the *chazzan*.

The service was held in the new Shul that was built in the area that used to be the courtyard of the Shul. In the woman's section, a very high partition had been constructed, one that exceeded a person's height. This was done in response to a directive from Rabbi Chodakov which, it appears, originated in the Rebbe's instructions. He said that if there would not be such a partition, the Rebbe would not come out for Selichos.

articles...

Rabbi Gansbourg and Charles

by Hensha Gansbourg

It was just after Passover, and we needed to do some repairs outside our home. Just that very morning I had spoken with my friend Chana on the phone. Chana lives in Manhattan and has wonderful connections with just about everyone. Just the previous year, I needed a man to hang wallpaper, and Chana immediately found Ron, an Israeli, to do the job. When Ron arrived, my husband immediately put Tefillin on him. My friend Chana felt so good to have been even indirectly involved with the mitzva of Tefillin.

I had been in a dilemma that morning. Who could I call to do the repairs? I spoke with Chana that morning, and a few minutes later she called back with the name Charles Christian, III.

Chana even jokingly remarked that perhaps my husband would put Tefillin on him as he did with Ron! "Sure," I said to myself, "with a name like Charles Christian, III."

Charles came to our home the following week to look over what the job entailed and to give us an estimate. As we were coming back in the house, he said, "You might not know this, but I'm part Jewish."

"Part Jewish!" I exclaimed. "From your mother's side or your father's side?" I inquired.

"Well, it's really my mother who is Jewish. She survived the Holocaust and felt that Jews were persecuted only for being Jews. She decided when she arrived in the United States that it was perhaps safer to live as a non-Jew. She settled in Pennsylvania and married my father, who is not Jewish."

At this point in our conversation, my husband, who was in another part of the house but had overheard this startling revelation, came over to Charles and asked if he would like to do a Jewish thing. Charles replied that he didn't know anything about being Jewish. My husband said it didn't matter. Soon, a pair of Tefillin were being wrapped around Charles's arm. He recited the Shema after my husband. He seemed visibly moved. My husband then proceeded to tell him that he was now "Bar Mitzvahed."

Charles was shaken by that revelation. He proceeded to tell us that he didn't know anything about being Jewish, and that, in fact, he had been raised as a non-Jew.

I looked around the room thinking: Here he's Bar-Mitzvah'ed – what an opportunity to give Charles a Bar Mitzvah gift. Just then I noticed Simon Jacobson's book, Toward a Meaningful Life, sitting on the bureau. I grabbed the book and gave it to Charles to read, since he said that he didn't know anything about Judaism. Charles was very touched.

A few weeks later Charles and his partner came back to do the repairs. My husband again put Tefillin on him, and Charles was obviously very happy to again be able to do something Jewish.

Towards the end of July, I had a question about the repair job that had been done. His partner, James, answered the phone and said that he was sorry to tell me that Charles had an accident and had passed away the previous Friday.

It says in the Talmud that the mitzva of Tefillin is so basic that "a head which dons no Tefillin is like a Jew who neglects the observance of the Torah precepts. Yet, a Jew who performs this mitzva even once becomes so spiritually refined that he is raised from that category and is consequently set on a path of growth and ennoblement."

I was stunned when I heard that Charles had died. I couldn't help but think of the Divine Providence. Here, a Jew who didn't even consider himself totally Jewish had the opportunity to put on Tefillin shortly before his passing.

May the memory of Charles be blessed. May we continue to see the workings of Divine Providence with our eyes of flesh. May we merit to bring more and more Jews into the tent of Torah and mitzvot, so that we finally see the Rebbe with our own eyes, together with all of the souls that he has embraced. May this be speedily in our days.

Reprinted with permission from the N'Shei Chabad Newsletter

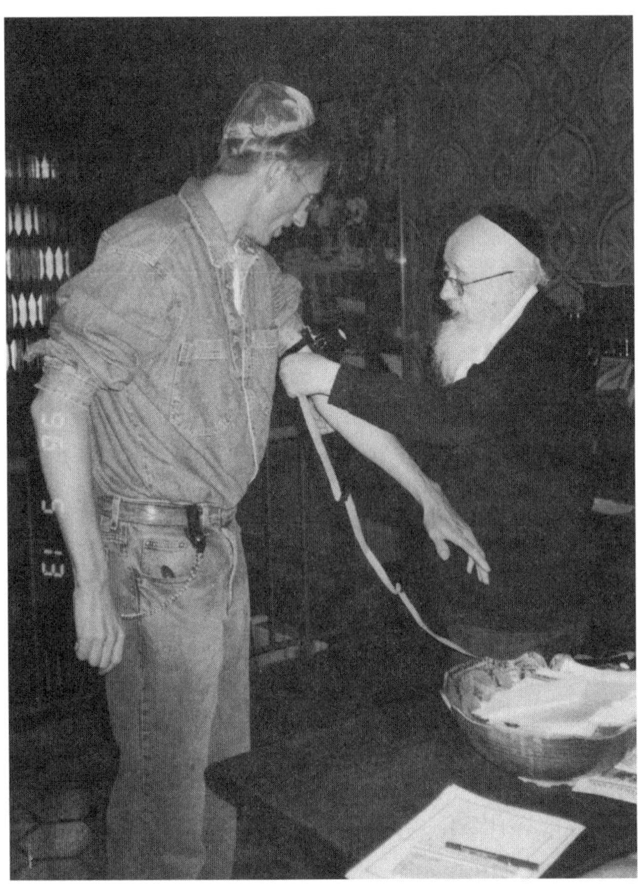

Through Water and Fire

By Mendel Jacobson

He sees the man dancing as if there are no worries in the world. His legs pump in a rhythm only his soul could produce. He looks like a flame, flickering on and on, reaching for a place beyond anything he has ever known. Wow, how could that man be so happy?

"Which man?"

Startled, the 14-year-old boy didn't realize he'd asked that question aloud.

"Which man?" His father asks him again.

"That man," the young boy points to the whirling man. "He must be the happiest man on earth."

As his father looks to where his son is pointing and he sees the black-bearded man with five children in tow, his eyes fill with tears and he sighs. "That man just lost his young wife six days ago."

"But then how can he be so happy, how can he possibly dance like that?"

"Because today is Simchas Torah and it is a mitzvah to dance and to be happy. This is what a Jew does; this is what a real Chassid does."

Although this story happened before I was born, I have heard it many times.

The year was 5730, 1969, and, on the second day of Succos, a young man lost his wife to leukemia. Every year, on Simchas Torah, the young man would take his five young children to a small Shul in East Flatbush where they would dance with the

Torah and rejoice with the community. That year, 1969, the young man did the same. The children's grandmother, their mother's mother, dressed them in their finest clothing and sent them off with their father to East Flatbush.

It was there, in that little Shul, that this dialogue between father and son took place.

After the dancing was over in East Flatbush, the young man and his five children walked back to Crown Heights. He dropped his younger children off at home with their grandmother and hurried to 770 where the Lubavitcher Rebbe was in middle of a *farbrengen*. Every year on Simchas Torah, before the dancing would begin, the Rebbe would speak for a number of hours, discussing the intricate energies of Simchas Torah and hakofos. At different times throughout the talk, the Rebbe would pause and the Hassidim would begin singing a *niggun*, a Hassidic melody sometimes dating back hundreds of years. The young man of whom we are speaking was the one who began the niggunim at the Rebbe's farberengens.

The Shul at 770 Eastern Parkway was packed from floor to ceiling; people were clinging to bleachers and rafters just as they did to the Rebbe's every word. As the Rebbe finished his talk, the crowd was eagerly waiting for the young man to begin a song. They all knew he had just lost his wife and were wondering what his choice of song would be.

Through the hush of thousands of people, a small but defiant voice could be heard: "*Mi vadiom nye patonyem ee v'agniom nye s'gorim*," a lively Chassidic Russian song meaning, "We in water will not drown and in fire will not burn." As the Rebbe began swinging his arms, the crowd became more and more excited, chanting, "We in water will not drown and in fire will not burn; we in water will not drown and in fire will not burn." Faster and faster they chanted, as if in a trance. People that were there could not believe this little man, swinging back and forth, singing, "We in water will not drown and in fire will not burn," as if G-d had not just taken his wife, as if he was the happiest man alive.

~

Fast-forward 20 years:

A phone call comes in to a major Jewish children's organization in Crown Heights.

"Hello," the voice on the other end of the line says. "I am so-and-so and I would like to sponsor children's programs for Simchas Torah."

"Ok, sure," the man working in the organization happily replies. "But, if I may ask, why do you have an interest in sponsoring children's programs for Simchas Torah?"

"Well, you see, when I was a boy, every Simchas Torah my father and I would go to a small Shul in East Flatbush to dance. One year, when I was fourteen, as I was watching the few people dancing in a circle, I noticed one man who looked so happy, as if everything in the world was perfect. I stood there transfixed, wondering how this man could exude so much joy. I asked my father this question, and my father told me that I should know this man just lost his wife but, because he is a real Hassidic Jew and the Torah says to be happy on Simchas Torah, he is happy. This made a very big impression on my 14-year-old mind – that a Jew could put aside all his pain and suffering and be happy just because it's a mitzvah to be happy was unbelievable to me – so I decided I would like to help other children celebrate the happiness and joy of Simchas Torah."

~

Fast-forward another 17 years:

On the 23rd of Cheshvon, 5767, 2006, the young man of this story, the one who lost his wife in 1969, rejoined her in the Garden of Eden. Yet, his (and her) grandchildren, their "life," live on. They have built families and communities, changed people's lives, and continue to make the world a better place.

The story of the young man has taught me much: even in the saddest of times, even when all seems lost, with a little joy, a little dance, everything can change.

"We in water will not drown and in fire will not burn." I myself am living proof. You see, my mother was one of those five children that walked with their father to that small Shul in East Flatbush those 37 years ago.

Reprinted with permission from the Algemeiner Journal

living on...

Original Hebrew Writings

דיוקנו
של חסיד

הרב צבי הירש גאנזבורג ע"ה
תרפ"ח-תשס"ו

יוצא לאור לרגל שמחת נישואין של נכדיו
הרב התמים **בנציון** וב"ג **ראשא** שיחיו **מארקוס**
ד' אדר ראשון ה'תשס"ח

ISBN 1-886587-17-5
Printed in the United States

The GJCF preserves the legacies of institutions and individuals that have built and advanced Jewish life. For more info: E-mail mylegacy@gjcf.net

מפתח הענינים

פתח דבר

בתודה להשי"ת הננו מוציאים לאור בזה את הספר "דיוקנו של חסיד", והוא ספר זכרון לזכרו של חמי, הרב התמים ר' צבי הירש גאנזבורג ע"ה, הידוע גם בתואר החיבה שלו ר' העסקע.

ספר זה כולל: 1) יומנים של ר' צבי הירש שנכתבו בשנים תש"ה ותש"ז בתל אביב, ובשנים תשי"א, תשי"ב, תשח"י ותש"כ בניו יארק. 2) צילומי מכתבים של כ"ק אדמו"ר מהוריי"צ וכ"ק אדמו"ר נשיא דורנו להרה"ח הרה"ת ר' משה דובער גנזבורג ע"ה, אביו של ר' צבי הירש. 3) כמה פקסימיליות של כתי"ק כ"ק אדמו"ר - הגהות לקונטרסים וספרים שונים שהוכנו לדפוס על ידי ר' צבי הירש, בתקופת שנת תשי"א (כפי שנזכר כמה פעמים ברשימותיו). 4) תמונות מהמשפחה. 5) תמונות מכמה חסידים ועסקנים מתקופה ההיא הנזכרים בהיומנים.

לתועלת הציבור הרחב הוספנו גם תרגום אנגלי מהיומנים, בשילוב צילומים, מכתבים ותמונות.

רוב החומר מתפרסם כאן לראשונה, ויש לציין שפרטים רבים המתגלים כאן שופכים אור חדש ומשלימים פרטים רבים ויסודיים בתולדות ימי רבינו ותנועת חב"ד באותה תקופה הרת גורל של "וזרח השמש ובא השמש", שכבר נכתב עליה רבות בספר "ימי בראשית" ופירסומים דומים*, כולל ובמיוחד בעבודת רבינו בתור יו"ר הנהלת קה"ת והתעסקותו בהוצאה לאור של דברי חסידות וכו'.

תודתי נתונה להת' יוסף יצחק שי' קרץ ור' אברהם שי' רייניץ שסייעו בעריכת החומר ובעימוד הספר.

ספר זה, כפי שמפורש בשמו, הינו "דיוקנו של חסיד" אמיתי הראוי

לשמו. מהו חסיד? חסיד מסור בכל מחשבתו, דיבורו ומעשיו ללמילוי שאיפותיו ושליחותו של רבו. וכבר ידוע הפתגם החסידי, שחסיד הוא "א שטיק רבי", כלומר, שאין לו שום זהות נפרדת לעצמו אלא הוא רואה ומרגיש את עצמו בתור חלק ו"התפשטות" מהרבי, בתור צינור למלאות את רצונו הק', אשר הוא הוא רצון הקב"ה אשר גילה על ידי עבדיו הנביאים. ואכן, ר' צבי הירש שימש דוגמא חיה ל"חסיד" במובן זה, אשר כל מהותו והליכותיו היו מוקדשים למילוי רצון כ"ק אדמו"ר נשיא דורנו. כל מי שהכיר את ר' צבי הירש ידע, שלא היו לו חיים עצמאים, כי אם, כל כולו הי' שקוע, מבוקר עד ערב, בעבודתו של רבינו. אפשר לומר, שר' צבי הירש קיים ברכת והבטחת רבינו אליו ביחידות לרגל יום ההולדת הכ"ב שלו: "א טייל פון דעם רבי'נס ענינים וואס דער רבי האט געוואלט דורך פירן זאל ער דורכפירן דורך דיר" (פנים הספר ע' סא).

ר' צבי הירש גייס עצמו לעסוק בכל מבצע ובכל הפעילות שיזם הרבי והי' מהעומדים בראש של פעולות רבות ומגוונות של תנועת חב"ד, כגון הכנת רשימות ושיחות הרבי לדפוס, עבודת ההוצאה לאור וההכנה לדפוס של ספרי ופירסומי קה"ת**, התייסדות צעירי אגודת חב"ד (צא"ח), חבר במקהלת ניגוני חסידי חב"ד (ניחו"ח), מנהל הניגונים בעת התוועדויות רבינו במשך ריבוי שנים, ביקורים לאחבנ"י בבתי הכלא, והכנסת אורחים בבית פתוח לכל איש. ר' צבי הירש היו מהעסקנים הציבוריים הבולטים בחצר המלכות, היא שכונת "כאן צוה ה' את הברכה".

התמסרות זו באה גם לידי ביטוי ברשימות, ביומנים ובכל המסמכים שנדפסו שבספר זה.

תקוותנו חזקה שספר זה, שבו מתגלים לעיני הקורא חייו של חסיד אחד, יעורר את לב כל קוראיו, בני המשפחה, הידידים, וכל אנ"ש שיחיו, לחזק התקשרותם לכ"ק אדמו"ר, ולשליחותו הק' - להפיץ המעינות חוצה, לכל החוגים, ובכל העולם כולו, אשר זה יזרז עוד יותר קיום הבטחת מלך המשיח להבעל שם טוב: לכשיפוצו מעינותיך חוצה אתי מר דא מלכא משיחא. ונזכה לראות את פני מלכנו, בקיום היעוד הקיצו ורננו שוכני עפר, ור' צבי הירש וכל החסידים, בתוככי כלל ישראל, בתוכם, ומלכנו בראשם, בגאולה האמיתית והשלימה עלי ידי משיח צדקנו.

ספר זה נדפס עתה לזכות נכדיו של ר׳ צבי הירש - יבחל״ח - ראשא וב״ג האברך בנציון שיחיו מארקוס, לרגל נישואיהם בשעטומ״צ ביום א׳, ד׳ אדר ראשון ה׳תשס״ח.

סימון יעקבסאן

יו״ד שבט תשס״ח

אנו פונים לקהל הציבור, שבאם יש להם מכתבים, רשימות או מסמכים הקשורים לר׳ צבי הירש גאנזבורג ע״ה, נא לשלחם לבני המשפחה, לכתובת זו: GJCF 508 Montgomery St., Brooklyn, NY 11225, או בדואר אלקטרוני, info@gjcf.net, כדי שנוכל להוסיפם בהוצאה הבאה, לתועלת הרבים.

*) וכדאי גם להשוות החומר בספר זה עם הנדפס בספר חייל בשירות הרבי, זכרונותיו של ר׳ יצחק גנזבורג ע״ה, אחיו של ר׳ צבי הירש ע״ה (הספר יצא לאור בשנת תש״ס בעריכת אברהם רייניץ).

**) גודל הזכות בזה – מובן מדברי רבינו אליו: ״כשתהי׳ על הציון תספר לכ״ק אדמו״ר כי סדרת חלק מהמאמר דר״ה״ (פנים הספר ע׳ סא).

סדר יוחסין

משפחת דענבורג - גאַנזבורג

סדר יוחסין של משפחת דענבורג - גאַנזבורג*

ראַשאַ גאַנזבורג איז די טאָכטער פון ר' ישעי' דענבורג און הענא חיענאַ דענבורג.

ר' ישעי' דענבורג האָט געלערנט אין ליובאַוויטש און איז געווען אַ געוואַלדיקער למדן, ער האָט געקענט גאַנץ ש"ס אויסנווייניק. במשך אַ געוויסער צייט האָט ער געטאָן ערד-אַרבעט און בשעת מעשה גע'חזר'ט גמרא אויסנווייניק.

ר' ישעי' איז געווען דער זון פון ר' יהודה לייב דענבורג און שרה דענבורג. ר' לייב האָט פאַרמאָגט אַן אייגענע פאַרם אין דעם שטעטל שטשעדרין אין מינסקער גובערניע אין ווייס רוסלאַנד.

שטשעדרין איז אַ שטעטל געגרינדעט דורך דעם רבי'ן דער צמח צדק נ"ע אין יאָר תר"ד וועלכער האָט אָפּגעקויפט אַ שטיק לאַנד פון דעם פריץ שטשעדרינאָוו און באַזעצט אַ סך אידישע משפחות צו טאָן דאָרט ערד-אַרבעט. אויך איז שפּעטער אין שטשעדרין געווען אַ טייל פון דער ישיבה תומכי תמימים ליובאַוויטש.

ווי געזאָגט איז ר' יהודה לייב געווען אַ פאַרמער. פון צייט צו צייט פלעגט ער פירן די פּראָדוקטן פון זיין פאַרם אין דער גרויסער שטאָט צום פאַרקויפן. אין יענע צייט זיינען נאָך אין רוסלאַנד קיין אויטאָמאָבילן ניט געווען און ר' יהודה לייב האָט געפירט זיינע פּראָדוקטן מיט אַ פערד און וואָגן. אויפן וועג פלעגט ער חזר'ן מדרש רבה וואָס ער האָט געקענט אויסנווייניק.

די משפּחה דענבורג האָט געשטאַמט פון דער שטאָט דינאַבורג אין לאַטוויע פון וואַנען זיי זיינען געקומען קיין שטשעדרין. דאָרט איז געווען הגאון ר' לייב בטלן, פון די באַרימטע חסידים פון צמח צדק.

שפּעטער איז די שטאָט גערופן געוואָרן דווינסק, וואו דער חסידישער רב איז געווען הגאון המפורסם ר' יוסף ראָזין – אָדער דער ראָגאַטשאָווער גאון – וואָס האָט נאָך קינדווייז זוכה געווען צו דער ברכה פון דעם צמח צדק.

*) נכתב על ידי ר' צבי הירש בשנת תשמ"ט, בעד פרוייקט בי"ס של נכדתו ראשא ליבערמאַן (מינקאָוויץ).

די משפחה דענבורג האָט אַ סך געשטיצט די ישיבות תומכי תמימים אין מאָנטריאַל און ניו יאָרק און זיי טוען דאָס ביז היינט צו טאָג.

ר׳ נחום דוב דענבורג, אַ ברודער פון ר׳ יהודה לייב, איז געווען אַ חסיד פון פריערדיקן רבין נ״ע. אין זיין זכות האָבן זיינע קינדער געדרוקט דעם תהלים אהל יוסף יצחק מיט די חסידות פון דעם צמח צדק אונטערן נאָמען יהל אור. אַ צאָל בריוו פון דעם רבי׳ן צום פעטער ר׳ נחום דוב זיינען אָפּגעדרוקט אין אלע ספרי תהלים אהל יוסף יצחק.

שרה דענבורג האָט געשטאַמט פון דער משפחה אָקון אויך פון שטשעדרין וואָס האָט אַרויסגעגעבן אַ סך לומדים און חסידים (צווישן זיי הגאון ר׳ ישראל זובער הי״ד ווען דער רבי נ״ע האָט געשיקט קיין שטאָקהאָלם, שוועדן, און איז שפּעטער געווען מנהל פון דער ליובאַוויטשער ישיבה אין באָסטאָן).

ר׳ ישעי׳ דענברוג האט חתונה געהאַט מיט העניא חיענאָ, די טאָכטער פון ר׳ יצחק און שיינע חי׳ נעמאַנאָוו פון באָברויסק.

ר׳ יצחק איז געווען אַ גרויסער ירא שמים, אַ סוחר באַליבט ביי אַלעמען. אין די לעצטע יאָרן פון זיין לעבן איז ער געוואָרן אַרעסטירט דורך די קאָמוניסטן און אין תפיסה איז ער קראַנק געוואָרן און אַ קורצע צייט שפּעטער נפטר געוואָרן בשם טוב. מ׳האָט אים מקבר געווען נאָענט צום קבר פון אדמו״ר ר׳ שמרי׳ נח נ״ע פון באָברויסק.

דער באָבע העניא׳ס ברודער איז געווען דער באַרימטער חסיד און משפיע ר׳ ניסן נעמאַנאָוו, ווען דער רבי ריי״צ נ״ע האָט איבערגעגעבן די הנהגה פון חסידים ווען דער רבי האָט פאַרלאָזן רוסלאַנד אין יאָר תרפ״ח.

ער איז אויך געווען מנהל און משפיע אין ישיבת תומכי תמימים אין פראַנקרייך.

ער איז פיל מאָל געווען אַרעסטירט אין רוסלאַנד וואו ער איז אויסגעשטאַנען גאָר אַ סך יסורים אָבער זיין בטחון האָט ער קיינמאָל ניט פאַרלוירן. ער פלעגט כסדר זאָגן אויסנווייניק תהלים און תניא.

ווען ס׳איז אויסגעבראָכן די צווייטע וועלט-מלחמה און היטלער׳ס ימח שמו אַרמיי האָט פאַרנומען שטשעדרין, האָבן זיי אויסגע׳הרג׳עט אַלע

אידן פון שטעטל. אָבער דער עלטער-זיידע מיט זיין משפחה האָבן שוין געהאַט פאַרלאָזן די שטעטל פון פריער.

די משפחה איז געלאָפן פון די דייטשע אַרמייען קיין מיטל-אַזיע, וואו דער עלטער זיידע ר׳ ישעי׳ איז נפטר געוואָרן אין יאָר תש״ג אין טאַשקענט, קאַזאַכסטאַן.

נאָך דער מלחמה, איז די עלטער באָבע הענא צוזאַמען מיט איר טאָכטער ראַשאַ און דעם זון ר׳ יהודה לייב, מיט נאָך אַ סך חסידים, צווישן זיי אַ צאָל פוילישע אידן וועלכע זיינען געווען אין רוסלאַנד אין צייט פון קריג, געקומען קיין דייטשלאַנד און געוואָרן איינגעאָרדנט אין פליטים לאַגער לעבן דער שטאָט פּאָקינג.

אין דעם זעלבן לאַגער איז אויך געווען די רביצין חנה נ״ע, די מוטער פון דעם רבי׳ן שליט״א - יבדל לחיים טובים - די באָבע הענאַ און דער פעטער ר׳ יהודה לייב האָבן דער רביצין אַ סך אַרויסגעהאָלפן, און די רביצין איז געבליבן אַ גוטער פריינט צו דער משפחה.

מיין מאַמע [שרה][1] און דער מאַמעס ברודער ר׳ ישעי׳ האָבן אַלס קינדער געקראָגן מתנות, זיסקייטן, פון דער רביצין נ״ע.

מיט דער הילף פון די קרובים דענבורג אין אַמעריקא און קאַנאַדע, איז די באָבע הענאַ צוזאַמען מיט איר טאָכטער די באָבע ראַשאַ און שפּעטער אויך דער פעטער ר׳ יהודה לייב געקומען קיין קאַנאַדע.

ר׳ צבי הירש גאַנזבורג, איז דער זון פון ר׳ משה דובער און דאבא גאַנזבורג.

דאבא גאַנזבורג איז די טאָכטער פון ר׳ יהודה לייב דאטליבאוו און נחמה דאטליבאוו. ר׳ יהודה לייב איז געווען אַ רב אין שטעטל ווערכנעדניעפּראָווסק אין אוקראַינע, וועמנס קינדער האָבן געלערנט אין ליובאַוויטש און אַ גרויסער טייל פון זיי זיינען אומגעקומען על קידוש השם.

די באָבע נחמה האָט געשטאַמט פון דער פּחה שאַפּיראָ אין סלאַוויטע,

1) היינו האם של ראשא ליבערמאַן, שרשימה זו נכתבה בעדה (כבהערה הקודמת).

די אייניקלעך פון הצדיק הקדוש ר׳ פינחס קאָריצער נ״ע.

די קינדער פון ר׳ פינחס קאָריצער, ר׳ שמואל אבא און ר׳ משה, זיינען געווען די באַרימטע דרוקערס פון דעם באַוואוסטן ש״ס בבלי אין סלאַוויטע. נאָך אַ בלוט בילבול מיט דער פאַלשער באַשולדיקונג אַז זיי האָבן געהאנגען אַ רוסישן אַרבעטער אין דער דרוקעריי זיינען זיי פאַר׳משפט געוואָרן צו דורכגיין צווישן צוויי רייען פון קאָזאַקן וועלכע האָבן די ברידער געשמיסן מיט זייערע נאַגאַיקעס (גומענע שווערע בייטשן).

ווען איינער פון די ברידער איז אַ דורך די קאָזאַקן-רייען איז ביי אים אַראָפּגעפאַלן די יאַרמולקע און ער האָט זיך איינגעבויגן אויפצוהויבן די יאַרמולקע ניט קוקנדיק אויף די מאָרדערלעכע שמיץ פון די קאָזאַקן.

ביים סוף פון דער ערשטער וועלט מלחמה זיינען פּאָרגעקומען מורא׳דיקע פּאָגראָמען אויף אידן אין ווייס רוסלאַנד און אוקראַינע. די באַנדעס פון פעטליוראַ און דעניקין און אַנדערע באַנדעס האָבן געמאָרדעט און גערויבט און געטאָן אַנדערע שוידערלעכע זאַכן צו די אידן.

ווען די באַנדעס זיינען אַריין אין שטעטל וואו דער זיידע ר׳ יהודה לייב און נחמה האָבן געלעבט און קומענדיק אין זייער הויז האָט איינער פון די קאָזאַקן אָנגעשטעלט זיין ביקס צו שיסן דעם זיידן, דאַן האָט זיין טאָכטער די באָבע דאבא, זיך געשטעלט אין פראָנט פון איר פאָטער און געזאָגט דעם קאָזאַק "שיס מיך!" ערשט דאַן האָט דער גזלן אַראָפּגעבויגן זיין ביקס.

די מידות טובות און מסירת נפש פון דער באָבע דאבאַ איז ניט צו באַשרייבן. איר הכנסת אורחים אין מאָסקווע, עטלעכע גאַסן פון קרעמלין, דער זיץ פלאַץ פון דער סאָוועטישער רעגירונג, איז ניט אָפּצושאַצן. זי האָט אָבער זוכה געווען צו האָדעווען חסידישע קינדער אין דער רויטער רוסלאַנד.

אין דער היים פון דער באָבע דאבא און דעם זיידן ר׳ משה דובער האָבן געפונען אַ געלעגער און עפּעס צום עסן אַ סך, גאָר אַ סך אידן וועלכע פלעגן קומען קיין מאָסקווע צו אָנגעבן אויף אַ דערלויבעניש אַרויסצופאָרן פון לאַנד.

זייער היים איז געווען אָפן פאַר אַלעמען, חסידים ווי מתנגדים, פרומע און ניט פרומע, ניט געקוקט אויף דער סכנה וואָס איז דערמיט געווען פאַרבונדן. זיי האָבן זיך דערוואַרבן אַ גרויסע צאָל פריינט.

ר׳ שמחה גינצבורג, דער פאָטער פון דעם עלטער זיידן ר׳ משה דובער גאַנזבורג, איז געווען אַ תלמיד פון משפיע ר׳ משה דובער לעכוויצער, וועלכער איז געווען אַ תלמיד פון ר׳ ישראל בער וועליזער, פון חסידי הצמח צדק און דעם מיטעלן רבי׳ן.

צו אַכצן יאָר האָט ר׳ שמחה געקראָגן סמיכת חכמים אויף די פיר חלקים פון שולחן ערוך.

זיין פאָטער ר׳ מרדכי יצחק גינזבורג איז געווען אַ חסיד פון צמח צדק און איז געוואָרן זייער רייך פון דעם צמח צדק׳ס אַ ברכה.

ר׳ מרדכי יצחק איז אַ זון פון ר׳ מנחם גינזבורג אַ זון פון ר׳ שניאור זלמן, וועמענס פאָטער איז געווען פון דעם אַלטן רבי׳נס חסידים.

ער האָט געשטאַמט פון די צדיקים נסתרים תלמידי הבעל שם טוב. די משפחה ציט איר יחוס פון ר׳ שמעון גינזבורג, דערמאָנט אין ספר "סדר הדורות".

ר׳ שמחה איז אין די יונגע יאָרן געווען אַ שמיד אָבער שפּעטער איז ער געוואָרן רב אין דעם שטעטל ווערכניעדניאָפּראָווסק (וואו ס׳האָט אויך געלעבט זיין מחותן ר׳ יהודה לייב דאטליבאָוו).

אויסער זיין לומדות און חסידות איז ער געווען זייער אַ לעבעדיקער מענטש, און די רביצין חנה נ"ע האָט אים עטלעכע מאָל דערמאָנט לטובה.

ער איז אומגעקומען על קידוש השם צוזאַמען מיטן גאַנצן שטעטל אידן הי"ד דורך די דייטשן ימח שמם.

ר׳ משה דובער האָט געהאַט אַ ברודער, ר׳ מנחם גאַנזבורג, ער איז געווען עלטער פון ר׳ משה דובער מיט זעקס יאָר און האָט געלערנט אין ליובאַוויטש אין די ערשטע יאָרן פון דער ישיבה. ווען דער רבי רש"ב נ"ע איז געפאָרן שפּאַצירן האָט געטראָפן אַז ער האָט דעם פעטער ר׳ מנחם

מיטגענומען מיט זיך.

ר׳ מנחם איז געווען אַ מקבל פון הרב הצדיק ר׳ לוי יצחק נ״ע, דער פאָטער פון דעם רבי׳ן שליט״א, אין דער שטאָט דניעפּראָפּעטראָווסק, וואו ר׳ לוי יצחק איז געווען דער רב הראשי.

ווען די סאָוועטישע רעגירונג האָט אין יאָר תרצ״ט אַרעסטירט דעם רבי׳נס פאָטער, און די רביצין חנה נ״ע איז געבליבן אָן וועלכער ס׳איז הילף, מצד דער סכנה פון קומען מיט איר אין באַרירונג, זייענדיק די פרוי פון אַ ״שונא פון פאָלק״, פלעגט דער פעטער ר׳ מנחם קומען צו איר אין מיטן נאַכט און ברענגען איר וואָס נאָר ער האָט געקענט באַקומען.

די רביצין חנה נ״ע שרייבט וועגן אים אין אירע זכרונות געדרוקט אין ספר ״אם המלך״.

דער עלטער זיידע ר׳ משה דובער האָט געלערנט אין ליובאַוויטש אין די יאָרן תר״ע-תרע״ג, ווען ער איז גענומען געוואָרן אין דער צאַרישער אַרמיי. ער האָט געדינט אין דער אַרמיי אַ סך יאָרן און אין דער ערשטער וועלט מלחמה איז ער גענומען געוואָרן אין געפאַנגענשאַפט פון די דייטשן. ווען ער איז באַפרייט געוואָרן און געקומען אַהיים זיינען שוין פאָרגעקומען די פּאָגראָמען און דער זיידע האָט אָרגאַניזירט די אידישע זעלבסט-שוץ צו באַשיצן די אידן.

אין יאָר תרצ״ח איז דער זיידע ר׳ משה דובער צוזאַמען מיט דער באָבען דאבא און דריי זין געקומען אין ארץ ישראל וואו ער איז געווען פון די הויפּט גרינדער פון דער ליובאַוויטשער ישיבה אין תל אביב. ער האָט אויך געהאָלפן אין דער גרינדונג פון די בתי ספר ״אהלי יוסף יצחק ליובאַוויטש״.

ער איז נפטר געוואָרן י״ט ניסן, חול המועד פסח תש״ך און מ׳האָט אים מקבר געווען אין צפת לעבן דעם קבר פון דעם רבי׳נ׳ס שליט״א - יבדל לחיים טובים - ברודער הרב החסיד וכו׳ ר׳ ישראל ארי׳ ליב שניאורסאָהן נ״ע.

יומנים

א.

תש"ה, תש"ז

מחיי אנ"ש בתל-אביב

ב.

תשי"א-תשי"ב

מ"בית חיינו" בתקופת קבלת הנשיאות

ג.

תשח"י-תש"כ

זכרונות מ"בית חיינו" והפעילות במסגרת צא"ח

כ"ק אדמו"ר מהוריי"צ

א.

תש״ה, תש״ז

מחיי אנ״ש בתל-אביב

תש״ה

יט כסלו, ש״ה

בעת ההתועדות במוצש״ק העבר, שהתקיימה אצל התמים ר׳ רפאל נחמן כהן, הנה לבד הבעה״ב, נוכח גם החסיד ר״מ דוואָרקין.

ר׳ מיכאל הנ״ל אמר על הפאַרברייינגען: שהוא כעין פאָרשפיל אשר היו עושים לפני החתונה במוצש״ק.

ר״ר כהן סיפר:

בנסעי בזאת השבוע לירושלים, הנה נסע אתי במרכבה יהודי אחד מווין – ר׳ נתן שמעון שמו – הוא גר בשכנות עם ר״ב פריז – ויספר אשר בהיותו גר בווין ראה הרבה אדמו״רים וביניהם את כ״ק אדמו״ר שליט״א[1].

ויספר דבר אחד מאתו, וזה הדבר:

בהיותו בווין הי׳ שם יהודי בשם ר׳ ישראל מרדכי טייטלבוים, הוא הי׳ גבאי אצל האדמו״ר ר׳ משה דוד טשאָרטקאָווער – בן כ״ק ר׳ ישראל הקדוש מרוזין – ובהיות כ״ק אד״ש מליובאַוויטש בעיר בסאַניטאָריום ״פורקערסדאָרף״ אשר אצל העיר נכנסתי לרי״מ הנ״ל, ואספר לו כי כ״ק נמצא קרוב להעיר, ויאמר לי אשר בהיותו זקן קשה לו לנסוע בעצמו ואם ארצה אלונו לכ״ק אדמו״ר שליט״א, ואסכים ברצון לבקשתו.

ונסע לכ״ק אד״ש, כ״ק אד״ש קבלו ויהיו אצלו כשעה ומחצה ואני לא זכיתי לשמוע רק את האמור להלן – כי אחרי שמעי את זאת רמזו לי כי אצא –

1) היינו כ״ק אדמו״ר מהוריי״צ, וכן בכל מקום שנזכר כ״ק אד״ש ברשימות אלו של תש״ה ותש״ז.

הרה"ח ר' רפאל (פולע) כהן

הרה"ח ר' מיכאל דווארקין

ואצא –.

ר' ישראל מרדכי סיפר סיפור אחד מכ"ק אדמו"ר הזקן נ"ע, – כפי הנראה שמעו מכ"ק אדמו"ר מטשאָרטקוב וזהו הסיפור:

לכל או"א מתלמידי הה"מ הק' נ"ע הי' מקום במזרח עם שטענדער, זולת כ"ק אדמו"ר הזקן נ"ע לא עמד במזרח ולא הי' לו שטענדער.

פעם בליל ר"ה כאשר הה"מ עם כל תלמידיו גמרו את תפלתם, ראו אשר כ"ק אדמו"ר הזקן לא גמר עוד את תפלתו, ויביטו התלמידים על רבינו, ויפן הה"מ הק' ויאמר:

טשעפּעט ניט מיין ר' זלמן'ען, בשעה שהוא אומר: וידע כל פעול כי אתה פעלתו ריהרט ער זיך ניט פון אָרט, ביז אז דער דומם ממש באַקומט ניט דעם דעת אַז כי אתה פעלתו.

בתוך הדברים ספר כ"ק אד"ש לרי"מ הנ"ל: איך האָב געהאַט אַ רבין, ר' שמואל בצלאל שמו – באַ אונז רופט מען אים רשב"ץ – אשר בהיותו אצל אאזמו"ר בעל ה"צמח צדק", הנה פעם אחת במעמד בניו הק' – גם הוא – הרשב"ץ – הי' באותו מעמד – אמר אדמו"ר בעל הצמח צדק, איך דאַרף רייסן קריעה כי בזו הרגע ממש איז נסתלק געוואָרן דער הייליגער רוזינער נבג"ם זיע"א.

הרה״ח ר׳ חיים יוסף רוזנבלום

הרה״ח ר׳ פנחס אלטהויז

שביעי ש״פ ש״ה

ישבנו היום אצל התמים ר׳ חיים יוסף רוזנבלום, הי׳ נוכח החסיד ר״מ דוואָרקין, אחר כך בא גם התמים ר׳ פנחס אלטהאוז ואחריו ר״מ גוראריי׳ ועוד כמה מהתמימים יחי׳.

ר׳ מיכאל התחיל לנגן את הניגון הנקרא זאוויל דעם חזנ׳ס. בתוך כך בא ר״פ אלטהאוז ויאמר שהניגון הוא של זאוויל דער חזן מניקאָלייעוו וניגנו אותו לפני כ״ק אדמו״ר (מהורש״ב) נ״ע.

לפני בוא רפ״א הנ״ל ספר ר״מ דוואָרקין:

א) הדבר הי׳ בשביעי של פסח שנת תרע״ו – היא השנה הראשונה אשר כ״ק אדמו״ר נ״ע הי׳ בגולה בראָסטאָוו – כ״ק אדמו״ר נ״ע ישב ואמר מאמר חסידות כנגדו עמד כ״ק אדמו״ר שליט״א, אני עמדתי מימינו, ומאחוריו בסוף האולם, הי׳ הדלת אשר דרך שם נכנסים הבאים, ושם עמד שלחן.

המאמר הי׳ נפלא גם נשמות הצדיקים באו לשמעו את המאמר – אף שבכל פעם באים נשמות הצדיקים לשמוע, אבל הפעם ראיתי במוחש –.

המאמר – המדבר בענין מציאות בלתי מציאות נמצא – הי׳ עמוק ביותר, ואני בעמדי נדמה לי כי נרדמתי, ואראה והנה על השלחן אשר בקצה האולם

הרה"ח ר' נחום גולדשמיד

הרה"ח ר' משה גוראריי'

ירד כ"ק אדמו"ר נ"ע מקאָפוסט, בבגדי ש"ק שלו עם השטריימל, ואזדעזע ואיקץ, ואמשיך לשמוע המאמר.

למחר בקר כאשר באתי לשתות חמין אצל כ"ק אד"ש – כי אמר לי שאוכל אצלו, ספרתי לו זאת – את האמור לעיל. אח"כ כאשר ישב כ"ק אדנ"ע לסעודה – ואני ישבתי בקצה השלחן – פנה כ"ק אדמו"ר שליט"א לאדמו"ר נ"ע ויספר לו ויפן כ"ק אדמו"ר נ"ע אלי ויאמר:

ווען איז ער... ניט פאַר שבועות, ואען: מלכות שביסוד ויאמר כ"ק אדמו"ר אלי: נו איז דאָס דען ניט פאַר שבועות . . .

ב) פעם הבאתי דורון לכ"ק אדנ"ע בערב הפסח שני כורסאות – קרעסלעס – כאלו שהיו אצל הגראפין ואביאם להיכל אשר לפני חדר היחידות, כי חשבתי, שאגיד להמשרת והוא יסדר זאת.

ואפתח את הדלת ואראה את כ"ק אדמו"ר יושב וסועד עם הרבנית נ"ע... בולקע מיט מילך...

ויברך כ"ק אדמו"ר אותי שאהי' גרף, ויפרש את דבריו: גיזונט, רייך, פרום.

ויסיים ר' מיכאל: ברוך השם גיזונט בין איך, רייך אויך, און צוא פרומקייט איז קיין שיעור ניטאָ.

ר׳ משה גוראריʼ ספר:

בהיותי אצל הרבי מבעלז [הרה״ק ר׳ אהרן] שליט״א למסור לו את המכתב שנתי עבורו מכ״ק אד״ש, ספר לי אודות ד׳ סימנים הראשונים הכפולים בשו״ע אדמו״ר הזקן שהעולם חושבים שהוא מהדורא בתרא. ויאמר:

כשהה״מ ציוה לו לסדר את השו״ע, חבר את ב׳ הסימנים הראשונים ויראה להה״מ ויאמר לו הה״מ, עס איז גוט עס איז פיין עס איז וואויהל נאָר עס איז ניט פאַר דער וועלט.

תש״ז

ב״ה, ב׳, וארא, כ״א טבת, ש״ז - תל-אביב
שעה רביעית אחה״צ. (בחנות הספרים של אבי שי׳ רח׳ מונטיפיורי 25)

על מכתבי האחרון לכ״ק אדמו״ר שליט״א – ובה בקשתי שירשני, ויורני את הדרך בה אעלה אל כ״ק – ששלחתי ביום א׳ כ״ג חשון, ש.ז., ענה כ״ק אד״ש ביום ט״ו כסלו ש.ז. ונתקבלה ביום ו׳, כ״א כסלו.

גם המענה לאחי יצחק נ״י ולמרדכי דובינסקי נ״י – ששלחו איתי בו ביום – הוא מאותו היום ונתקבל בו ביום. גם הבחור שלום דובער גולדשמיט, ששלח בקשתו בטלגרמה – ביום ב׳ כסלו – נענה באותו היום ונתקבל בכ״ז כסלו.

במענה נאמר שכ״ק מסכים על הצעתי, ״ויתדבר עם ההנהלה אודות התעודות הנחוצות לזה״ ומברכני: ״ויצליח בלימוד הנגלה והדא״ח, ויהי׳ ירʼ״ש חסיד ולמדן״. גם הנ״ל קבלו באותו הלשון בדיוק – חוץ משד״ג שקבל בשינוי לשון קל – כמובן אשר המענה הוא בחתימתו של המזכיר ח. ליבערמאַן.

במוצש״ק אור ליום כ״ט כסלו ערכנו בקשה להנהלת הישיבה בברוקלין שישתדלו עבורנו וישלחו לנו את התעודות הנחוצות בהקדם, ואת הבקשה שלחנו ע״י הרב ר׳ מאיר אשכנזי – רב בשנגהאַי – שיצא את הארץ – במטוס – למחרת – דרך קהיר – לארצה״ב.

בו ביום יצאה גם הרבנית גולדשמיד – בת החסיד ר׳ יחיאל צבי – או ר׳ הערשל – גוראריʼ ואשתו של המשפיע הרב ר׳ נחום ב״ר יצחק גולדשמיד – לארצה״ב.

הרה"ח ר' חיים ליברמן

חדב"ן הרה"ח הרב שמריהו גוראריי (הרש"ג)

ביום ב' א' דר"ח שבט הגשנו בקשתינו להממשלה – אשר משכנה הוא ברחוב אלנבי 138 – לתעודות להתאזרחות. בקשתנו לתעודות יושר הגשנו ביום ב' ג' שבט בירושלים במשטרת מוסטשפה – מחנה יהודא –.

ביום א' ו' שבט כתבנו עוד הפעם להנהלת הישיבה בברוקלין בהכפלת בקשתנו – שלחנו בדואר האויר.

הקונסול דורש כזאת מכאו"א: פספורט, תעודת לידה – אגב את התעודות לידה סדרנו בירושלים, תעודת יושר – מהמשטרה, תעודות הרופאים. כמובן שכ"ז הוא חוץ מהדרישה – אפידייוועט – והערבות הבנקאית מהתם. התמונות להויזה צריכים להיות על רקע לבן.

אם כי נתקבלו ידיעות שהרב אשכנזי והרבנית גוראריי הגיעו לאמריקה, עוד לא נתקבלו מכתבים מפורטים מהם.

ר' שמריי ב"ר נתן בר' זלמן גוראריי הגיע ביום הש"ק פ' שמות לנמל חיפה מארצה"ב. שלשם נסע בכוונה לחזות את פני כ"ק אד"ש.

אגב: ר' רפאל נחמן ב"ר ברוך שלום כהן קבל מענה מכ"ק אד"ש כי "בנו יואל אין צריך לנסוע לכאן".

ר' שמריי גוראריי הביא מכתב מכ"ק אד"ש להחסיד ר' מיכאל דוואָרקין,

ר׳ צבי הירש, ר׳ מרדכי דובינסקי ור׳ שלום דובער גולדשמיד

בו כותב כ״ק אד״ש שחפץ מאד להתראות עם החסיד הנ״ל ויבוא לארצה״ב לזמני הקיץ.

זה זמן מרובה – יותר משנה – אשר ר׳ מיכאל דוואָרקין רוצה לנסוע לכ״ק אדמו״ר שליט״א, וכבר הי׳ זמן אשר כמעט שקבל את הויזה מהקונסול האמריקאי, אולם הוא חולה ל״ע במחלת ״דלקת הריאות״ ועוד דבר מה, המחלה הנ״ל החלישתו במאד, אולם כאשר קם ב״ה על רגליו מחליו, בקש מכ״ק אד״ש שירשהו לנסוע וכ״ק אדמו״ר שליט״א ענהו שאינו צריך לנסוע, וכאשר נסע ר׳ ש״ג הנ״ל לכ״ק אד״ש בקשו רמ״ד – שמעתי שבקשו בדמעות שליש – שיעביר את בקשתו לכ״ק אדמו״ר שליט״א עוד הפעם.

רש״ג מילא את שליחותו בהכנסו לכ״ק אד״ש, אד״ש ענהו שידבר מזה עוד, ולפני חזרתו לא״י צוהו כ״ק אד״ש שישלח מברקה – טלגרם – לרמ״ד שהוא מביא אתו מכתב אליו מכ״ק אד״ש, ובבואו מסר לו את המכתב הנ״ל.

גם האברך ר׳ ברוך ב״ר אברהם פריז קבל מענה מכ״ק אד״ש שיבוא לזמני

הקיץ.

כידוע שמר זלמן לוין המיועד להיות חתנו של ר' אברהם פריז קבל מענה מכ"ק אד"ש שהחתונה תהי' בזמנה ויבוא צלחה לארה"ב.

גם הבחור נתן ב"ר ש. גוראריי' הנ"ל קבל מענה – ע"י אביו שיבוא ללמוד בישיבת "תומכי תמימים" בברוקלין.

חתונת התלמיד מנחם ישראל ב"ר שמואל מלוב, נתקיימה בשעטו"מ ביום י"ז כסלו באולם הפועהמ"ז רח' אחה"ע 103.

מ. מלוב הנ"ל והבחור יעקב פלאסק – מטאלנעשט – הקימו בהצעת אבי' שי' – בית חרושת קטן לשפולן. יה"ר שיצליחו בעבודתם.

בליל ערש"ק העבר נפטר בביה"ח בילינסון – ליד פתח תקוה – מר ד"ב שלונסקי מיקאַטערינאָסלאוו. תנצב"ה.

ביום ש"ק העבר נפטר בביה"ח הנ"ל, הרב ר' פתחי' מענקין, שהי' רב בכמה עיירות חסידיות – חסידישע שטעטלעך –. תנצב"ה.

בפעם הראשונה ראיתי את הרב מענקין הנ"ל בחודש אדר ת"ש בחתונת מר יוסף שערמאַן עם בתו של מנהל ישיבתנו – היום – הרב ר' משה אקסלרוד בר' ג. הוא שימח את הקהל ברוב פרפראות וגימטריאות ובריקודו היפה. אם כי הי' אז רק חודש ימים מקומו מחוליו אשר חלה את רגליו.

לפני זמן לא רב חלה עוד הפעם את המחלה הנ"ל והמחלה הזאת הכריעתו.

התמים ר' משה גוראריי' מסר שהערב נלמד אצלו בשעה 7:30 בבית החסידים דגור ר' אחה"ע 55.

בפעם הראשונה למדנו אצלו ביום י"א – בערך – טבת ש"ו, ומאז אנו לומדים אצלו בממוצע פעמים בשבוע.

התלמידים הלומדים אצלו הם, יואל ב"ר פאָליע כהן, נתן ברמ"ג הנ"ל, אחי יצחק, ואני. גם התלמיד אברהם יצחק שאולזאָן למד אצלו זמן מה אבל לא

ב'וואָרט' של ר' שלום חסקינד. משמאל לימין: ר' שלום חסקינד, ר' משה גוראַרי',
הרב נתן אייכנשטיין, ר' דניאל חסקינד, ר' שמריהו ובנו ר' נתן גוראַרי'

יותר.

הבחור א.י. שאולזאָן הנ"ל מירושלים – נכנס לישיבה בזמן העבר – כתב לכ"ק אד"ש בדבר רצונו לנסוע לכ"ק ויחכה לתשובה.

גם התמים ר' מאיר בליזינסקי כתב לכ"ק אד"ש שברצונו שבנו שמואל נ"י יסע לכ"ק, וגם הוא מחכה לתשובה.

הישיש ר' שלמה תומרקין קבל מכתב מנכדו שלום חסקינד מברוקלין, שהי' ביחידות אצל כ"ק אדמו"ר שליט"א וכ"ק אדמו"ר שליט"א אמר לו: (אינני זוכר את הלשון בדיוק)

"שמעתי אַז דו האָסט גוטע כשרונות אויף לערנען, לערנען איז נאָך ניט אינגאַנצן, דאַוונען איז אויך ניט אינגאַנצן, טאָן אַ אידן אַ טובה איז אויך ניט אינגאַנצן.

"מיא דאַרף לערנען, און טאָן אין עבודת התפילה און טאָן אַמאָל אַ אידן אַ טובה.

"זאָלסט לערנען יורה דעה, און אין משך פון אַ האַלב יאָהר, ניט מער וויא

דריי פערטל יאָהר, זאָלסטו קומען צו מיר אַ פאַרטיגער רב, מ'דאַרף זיין אַ איד און אַ רב, אַ איד איז נאָך ניט דער ענין פון רב.

"ריידין אין מיטן לערנען דאַרף מען ניט אַפי' בעניני חסידות אויך ניט, אויף ריידן בעניני חסידות איז פראַן אַ ספעציעלע צייט דאָנערשטאָג ביינאַכט און מוצש"ק פאַר שבת און נאָך שבת. מיא דאַרף חזר'ן חסידות און ניט נאָר זאָגן אַז יענער זאָל חזר'ן".

התלמיד שלום חסקינד הוא בנו של התמים ר' דובער האַסקינד.

ב"ה ג, כ"ב טבת, ת.א.

שעה אחד עשרה לפנה"צ (בביתינו הר-סיני 1)

היום בוקר בקר אצלנו בבית ר' ראובן גשייד מכפר אתא – על יד חיפה – המיועד להיות חותנו של התלמיד החשוב מר שלמה בהרב ר' אלתר בצלאל קופטשיק.

הוא בקר אצלנו לשם שיחה אם אבי מורי שי' בדבר הענינים השייכים להמיועד להיות חתנו.

את המכתב הראשון שכתבתי לכ"ק אד"ש – יחד עם אחי יצחק שי' – בדבר נסיעתינו לברוקלין, ביום י"ב סיון ש"ה ובר"ח אלול ענה כ"ק, והמענה נתקבל באמצע חודש תשרי ש"ו.

המענה הנ"ל נתקבל על אדרסתו של הר"מ גוראַרי' – בניגוד להמענה האחרון שנתקבל ישר על אדרסתי – וכן גם האחרים קבלו כנ"ל ג"כ בניגוד להמענה האחרון שנתקבל כמו"כ על אדריסתי, חוץ מרד"ג שנתקבל ע"י הרמ"ג.

בדבר התלמיד מר נתן בר"ש גוראַרי', שמעתי מהתלמיד ש.ד. גולדשמיד – כשבקרנו יחד את הישיש החסיד ר' שבתי בערמאַן המתגורר אצל בתו

בירושלים – שכשנכנס אביו ר"ש לכ"ק אד"ש והציע לו שבנו יבוא על משך כמה חדשים לכ"ק אד"ש, ענהו כ"ק שעוד ידבר מזה.

וכן הי' עוד פעם או פעמיים ואד"ש ענהו כנ"ל.

בפעם האחרונה שדבר עם כ"ק מזה אמר לכ"ק שרצונו שבנו יבוא לברוקלין כי הזמן בארץ איננו שקט, ואז ענהו כ"ק שמזה אין מה לפחד, רק אם רצונו לבוא ללמוד, יבוא.

אור ליום כ"ד טבת[1] הלולא של כ"ק אדמו"ר הזקן נבג"מ זי"ע.

שעה שמינית ערב.

היום נתמלאה שנה לבואו של הבחור מנחם דב מוסטוביץ לביתינו.

הבחור הזה הוא בנו של ר' יצחק מוסטוביץ מחסידי האדמו"ר מגור שליט"א, הוא הי' אחד הגבירים החשובים והאדירים של עיר הנופש אָטוואָצק. בעל נחלאות גדולות בעיר אָטוואָצק שנמשכו על כמה מרחובותי', חוץ מהבתים ובית החרושת ליין ויי"ש שהיו לו בעיר ראַדום.

זמן קטן לפני המלחמה האחרונה נמצאה הישיבה הק' "תומכי תמימים" ליובאַוויטש באחת מחווילותיו הנאות.

בנו הבחור מר מנחם דב הנ"ל למד זמן מה בהישיבה "תו"ת", בזמן המלחמה נמצא הוא ואחותו דבורה תחי' בין הנכרים בפולין.

אמו, אחיו הקטן ואחותו נהרגו על קדוה"ש בעיר אָטוואָצק, אביו ר' יצחק הנ"ל נשלח ע"י העמלקים הארורים לכבשני האש בטרבלינקה.

ז"א אשר רק הבחור הנזכר ואחותו הנזכרת נשארו בחיים מכל בני המשפחה.

הוא נמצא כעת בביתינו ועובד בעבודת האריגה – כ"ק אדמו"ר שליט"א כותב לו "ובטח התמימים יקרבוהו" – ואחותו נמצאת בהפנימי' "בית יעקב" בירושלים וגם לומדת שם בהסמינריון.

מוצש"ק וארא, אור ליום כ"ז טבת ת"א

שעה שביעית

1) פה נרשם: "ד', כ"ג טבת ת.א. אעתיק בזה כמה מרשימותי הקודמים". ומעתיק הרשימות די"ט כסלו ושביעי של פסח תש"ה (נדפסו לעיל ע' יט-כג).

ביום חמישי ערב ספרה אמי תחי' אשר בעת הניתוח שניתחוה במוסקבה הנה לפני הניתוח נראה לה אבי' – הוא אבי זקנה הרב ר' לייב ע"ה מוויערכניעדניעפראָווסק – ויאמר לה:

"מיין קינד זאָג בידך אפקיד רוחי כו'". בו בערב נזכרה אשר לפני שנה באותו ערב – שהי' בסעודת ש"ק – סעודה ראשונה – בחוץ הי' "עוצר" חמור שהתחיל ערב לפני כן, בביתינו ישבנו לסעודה וגם אורח הי' לסעודה הסטודנט חיים לפשיץ והנה מישהו דופק בדלת ונפתח את הדלת והנה הבחור יונתן בלטר עומד ע"י הדלת ויספר: שבצהרי יום הלך – עם התלמיד הנער הלל לווינזון – להרבנית זיסלין לקחת לחם לשבת, והנה הבחין בהם חייל בריטי, הנער הלל הספיק להסתתר בחצר אחד הבתים – אח"כ שמעתי שהסתתר בביתו של הרב ברנדוויין – ואותו לקחו באוטו צבאי לבית הדר ובערב שכבר הי' ש"ק – הי' המשפט והפסק דין הי' שיתן 200 לא"י קנס ומפני שהי' הש"ק לא הי' באפשרותו לשלם והתנדב אחד מהשוטרים לשלם עבורו. ויתנו לו רשות ללכת לביתו – והנה הוא עובר ע"י ביתנו ויכנס אלינו, והוא הולך עכשיו.

בערש"ק בבקר הגיע לחיפה בן שכנינו – הה"ג ר' ירוחם וורהפטיג – מר זרח וורהפטיג – חבר האקזקוטיבה של המזרחי העולמי, ובערב לפני הדלקת הנרות בא לבית הוריו.

לפני המלחמה הי' עו"ד קטן בפולניא, ובזמן המלחמה עזר הרבה להצלת בנ"י ובעיקר להצלת בני ישיבה, הוא ברח – יחד עם הרבה פליטים – לשנגהאַי, ומשם הגיע לארצה"ב של אמריקה.

ע"י התאמצותו הרבה בדבר הצלת בני ישראל – וגם במסירות נפשו – נתפרסם שמו בעולם.

לפני כשנה נסע לאירופא להציל את ילדי הקדושים מהמנזרים הנוצרים.

הוא נבחר כציר להקונגרס הציוני בבזל ומשם נסע להתראות עם הוריו.

הוא מספר אשר באוטבוצק נמצאו כתביו של ר' יחזקאל פייגין – מזכירו של כ"ק אד"ש – וגם כמה מכתביו של כ"ק אד"ש – שלא הספיק לקחתם בהמלטו מפולין – ועוד כתבים של כמה מחסידי חב"ד, הכתבים נמסרו להרב כהנא.

הוא מסר פר"ש מהישיבות "תו"ת" באמריקה. "הרושם שהוא עושה איננו רע כל עיקר".

היום לסעודה השלישית נמשך הדיבור אודות הרב ר׳ שמעון מנשה – שהי׳ רב בחברון בימי כ״ק אדמו״ר צמח צדק נ״ע ויספר ר׳ מ״מ סלונים:

אביו החסיד ר׳ שניאור זלמן סלונים הלך להתברך - בענצען זיך - להר״ר ש״מ הנ״ל ויאמר לו בניגון: איך דאַרף דיר בענטשן? ובכ״ז בקשו עוד הפעם שיברכו ויאמר לו ״בא אַ אידן דאַרף זיין כל מעיני בך, כל מעיני בך, כל מעיני בך״.

כנגד ביתו עמדו כמה בתי חומה של ארבעה או חמשה קומות, ויהי בצאתו מלפניו וירא את הבתי חומה, ויאמד תוהה בחשבו האם זהו דמיון או מציאות.

הוא נתן פתקאות לאנשי שלומו להלות להם כסף וכ״כ הרבה כסף הלווה להם עד שנתקבץ לסך 20,000 רובל, ויבואו ויספרו לכ״ק אדמו״ר הצ״צ, ויאמר לכ״ק אדמו״ר הצ״צ:

אויף מיין שמעון מנשה׳ן, אויף מיין צדיק זאָלט איר ניט ריידן.

הוא הי׳ מופשט מהגשמיות.

היום שמעתי שנתקבלה טלגרמה מהבחור מר יונתן בלטר הטלגרמה נתקבלה אצל דודו – מר צפירירי – מורגענשטערן בה הוא כותב שנמצא כעת בפריז.

מר י. ב. הנ״ל יצא מוילנא עם שאר תלמידי ״תו״ת״ ונמלט לקאָבאָ, יפאַן – ומשם בא ארצה, ויכנס לישיבה ״אחי תמימים״ דכאן, בחודש מנ״א ש״ו יצא את הארץ לאירופא – באמרו שהוא נוסע לחפש את אמו – במשך הזמן כמעט שלא היתה ממנו ידיעה.

מר יצחק יודאַסין – שגם הוא נמצא כעת באירופה בשליחות האגודה כתב לאביו – הרב ר׳ אלכסנדר סנדר יודאַסין רב בכמה שכונות ביפו – ששמע שמר י.ב. כבר עבר את הארצות דלהלן: מצרים, איטליא, שווייץ, צרפת, האָלאַנד, בלגי׳, אשכנז ״ועוד ידו נטוי׳ה״.

שמעתי שרצונו של ר׳ משה גוראַרי׳ להיות על חה״ש הבע״ל אצל כ״ק אדמו״ר שליט״א, וכנראה שהוא כבר עוסק בהכנות לנסיעה.

ב"ה ד' ח שבט ש"ז ת.א.

בש"ק העבר בעת סעודה ב' נמשך הדבור אודות מאכלי שבת שאינם מקלקלים, ויספר ר' חיים בער לערמאַן:

שמעתי מר' יצחק יואל ראפאלאָוויטש, שפ"א בא על ש"ק לליובאַוויטש וכ"ק אדמו"ר הזמינו לסעוד על שלחנו. ר' יצחק יואל סבל אז ממחלת הקיבה הנקראת קאטאר זשעלודקא.

ויהי בעת הסעודה הביאו כמה מיני מאכלים לשלחן ור"מ הנ"ל לא רצה לאכול מפני המחלה הנ"ל.

ויאמר לו כ"ק אדמו"ר שמאכלי שבת אינם מקלקלים. על השבת הבאה בהיותו בביתו צוה להכין לו כמה מיני מאכלים באמרו לפני ב"ב את אשר אמר לו כ"ק אדמו"ר. בשבת הביאו לפניו את המאכלים והוא אכלם, ואז תקפוהו חבלי מחלתו אשר כמעט שנשאר בחיים.

עוד ספר רח"ב הנ"ל:

שמעתי בירושלים שהה"ג הרה"ח ר' ברוך מרדכי מבאָברויסק אמר ע"ע – מבטאו הי' דומה למבטא יהודי גאַליציא –

"לערנען בראך איך נישט ווייל איך קאָן שוין, קאָנען בראך איך נישט ווייל איך בין שוין אַ מפורסם".

קשורי התנאים בין בתו הבכירה של ר' משה גוראַרי' עם הבחור העשיל ברוידא – מתלמידי חברון המצוינים – שהיו צריכים להתקיים ביום השני ערב, ונדחו מפאת העוצר, נתקיימו אתמול בערב בביתו של רמ"ג.

אחי מר יצחק שי' קבל במוצש"ק העבר מכתב מכ"ק אד"ש – ע"י רמ"ג –, המכתב הזה הוא מענה על מכתבו ששלח בהצעתו של הישיש ר' שבתי ברמן ביום י' כסלו. המכתב הוא מיום ג' טבת, ובו כותב לו כ"ק אד"ש: (הלשון איננו מדוייק).

בטח קבל את מכתבי מיום ט"ו כסלו, כעת קבלתי את מכתבו מיום י' כסלו ובו הצעת אביו

שי׳ שהיא הצעה נכונה, ואם כי חפצו הטוב להתראות, אמנם כעת צריכים לדחות את הנסיעה, ויסתדר בעז״ה בשידוך טוב, ויהי׳ לעזר לידידי אביו שי׳ בענין הפרנסה והש״י ישלח לו שידוך הראוי לו, ויהי׳ להם פרנסה בהרחבה

בשם כ״ק אד״ש

מזכיר ח. ליבערמאַן.

אבי שי׳ שלח ביום הששי העבר מכתב – בדאר אויר – לשא״ב הר״ר משה דובער ריבקין שישתדל עבורינו בענין האפידייוועט.

מוצש״ק יתרו, ח״י שבט.

במוצש״ק העבר כתב ר׳ משה דובינסקי מכתב לר׳ דובער חסקינד בדבר נסיעתנו לארה״ב, המכתב נשלח ביום א׳, ביום ב׳ שלחנו מכתב להר׳ מאיר אשכנזי כנ״ל.

ביום השני העבר נתקיימו קשורי התנאים בין בתו הבכירה של ר׳ שמרי׳ גורארי׳ ובין הבחור הר׳ נתן אייכנשטיין בנו של האדמו״ר מזידיטשוב. נכחו

הרה״ח ר׳ שמריהו גורארי׳ והאדמו״ר מזידיטשוב מלווים את החתן, ר׳ נתן אייכנשטיין לחופה

מימין לשמאל: ר' מכאל דווארקין; ר' שלמה אורנשטיין;
ר' פיניע אלטהויז; ר' משה אשכנזי ור' צבי גינזבורג

כמה מהאדמו"רים.

ביום הש"ק פ' בא נולד לראש ישיבתנו הר"ר דוד חנזין בן למז"ט והברית מילה הי' בזמנו בפ"ת.

בש"ק העבר הי' בביתהכ"נ חב"ד המרכזי קידושא רבא. השמש ר' צבי הירש גינזבורג – בנו של הרב מיאקאבשטט הי' מבוסם, וסיפר:

זוכר הוא אשר בבואו לביתו מהישיבה – הוא למד בכמה ישיבות של האשכנזים ובתוכם ישיבת ראַדין – הנה פעם אחת ישבו אביו זקנו ואביו ליד השלחן ומזגו כוסות יי"ש. וא"ז סיפר: אשר בהסתלקות כ"ק אדמו"ר בעל "צמח צדק" קרעו את בגדיו וחלקום ולו – ז"א לא"ז – עלה לזכות בקעשענקע ממכנסיו של כ"ק אדמו"ר צ"צ.

גם ספר:

בימי כ"ק אדמו"ר צ"צ נודע בעולם שכשנכנסים לכ"ק אדמו"ר מזדעזעים, ויאמר אחד מהמשכילים, שהוא יכנס ולא יזדעזע.

כשנכנס לכ"ק אדמו"ר, שאלו כ"ק אדמו"ר:

פון וואַנען קומט אַ איד, ויענהו:

פון אַ פאָר פאָלק.

ויאמר לו כ״ק אדמו״ר: אידן זיינען מעם אחד מדאמר פון אַ פאָר פאָלק שמע מינא ממזר הוא. החסידים העומדים בחצר כששמעו, בדקו אחריו ומצאו כדברי כ״ק אדמו״ר.

ב״ה ד׳ תרומה ער״ח אדר ש״ז

שעה אחת עשרה לילה

היום בשעה הרביעית נתקבל בהישיבה רח׳ הרב קוק 16 האפידייוועט מישיבת ״תומכי תמימים״ בברוקלין. המעטפה של הא״ד נתקבלה על שמו של מר שד״ב גולדשמיד.

כשנתקבלה, שלח הרח״ש ברוק את התלמיד מר שלמה קופציק להודיע מזה לש״ד גולדשמיד – כידוע, אשר תלמידי הקיבוץ לומדים בהשטיבל של האדמו״ר מלוצק ע״ה, ברחוב האר״י 9 – והוא עם (התלמיד הנכבד) מר מ. דובינסקי באו להודיעני.

האפידייוועט נתקבל במפתיע, כי מסרנו את בקשתנו ע״י החסיד ר׳ מיכאל דוואָרקין – היוצא מחר לארצה״ב דרך אלכסנדרי׳ – קאַהיר.

להאפידייוועט הי׳ מצורף גם מכתב מחדב״נ הר״ר שמרי׳ גוראריʼ יו״ר ועד הפועל, בו הוא כותב: אשר נפנה להקונסול ובטח נקבל את הניירות הדרושים והוא מקוה לראותנו יושבים על התורה והעבודה. נ.ב. נא להודיעני ממהלך הענינים...

(האפידיוועט׳ס הם על שמי, ושם אחי יצחק, וש.ד. גולדשמיד. ומ. דובינסקי).

היום מתקיימת החתונה בין בתו של התמים השו״ב ר׳ שמואל זלמנוב, ובין מר קפוסטה בהיכל המלאכה.

היום בקר בשעה אחת עשרה נתקבל טלגרמה מכ״ק אד״ש וז״ל: ״לכ׳ גנזבורג מונטיפיורי 25. יהי׳ להצלחה בגו״ר. רבי שניאורסאָהן. בראשה נרשם Brooklyn NY 18, 1334״ הטלגרמה הי׳ תשובה על הטלגרמה ששלחו הורי לכ״ק, בדבר הצעת שידוך לאחי מר שלום יודא לייב עם בתו של מר מנחם זאב בוטשאַן חסידה מוורשה דזיקא 24 הגר כעת בירושלים, הט״ג נשלחה בליל א׳ פ׳ יתרו, ומאז עברו שבועיים ולא נתקבל מענה. בליל א׳ ש.ז. שלחו טלגרמה למר ד. חאַסקינד שיכנס לכ״ק אדמו״ר, והיום נתקבל המענה כאמור. השדכן הוא ר׳ ראובן גשייד מכפר אתא.

האח, הרה"ח ר' יצחק גנזבורג

האח, הרה"ח ר' יהודה לייב גנזבורג

א' תשא. י' אדר

שעה רביעית אח"צ

ביום השני העבר ד' אדר נתקיימו קשורי התנאים של אחי מר שלום יהודא לייב עם ב"ג מרת גאָלדא מלכה בת ר' מנחם זאב בוטשאַן (חסידה).

קשורי הת' נתקיימו בירושלים בבית אבי הכלה – בית ישראל רח' באר שבע 8, והיו נוכחים מלבד המחותנים וקרוביהם כמה עשיריות אנשים.

את זמן החתונה קבעו לא יאוחר מחדש אלול, אמנם יכול להיות אשר תהי' גם בתוך הזמן.

– במוצש"ק העבר נתקיימו קשורי התנאים בין התמים יעקב ב"ר טובי' פלאסק ובתו של ר' שמואל מלוב. ביום השלישי העבר נתקיימה החתונה של מר זלמן לוין עם בתו של ר' אברהם פריז. החתונה התקיימה בביתהכ"נ ברית יצחק (רמת גן ב').

אחרי החתונה חושב הוא לנסוע לארה"ב – כפי שהורה לו כ"ק אד"ש.

התלמיד יואל ב"ר רפאל נחמן כהן, קבל ביום החמישי מכתב מכ"ק אד"ש: וזאת העתקתו כפי השמור בזכרוני.

הרה״ח ר׳ יואל כהן

ב״ה כ״ו שבט, תש״ז, ברוקלין

ידידי התלמיד החשוב מר יואל שי׳ כהן

ידידי אביו שי׳ כותב אלי (או קבלתי את מכתב אביו שי׳) כי שוקד הוא בלימוד, ונהנתי במאד, יוסיף אומץ בלימודו.

ובזמנים קבועים יתעסק בעבודת התפלה ובהנהגה ביראת שמים ובקניין המדות טובות. והש״י יעזרהו ויצליחהו בלימודו ובעבודתו ויהי׳ יר״ש חסיד למדן המברכו

[חתי״ק]

רחש״ב מספר:

בזיטאָמיר הי׳ אצל יהודי יר״ש (חייט) משרת יהודי וגם משרתת נכרית. ויחשוד הבעה״ב את משרתו כי עסק לו עם הנכרית. הוא ספר הדבר לפני ראשי הקהל, ויצא הפסק כי יכפתוהו עם הנכרית ויעבירום ברחובות העיר בריש גלי׳.

הבחור לא הי׳ אשם בדבר ובעברו על פני ר׳ וואָלף מזיטאָמיר אמר לו כי איננו אשם. ויאמר לו ר׳ וואָלף: באם נכון הדבר כי אינך אשם תזכה אשר בך יתחתנו גדולי הדור.

אחרי אשר קיימו את הפסק עזבו אותו לנפשו. הוא שלח ידיו במסחר והתחיל לעלות בסולם ההצלחה. ויעזוב את העיר ויצא לעיר אחרת ושם התחתן, ויהי לאחד מנגידי העיר.

בתחלה התחיל להתעסק בעניני הקהילה, אם בהיותו ממקום פשוט מוצאו

התחילו נגידי העיר להתקוטט עמו, ומשום מה יצא לו שם "הגוי החסידי" – דער חסידישער גוי – ובראותו את הריחוקים שנגידי העיר ריחקוהו התחיל גם הוא להתרחק מהם, ולא הלך כפעם בפעם אליהם.

עברו כמה שנים ובתוך הזמן נולד לו בן, להנער היו כשרונות מצוינים ויהי לעילוי.

לימים עבר ר' ברוך ממעזיבוז קרוב להעיר ויודע הדבר כי חושב הוא להתאכסן בהעיר, וכל נגידי העיר יצאו עם כרכרותיהם ועגלוניהם, מחוץ לעיר, מקום אשר ר' ברוך הי' צריך להגיע, בחשבם לזכות בכבוד אשר ר' ברוך'ל יכבדם לשבת במרכבת אחד מהם.

העשיר – המשרת – לא רצה לצאת עם שאר הנגידים בהיות אשר נתרחק מהם, ותאמר לו אשתו מדוע לא תצא לכבודו של ר"ב ויעני' כנ"ל, ותפציר בו עד בוש, עד אשר אסר מרכבתו ויצא גם הוא לכבודו של ר"ב ויעמד מאחורי כל העגלות.

ר"ב בבואו התבונן לכיוון העגלות אשר עמדו על הככר וירמוז – להשתוממות כולם – להעשיר המשרת כי יתקרב אליו, ויתקרב. ויכנס ר' ברוך'ל למרכבתו וישב בה, ויפן העגלון את הסוסים ויסעו העירה וכל העגלות אחריהם.

הוא שלח להגיד לביתו כי ר"ב נוסע במרכבתו ויתאכסן בביתו. בבוא השליח ויבשר לאשתו את כל הדברים האלה נתרגשה האשה במאד ותתעלף. ור' ברוך עודנו נוסע עם הנגיד במרכבתו, וישאלהו ר"ב על דבר משפחתו ועסקיו, ויענהו כי ה' הרים קרנו בעסקיו, וגם נער יש לו וימסרהו על יד מלמדים מועילים ויהי לעילוי, וישאלהו ר' ברוך אם רצונו להשתדך אתו – לר' ברוך היתה נכדה עומדת על פרקה – ויהי בעיניו כמצחק, אמנם בראותו כי ר"ב מדבר על זה ברצינות ענהו: הלואי שהרבי ירצה להשתדך אתי – עוד הם מדברים והנה השליח בא ויספר כי האשה נתעלפה, ויאמר ר' ברוך, לך ובשר לה כי רצוני להשתדך אתה והבשורה הזאת תוציא אותה מהתעלפותה וכך הוה.

בבואם לביתו ור"ב נח מעמל הדרך, כתבו התנאים ויתקשרו בקנין כת"ק ויגבילו את זמן החתונה.

בבא הזמן והמחותנים עם הקרואים באו להחתונה ויגש ר"ב להמחותן ויתחיל לצעוק עליו, אתה בור, עם הארץ ועוד ועוד, וילך מלפניו, ויעבר זמן מה ויבא לפניו ויצעק עליו שנית וכ"ה הי' עוד כמה פעמים. עד שר"ב צוה ללכת להחופה.

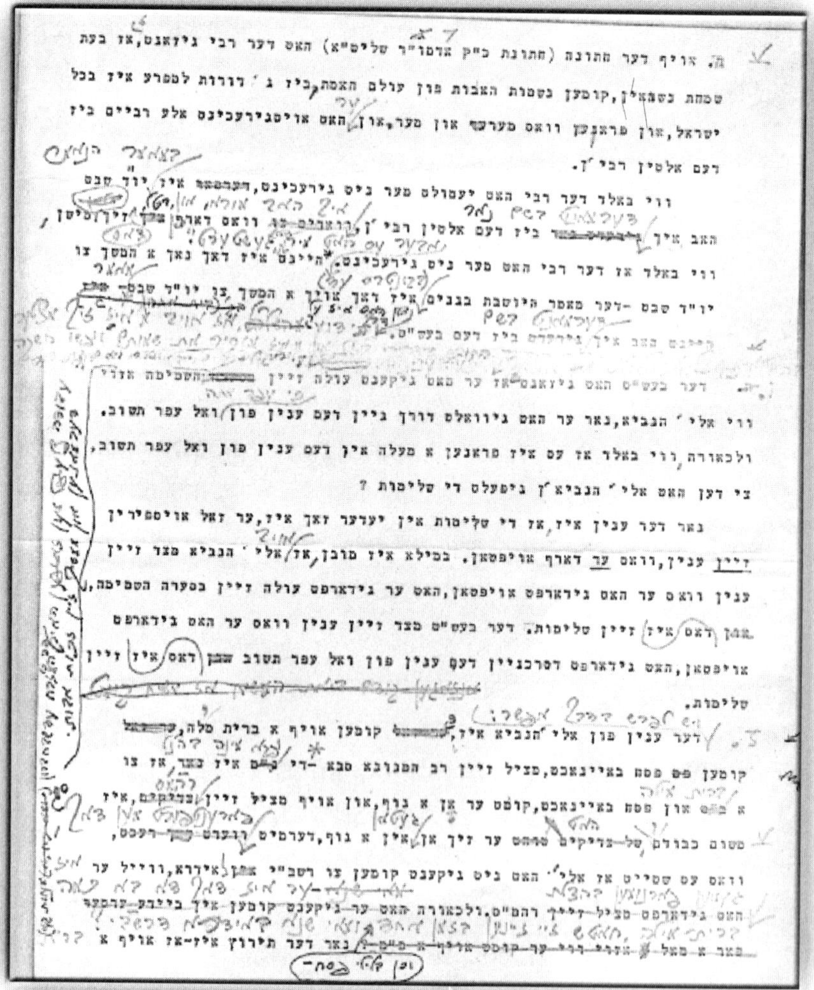

ה. אויף דער חתונה (חתונת כ"ק אדמו"ר שליט"א) האט דער רבי גיזאגט, אז בעת שמחת נשואין, קומען נשמות האבות פון עולם האמת, ביז ג' דורות למפרע איז בכל ישראל, און פראנקן וואס מערער און מער, און האט אויסגירעכינט אלע רביים ביז דעם אלטין רבי'ן.

ווי באלד דער רבי האט יעמולט מער ניט גירעכינט, דערמאנט איז יוד שבט האב איך בין דעם אלטין רבי'ן, וואס דארף זיך דערמאנען, ווי באלד אז דער רבי האט מער ניט גירעכינט. היינט איז דאך נאך א המשך צו יו"ד שבט - דער מאמר היושבת בגנים איז דאך אויך א המשך צו יו"ד שבט, היינט האב איך גירעדט בין דעם בעה"ס.

ו. דער בעש"ט האט גיזאגט אז ער האט גיקענט עולה זיין השמיטה אזוי ווי אלי' הנביא, נאר ער האט גיוואלט דורך גיין דעם ענין פון ואל עפר תשוב. ולכאורה, ווי באלד אז עס איז פראנען א מעלה אין דעם ענין פון ואל עפר תשוב, צי דען האט אלי' הנביא'ן גיפעלט די שלימות?

נאר דער ענין איז, אז די שלימות אין יעדער זאך איז, ער זאל אויספירין זיין ענין, וואס ער דארף אויפטאן. בכילא איז מובן, אז אלי' הנביא מצד זיין ענין וואס ער האט גידארפט אויפטאן, האט ער גידארפט עולה זיין בסערה השמיטה, אמן דאס איז זיין שלימות. דער בעש"ט מצד זיין ענין וואס ער האט גידארפט אויפטאן, האט גידארפט דורכגיין דעם ענין פון ואל עפר תשוב אמן דאס איז זיין שלימות.

ז. דער ענין פון אלי' הנביא איז, קומען אויף א ברית מלה, קומען פס פסח באיינאכט, מצד זיין רב המנונא סבא - די נשמה איז נאר, אז צו א בית און פסח באיינאכט, קומט ער אן א גוף, און אויף מציל זיין, איז משום כבודם של צדיקים מוזמן ער זיך אן אין א גוף, דערמיט ווערט רעכט, וואס עס שטייט אז אלי' האט ניט גיקענט קומען צו רשב"י אין אידרא, ווייל ער האט גידארפט מציל זיין רהמ"ס. ולכאורה האט ער גיקענט קומען אין בילבע, נאר א מאל א אזוי ווי ער קומט אויף א פסח נאר דער תירוץ איז - אז אויף א

הגהות רבינו לשיחת י"ג שבט תשי"א אודות הדורות הבאים לחתונה (נדפס בלקו"ש ח"ב ע' 515).

אחרי החופה בטוב לבו של המחותן עליו, שאל את ר"ב מדוע צעק הרבי עלי האם אני הוא שהצעתי על השידוך, הלא הרבי הוא שהציע אתו ומדוע יצעק אלי ויביישני האם לא ידע כי בור ועם הארץ אני.

ויענהו: תדע שבכל חופה בא אלינו אבותינו ואבות אבותינו, והנה בהגיע זמן החופה, אבותי באו, ואבותיך לא רק שלא באו אלא שגם לא יכולתי למצוא מקומם, ולכן צעקתי עליך וכן בפעם השני' וכו' עד אשר מצאתים והבאתים אל החופה.

בשעה שתים עשרה חצות בלילה הוכרז ברדיו על עוצר. בשעה אחת עשרה לפנה"צ הוכרז על משטר צבאי.

פירושים אינם ידועים עוד, ולא אכתבם כי בודאי ירשמום בעיתונים.

ב"ה יום ד', צו, ה' ניסן ש"ז.

בדירתנו החדשה רח' טיומקין 10 פנת אבן גבירול.

אחרי אשר ביום השני ח"י אדר בוטל המשטר הצבאי, הנה ביום הרביעי כ' אדר נכנסנו לדירתנו הפרטית החדשה להצלחה ולמז"ט. הסיבה לזה הוא רצונו של הבעה"ב של דירתנו הישנה להרוס את הבנין כולו ולבנות חדש במקומו. גם השכנים האחרים יצטרכו לצאת משם. הדירה נמצאת בלב ת"א ברח' טיומקין 10 פנת אבן גבירול, בקומת הקרקע, הדירה הראשונה לצד ימין.

הבנין אשר בו נמצאת דירתנו הוא בנין חדש בן 4 קומות, אשר מר כהנא – בעל המגרש הקודם – בנאו לשם מכירה לבעלי הדירות הפרטים, ונקרא שמו בישראל "בית משותף".

הבחור מר יששכר דובער פרידמן [אודותו צריך לרשום פרק מיוחד] מספר על מר כהנא הנ"ל, מה שספר לו דודו שבת"א, שעוד בעיירתו חיוסט באונגריא, אמרו עליו: – בהיותו שם בבנין הרבה דברים – וואָס עס פאַלט איין בוייט ער און וואָס ער בויט פאַלט איין.

לדירה זו יש מעלות וחסרונות, כמו לדירות אחרות, אמנם חסרונה העיקרי הוא: שהיא נמצאת מול מצודת חיילי הוד מלכותו המלך ג'ורג' הששי יר"ה. בבית הדר וסביבתו, ובהתקיף חברי הארגונים הטרוריסטים את "המצודה" – או כשנדמה להחיילים שהתקיפותם – מתחילים החיילים לירות בקנה רובה ומכונות ירי' אוטומטיים למקום אשר כפי רצון הרוח ללכת. כמו שהי' במוצ"ש פ' תצוה, ועוד היום יכולים למצוא בהרחבה חורים בביתנו – אם כי בדירות העליונות – שנתהוו מהכדורים.

במוצש"ק פ' ויקרא אור ליום ב' ניסן, הילולא של כ"ק אדמו"ר זי"ע, היתה התועדות בהישיבה. ר' מנחם מנדל סלונים ספר: כשהי' אבי – הוא הרה"ח ר' שניאור סלונים רב דחסידי יפו – ביאלטא אצל כ"ק אדמו"ר בשנת תרמ"ז בערך, הנה הסדר הי' אשר כ"ק הי' הולך בכל יום לטייל ששה שעות שלש

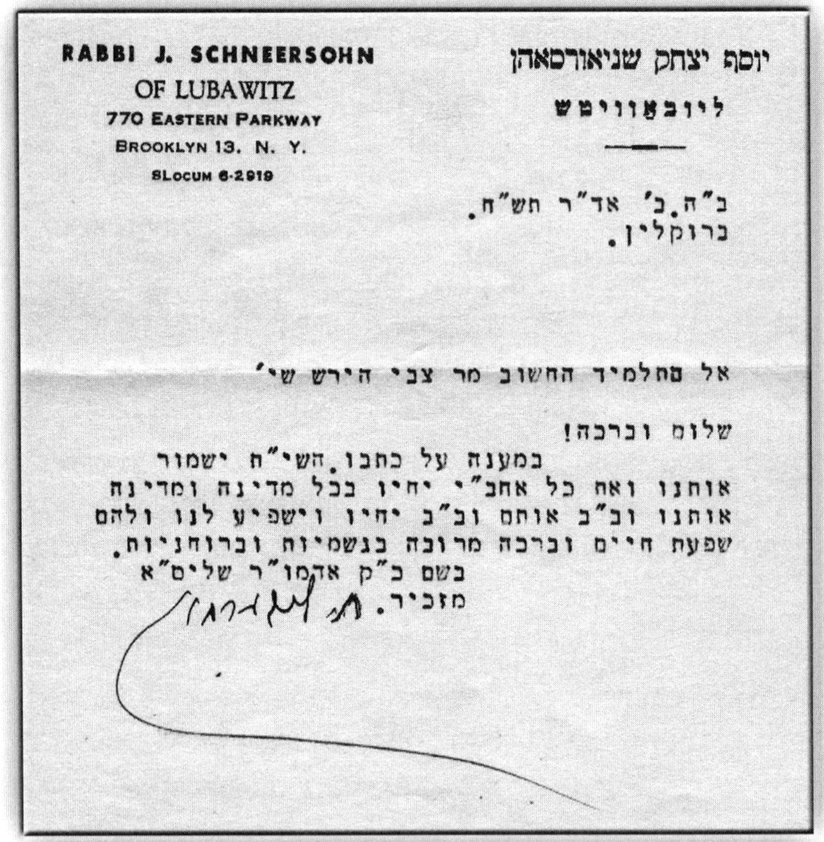
יוסף יצחק שניאורסאהן
ליובאוויטש

RABBI J. SCHNEERSOHN
OF LUBAWITZ
770 EASTERN PARKWAY
BROOKLYN 13. N. Y.
SLocum 6-2919

ב"ה, כ' אד"ר תש"ח.
ברוקלין.

אל התלמיד החשוב מר צבי הירש שי'

שלום וברכה!

במענה על כתבו, השי"ת ישמור אותנו ואת כל אחב"י יחיו בכל מדינה ומדינה אותנו וב"ב אותם וב"ב יחיו וישפיע לנו ולהם שפעת חיים וברכה מרובה בגשמיות וברוחניות.

בשם כ"ק אדמו"ר שליט"א
מזכיר. ח. ליבערמאן

ברכת אדמו"ר מהוריי"צ באדר תש"ח לשמירת אחבנ"י בכל מדינה ומדינה

שעות הלוך ושלש חזור, ולקח גם את אבי אתו.

בששה שבועות הראשונות לא דיבר כ"ק אדמו"ר מאומה וכפי הנראה אַז ער האָט גיפלאַנעוועט את הענין אשר רצה לדבר. ואחר הזמן הזה דבר ענין אחד כל זמן טיולם, ובכל יום כשבא אבי הביתה הי' רושם את אשר שמע מכ"ק.

בבוא העת להפרד מכ"ק הנה יומיים או שלשה ימים לפני פרידתם הראה אבי את רשימותיו לכ"ק לבקרם. כ"ק אדמו"ר לקח את הרשימות, ואז הי' זמן החורף, ובתנור בית החורף בער אש להחם את הבית,

וכאשר כ"ק אדמו"ר לקח את הרשימות דיפדפם זמן מה ויזרקהו לתוך האח הבוערת.

ויתחיל אבי להתאונן ולאמר: מדוע יעשה רבינו ככה הלא אנכי יגעתי ע"ז הרבה חדשים, ולבד זאת כאשר רשמתי את כל אשר שמעתי לא נתתי את לבי לזוכרם בטוב, ומדוע יעשה רבינו ככה.

ויענהו: אין רצוני שאתפרסם לרבי.

ר' רפאל נחמן כהן ספר:

זוכר אני את ר"ש סלונים היטב, פעם אחת – זה הי' בשנת צ"ה-ו – לא הי' ר"ש הנ"ל בביתו כי נסע להתרפאות, ובהיותו רב ביפו הי' לומד לפני העולם דא"ח, בהעדרו, שלחוני ללמוד דא"ח במקומו, והייתי לומר תו"א ולקו"ת, ופעם כתבים מאמרי כ"ק אדמו"ר.

כשחזר מנסיעתו ובערב שבת קודש בערב ישבתי כדרכי בבית הכנסת ולמדתי כדרכי, הנה באמצע הלימוד, נכנס ר"ש לבית הכנסת, כמובן שכל הנמצאים בבית הכנסת עמדו על רגליהם לכבודו, ואני הפסקתי את לימודי, ויאמר כי נמשיך את לימודנו כרגיל.

ועוד ספר:

אהלו של כ"ק אדמו"ר ברוסטוב-דאָן נמצא בביתה"ק, וממול אהלו בצד – כפי הנראה זה הי' חוץ מביתה"ק – קבורים הקראים כי לא רצו לקוברם בקברי בנ"י.

– כ"ק אדמו"ר שליט"א אמר ע"ז כי סימנך הוא כמ"ש אצל משה רבינו מול בית פעור –

פעם אחת זכיתי לראות כשכ"ק אד"ש הלך להשתטח על האהל, האהל הוא בלי כיפה ובראותנו אני עם עוד תמימים כי כ"ק אד"ש הולך על האהל עלינו על הגדר להסתכל ולראות את הנעשה, ונראה: כשכ"ק נתקרב אל האהל פתח ספר תהלים ויאמר דבר מה ואח"כ סיבב את האהל ויאמר עוד דבר מה וכסדר הזה נהג זמן מה.

אח"כ ראינו כי כ"ק אדמו"ר מכוין עצמו לאיזה דבר והכנתו היתה בדיוק כהכנתו לשמוע אמירת דא"ח מכ"ק אדמו"ר זי"ע, אחר הכנתו א"ע עמד מול כ"ק אדמו"ר בדיוק כעמדו בעת אמירת דא"ח מול כ"ק אדנ"ע.

וכה עמד זמן רב, ואח"כ פתח עוד את ספר התהלים ויאמר דבר מה וראינו שהכין עצמו לצאת מהאהל, וכמובן אשר חיש מהר ירדנו מהגדר ונסתתר.

ר' ח"ש ברוק ספר:

הרה״ח ר׳ חיים שאול ברוק

הרה״ח ר׳ אברהם דריזין (מאיור)

ר׳ ברוך׳ל מעזבוזער נהג אשר אף אחד מהבאים לפניו לא ישב אצלו, פשוט עס איז קיין ביינקל נישט גישטאַנען. ואחד מן האדמו״רים (הוא אמר את השם אמנם אני לא שמעתי ברור) בא לפניו עם משמשו ומשמשו הביא כסא עבורו, ויכנס לר״ב וישב על הכסא.

האדמו״ר הזה הי׳ מפורסם בחכמתו, ויאמר לו ר״ב הלא אנכי הנני חד בדרא ויענהו: גם אנכי הנני חד בדרא, וישאלהו ר״ב: ואיך אפשר להיות שני חד בדרא, ויענהו: איהר זייט אַ חד בדרא אין צדקות און איך בין א חד בדרא אין חכמה.

ויאמר לו ר״ב: אַזוי אַזוי אם אתם חד בדרא בחכמה נו זאָגט מיר איזה קטרוג הי׳ בר״ה האחרון על ישראל ויענהו: הקטרוג הי׳ אשר בנ״י מקיימים את התומ״צ למענם ולא לשם השי״ת.

ויאמר לו ר״ב: נו איז וואָס האָט איר געענטפערט: ויענהו: אני עניתי: רבוש״ע עשה להם מדה כנגד מדה, עשה למענך אם לא למעננו.

שעה אחת עשרה לילה

לר׳ ישראל צבי הבר נולד בן ביום ה׳ אדר, ונקרא שמו בישראל שמואל.

הרה"ח ר' אברהם פריז

הרה"ח ר' ניסן נמינוב

בנו הראשון נקרא בשם אברהם אלטער, השם אלטער הוא על שם ר' אלטער משפיע פאָצעפער. המוהל הי' מר פליישמן. לר' שלמה פוטשין נולד בן, בתחלה לפני שנתיים או שלש נולדה לו בת והוא כתב לכ"ק אד"ש בטלגרמה, וכ"ק ענהו במז"ט על הולדת בנו ואמר אז ר' פנחס אלטהאוז בטח אשר גם בן יולד לו והמוהל הי' מר שכטר.

מר חיים חנוביץ יצא לארה"ב.

מר א. קפלן חזר מביקורו באירופא.

הוא בקר אצל אחותו הנמצאת כעת באירופא, הוא מספר הרבה דברים מאשר ראה ושמע מהתמימים בהמחנות. הוא מספר:

שמעתי את התמים ר' ניסן משפיע – דער געלער – זלאָבינער אמר תניא ונדמה לי כי יושב הנני בליובאַוויטש ושומע תניא מהמשפיע, רק האולם הגדול חסר שמה.

זיי טייגן אויף אַריין שטעלין זיי אין אַ מוזעאום, אומר א. קפלן הנ"ל על התמימים שבקרם, כולם רוצים לנסוע לכ"ק אדמו"ר שליט"א.

הוא הי׳ גם בפאַריז ומספר אשר בהיות שר׳ זלמן שניאורסאָהן נסע לכ״ק אדמו״ר שליט״א, הנה ממלא מקומו הוא ר׳ מיכאל חתנו של ר׳ אלי׳ פאר.

כל התמימים עובדים במרץ רב. וחומם הוא פלאי פלאים.

מר א. קפלן למד בליובאַוויטש אמנם הוא התרחק הרבה. הוא מקרוביו של הרח״ש ברוק.

הרב ר׳ שאול דובער זיסלין קבל סרטיפיקאַטים עבור נכדו הנמצא בפאָקינג ונכדתו הנמצאת בלינץ, ומקוה כי בקרוב יבואו ארצה. הוא קבל לפני זמן מה מכתב מכ״ק אדמו״ר והוא מברכו שיצליח להעלות את נכדיו לארץ ישראל כשורה.

ביום השני ג׳ ניסן אפינו מצות שמורה. האופים היום כמעט כל תלמידי הישיבה וגם הרב ר׳ ש״ד זיסלין, המשגיח הוא ר׳ צבי גינזבורג. אפינו בהפאדראד של ר׳ משה ירוסלבסקי בנו של ר׳ אהר׳לי האביטשיץ בקרית יוסף גבעתיים.

ב, תזריע כ״ד ניסן

שעה תשיעית ערב.

ביום 12 מרץ ש״ז שלח לנו הקונסול דארה״ב מכתב ובו כותב הוא לנו שאנו צריכים להוכיח כי נבוא חזרה וההוכחה תהי׳ במשפחה, במסחר או ברכוש. וכפי שאמר לנו מר יוסף סיטון צריכים היינו לאשר א״ז על מוסד מוסמך. מר ש.ד. גולדשמיד ומר מ.דובינסקי אשרו בועד הקהילה בירושלים בעדותו של מר סגל, ואני אשרתי בהרבנות הראשית בת״א בעדותם של ר׳ מנחם מענדל סלונים והרב א. פריז. ובחתימתם של הרבנים הראשיים הרב יעקב משה טולידאנו והרב איסר יודה אונטערמן.

ר׳ מנחם מענדיל סלונים התעסק עבורי והלך אתי להמזכיר ר׳ שלמה רוהלד ובקשו שיסדר עבורי תעודת אישור כנ״ל, וגם אח״כ הלך להרב י.מ. טולידאנו שיחתום, ומבלעדיו היו עוברים כמה ימים עד שהיו מסדרים לי את התעודה, כי הדוחק בהרבנות גדול הוא במאד.

תמול קבלנו מהקונסול מכתב ובו הוא כותב שכפי הנראה לא הבננו את

דבריו מיום 12 מרץ כי צריכים אנו לאשר במוסד כספי כי יש לנו אמצעים לבוא חזרה, ועוד כמה פרטים.

ביום החמישי קבלו אבי שי' ואחי מר ש.י.ל. מכתבים מכ"ק אד"ש מיום ט' ניסן ובהם ברכות מז"ט, ולאחי כותב כ"ק אד"ש שנכון הדבר שיסתדר, שיתעסק באומנות השו"ב. נוסף על הטלגרמה שקבל מכ"ק אד"ש לפני כמה חדשים ובו כותב כ"ק: הנני מסכים להסתדרותו באומנות השו"ב. המכתבים הם בחתימתו של כ"ק אדמו"ר שליט"א.

אצל הרב ר' הנדל האַוולין מנהל ישיבת "תורת אמת" בירושלים, מכתב מהתמים ר' נחום זלמן הורביץ חתנו של ר' דובער ליעוויערטאָוו – או כפי שקוראים אותו בערל קאַבעליאַקיער – מאחת המחנות באוסטריא.

במכתבו הוא מזכיר את אבי שי' ואת רר"נ כהן, מהר"ר נ. עבער, וגם הוא כותב שימצאו את הפליעמעניקע של אמו מרת מינה הורביץ, ושמותם שלמה, ושמחה חיין, מאווראוויטש. מר זלמן לייבוביטש-אריאלי שגם הוא מאווראוויטש הגיד לנו – לי ולאחי יצחק יחי' – כאשר בקרנו בביתו ברח' בן עמי 8 בת"א – כי מכיר הוא את שניהם, אחד מהם הוא קבצן גדול, אשתו מתה עליו לפני זמן והוא הי' בא לביתו לקבל את תמיכתו, ואת כתובתו איננו יודע, והשני שינה את שמו, לש. בן-ישראל ונמצא כעת בטבריא והוא מורה בבית הספר העממי שם.

מר זלמן ליבוביץ הנ"ל למד בליובאַוויטש שלש שנים. הוא למד בשנות תרס"ג בערך. אחר שיצא מליובאַוויטש בשנת הט"ו לחייו הלך לרעות בשדות זרים, ואח"כ הי' מורה בבית הספר של חברת מפיצי השכלה במאָסקווה – כפי שספר לנו כאשר בקרנוהו בביתו – שם הי' נפגש לפעמים עם חברו התמים ר' אייזיק ב"ר גרונם אסתרמאַן.

זוכר הוא כמה מחבריו אשר למדו אתו בהאָראָדישץ ומהם את ר' שלמה ליב פאַריטשער, ואת מורו הרב ר' זלמן האַוולין, שהי' אז המשפיע.

כעת הוא רחוק בכלל מחיי היהדות והוא כעת המנהל הכללי בבית הספר "ביאליק" ברח' לוינסקי בת"א.

גם ספר לנו שאחד מקרוביו – שהם גם מקרוביו של הת' מר שלמה פיאטשין

– ושמו ר' משה אברהם גרינשפאַן הנמצא כעת בפאַריז נוסע עם ביתו לאה"ב לחסות בצל כ"ק אד"ש.

בחוהמ"פ הגיע לתל-אביב מר לוין – גיסו של מר משה דימנד גיסו של הת' נפתלי בהרה"ג שמואל אבא דאָליצקי – שיצא לפני שמונה או תשעה חדשים ממאָסקוואַ, הוא הגיע הנה מפריז, בנו נמצא עדיין בפאַריז וחושב לבוא ארצה.

ב"ה, כ"ו ניסן

שעה עשירית בקר

היום בשעה רביעית לפני עלות השחר נתלו ארבעה יהודים מהנידונים למוות בעכו, משעה רביעית הוכרז עוצר בכל הארץ עד להודעה חדשה.

מפני אי היכולת ללכת להתפלל לבהכ"נ מפני העוצר התפללנו במנין עשרה בביתו של מר שלמה, בביתינו בקומה הב'.

באותה הקומה גר גם הרב יוכט וחתנו מר משה ספוקלינה.

ארשום בזה פרשת התמים ר' הירשל ליבערמאַן.

כפי ששמעתי מהוריי וכפי השמור בזכרוני התמים ר' הירשל ליבערמאַן – אחיו של התמים ר' חיים ליבערמאַן מזכירו של כ"ק אדמו"ר שליט"א – הי' מקודם שוחט בפנים רוסי' בעיר אָרענבורג, ואח"כ עבר למאָסקוואַ הוא ואשתו ושני בניו. ובהיות אשר לא מצאו דירה מתאימה במרכז העיר – כי בימים ההם קשה הי' להשיג דירה בעיר – עברו לגור לפרובה ושכרו דירה בפרור טשעריאָמאָשקע.

אשתו של מר ליבערמאַן בת חייט היתה וגם היא היתה חייטת, ותתחיל להשתכר בעבודתה בביתה. אם כי הרבה עבודה לא הי' לה.

הוא בעצמו הי' סטאַראַז' (שומר), במוסקווה.

שאלת החינוך היתה די קשה עד אשר לא הי' יכול לפותרה, ויהי' בניו מתרועעים עם נערי הכפר (השקצים), ותאמר אליו אשתו: לא יוכל הדבר להיות

הרה"ח ר' הירשל ליבערמאן

ככה, הלא המה הולכים ומתגדלים בלא חינוך אפי' להיות אנשים, אפי' לא יהודים ח"ו, וביזמתה הלכה ותרשום אותם לביתה"ס הכללי.

הדבר הזה לא מצא חן בעיניו, וגם כל מאמצי כוחותיו רצה לפעול עלי' אשר תוציא את הנערים מהשקאָלע.

ויתחיל למרר לה את החייה, ובכל ערב, בבואו לביתו, לקח בקבוק יי"ש וישת עד תומו, כדי שהדבר ימאס לה ותלך ותוציא את ילדי' מביה"ס. גם סיפרו שהוציא דבר קללה מפיו על אשתו ובניו (אם כי לא אדע אם נכון הי' הדבר).

בימים ההם התחיל אבי לעבוד את העבודה הבאה: ציפוי מהדקי שערות נשים בצעלעלויד, את הצללויד היו לוקחים מסרטי הקולנוע, הארוכים והיו רוחצים אותם עד שיהיו נקיים, ואז היו מחממים אותם ע"ג האש, ואחר שחתכום ציפו בהם את ראשי מהדקי השערות.

גם ר"ה ליבערמאַן התחיל לעבוד את העבודה, הוא עבד את העבודה בביתו.

דירתם היתה בצריף עץ, מצא אבי עבורו חדר מתאים להעבודה הנ"ל, והשתדל שיעבוד לא בביתו אלא מהחדר שמצא עבורו.

בערב האחרון שהי' בביתינו במאָסקוואַ, הזהירוהו אבי אמי וא"ז הו'בנית מרת נחמה ע"ה כי לא יעבוד בביתו כי הצללויד נוח להתלקח וביתו צריף עץ הוא, אמנם הוא לא שמע להאזהרות וימשיך את עבודתו בביתו.

את רוב עבודתו הי' עובד בלילה.

בערב אחד עבד כדרכו. השעה היתה מאוחרת. אשתו וילדיו כבר ישנו במיטותיהם, הוא רחץ את הסרטים ויניחם על גבי המחצלות ליבשם.

מכונת הנפט – קנויט מאַשינקע – בערה, וכנראה אשר הוא הוציא סיגרי'

מאמתחתו וחפץ להבעירה.

ויקח את אחת הסרטים – אשר היתה יכולה לעמוד כעין מקל – ויבעירה בהמכונה, ויתחיל להגישה לפיו להבעיר הסיגרי׳, אמנם הסרט נשבר, והאש נפלה על אחד הסרטים המונחים על מטת אשתו וכרגע כמימרא, התלקחו הסרטים שעל מטת אשתו ואחריהם הסרטים האחרים המונחים על מיטות בניו, וכעבור רגעים אחדים כל הצריף הי׳ אחוז בלהבות.

לקול צעקותיו נתעוררה אשתו ושניהם קפצו דרך החלון להנצל מהאש הבוערת, אמנם תיכף קפצו חזרה לחדרים כדי להקיץ את בניהם האחוזים בשינה עמוקה. הם התחילו לעוררם ובשום אופן לא עלה בידם, האש אחזה גם בהם בעצמם, ויקפצו דרך החלון הבוערת אל החצר.

הדבר הי׳ בימות החורף, ובחצר הי׳ מונח שלג רב, היא נפלה לתוך השלג להתגלגל ולהצטנן מהאש הבוערת, ותקבל הצטננות חזקה, ותקבל דלקת הריאות.

מתוך כך בער הצריף כולו, את הבנים הוציאו אחד כבר הי׳ מת, והשני מת כעבור רגעים אחדים.

אותו ואת אשתו העבירו לבית החולים.

– אבי הלך אח״כ לחפש במטת הצריף השרוף וימצא כמה מאצבעות ידי בנו. אבי לקחם ויקברם בבית החיים, הוא גם לא ידע מזה. –

אשתו הבינה אשר הבנים נשרפו, וכעבור ימים אחדים הלכה גם היא לעולמה מתוך מכאובים נוראים.

הוא שכב בבית החולים עוד כמה חדשים, ומביתנו הביאו לו בכל יום אוכל, וגם בחג הפסח קנו לו כלים חדשים וגם הביאו לו את האוכל מביתינו.

בהגיע העת לצאת את ביה״ח, לא רצה ללכת לקרוביו אשר גרו במאָסקוואַ, וכאשר שאלוהו למי ילך ענה, שלא ילך כ״א לבערל גאַנזבורג, אם כי אבי לא הי׳ שבע רצון מזה בחשש אשר בזה יוסיפו את מכאוביו שימצא בבית עם ילדים כ״י.

כל היום לא הי׳ נראה עליו כלום רק בלילה הי׳ נשמע יללה חרישית ממטתו. אח״כ שכר לו אבי חדר לעצמו. בהיותו בביתנו ספר כמה סיפורים ובדיחות בהיותו בעל פה שנון ומפיק מרגליות ואי״ה עוד ארשום כמה מסיפוריו.

ב"ה ב, בדר"ח אייר ש"ז (בביתינו)

ארשום בזה כמה מסיפוריו של התמים ר' הירש'ל ליבערמאַן אשר ספר בעת היותו בביתינו במאָסקוואַ.

"סיפורי גנבים"

בזמן היותי שוחט באָרענבורג היו שם גנבים נודעים לשמם, תכסיסי גניבותיהם יפליאו את השומעים אותם.

א) באחד מימי השוק בימות החורף לפני עלות השחר בא אחד מהסוחרים הרוסיים עם עגלתו המלאה סחורה לאחת מסימטאות השוק, ויעמיד עגלתו, ובהיות אשר השעה היתה מוקדמת ביותר, כיסה את סחורתו במכסה, ויעלה על העגלה וישכב עלי', פניו למטה ואחוריו למעלה, החורף הי' בתקפו, ויקח את אדרתו – שובַא – אדרת החורף וישימה על כתפיו וישן.

הוא לא הספיק להעמיק בשנתו וירגיש אשר מישהו התחיל לחלוץ את מגפיו – שטיוועלאַך –, ויאמר בלבו, מה לו לפתי זה ולמגפי, האם לא ידע כי מרגיש הנני ובעוד רגע אקפוץ מהעגלה ואתפסו, אמנם הגנב כנראה לא חשש למחשבותיו, ויחלוץ אחד ממגפיו עד החצי וילך לו. ויאמר הסוחר בלבו: כנראה שהגנב הרגיש מי אני, ומה אוכל לעשות לו, ומשו"ז הלך לו. כעבור איזה רגעים הרגיש שחולצים לו את מגפו השנית. וגם בה חלץ הגנב עד החצי וילך לו.

ויחשוב הסוחר בטח כעת לא ישוב הגנב עוד, כי הלא בטח יודע הוא אותי ואת נחת זרועי.

בפתע פתאום, חטף הגנב את אדרתו ויתחיל לנוס, אמנם הוא קפץ כרגע מעל העגלה ויתחיל לרוץ, אבל כרגע נפל לו, כי בהיות אשר הגנב חלץ לו את מגפיו, עד החצי לא יכול לרוץ, וגם לא יכול לחלצם או ללבשם במהירות.

ב) שני סוחרים רוסיים, לבושים אדרות פרוה יקרות סיימו מלאכתם ביום השוק, הם מכרו את כל סחורתם שהביאו אתם לשוק.

כאשר סיימו את מלאכתם לקחו את כל כסף הפדיון – שעלה לסך מסוים, וילכו אל מחוץ לעיר, לספרו.

מחוץ לעיר היו מונחים קורות עץ מהוקצעים ביחוד, לקבעם כעמודי טלגרף גופות גופות, וישבו שני הסוחרים על אחת מגופות העצים ויפשילו

את אדרותיהם לאחוריהם, אחד מהם הסיר כובעו והניחו ע"י ברכיהם, ויוציאו את צרור הכסף, ויתחילו למנותו לתוך הכובע. בהיותם מונים את כספם ראו מרחוק צעיר רוסי, לבוש מצנפת, עובדי הדואר והטלגרף, הולך ומכה בפטיש קטן, על הקורות ומטה אזנו לשמוע דבר מה.

כאשר הצעיר נתקרב אלהם שאלוהו מה עבודתו? ויענם: בהיות שהוא עובד בעבודת הטגלרף, צריך הוא לבדוק את הקורות אם לא עלה לתוכם הריקבון או התולעת, וע"כ מכה הוא בפטישו ומטה אזנו לשמוע את הקול היוצא מהקורות, כי הקול היוצא מהקורות הרקובות, אחר הוא מהקול היוצא מהקורות הבריאות.

כאשר הצעיר הסביר להם עבודתו, כבשו הם את פניהם לתוך הכובע עם הכסף, וימשיכו את עבודתם – מניית כסף הפדיון.

זמן מה שמעו עוד את הקשת הפטיש, ולפתע פתאום ראו שהצעיר חטף את הכובע עם הכסף וינוס, הם חפצו לרדוף אחריו אך כאשר רצו לקום ממקום מושבם הרגישו שהאדרות צמודות להקורות במסמרים...

ב"ה ב' כ"ד אייר ש"ז

שעה תשיעית ערב.

זה כשעתיים שבאתי מירושלים, יצאתי באוטובוס האחרון – מפני עוצר הדרכים המתחיל בשעה 7 – היוצא בשעה 5.

לירושלים באתי בשעה האחת עשרה בקשר לבדיקת הרופאים הממונים ע"י הקונסול האמריקאי.

לפני כשבועיים קבלתי מכתב מהקונסול, לבוא אליו ביום ה-20 למאי, עם פספורט ו-3 תמונות בלי לוית מישהו ממשפחתי בשעה 10.00 בקר. אגב את הפספורט קבלתי ביום 27 לחדש אפריל חדשיים להגשת בקשתי ביום 27 לחדש פברואר. גם מר מרדכי דובינסקי קבל מכתב לבוא באותו יום בשעה 9:30 בקר, אמנם למכתבו היו מצורפים שני טפסי רופאים, וגם במכתב הקונסול כתוב שילך להבדק להרופאים הבאים, ד"ר דג'אני מרחוב ממילא. או ד"ר מ. ניומאַן, מרח' בצלאל קרוב למלון עדן – רופאים כלליים – קליניקה ע"ש סט. ג'והן, סמוך לתחנת הרכבת – רופא עינים –.

מר מרדכי דובינסקי הלך תיכף להרופאים אמנם אני לא הלכתי, כי חסרו

לי הטפסים, וגם הקונסול לא רמז ע"ז במכתבו אלי, אם כי הבנתי שנפל שם איזה טעות. לפני כמה ימים קבל גם ש.ד. גולדשמיד מכתב מהקונסול כמו אצל מ.ד. ולבוא אליו ביום 28 לחדש מאי, מבלי לסמן את השעה.

כמובן שמר ש.ד.ג. הלך גם הוא להרופאים ובהיותו אצל ד"ר ניומאַן ספר לו אודותי, הוא ענהו שהטפסים נמצאים אצלו, ואבוא אליו ביום החמישי, והוא יטלפן להקונסול. והיום הייתי אצלו, הוא מילא את הבטחתו, ובבואי נתקשר בטלפון עם הפקידה בקונסולי' האמריקאית בשם גב' סולומון, והיא צותה לו ליתן לי את הטפסים.

הוא ספר לי שאביו הי' מגרודנה והוא בעצמו נולד בירושלים ולמד בישיבת תורת חיים, ואח"כ יצאתי לתרבות רעה, סיים בחיוך.

הד"ר ניומאַן הוא איש כבן שבעים דיבר בשפות, עברית אנגלית ואידיש וגרמנית בפני.

ממנו הלכתי לרופא העיניים האנגלי (המדבר רק אנגלית), ואח"ז שלחתי את הטפסים להקונסול.

את התעודות מהבנקים שלחנו זה כבר להקונסול, וגם את מכתבנו ומכתבי ההורים.

אבי קבל את האישור מבנק למלאכה.

מ. דובינסקי מבנק בריטני' א"י.

ש.ד. גולדשמיד מהג'וינט ומבנק אנגלו-פלשתינה.

ואחר שהקונסול קבל את מכתבינו שלח לנו את המכתבים הנזכרים לעיל.

כפי ששמעתי הנה הרב ר"א קרסיק ור"מ גוראריי' מתעסקים בדבר נסיעתם לכ"ק אדמו"ר שליט"א לאה"ב.

כנראה ששניהם רוצים לנסוע בתור סוחרים, ור"מ גוראריי' יסע כנראה בתור סוכן בית החרושת לשוקולדה "ליבר" שהוא כעת סוכנם בארץ. אחיו ר"ש נסע בתור סוכן ביהח"ר לסיגריות "דובק" שהוא סוכנם גם בארץ.

ב"ה ד' בהעלותך

ביום ג' ר"ח סיון הלכתי עם מר מרדכי דובינסקי להקונסולי' האמריקאית – הכניסה למשרדי "ויזות למהגרים" היא מהחצר והמשרד עצמו צריף אבן

מצופה פח בצורה עגולה –

כאשר דפקנו בדלת יצא לקראתנו השוער הערבי במדי הקונסולי׳, וכאשר הראנו לו את הזמנות הקונסול פתח עבורנו את הדלת ונכנסנו.

– משרד הויזות למהגרים הוא חדר די גדול אשר מחיצת ארונות מפסקת בו בין החלק הראשון הקטן (ע״י הדלת) שהוא חדר ההמתנה, להחלק השני הגדול אשר בו ישב הקונסול – כמובן הסגן השייך להויזות – ע״י הארונות, והפקידות הכותבות –

אחרי אשר מסרנו להשוער את ההזמנות, הלך כנראה אל הפקידה הראשית ובחזרו לקח ממנו את טביעת אצבעותינו.

הסדר בלקיחת טביעת האצבעות כך הוא: בהן היא הימנית ואבריך האצבעות האחרות כל אחד לחוד, וכן בהיד השמאלית, פעמיים.

אחרי שלקח טביעת אצבעותינו הכניסם כנראה שוב להפקידה. כעבור זמן מה קראו את מ. דובינסקי, הוא נגש אל הפקידה, הפקידה אמרה שכנראה אין אנו מדברים אנגלית ע״כ דברה עברית, וחקרה את כל הפרטים, כעבור חצי שעה קראו גם אותי כנ״ל.

אחרי אשר חקרונו ״נשבענו״ במעמד הסגן קונסול G. Cattal, השבועה היא שהפקידה אמרה אני נשבעתי שכל הנ״ל אמת ואחרי עבור זמן לימודי אחזור לארץ ואנו הרמנו את ידינו, אח״ז אמרו לנו לבוא למחר בשעה 1, ולמחר נתנו לנו את הויזות, מס׳ הויזה של מ.ד. הוא 363 ושלי 364, הויזה היא על ארבע שנים ואנו יכולים להתעכב עד כניסתנו לאמריקה 4 חדשים. שלמנו כ״א 2,500 שהם 10 דולאר.

כעבור שבוע קבל גם מר ש.ד. גולדשמיד את הויזה.

אם כי הגשנו בקשות להקונסולי׳ לתן לנו מקומות באני׳ ״מריין קארפ״ היוצאת ביום 13/6 47, וגם הבאנו מכתב מהישיבה, בכ״ז דחו את בקשתנו והבטיחו לנו לתת מקום באותה האני׳ ליום ר״ח אב לערך.

ביום החמישי העבר עזב מר נ׳ גוראריʼ את הארץ באוירון בדרכו לאה״ב והגיע לשם ביום א. ש.ז.

הרב טקץ היוצא מטעם ישבתנו לאה״ב עזב את הארץ באני׳ ״רוסי״ שיצאה

לפני כמה שבועות מחיפה, - בעיתונות נמסרה ידיעה שהאני' כבר הגיעה לניו יאָרק – בצאתו את הארץ נתקבלה טלגרמה מכ"ק אד"ש שהשליח מהישיבה יצא רק לחדש אלול, ולא קודם, חושבים שזהו מפני פגרת הקיץ החלה כעת באמריקה.

בשבועות הללו צריך להגיע לארץ הרב ר' שמרי' גורארי' חדב"נ, הרב ח. הבלין השתדל עבור הרשיון.

אצל ר' ישעי' גינזבורג נתקבלה טלגרמה שהרב ר' ניסן טעלושקין מהמתעסקים החשובים באגודת חסידי חב"ד בארה"ב יצא בדרכו לארץ.

ביום ל"ג בעומר בערב התקיימה חתונת התלמיד החשוב מר שלמה קופציק עם בת ר' ראובן גשייד מחסידי פיאַסעצנא, בכפר אתא הרבה מתלמידי הישיבה והתמימים נוכחו על החתונה וכמה מהתלמידים נשארו על ש"ק.

בחג השבועות הי' רש"ק הנ"ל אורחינו בת"א.

הרב ר' שאול דב ספר:

לר"ש גרונם אסתרמן המשפיע הי' בן בשם מאיר, ובהגיע הזמן אשר הבן הנ"ל הי' צריך להלקח לעבודת הצבא, הי' נחשב בין בעלי הליגאטא השני', כששאלו את כ"ק אדמו"ר נ"ע מה לעשות ענה שצריכים לתת כסף.

הוא הי' צריך לעמוד לפריזיב בעיר באָריסאָוו, ויסע לבאָריסאָוו ויתאכסן בבית חותני ר' חיים יאיר. בעיר באָריסאוו הי' אחד מהפקידים הגבוהים בשם פערדינאַנד, האיש הזה בקשרים טובים עם כ"ק אדמו"ר והוא ידע קצת מכ"ק אדמו"ר.

כאשר הגיע מאיר לבאָריסאָוו הלך עם חותני לפערדינאַנד הנ"ל, ורצו לתת לו סך 150 רובל, פערדינאנד ענם שאיננו רוצה לקבל את הכסף, בהיות אשר

חסרים הרבה מהמועמדים ע״כ בטוח הוא שיקבלוהו וכסף לחנם איננו רוצה לקבל. הם דחפו לו את הכסף לידו והוא בשום אופן לא קבלו.

כאשר באו לביתם כתב מאיר מכתב לאביו, רש״ג וכתב לו את המצב ואשר מר פערדינֵנד אינו מקבל את הכסף.

רש״ג הלך לכ״ק אדמו״ר – אנכי עמדתי אז בהחדר אשר לפני כ״ק אדמו״ר – ויראהו את מכתב בנו ויאמר לו בהיות אשר את הכסף אין רוצים לקבל שואל הוא מה לעשות.

כ״ק אדמו״ר נשען על ידי קדשו, און האָט זיך פאַרטראַכט כעבור רגעים אחדים, הגביה את ראש קדשו ויאמר:

דו פרעגסט וואָס זאָלסטו טאָן, קיין רוח הקודש האָב איך ניט, איך האָב דאָך געזאָגט אַז מען זאָל געבן געלט, מען דאַרף מאַכן אַ כלי אין וואָס די ברכה זאָל שורה זיין.

כאשר יצא רש״ג מאת כ״ק אדמו״ר ספר לי מה שאמר כ״ק אדמו״ר.

רש״ג כתב זה תיכף לבנו, וילך שוב עם חותני למר פערדינַנד וכאשר ספרו לו מה שאמר כ״ק אדמו״ר קבל את הכסף.

לפתע פתאום נשמע בעיר באָריסאוו שפטרו את חברי הועדה העוסקים בעניני הפריזיוו, נתקבלו נגדם האשמות חמורות והם פוטרו, ובמקומם באו חברי הועדה מעיר ליעפלי.

חברי הועדה מעיר ליעפלי באו לבאָריסאוו ועמם באו גם החאדאטאייעס – הַלָכים – מליעפלי.

באחד הערבים ומאיר הנ״ל ישב בבית חותני נכנסו שני אנשים צעירים וישאלו את חותני אם מתאכסן אצלו צעיר בשם מאיר אסתרמן, ויראה עליו. הם נכנסו אתו לחדר מיוחד ויספרו לו שגם הם הנם ליעגאטשיקעס והם דברו עם חברי הועדה מליעפלי, והם ענום שהדבר קשה הוא שישחררום רק אם יאספו בין כל הליעגאטשיקעס סכום של אלפיים רובל, ישחררו את כולם. הם לקחו ע״ע את העבודה לקבץ את הכסף ומקבצים אותו לפי הערכה ועליו העריכו לתת 50 רובל הוא נתן את הכסף, ושוחרר מעבודתו בצבא.

מוצש"ק פ' שלח, כ"ו סיון.

הרה"ח ר' ניסן טעלושקין

בעש"ק בקר עלה בנמל חיפה הרב ר' ניסן טעלושקין מניו יאָרק.

הר"נ טעלושקין הוא אחד מהעוזרים בעבודת הקדש של כ"ק אדמו"ר שליט"א.

הוא מתאכסן אצל בן עירו ר' ישעי' גינזבורג. היום הי' אצל י.ג. הנ"ל קידוש לכבוד האורח הנכבד. האורח ספר כמה דברים וביניהם הדברים הבאים:

א) כשהגיע כ"ק אד"ש לארה"ב בהקבלת פנים שערכו לכבודו אמר:

אצל משה כשחזר מאת יתרו למצרים אמר לו הקב"ה, על אהרן "וראך ושמח בלבו" והפירוש הוא, ששמחת אהרן על ראיית פני אחיו היא רק בלבו אבל על פניו אין היא ניכרת, כי אהרן הי' שבור ורצוץ מצערם של ישראל במצרים.

כן גם אנכי מבלי להביט כי שמח אני מראיית פני אחיי אשר באמריקה שבור ורצוץ הנני מצערם של ישראל מעבר לים.

ב) כ"ק אדמו"ר שליט"א אמר לי ביחידות אודות ההבדל בהמצב הרוחני של אחינו בנ"י באמריקה למצבם מעל"י. וזהו:

שניהם יש בתוכם אש וההבדל הוא כההבדל בין האש הנאחז בעצים להאש הנאחז בבנזין. האש הנאחז בעצים הנה גם אחר אשר יבער את כל האש ישארו גחלים, ובבנזין אחר אשר יבער הבנזין לא ישאר כלום: והעצה ע"ז היא שיהי' האש בוער תמיד.

בקשר לבואו נתקבל מכתב מכ"ק אד"ש לאנ"ש והתמימים מת"א, לחזק את שיעורי הלימודים בנגלה ובדא"ח, בבתי כנסיות חב"ד, וליסד במקומות אשר אינם מתקיימים עוד. ובהיות אשר הרה"ג הידוע, לתהלה ותפארת וו"ח

אי״א מוהר״ר הר״נ טעלושקין מתכונן לעלות ארצה לכבדו בכבוד הראוי ויביא פ״ש מאת כ״ק אד״ש ומאת אנ״ש והתמימים והמוסדות אשר בארה״ב, וזה יביא בטח התעוררות. המכתב הוא בחתימת כ״ק אדמו״ר שליט״א.

ובהתאם למכתב כ״ק, נסעו לחיפה לקבל פניו ר׳ שמואל זלמנוב ומנהל ישיבתנו הרב ר׳ משה אקסלרוד.

כ"ק אדמו"ר נשיא דורנו

ב.

תשי״א, תשי״ב

מ״בית חיינו״ בתקופת קבלת הנשיאות

תשי״א

ב״ה ה׳ ג׳ תשרי צום גדלי׳ תשי״א
ברוקלין, שעה הי״א בוקר

ביום כ״ז אלול ש״ק פ׳ נצבים מלאו לי למז״ט כ״ב שנה. ולרגל מאורע זה נכנסתי ליחידות לכ״ק אדמו״ר שליט״א. ביום ה׳ כ״ה אלול בשעה חצי האחת עשרה בערב לערך.

במוצש״ק פ׳ תבוא הלכתי לאסיפת חברים בחברת אגודת אחים אנשי באברויסק לבקשם כי יואילו לקבלני, או יותר מדויק לרשום אותי, בתור רב בחברתם כי כ״ק אדמו״ר הורה לי שאמצא איזה בית כנסת שתרשום אותי בתור רב מהיום ולהבא, וזה יאפשר לכתוב כי מכהן אני . . .

וע״פ הצעת כ״ק אדמו״ר שליט״א ביקרתי יחד עם התמים הר״ר יעקב העכט את בן דודו העורך דין העכט בנויארק, וגם הוא הסכים להצעת כ״ק.

וטרם בואי מסרתי ע״י הרב – ר׳ חיים מרדכי אייזיק ב״ר שלום ישראל חדקאוו, לכ״ק אדמו״ר שליט״א כי הולך הנני לאסיפתם.

אחרי אמירת הסליחות

– הסליחות אמרו בבית המדרש. והעובר לפני התיבה הי׳ הר״ר שמואל ב״ר שרגא פייוויש זלמנוב. הוא הי׳ הבעל תפלה גם אצל כ״ק אדמו״ר הכ״מ.

כ״ק אדמו״ר שליט״א לא עמד על מקומו הרגיל במזרחית דרומית

(– מקומו עד עתה הי׳ לא בקרן מזרחית דרומית מקום שם עמד השטענדער של כ״ק אדמו״ר הכ״מ, ושם הי׳ מתפלל כ״ק אדמו״ר הכ״מ בימים נוראים בשנים הראשונות לבואו לארה״ב [את השטענדער פרקו ביום הלוית כ״ק אדמו״ר הכ״מ ואת הקרש העליון העמידו לראש כ״ק אדמו״ר הכ״מ בתור גולל. חתיכה קטנה מהשטענדער נמצאת אצלי], אלא על יד הדלת הפונה לחדר שני לימין כ״ק אדמו״ר הכ״מ משוך כאמתיים או שלוש לצד מזרח –)

אלא עמד ליד השולחן בחלק מזרחי צפוני של הבית המדרש.

את הסליחות התחילו להגיד כמה רגעים אחרי שעה ראשונה היא חצות לילה לפי השעון הרגיל. –

[הנה לאחרי הסליחות] רמז לי כ״ק אדמו״ר שליט״א שאתקרב אליו, וישאלנו מה היו תוצאות ביקורי בהאסיפה.

אנכי סיפרתי לו כי השיבו את פני ריקם באמרם שיראים הם כי אחרי כתיבת החוזה – הקונטראקט – אתבע מהם את הסכום הנקוב בהחוזה. וגם בקשת הר״ר ישראל דזייקאבסאהן היתה ללא הועיל.

כ״ק אדמו״ר אמר ע״ז כי הייתי צריך להציע להם להכניס את כל הכסף אשר יכתבו בהחוזה על משך שנה אחת ואמר: ״מען האט עס געקענט באווארענען פריער״. גם אמר שאודע שם הפרעזידענט ואפגוש אתו ביחוד להודיע לו לתת את הכסף כאמור.

בגמרו לדבר, סיפרתי לכ״ק כי ביום הש״ק ימלאו לי כ״ב שנה וארצה לדעת באיזה זמן אוכל להכנס ליחידות. כ״ק אד״ש ענני שאוכל להכנס ביום ועש״ק או ביום החמישי לילה.

כאשר נכנסתי ישב כ״ק שליט״א ליד השולחן פניו למזרח, הי׳ לבוש בגדו העליון – הקצר – וכבעו השחור על ראש קדשו.

בהכנסי נשארה הדלת פתוחה. כ״ק אדמו״ר שליט״א אמר לי שאסגור את הדלת. סגרתי הדלת ואגש אל כ״ק שליט״א והגשתי לידו הק׳ את הפ״נ, בו הודעתי כי ביום הש״ק ימלאו לי כ״ב שנה ובקשתי ברכה.

בלקחו את הפ״נ מידי הי׳ פניו רציניים מאד. ויקראהו בשים לב. הקריאה ארכה זמן רב בערך השורה היחידה אשר כתבתי.

ויגביה עיני קדשו ויבט עלי ויואיל לאמר:

״נו, זאלסט וואקסן א חסיד – ויפסיק רגע – א ירא שמים און א למדן.

"דעם רבי'נס ברכות זאלען מקוים ווערן, און א טייל פון דעם רבי'נס ענינים וואס דער רבי האט געוואלט דורך פירן זאל ער דורכפירן דורך דיר.

"במשך פון דעם יאהר זאל מען דיר מציע זיין א גוטע הצעה וועגן א שידוך און זאלסט זיך מסתדר זיין (ווי עס דארף זיין).

"דעם טאג וועסטו מסתמא אוסניצן אויף לערנען דעם רבי'נס מאמר פון ג' סליחות.

"מסתמא וועסטו מארגן פארן אויפן ציון".

את המוסגר אינני זוכר ברור.

אמרתי שאם צריכים לנסוע אסע.

ויאמר כ"ק אדמו"ר שליט"א:

זאלסט פארן און זאלסט דערציילן דעם רבי'ן אלץ אזוי ווי דא.

שאלתי האם לכתוב פ"נ ויענני בוודאי. גם שאלתי האם להניח את הפ"נ על הציון ויענני בחיוב.

גם אמר:

כשתהי' על הציון תספר לכ"ק אדמו"ר כי סדרת חלק מהמאמר דר"ה. דו האסט געזעצט א טייל פון דעם ראש השנה'דיקן מאמר אויך? זאלסט דאס דערציילן דעם רבי'ן.

כאשר אמר שאלמוד המאמר דג' דסליחות הרגשתי כי התיישב בדעתו הק' אם לצוות עלי ללמוד את המאמר דר"ה או המאמר דג' סליחות. ויאמר: דעם מאמר פון ג' סליחות, בהדגשה.

ו עש"ק ד תשרי תשי"א ברוקלין (המשך להנ"ל)

למחרת אחר חצות היום נסעתי על האוהל וקיימתי ככל האמור.

אחר קבלת שבת ותפלת ערבית

– מתפללים בחדרו של כ"ק אדמו"ר הכ"מ. מקומו של כ"ק אדמו"ר שליט"א על יד השולחן בצד דרום, ולתפלת ש"ע בקרן דרומית מזרחית ליד הדלת. העובר לפני התיבה עומד ליד השולחן הקטן מקום שם הי' יושב כ"ק אדמו"ר הכ"מ כשהי' עובר לפני התיבה.

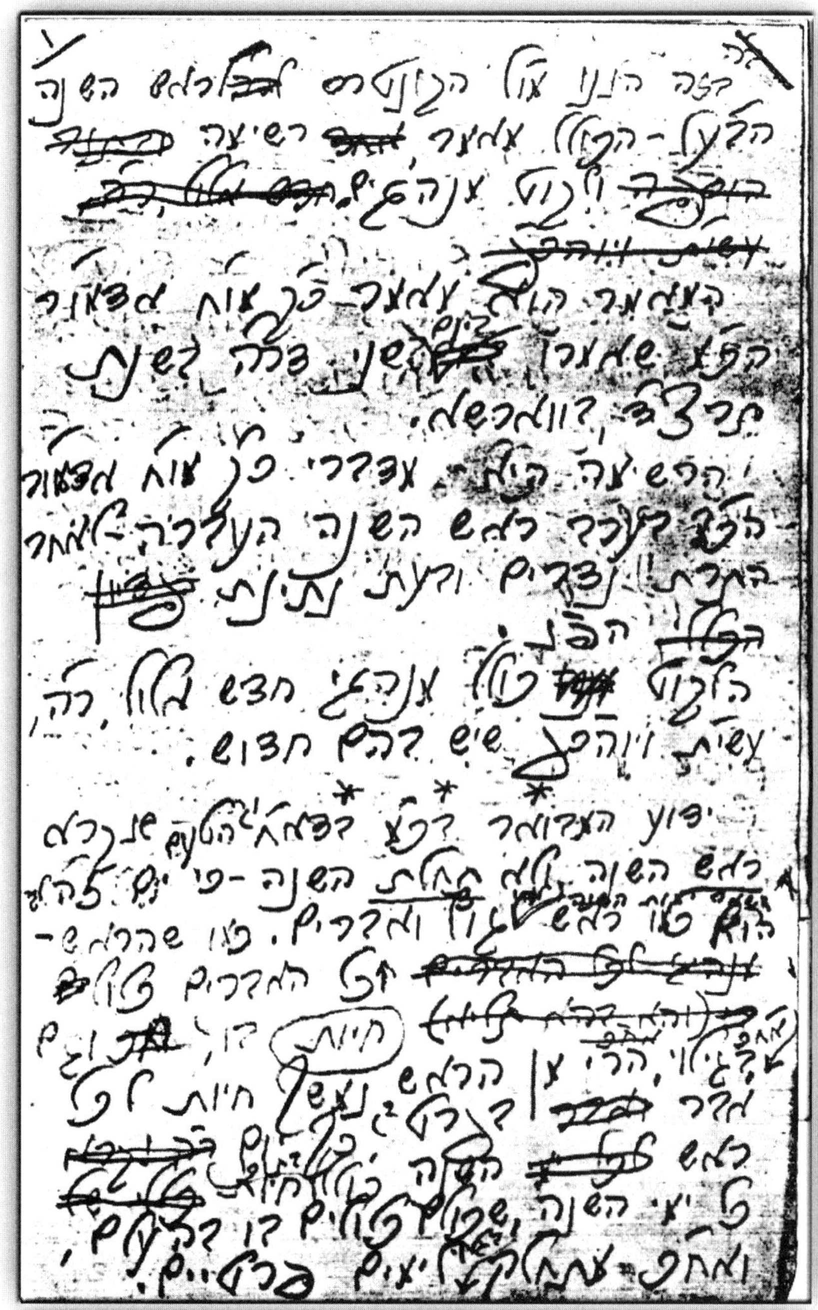

פתח דבר לקונטרס ראש השנה תשי"א, שעליו צוה רבינו לר' הירש להזכירו על הציון
("כשתהי' על הציון תספר לכ"ק אדמו"ר כי סדרת חלק מהמאמר דר"ה")

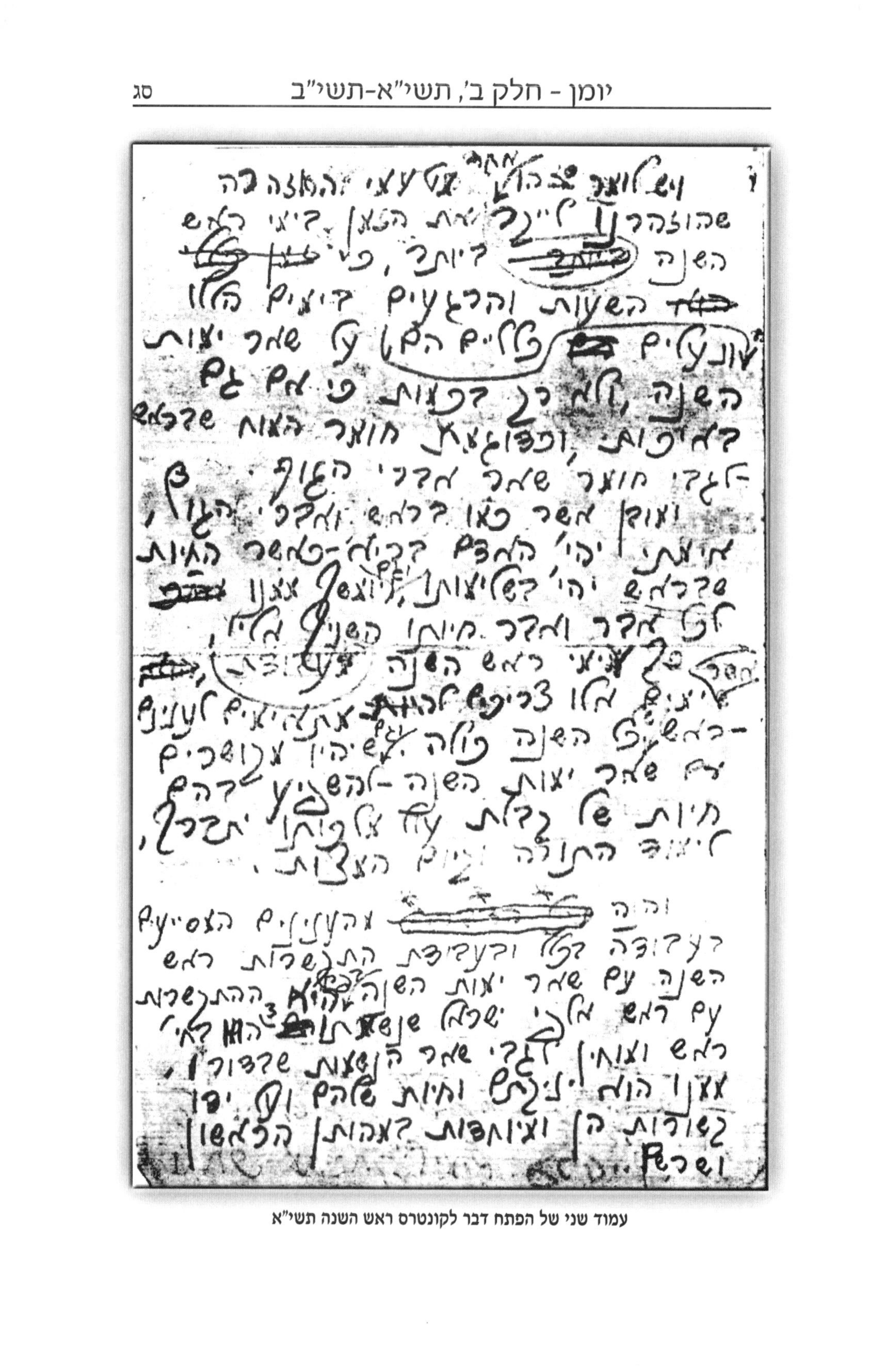

עמוד שני של הפתח דבר לקונטרס ראש השנה תשי"א

3 ויבאו כו' בלב אחד ואחת עצתנו

ע"י ההתקשרות עם נשיא

וראש דורנו, הוא כ"ק מו"ח אדמו"ר

הכ"מ - ובדרך דיבר אשר ההתקשרות

היא ע"י לימוד תורתו והליכה בדרך

הישרה אשר הורנו מדרכיו ונלכה

באורחותיו - היא היא אשר תסייע

בעבודת ימי ראש השנה[4]

והתקשרותם עם שאר ימות השנה,

ותהי' הבעל"ט בכל דו"ו ואשפו הכתיבה וחתימה

טובה, בטוב הנראה והנגלה,

ברוחניות וגשמיות - ~~ולהאשיפו~~

בכל השנה כולה.

דימי ראש השנה ומוסף

יום ראשון דסליחות
השי"ת, ברוקלין נ.י.

מנחם מענדל
בן חנה שניאורסאהן

1) ראה לקו"ת ר"פ תבוא. עטרת ראש בתחלתו.
אוה"ת ר"ה בשנת תש"א, תש"ד. ועוד.

2) עיין תניא פמ"ו.

3) תניא פל"ד. וראה אגה"ק דהקדמות קונטרס
י"ד תמוז (קונטרס פ').

עמוד שלישי של הפתח דבר לקונטרס ראש השנה תשי"א

על השולחן חמשה נרות דולקים. בג' מנורות, במנורה האמצעית ג' נרות, ובמנורות הצדדיים נר אחד.

אחרי אמירת גוט שבת לכ"ק אדמו"ר ואמירת גוט שבת בפה קדשו, הוציא כ"ק אדמו"ר שליט"א מסידורו

– סידור תורה אור הוצאת אגודת חסידי חב"ד בנויארק. – כפי אשר שמעתי הוא סידורו של כ"ק אדמו"ר הכ"מ – בהסידור מונחים כמה מאמרי דא"ח, מקונטרסים שיצאו לאור אחרי הסתלקות כ"ק אדמו"ר הכ"מ –

ומסר לידי מכתב כתוב במכונת כתיבה על טופס המרכז לעניני חינוך. ובו מברכני שאזכה להיות כלי ראוי' שיתמלאו ברכותיו של כ"ק אדמו"ר הכ"מ במילואן. ושבטח ראיתי הכתוב בהיום יום לי"א ניסן אודות יום הולדת, ומורה לעיין בקדושין ל"א דלחד מ"ד עד כ"ב. ומסיים בברכת כוח"ט ובכי"ק: ובהסתדרות טובה באופן המתאים לפניו בגו"ר. וחותם מ. שניאורסאן. התאריך הוא מיום ו עש"ק כ"ו אלול*.

בליל ער"ה בשעה האחת עשרה הייתי ב770 להודע האם יש לכ"ק אדמו"ר דבר מה למסור על ידי בהנוגע לקונטרס ש"ש מוצאי יו"כ, עמדתי במסדרון וכ"ק אדמו"ר שליט"א עבר על ידי: ויפן אלי בשאלה: האם ראיתי את לייבל גראנער? כי מסרתי לו דבר מה למסור על ידך. על שאלתי האם ישנם כבר ההגהה והערות על הקונטרס ענה: וואו? איך האב נאך אפילו ניט אנגעהויבן.

בשעה הששית בקר בעת אמירת הסליחות בביה"מ מסר לי התלמיד ליב גראנער את אשר נתן לו כ"ק אד"ש למסור לי עבור שותפי ר' מרדכי שוסטערמאן, והוא: ספר – השייך להר"ר אברהם יהושע העשל הרבי מקופישניץ – חותנו של ר' זלמן גורארי' – שמכורכים בו כמה ספרי מוסר וחסידות וביניהם צוואת הריב"ש, לסדר מזה את הפיסקא הראשונה מהצוואה. כן הי' על גליון בפ"ע הערות להפיסקא הראשונה. כן מסר לי קונטרס ההשתטחות מכ"ק אדמו"ר האמצעי לסדר מזה את הפיסקא הראשונה עד תיבת והב'. ולמסור ע"פ לשותפי כי יסדר הלאה מהספר אור תורה להה"מ ממעזריטש, ולתת א"ז חזרה לכ"ק אד"ש עד הדלקת הנרות.

בשעה השני' נסע כ"ק אד"ש להציון ואתו עמו נסעו גם חלק גדול מאנ"ש

*) נדפס באגרות קודש כרך ג' ע' תפג-תפד.

הרה"ח ר' שמואל זלמנוב

הרה"ח ר' יהודה לייב גרונר עומד ליד הרבי

והתמימים. נסענו בשני אוטובוסים, וכ"ק אד"ש נסע בהשני', וישב כדרכו על הספסל הראשון לצד ימין. על ידו ישב הר' חדוקוב, מנהל המל"ח, כדרכו בכל פעם שנוסעים על הציון.

קריאת הפדיונות ארכה כג' שעות ומחצה לערך ובבואנו חזרה כבר הי' עשרה רגעים על השעה השביעית.

הי' גשם שוטף ודולף. כ"ק אדמו"ר עמד על מקומו לרגלי כ"ק אדמו"ר הכ"מ. הת' משה קאזארנאווסקי אחז מטרי' על ראש כ"ק להגן מפני הגשם. עמד משמאל כ"ק אד"ש, כי כן צוהו.

לפני הנסיעה צוה להת' לייב גראנער לקחת אתו הרבה מעטפות ואחרי קריאת כל חלק קטן מהפדיונות פתח ל.ג. אחת המעטפות וכ"ק אד"ש שם בה הפדיונות.

כי דרכו של כ"ק אדמו"ר שליט"א לסדר הפדיונות לכמה חלקים – בכל חלק מעשרה עד חמישים פדיונות לערך, וכל חלק מחובר במהדק. וכמה חבילות קטנות יסדרם יחד וישימם במעטפה.

אמנם עד הנה הי' שם את החבילות חזרה לאותם המעטפות שמהם הוציאם, אמנם בערב ר"ה חדשה נהיתה כאמור.

בהזמן הראשון הי' שם את הפדיונות בקרקע הציון קדש, אבל זה הי' רק

פעמים אחדות.

אח״ז הי׳ שם את הפדיונות לכיס מעילו, ואחרי זה הי׳ שם במעטפה כנ״ל.

לפני הנסיעה מסרו לו כל הקהל הפדיונות עם כסף לפ״נ. גם אני מסרתי לו ד׳ פדיונות. א. עבור הורי ועבורי. ב. עבור אחי הבכור וזוגתו. ג. עבור אחי יצחק וזוגתו. ד. עבור דודתי לאה ובני׳. ולכל צעטיל שקל אחד לפ״נ.

בהכנסי לכ״ק אדמו״ר שליט״א ומסרתי לידו הפדיונות עם הכסף שאלני האם כתבתי את שם אבי ואת שמות כולם, ואמר אפשר - או מסתמא – האבען זיי אויך געשריבן.

מכתב

ב״ה אור ליום ו׳ עש״ק פ׳ במדבר ד׳ סיון תשי״א ברוקלין נ.י.

כבוד ידיד נפשי יקר וחביב, מקשישי התמימים משכיל על דבר טוב עושה ומעשה התמים ר׳ לייב שי׳ הורוויץ נ״י.

שלום וברכה!

בודאי קבל את המכתב ששלחו ידידינו תלמידי הישיבה אודות ה״חבר פעילי המחנה התורתי״ באר״י. וכעת הנני להשלים הדבר ולהסביר לידידי החביב את הדבר באשר הוא:

ליבער פריינד!

ווי באַוואוסט ווערן געבראַכט היינט צו טאָג קיין ישראל צעהנדליקער און הונדערטער טויזענטער אידן צווישן זיי פיעלע אידן פון די אַראַבישע לענדער: איראַק, מאַראָקאָ, אַלזשיר, א.ד.ג.

די געבראַכטע אידן ווערן אויסגעהאַלטן אויפ׳ן חשבון פון ישראל רעגירונג וועלכע באַזאָרגט זיי מיט אַלעם נויטיגן אין גשמיות.

אבל דא עקא, די אידישע פאַמיליעס זיינען קומענדיג אין ישראל אָרים מאַטעריעל און צובראָכן אין גייסט, דעריבער זיינען זיי איבערגעגעבן צום

חסד פון די מענשן וואָס באַהאַנדלען זיי.

די מענשן וואָס באַהאַנדלען די קומענדע אידן אין די קעמפּס – אָדער "מעברות" ווי מען רופט זיי אין ישראל – זיינען רובם ככולם פרייע מענשן, חברים פון "שומר הצעיר" און אַנדערע אַנטי-רעליגיעזע פּאַרטייען, וועלכע זוכן מיט ? זייערע כחות צו באַאיינפלוסן די נייע געקומענע, און ווירקן אויף זיי מיט אַלע מעגליכקייטן.

לויט די ידיעות וועלכע קומען אָן אַהער פון פּאַרלעסלעכע קוועלן, רייסן די אויבן דערמאָנטע עלעמענטן, אַוועק די קינדער פון די ניי-געקומענע, פון זייערע עלטערן און גיבן זיי אַן ערציהונג וועלכע געפעלט זיי.

די לאַגע איז פּשוט אַ **קריטישע**, הונדערטער און טויזענטער קינדער, ווערן מיט גוואַלד אַוועקגענומען פון עלטערן וועלכע זיינען ברובם ערליכע און פרומע אידן. און מען גיט זיי אַ חינוך וואָס איז ניט נאָר ניט קיין פרומער נאָר אַ חינוך פון **כפירה ממש ר"ל**.

שומו שמים!

ביז ווען וועלן מיר שווייגן און לאָזן אַוועקרייסן די קינדער פון אידישן פאָלק. לאָמיר ניט פאַרגעסן אַז אויב אין דעם מאָמענט וועלן מיר שווייגן און גאָר ניט טאָהן וועט ח"ו די שולד פאַלן אויף אונז.

אין ארץ ישראל האָבן זיך אָרגאַניזירט אַ געוויסע צאָל תלמידים פון **אַלע ישיבות**, וואָס האָבן אויף זיך גענומען די פליכט צו ראַטעווען די אויבן דערמאָנטע קינדער פון די מחריבי הדת, און אַריינברייינגען זיי אין פרומע אינסטיטוציעס און אויך גרינדן נייע חדרים און ישיבות פאַר די קינדער.

די אַרבעט זייערע, איז ניט נאָר וואָס איז פאַרבונדן מיט שוועריגקייטן, נאָר עס איז אויך פאַרבונדן **מיט סכנת נפשות ממש**.

אַריינגיין אין אַ מחנה וואָס איז אין די הענט פון מסיתים ומדיחים, און איינרעדן עלטערן אַז זיי זאָלן ניט מורא האָבן פאַר די פאַרוואַלטונג פון דער מחנה, און איבערגעבן די קינדער צו פרומע ערליכע הענד איז אַ זאַך וואָס שמעקט מיט געשלעג און נאָך ערגער, עס איז זאָגאָר געקומען צו רציחות.

אָבער ניט געקוקט אויף דערויף זיינען זיך די אויבן דערמאָנדע תלמידים **מוסר נפש**, און גיבן זיך איבער צו דער הייליגער אַרבעט, און מיט דעם אויבערשטנס הילף וועלן זיי געוויס מצליח זיין.

עס איז אָבער אַ זאַך וואָס איז פאַרבונדן מיט ריזיגע הוצאות.

– עס איז איבעריג צו זאָגן אַז זיי אַרבעטן ניט באַקומענדיג קיין געהאלט. –

איך וועל אייך שרייבן אַ פאַל פון וואָס איר וועט זעען אין וואָס די הוצאות באַשטייען:

היינטיגע וואָך האָבן מיר ערהאַלטן אַ בריף פון דעם סעקרעטאַר פון דער ליובאַוויטשער ישיבה אין לוד – דער סעקרעטאַר איז זיינער אַ חבר פון ישראל – וואָס ער שרייבט פאָלגענדעס:

אַ גרופע פון די אויבן-דערמאָנטע תלמידים האָבן אַרויסגעשלעפט פון אַ געוויסן אָרט אַ צאָל פון 60 תלמידים, מיט ספרד׳ישע קינדער וועלכע זיינען געוועזן גרייט צו גיין אין אַ ישיבה.

די קינדער זיינען געווען אינגאַנצן אָפּגעריסענע און באָרוועסע בפועל ממש. און די קינדער האָבן געזאָלט אַריינגענומען ווערן צו אונז אין ישיבה, **<u>אָבער צוליב דעם וואָס די ישיבה האָט ניט געהאַט די מעגליכקייטן צו אויסהאַלטן די קינדער זיינען די קינדער צוריק אַוועק פון וואַנען זיי זיינען געקומען.</u>**

עס איז שרעקליך און שוידערליך!

בפקודת כ״ק אדמו״ר שליט״א האָבן מיר די תלמידים פון דער ישיבה תומכי תמימים אין ברוקלין אָנגענומען אויף זיך צו שאַפן – לכה״פ אַ בעדייטענדן טייל – פון די געלט וואָס איז נויטיק אויף צו אַרויסרייסן און אויסהאַלטן די אויבן – דערמאָנטע קינדער.

טייערער פריינד!

איר קענט מיר גאַנץ גוט און איך גלויב אַז איר ווייסט אַז אומזיסט וואָלט איך צו אייך ניט געשריבן.

איך בעט אייך בכל לשון של בקשה אַז איר זאָלט מאַכן אַלע אָנשטריינגונגען און באַמיאונגען צו שאַפן די אויבנדערמאָנטע פאָנדן און אויסשטרעקן אַ האַנט צו דער הייליגער אַרבייט.

אויב עס איז נאָר מעגליך זאָלט איר זיך צונויפריידן מיט אונזערע פריינד אין באָסטאָן און אומגעגנד, און אויב מעגליך מאַכן **<u>אַן אַפּיל</u>** אויך ביי אונז אין שול.

לייענט איבער דעם בריף וואָס די תלמידים האָבן צו אייך געשיקט און די

ווערטער פון כ"ק אדמו"ר שליט"א זאָלן דינען ווי אַ וועג ווייזער צו אייך און אַלע וועלכע זיינען פאַראינטערעסירט אין קיום פון תורה-אידישקייט בכלל און אין ישראל בפרט.

האָט קיין פאַראיבל ניט וואָס איך באַלעסטיג אייך, אָבער **<u>ההכרח לא יגונה</u>**.

בברכת חג שמח וקבלת התורה בפנימיות.

אייער פריינד צבי הירש גנזברוג.

א, ט"ו אלול תשי"א, ברוקלין.

תמול ביום הש"ק אחר תפילת המנחה

– מתפללים בכל ש"ק בשעה 1:30 כפי רצון כ"ק אד"ש –

פנה כ"ק אד"ש להרה"ח התמים ר' זלמן שי' דוכמאַן (נכד החסיד ר' מרדכי יואל נ"ע מהאָמעל) שבא לא כבר מברית המועצות – ר' זלמן עבר לפני התיבה בתפילת שחרית וכן בתפילת מנחה כי בעל שמחה הוא כי חתונת בנו תתקיים היום בפאַריז – ויאמר: היינט איז דאָך אין די שבעת ימי המשתה פון דעם רבי'ן דעם שווערס חתונה. די חתונה איז געווען ביום י"ג אלול.

חתונת אדמו"ר נ"ע היתה גם ביום י"ב או ביום י"ג אלול.

אין די שבעת ימי המשתה האָט דער שווער געדאַרפט שטיין צום פריזיוו אין וויטעבסק הגם ער איז אַלט געווען נאָר 17 יאָהר. אַמאָל פלעגט מען שטיין צום פריזיוו פאַר דער צייט און בכדי אַז מען זאָל ניט דערקענען זיין עלטער האָבן חסידים געגעבן אַן עצה אַז מען זאָל אויסשמירן זיין פנים אין סאַזשע, און אַזוי איז ער געפאָרן קיין וויטעבסק.

על שאלת הר"ז דוכמאַן ענה: אימיצער פון די חסידים איז מיט איהם מיטגעפאָרן. אין דעם זעלבן טאָג איז ער מסתמא געקומען צוריק קיין ליובאַוויטש.

אַז דער רבי (מוהרש"ב) נ"ע האָט געדאַרפט שטיין צום פריזיוו האָט זיך דער גובערנאַטאָר איינגעשפאַרט. האָט צו איהם געשיקט כ"ק אדמו"ר

הרה״ח ר׳ זלמן דוכמאן

מוהר״ש, אַז ער גיט אים די ברירה: אויב ער וויל זאָל ער אים באַפרייען און פאַרשפּאָרן איהם די טרחה פון פאָרן קיין פּעטערבורג, און אויב ניט וועט ער דאַרפן פאָרן קיין פּעטערבורג אָבער אויספירן וועט ער אַלץ איינס, און איהם וועט עס ניט לוינען.

דער גובערנאַטאָר איז געווען אַ צורר היהודים און האָט זיך איינגעשפּאָרט אַז ער וועט איהם דוקא נעמען, און דער רבי מהר״ש איז געפאָרן קיין פּעטערבורג און האָט ער דורכגעפירט, עס האָט אים געקאָסט 10 טויזענד, ער האָט געקויפט אַ בילעט און מען האָט איהם באַפרייט.

אַז כ״ק אדמו״ר מהר״ש איז געקועמן צוריק קיין ליובאַוויטש איז דער גובערנאַטאָר געוואָרן געפערליך קראַנק, האָט ער געשיקט - ד.ה. די ווייב האָט געשיקט, אַז זי האָט חרטה און ער האָט חרטה.

דערויף האָט געענטפערט דער רבי מהר״ש אַז ער איז צו שפּעט, און אין דריי שעה אַרום איז ער געשטאָרבן.

ר׳ יוחנן גורדון הי׳ קצת בגילופין - כי ביום הש״ק הי׳ העלי׳ לתורה (אויפרופן) של התמים דובער זוסמאַן, והי׳ קידוש, און מען האָט גענומען צו ביסלאַך.

ופנה לכ״ק אד״ש, ויאמר: היות שהר״ז דוכמאַן האָט געמאַכט קידוש און איז בגילופין דערפאַר האָט ער געדאַווענט מנחה אַזוי פרייליך.

ויאמר כ״ק אד״ש, צו שחרית איז אויך געווען גאַנץ פרייליך . . .

פתח דבר לקונטרס שמע"צ ושמח"ת תשי"א

ומין.. צ"ע: דהא דמה אורח לדוגמא ע"ד-
בספר דשו"ע. אות [illegible]

ובאו"ש דצ"ח: להעיר [illegible] החוצה [illegible] ואילך..
[illegible] לא חשיב פסוק

ד"ה ע"פ כן: ואמרו [illegible] ואילך. ועוד.

ובמאמר מי: ראה [illegible]

[illegible]

וכתיב [illegible]: קהלת [illegible]

איתא דבהר: [illegible]

ופירוש [illegible]: ראה [illegible] שאול [illegible]

[illegible] ועוד.

[illegible]: [illegible]

דאיתא דבהר: [illegible] ועוד.

באו"ש דצ"ח: להעיר [illegible]. סידור [illegible]

ואיתא [illegible]

ובאו"ש [illegible]: להעיר [illegible] ד"ה
[illegible] ד"ה והדריה [illegible]
[illegible]. ועוד.

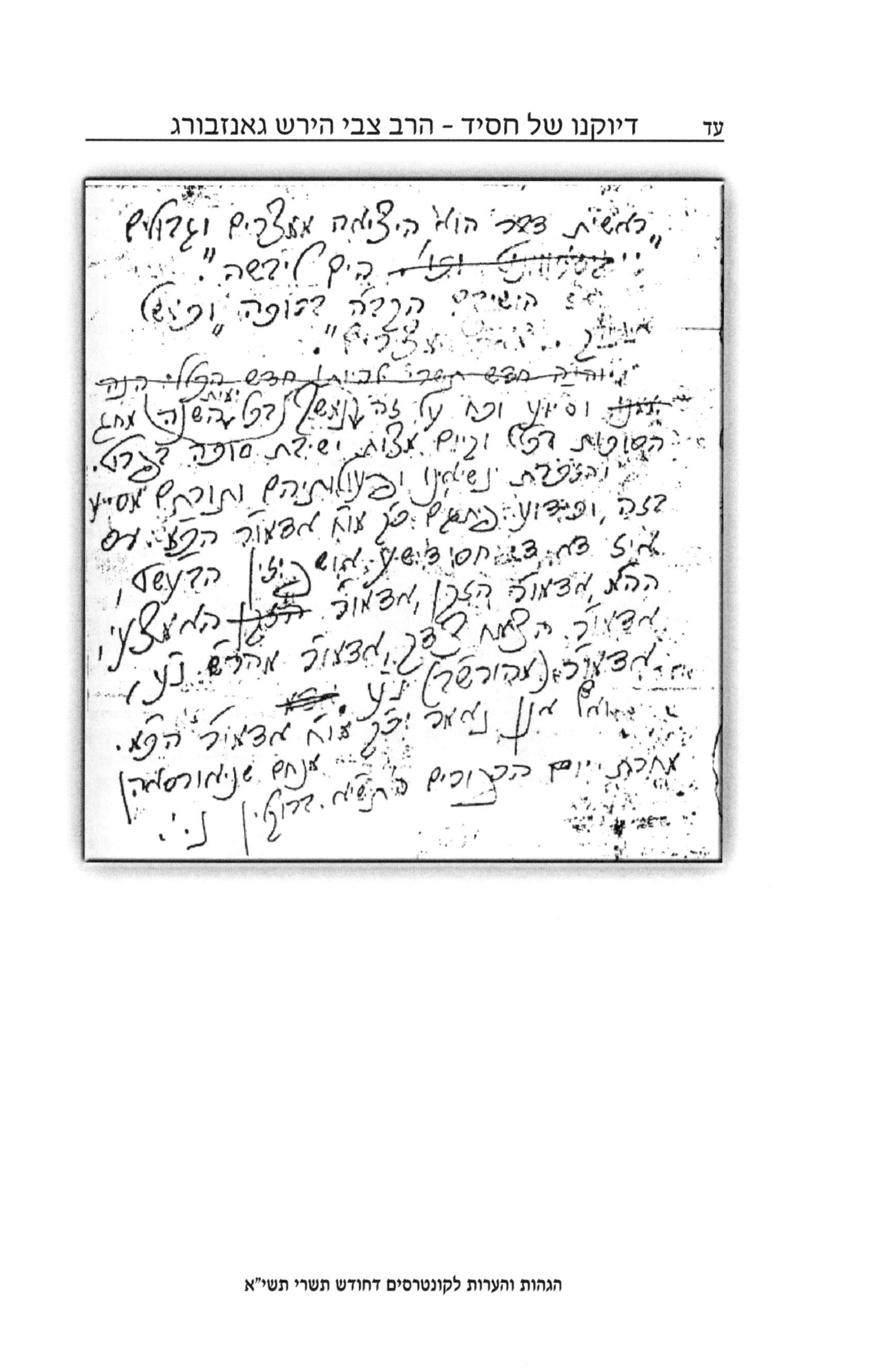

לקוטי מנהגים　　　　עמוד ג

ביום ראשון שלאחריו אומרים גם ה"הושענא" דיום השבת, אבל אין מקיפים אלא פעם אחת. (באמירת ההושענא דיום זה).

במוסף - אמירת ומנחתם ונסכיהם כו' אחרי קרבנות כל יום דיום.

בתיקון ליל הושענא רבה גם פרשת ברכה אומרים רק מקרא ופעם אחת. (אמירת שנים מקרא ואחד תרגום הוא בערב שמחת תורה).

אמירת תהלים בליל הושענא רבה - אחר חצות ובחגירת אבנט. ואין מאריכין באמירתו.

בהושענא רבה קודם הלל - מסירים שתי הכריכות אשר על הלולב ואין נשארים אלא ג' הכריכות המאגדים את הלולב הדסים וערבות.

ה ק פ ו ת: בליל שמיני עצרת ובליל שמחת תורה - שבע פעמים. ביום שמחת תורה - שלש פעמים וחצי. אבל גם אז אומרים כל סדר ההקפות.

בשמיני עצרת מקדשים ואוכלים ושותים בסוכה - הן בלילה והן ביום.

בשמיני עצרת ושמחת תורה - אין טובלים פרוסת המוציא בדבש.

המסורת שמיני עצרת - ויהי ככלות - ולישראל עמו.

בשמיני עצרת לעתות ערב נכנסים לסוכה (ואוכלים או שותים דבר מה) „צו געזעגנען זיך", אבל אין אומרים ה„יהי רצון".

אין קוראים בתורה בליל שמחת תורה.

נשיאת כפים בשמחת תורה - בתפלת שחרית.

אין נוהגין לפרוס טלית על ראשי העולים לחתן תורה או לחתן בראשית.

גם העולה לתורה אומר חזק חזק ונתחזק.

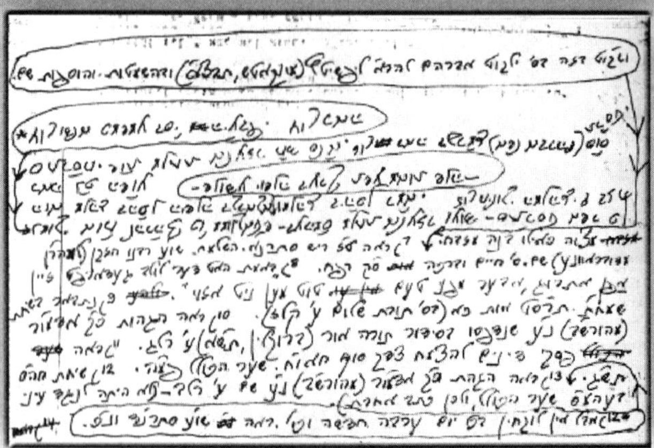

הגהות והערות לקונטרסים דחודש תשרי תשי"א

תשי"ב

ב"ה, ה' לסדר ועשו לי מקדש, ב' אדר תשב"י. ברוקלין.
דירת ר' משה דובינסקי שי' - 767 איסטערן פּאַרקוויי

ביום הש"ק העבר שבת מברכים אדר פ' משפטים יצא כ"ק אדמו"ר שליט"א מחדרו בשעה 12:35 ונכנס לבהמ"ד דרך הדלת האחורית (החדר שני) בכיוון מקומו בראש השלחן העומד בצד מערב, משוך לצד דרום (מקום שם יושב כ"ק אדמו"ר שליט"א להתועדות בכל שבת מברכים, בניגוד לשאר זמני התועדות שמסדרים עבורו בימה מיוחדת ועלי' מעמידים שלחן).

כאשר ראה שהעמידו עבורו כסא מיוחד (כסא רחב מרופד, בצבע תכלת), עשה תנועה בראש ק', כאילו אומר שהוא מתפלא על הדבר החדש, ובכל זאת ישב על מקומו.

כעבור כמה רגעים התחיל לומר את המאמר: לא תהי' משכלה ועקרה.

(כמו בכל פעם לפני אמירתו דא"ח הי' גם הפעם מרוגש ביותר ופניו לבנים).

(מיום היא"צ האחרון של כ"ק אדמו"ר נבג"מ זי"ע, חדשה נהיתה, אשר כ"ק אדמו"ר שליט"א אינו אומר לפני המאמר איזה מלים, כאשר הי' מנהגו בכל פעם באמרו דא"ח ברבים, מהפעם הראשון ביום יו"ד שבט בשנה העברה עד ש"ק מברכים שבט באמרו את המאמר וארא אל אברהם).

המאמר ארך כחמישים וחמש רגעים.

באמירתו בכה הרבה מאד, ובכמה מקומות לא התאפק ויבך בקול.

כאשר באר את הענין של: את מספר ימיך אמלא, אשר השי"ת נותן לכל אדם ימים קצובים אשר בהם ישלים עבודתו, כאמור: ימים יוצרו ולו אחד בהם, וכי הימים הם מדודים ביותר, ולא רק הימים אלא גם השעות והרגעים מצומצמים המה ומוכרחים להשלים העבודה של כל רגע ורגע במילואה, וכי דבר זה אינו נותן מנוח און מען איז פאַרדריקט, פאַרקוועטצט און פאַריאָגט, אַז מען זאָל לכל הפחות ווי עס איז קענען טאָן אין יעדער רגע וכו' וכו',

הנה באמרו את הדברים הנ"ל האָט מען געזעהען אַז ער לעבט יעצט דורך אָט די התבוננות, ובאמרו זאת בכה מקירות לבו ולא יכול להמשיך את דיבורו,

התוועדות בשנת תשי״ב. משמאל (מסומן בעיגול) נראה ר׳ צבי הירש גנזבורג

והניח את ראשו הקדוש על יד ימינו ויבך כמה רגעים.

בלתי אפשרי הוא לתאר את הדבר הזה בעט סופר. והנני מבקש מהשי״ת שהתמונה הזאת לא תסור מנגד עיני כל ימי חיי.

בגמרו את המאמר, אמרו הנוכחים לחיים לכ״ק אדמו״ר שליט״א, כנהוג, וכ״ק אד״ש ענה לכ״א בפרט לחיים ולברכה כדרכו.

הישיש ר׳ ישראל גאָטעסמאַן שי׳ הנק׳ ר׳ ישראל בעל שם באמרו לחיים, אמר לכ״ק אד״ש כמה מלים, וכ״ק אדמו״ר שליט״א ענהו: ״עס וועט זיין את מספר ימיך אמלא, מען דאַרף נאָר דעם ועבדת את ה׳ אלקיך״.

כ״ק אד״ש שאל על הת׳ שלום מרזב אם כבר התפלל וכאשר ענהו בשלילה שאל:

״קיין שחרית אויך ניט, נו, אויב אַזוי קען ער דאָך זאָגן לחיים״.

אח״כ היתה שיחה בענינים הנזכרים בהמאמר. השיחה ארכה זמן מועט, וגמרה בברכה: (המלים אינן מדויקות)

״אָט די וואָס זיינען נאָך ניט נפקד געוואָרן, זאָל זיי דער אויבערשטער העלפן אַז במשך פון דעם יאָהר זאָלן זיי נפקד ווערן בזרעא חייא וקיימא, די וואָס פעלט זיי אין בריאות זאָלן זיי האָבן בריאות הנכונה, און די וואָס פעלט זיי פרנסה זאָל דער אויבערשטער העלפן אַז זיי זאָלן האָבן פרנסה בהרחבה ווי דער אויבערשטער קען מידך המלאה הפתוחה והרחבה און מען זאָל זוכה זיין לביאת גו״צ למטה מעשרה טפחים במהרה בימינו אמן!

ג.

תשח"י

זכרונות מ"בית חיינו"
והפעילות במסגרת צא"ח

תשח"י

ב"ה. מוצש"ק תצוה, פ' זכור. ט' אדר תשח"י, ברוקלין,
בשעה השמינית בדירתנו 763 איסטערן פאַרקוויי, מס' E-21.

היום בוקר בשעה 8:50, בבואי לבית המדרש של כ"ק אדמו"ר שליט"א, תיכף בהכנסי ראיתי את ר' דוד ראַסקין נחפז אל התלמידים, וכעבור רגע, והנה כל התלמידים קמו בבהלה ממקומותיהם ובקול המולה מיהרו אל חדר המדרגות בו נמצאת הדלת לחדרו של כ"ק אדמו"ר שליט"א.

בלי לחשוב הרבה, פשטתי את מעילי העליון ואת הטלית ואדחק עצמי לדלתו של כ"ק אד"ש, כי סיפרו לי, אשר כ"ק אד"ש נכנס לפני רגעים מספר לבית המדרש וגם לחדר השני. אחרי זה קרא את ר"ד ראַסקין ואמר לו בלשון זו: "די וואָס ווילן הערן חסידות זאָלן אַריין אין צימער".

כעבור רגע או שני רגעים (לא יותר), נפתחה הדלת והעומדים צפופים על יד הדלת, כשלשה מנינים - ביניהם אך כחמשה אברכים - נכנסו אל החדר פנימה. ואני תפסתי את מקומי על יד החלון. המקום הראשון מצד זה אל השלחן. כמה מהתלמידים היו בהבנין בעת שקרא כ"ק אד"ש לאמירת דא"ח ולא הספיקו להגיע לדלת לפני שנסגרה. ושמעתי כי גרשון מענדל גאַרעליק האָט געוויינט מרוב עג"נ שלא זכה לשמוע את אמירת המאמר.

כ"ק אד"ש ישב על כסאו חבוש מגבעתו ופניו פונות ממולו נוטה מעט לשמאלו, באמצע אמירת המאמר פנה יותר לשמאלו לצד הקיר וממול פניו עומד כסא ריק, וכן הי' כל זמן האמירה. זייער אָנגעצויגן. עוד מעט ויפרוץ בבכי. ויאמר לסגור הדלת. כאשר שאל שוב אם הדלת סגורה והבטיחוהו ע"ז, התחיל לאמר את המאמר ד"ה זכור את אשר עשה לך עמלק, מחה תמחה את זכר עמלק. ותוכנו ביאור כפל המצוה דזכור ותמחה, וביאור ראשית גוים כו' ואחריתו, הפרש עמלק וז' עממין, כמבואר במאמר זכור תרס"ה וזכור תרפ"ז. אלא ששינה בסדר הענינים. בדברו בענין חומת בת ציון נשבר קולו כמבקש לבכות. גם בסיום המאמר ניגב את עיני קדשו.

– המאמר זכור תרס"ה ניתן אלינו לפני כשבועיים לסדרו מביכל סימפסאָן ואני סידרתיו כולו, וכפי שאמר לי ר"ל גראָנער הנה סופו הוא הנחה מאחד השומעים וביום החמישי בשבוע העברה ניתן גם סיומו העתקה מכתי"ק אדנ"ע, ומקוים כי המאמר יודפס לחג הפורים הבע"ל. –

המאמר ארך כחמישים רגעים. ובגמרו יצאו הנוכחים מחדרו של כ"ק אד"ש. ר' דוד ראַסקין ניגש אל כ"ק אד"ש ואמר לו, כי הצעירים מסדרים התועדות אחרי התפלה, כי היום הוא יום ט' אדר, יובל שנת ח"י מביאת כ"ק אדמו"ר (מוהריי"צ) לאמעריקא. כ"ק ענה: זייער אַ גלייכע זאך. ובהנוגע להשתתפותי – המאמר הוא ההשתתפות הטובה ביותר.

התל' אברהם יצחק שם-טוב חזר על המאמר, בעזרתו של יעקב יצחק קאַדאַנער, אפרים ראָזענבלום ועוד. גם אני עזרתי קצת כי ידעתי הענינים מסידור המאמר דתרס"ה.

ר' יואל שי' לא הי' בעת האמירה, ובבואו סיפר לי כי בבית למד את המאמר זכור-תרפ"ה בחשבו כי כ"ק שליט"א ידבר בעניניו (אחר התפלה – כמובן). ולא ידע רוב הקהל כי הסדר ישונה ליום זה והמאמר יאמר לפני התפלה. כמובן אשר אחרי החזרה יודע הוא את המאמר טוב ממני.

אחרי התפלה היתה התועדות. אברהם שם-טוב חזר שוב על המאמר. ודיבר ר' שמואל לויטין כמה דיבורים, ר' אלי' חיים רויטבלאַט האָט גענומען אַ קאַפעטשקע און האָט זיך צוזווערטעלט מיט ר' זלמן דוכמאַן וכו'...

הרה״ח ר׳ שמואל לויטין

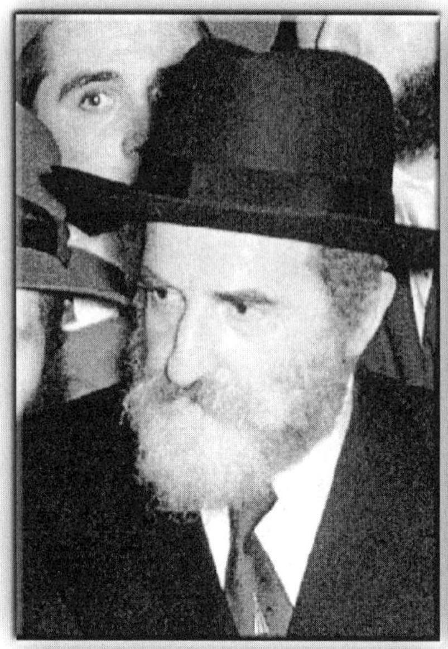
הרה״ח ר׳ אליהו סימפסון

במוצש״ק העבר היתה התועדות רבתי, מלוה מלכה ע״י צעירי אגו״ח, נוכחו כמאה איש וביניהם כשמונים אברכים. ההתועדות היתה בבית הכנסת הרב נאָוויק ברחוב טראָי. ר׳ דוד ראַסקין נתן סקירה כללית על הפעולות, הרב ר׳ שניאור גאַרעליק האורח קרא את המכתב של כ״ק אד״ש לסניפי צא״ח מיום ר״ח שבט (כפי שנודע נשלח בעיקר לריאו די זשאַנירו, בברזיל) ותוכנו ביאור הפסוק ויהי באחד עשר חדש באחד לחדש הואיל משה באר את התורה כו׳ . . .

הרב מרדכי מענטליק נאם נאום נלהב ותוכן דבורו: להיות מסור לפעולות כ״ק אדמו״ר שליט״א, והציע שכמה אברכים ימסרו א״ע אשר כל ענינם יהי׳ לבצע משימותיו של כ״ק אד״ש. ער האָט גערעדט ווי אַ חסיד, עד שגם ר׳ שי׳ המבקר הגדול נתרשם מדיבוריו. .

ביום הראשון היתה הצגת ילדות בית רבקה לטובת ישיבת אהלי תורה של ר״מ טייטעלבוים, הראו גם את סרט ל״ג בעומר משנה העברה.

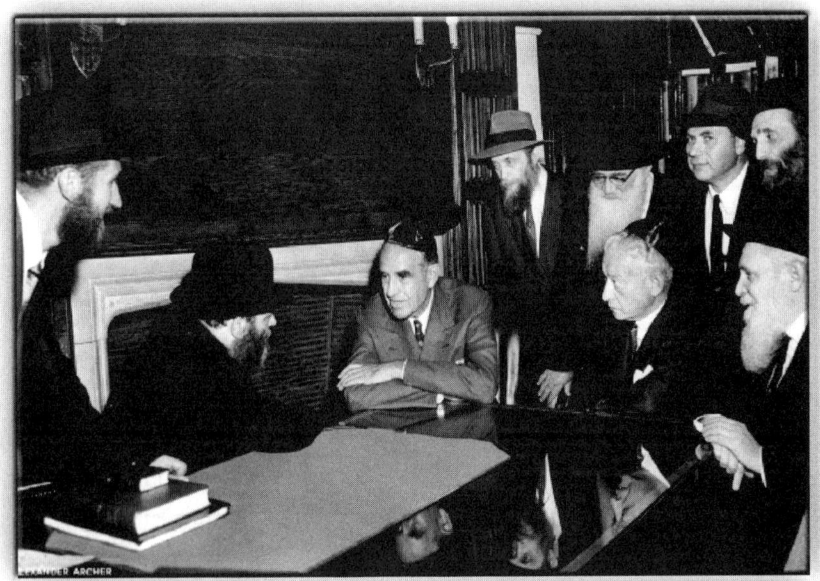

אנשי מימשל ביחידות אצל הרבי

מימין לשמאל: חדב"ן הרש"ג, הרה"ח ר' בנימין גורודצקי, הרה"ח ר' ניסן מינדל, הרה"ח ר' שלמה אהרן קזרנובסקי, הרה"ח ר' חיים מרדכי אייזיק חדקוב. בצד שמאל: הרה"ח ר' יעקב העכט

אני נאמתי בפני הנשים הנאספות. תוכן נאומי: סיפור ממאמר וקבל היהודים תרפ"ז, ושיחת כ"ק אד"ש בחג הפורים העבר בסיפור המדרש מכ"ב אלף ילדים שלימדם מרדכי.

ביום השני אסיפה בבית יואל שי' בסידור הנגינה לחג הפורים, כי הרב חודקוב עורר שוב בנחיצות הדבר, וצריכים לעשות דבר מה אודות זה, החלטנו כי יתנו לנו מקום מיוחד בעת ההתועדות, ונאסוף כחמש עשרה אנשים שינצחו על הנגינה. אולי יצא דבר מה מזה.

כן בחרנו ורשמנו סימנים לכ' ניגונים בערך, לנגנם.

ביום ג' שיעור לימוד מחברינו בביתנו, למדו שו"ע הל' פסח והמשך כימי צאתך תש"ח. בסוף הלימוד נשארו ר"מ גאָלדמאַן ויואל שי' ושוחחנו ארוכות על תפקידה ועתידה של צא"ח עד שעה מאוחרת ביותר.

ביום הרביעי ביקרני יואל שוב. ואני הנני עסוק בהגהת ספרו של הר"מ רי"י פיקאַרסקי על שו"ע אדה"ז הל' נדה. שוחחנו כמה שעות על דא ועל הא. עס איז מיט איהם גאַנץ אינטערעסאַנט צו פאַרברייינגען.

ביום החמישי אסיפת חזרה (רעפעטיציע) על הניגונים שננגן אי"ה בהתועדות חג הפורים. רוב האברכים שהבטיחו לא באו, והיו כמה אברכים וכמנין בחורים. וניגנו עד שעה חצי השתים עשרה בערך. יעזור השי"ת שיהי' טוב, כי אינני רואה עדיין שום תקוה לעתיד מזהיר בזה. נאָר אויב מען וועט טאָן וועט עפעס ווערן.

הילדים קצת חולים און מען לאָזט בייינאַכט ניט שלאָפן. יעזור השי"ת שיהיו בריאים ושלמים וגדלים כברכת ה'.

הנני מוכרח להפסיק כי עלי עוד לנאום לפני הנשים הערב בביתה של מרת פאָפאַק, ואחרי זה אסיפה של צא"ח בביתו של חיים אשר גאָרפינקל.

ב"ה, ב', י"א אדר, תשח"י. שעה 9:15 ערב

במוצש"ק נאמתי בפני נשי חב"ד, התוכן: סיפור כ"ק אדמו"ר ברשימת תרנ"ג שנדפסה בקונטרס י"ב תמוז תשי"א.

בשעה עשר ורבע בערך באתי לאסיפת צא"ח בביתו של ח.א. גארפינקל –כהנוב – הנוכחים: משה פסח גאָלדמאַן – המזכיר דצא"ח, ח.א. כהנוב, יודא קרינסקי ודובער אלעניק ואח"כ באו גם דוד ראַסקין ומשה קאַזאַרנאָווסקי.

דנינו בדבר ביקור אצל הרבנים דאיגוד הרבנים וכן אודות שיעורי הערב שנתיסדו באחרונה, אודות עניני הדפסה, שיחות כו'.

האסיפה נגמרה כשעה אחר חצות לילה ונקוה כי יהיו תוצאות טובות עקב אסיפה זו.

תמול ערב ואני עסוק בהגהת ספרו של הראש ישיבה, הרב פיקאַרסקי, ביקרני יואל שי', כי רצה לשאול אצלי ביכל תר"ס-ס"ה, וישב כמה שעות ושוחחנו בעניני לימוד כמו ספק ספיקא, מתהפך ואינו מתהפך, והזכירני תוכן דברי כ"ק אדמו"ר שליט"א ביום כ"ד טבת תשי"א בהתועדות סיום הש"ס, בסוף מס' נדה במחלוקת ב"ש וב"ה בדין שומרת יום כנגד יום, מחלוקתם בהדלקת נרות חנוכה ובדין כוורת דבש אם מחשבה מטמאתן או דוקא עשייתן, ז.א.: משיהרהר או משירסק. בלע"ה זכרונו טוב והבנתו עמוקה.

אחרי שעזב את מעוננו גמרתי את הגהת הספר הנ"ל בשמו, חקרי הלכות ח"ב, כפי שנדברנו ישלם לי 50 סענט עבור עמוד, והיו יותר על מאה עמודים.

אתמול נמסר המאמר זכור-תרס"ה מוגה למען לגמרו ולהדפיסו, והיום נגמרה הדפסתו.

כפי שאמר לי ליב גראָנער הי' בדעתו של כ"ק אד"ש להדפיס את, או רק להוציא חלק מן, סיום המאמר שנסדר בתחילה מההנחה שבביכל סימפסאָן, אמנם בסוף דבר נדפס המאמר בלי הסיום שבהנחה אלא כפי שנרשם ע"י אדנ"ע.

(הפסקתי את הכתיבה, כי בקרני שלום בער בוטמאַן הדר בביתנו בקומה הרביעית, ירדתי לדירתו והיו שם גם יואל ואייזיק שוויי וקראנו כמה ממכתביו של כ"ק אד"ש, כי יש לו אוצר גדול מהעתקות מכתבים. כן נדברתי אתו אשר מחר אי"ה בשעה חצי השמינית יבקר איתי את הרב שלמה גאָלדמאַן כפי המדובר באסיפה האחרונה, כי יודא קרינסקי כבר קבע את הראיון עם הרב גאָלדמאַן. צלצלתי אודות זה גם למ.פ. גאָלדמאַן ולא הי' בביתו כי הלך לחתונת יוסף וואַלדמאַן, וצלצלתי לדוד ראַסקין והוסכם אשר יודל קרינסקי יתן את החומר – קובץ ליובאַוויטש, בטאון, ותניא – לש.ב. בוטמאַן).

בבואי היום אחרי העבודה בשעה 7 – אשר כרגיל מתפלל כ"ק אד"ש תפילת ערבית עם המנין הקבוע של בני הישיבה בשעה 6:45 – הנה כ"ק אד"ש לא התפלל עדיין, כי קבל ליחידות את ר' בנימין גאָראָדעצקי שבא היום, והתפלל ערבית בשעה 7:30, אחרי גמר היחידות.

ג, י"ב אדר, שעה 12 לילה.

היום בשעה השמינית בערב בקרנו, אני ושד"ב בוטמאַן את הרב שלמה גאָלדמאַן ברחוב פעניסילוועניע. שוחחנו אתו כחצי שעה אודות פעולות צא"ח ועוררנוהו לסדר שיעורי ערב מתלמידי התלמוד תורה שעזבו לימודם, והבטיחנו לעשות בזה. סיפר לנו כי הי' כמה פעמים אצל כ"ק אדמו"ר (מהוריי"צ) וגם - יבלח"ט - אצל כ"ק אד"ש, כן היו לפני חתונתם הוא ורעיתו אצל כ"ק אדמו"ר לקבל ברכתו. השארנו אצלו קובץ ליובאַוויטש, בטאון חב"ד ותוכן השיחות ועוד כמה דברים.

היום למדנו אצל מ.פ. גאָלדמאַן, היו יותר ממנין מתאספים, וכמו בכל פעם למדנו עד שעה 10:30 ואח"כ נשארנו לשוחח קצת אודות פעולות צא"ח. דברנו בנחיצות הדבר לעורר - אויפלעבן - את המבצע "מבית לבית", אשר נעזב בזמן האחרון. ישנם הרבה נקודות במה להתעסק, אבל הדברים אשר עורר עליהם הרב חודקוב, ומסתמא הוא בהוראת כ"ק אד"ש, בהם צריך לעשות בתוקף יותר.

לייב מוצקין סיפר, כי אמר לו אחד מהמקורבים (לא אמר מי) שכ"ק אד"ש אמר לו כי הוא מודאג מזה שאין עוסקים כהלכה בעניניו, וכאשר שאל הלה: הרי כ"ק חותנו אדמו"ר הי' מעורר על כל הדברים בעצמו, אמר: איך האָב אַן אַנדער דרך, והוא רוצה שיהי' באופן מלמטה למעלה, אתערותא דלתתא.

קהת ווייס - חתנו של ר' משה דובינסקי - סיפר את אשר שמע, שלפני המשתה - דינער - שהי' עבור הישיבה תו"ת בחודש טבת או שבט, הי' הרש"ג שי' על יחידות אצל כ"ק אד"ש בעש"ק כעשרים רגעים לפני הדלקת הנרות, ואמר שיש לו דאגה, היות אשר הזמין את מר לעפקאָוויטש, התובע הכללי של ניו יורק, להדינער והלה הבטיח כי יהי' נוכח, ועכשיו אין לו מי שיוכל להתרועע אתו בעת הדינער, ז"א מישהו ממכיריו וואָס זאָל אים קענען אונטערהאַלטן. וישאלהו כ"ק אד"ש, מיהו אשר הי' בדעתו מתחילה לזה. ויאמר, או השופט קליינפעלד או מר יקותיאל קרעמער - אחד מהמתעסקים להביא את כ"ק אדמו"ר לאמריקה, והוא ואחיו מראשי הפעילים בהחזקת הישיבה מיום הוסדה - אולם מר קליינפעלד בטח לא יהי' וגם מר קרעמער נמצא כעת בפלאָרידאַ לבלות חופשתו. ויאמר לו כ"ק אד"ש שיצלצל למר קרעמער שיטוס לניו יאָרק להיות נוכח בהדינער. וכאשר ראה שאין הרש"ג שי' נכון לעשות דבר זה, כי כנראה שירא שלא ירגוז מר קרעמער עליו

שמבלבל מנוחתו, אמר כ"ק אד"ש: אויב איר ווילט קענט איר אים רופן אויף מיין חשבון. כל יום השבת לא הי' יכול הרש"ג להחליט אם בכלל לצלצל אליו, ובמוצש"ק החליט שיצלצל. אמנם לא יזכיר לו דבר מביאתו לניו יאָרק. וראה זה פלא, כאשר דיבר אתו על הטלפון אמר לו מר קרעמער בעצמו שהחליט לבוא להדינער וכבר יש לו הכרטיסים מוכנים לזה. וכן הי' שבא לניו יאָרק והי' נוכח על הדינער.

ד', תענית אסתר, שעה 12 לילה

היום באו מפיטסבורג כשתים עשרה תלמידים לחג הפורים, ומטעם צעירי חב"ד סידרום אצל אנ"ש. כן בא מר ליטוין מבאָסטאָן עם בני ביתו, והוזמן להיות אצלנו לסעודת פורים מחר אי"ה.

תפילת ערבית היום הי' בשעה 6:30, והקורא המגילה הי' ר' מרדכי שוסטערמאַן.

בודאי מתועדים באיזה מקום שהוא. נדמה לי אשר יואל מתועד עם התלמידים הספרדים מארגנטינה. כי טוענים הם שאין מבינים אידיש, ולכן צריכים הם להתועדות מיוחדת.

כנראה שנתקררתי קצת, גם הנני יגע מהתענית וקשה לי ללכת להתועדות.

מוצש"ק פ' תשא, שעה 12 לילה

ביום חג הפורים התפלל כ"ק אד"ש עם המנין וקראוהו לעלות לס"ת, קרה"ת ע"י דוד ראַסקין. קריאת המגילה בלילה וביום ע"י ר"מ שוסטערמאַן.

היום באו אצלינו משפחת ליטוין מבאָסטאָן ונמצאים עדיין אצלינו ויסעו מסתמא מחר בקר אי"ה. יש להם קירובים נעלים מכ"ק אד"ש, כי הם כעת יהודים שומרי תומ"צ, וגם עוסקים הרבה להחזקת הישיבה בבוסטון, ובאחרונה עזרו לקנין הבנין הגדול עבור הישיבה דשם. הבנין הי' מקודם בית תפלה לקונסרבטיבים. הוא בנין גדול מתאים לישיבה וגם לבית מדרש, וכ"ק נתן ברכות הרבה לזה.

ההתועדות דחג הפורים הותחלה בשעה 8:30 ונמשכה עד שעה 5:30 בקר. היו ענינים נפלאים מכ"ק שליט"א וגם הרבה גילויים.

תוכן השיחות אינני זוכר וגם מה שדיבר בקול נמוך ומה שדיבר לאנשים פרטיים הרבה לא שמעתי כי עמדתי קצת בריחוק מקום. משה לברטוב הבטיחני להלוות לי רשימותיו מהשיחות וקטעי שיחות ואעתיקם בל"נ אי"ה.

בתחילה הי' בשמחה רבה וציוה לנגן ניגונים שמחים, ואנחנו המנגנים אשר עמדנו מימינו אצל הבימה עשינו כמיטב יכולתנו. נדמה לנו כי הנגינה היתה קצת טובה מפעמים הקודמות, אם כי אין זה מספיק וחסר בזה הרבה, הרבה מאד.

אחרי כמה שיחות נשמע רעש באולם, כי היו הרבה מאוד נאספים בלי ע"ה, וקשה מאד להשתיקם וגם הרם-קול לא עבד כדבעי, וכנראה שגם דברים אלו פעלו עליו נמיכת הרוח - כמדומה לי, וכבר אמר כי כל הדברים הם הוראה כו', - וציוה לנגן את הניגון "היי צמאה" (וכמדומה לנו שמצוה לנגנו בעת שמשהו אינו כדבעי) גם התחיל בעצמו ניגון "דרכך" וגם כאשר התחלנו לנגן ניגון שמח לא הועיל.

אמנם כנראה שבאמצע פעל משהו שוב בטוב. וכאשר גמרנו לנגן ניגון ישן לבבי אמר בחיוך: דאָס איז דאָך אַן אסתר-תענית ניגון, איצטער זאָל מען זינגען אַ פורים'דיקן ניגון, וניגנו ניגון שמח בשמחה, והי' בשמחה רבה. וכאשר גמרנו לנגן התחיל בעצמו ניגון א' דשמח"ת בשמחה גדולה ובמחיאת כפים.

אמר המאמר חייב אינש לבסומי שארך יותר משעה. מאמר עמוק בביאור עץ חמישים אמה, עדן, נהר, גן, אאלפך חכמה כו', פנימיות הרצון, חיצוניות הרצון כו'.

באמצע ההתועדות קרא את התלמידים שבהם נתייסדה ישיבת תו"ת באמריקה לפני ח"י שנה ביום שושן פורים, וקראם בשמותם ביניהם היו: זאב שילדקרויט, אברהם באַרנעצקי, מענדל פעלדמאַן, מרדכי אַלטיין, יצחק קאַלאדני, יהושע גודמאַן ועוד, כמה מהם לא היו בעת ההתועדות, ואמר כי היום נתמלאו ח"י שנה ליסוד הישיבה באמריקה, ודיבר הרבה בשבח הישיבה. נתן להם משקה בעצמו בידיו הק', וצוה להם לנגן ניגון שמח ולרקוד, וגם רמז להרב מענטליק לרקוד עמהם וקפץ הר"מ לתוך המחול ובעצמו עמד מלוא קומתו לרקד במקומו. וכן רקד הר"י דזייקאָבסאָן והרב שניאור גאַרעליק. ורקדו משך זמן, ואז התחיל לדבר אודות השיחה כל היוצא למלחמת בית דוד.

דיבר הרבה אודות הישיבה ורמז לההנהלה וכנראה להרב סימפסאָן

ביחוד. ואולי יהיו לי לכה"פ קטעי הרשימות.

הרה"ח ר' מרדכי מענטליק עומד ליד הרבי

שתה הרבה משקה, ושפך מהבקבוק בענעדעקטין כוס מלא (פשוט א גלאָז) ושתה את כל הכוס בשתי פעמים עד גמירא, וביקש עוד משקה בענעדעקטין ולא הי', ובנימין לויטין נסע לביתו והביא את המשקה ולא נתנו הרש"ג שי' ליתן את המשקה לכ"ק שליט"א כי חס על בריאותו וכ"ק אד"ש אמר להרב מענטליק שישפוך בכוסו משקה ולא נתן לו הרש"ג וא' האברכים חטף את הבקבוק ונתנו להרב מענטליק אמנם הזקנים שי' עשו כמה תחבולות וסוף דבר הי' כי לא נתנו לכ"ק אד"ש את המשקה ואחד הזקנים שפך לכוסו ממי הגזוז שעמדו על השלחן וכ"ק שליט"א לא הי' נוח לו זה, והראה זאת בתנועה ושפך את הכוס על הארץ.

הר"ד ריבקין שם ידו תחת אגרופו של כ"ק אד"ש כשהכה על השלחן, ואמר כ"ק: מען וויל פאַרהיטן מיין געזונט, מען דאַרף פשוט טאָן אין תו"ת.

ליב מוצקין קרב להשלחן וביקש ברכה עבור בריאות אמו תחי' וכן פנה להרב חודקוב: אפשר וועט איר אויסרופן אַז די האָספּיטאָלס זיינען געשלאָסן וכן די עקאָנאָמישע זאַכן כו', וכעבור איזה זמן שפך לכוסו של ליב מוצקין ומלאו במשקה (אינני כותב בסדר קדימה ואיחור כי אינני זוכר הסדר).

הי' רעש גדול באולם והמסדרים לא יכלו לעשות סדר. ור"ז דוכמאַן רצה לעמוד ולהכריז שיהי' סדר ואמר כ"ק שליט"א: דאָס האָט מען געדאַרפט נעכטן באַוואָרענען, און איצט זעצט זיך אַוועק.

בקול נמוך נתן ברכה כללית על בני חיי ומזוני, והיתה ברכה ארוכה ופרט: בני, שיהיו בנים בריאים, אלו שאין להם בנים שיהיו להם בנים, ואלו שיש להם ילדות יהיו להם גם בנים זכרים. וכן בחיי, שיהי' בריאות בהפלגה וכן במזוני לא רק שתהי' פרנסה מצומצת אלא פרנסה בהרחבה. וכל הדברים היו באריכות רבה, וימלא השי"ת ברכותיו.

אמר לבאַרנעצקי שיתן בניו לתו״ת ודיבר הרבה אודות זה, ואמר גם שמענדל פעלדמאַן יתן בנו לתו״ת און הגם איך האָב אים מסכים געווען שיוציאו בכל זאת יתנו לתו״ת. ודיבר שיחה ארוכה לבנו של באַרנעצקי שירצה להכנס לישיבה.

כמה שיחות היו מיוסדות על מאמרו של כ״ק אדה״ז ליהודים היתה אורה ל׳ נקבה וכמה שיחות התחיל במאמר זה. גם צוה לנגן ניגון אני מאמין.

כאשר דיבר אודות תו״ת אמר שכל אחד ישתתף בהישיבה בגופו בנשמתו כו׳ ולא ישכח גם על ממונו. בסוף ההתועדות עשה המגבית דפורים לקופת רבנו. זה הי׳ בשעה החמישית בערך וצוה לנגן ניגון הבעש״ט. וצוה לנגן ניגון ד׳ בבות והבבא אחרונה רק פעם אחת.

כאשר יצא מהפאַרבריינגען כנראה שלא הרגיש בטוב . . והשי״ת יחזק בריאותו. כעבור כמה רגעים כבר האיר השחר.

ב״ה, ה׳ כ״א אדר, שעה חצי השתים עשרה לילה.

לצערי לא יכולתי להאריך בכתיבה במוצש״ק העבר, כי באמצע הכתיבה נכנסו מר ומרת ליטוין והוצרכתי לדבר עמהם. בשעה השמינית היו ביחידות אצל כ״ק אד״ש, ושהו כשלשת רבעי שעה.

בעת ההתועדות דפורים קרב מר ליטוין לכ״ק אד״ש עם בתו הקטנה שמלאו לה 4 שנים לאוי״ט, וביקש ברכה, כ״ק אד״ש נתן לה חתיכת מזונות וצוה לה לברך, וברכה וכ״ק ענה אמן.

ביום הש״ק היתה התועדות בחצר בית המדרש, וכ״ק נכנס בשעה 1:30 וישב קרוב לשתי שעות. היו כמה שיחות, וצוה לנגן ניגון אני מאמין, וסיפר אודות החסיד ר״פ רייזעס, שנקרא ע״ש חותנתו ששמה הי׳ רייזע, ולא ע״ש אביו הגאון משקלאָוו:

חמותו של החסיד ר״פ רייזעס היתה אשה עשירה בשקלאָוו, והיו לה ג׳ חתנים, וכאשר הי׳ כ״ק אדמו״ר הזקן בשקלאָוו פעל עליה רושם אדיר, באמרה שבא מגיד אחד מסביבות וויטעבסק, שלא שמעו ממנו קודם, ועל כל אשר שאלו ממנו גאוני שקלאָוו ענה בטוב טעם ועל שאלותיו לא ענו רק אחת משלשה, ואמרה אשר מי מחתני׳ שיסע לכ״ק אדה״ז לליאָזנא ויהי׳ שם משך זמן תתן לו את כל הונה.

ר"פ רייזעס נסע לליאזנא ושהה שם כג' חדשים, ובחזרתו הביא אתו מכתב לאשר כי הי' בליאזנא, ואז נתנה לו את כל הונה שעלה לסכום רב. ר' פנחס חזר לליאזנא ומסר את כל הכסף לכ"ק אדה"ז, ואז ברכו אדה"ז עס זאָל ביי אים זיין תורה וגדולה, וביקש גם עוד דבר (הכוונה כנראה לבנים) ולא ענה כ"ק אדה"ז.

מחוזרי המאמרים אצל אדה"ז הי' אדמו"ר האמצעי, אחיו ר"ח אברהם ור' משה, וכן דער פעטער ר' לייבעלע ועוד, והטוב שבין החוזרים הי' הר"פ כי הי' מדקדק להניח על הכתב כלשונו ממש, וכאשר כ"ק אדה"ז הי' מתגלגל על הארץ לרוב דבקותו, הי' ר"פ מרכין אזניו לשמוע המלים שיצאו מפה ק' ובאם לא שמע כמה מלים, הניח בהכתב כמה שורות חלק, לסימן כי חסר משהו. ולכן לפעמים בתו"א שבנוי הרבה על הנחות הר"פ חסר בכמה מקומות קישור הענינים, ורק שכ"ק אדהצ"צ קישר את הדברים ובכל זאת בכמה מקומות קשה הקישור.

כ"ק אד"ש הי' בשמחה בעת ההתועדות והסביר, שאם שהמצות הקשורים בפורים מצותן רק עד יום ט"ו אדר, כמו מקרא מגילה, משלוח מנות כו', אבל ענין השמחה שייך לכל החדש.

בש"ק אחר התפילה קרא כ"ק אד"ש (ע"י הרב חודקוב) את יואל שי' ואת הת' אברהם שם-טוב (הוא בעל כשרונות ואחד החוזרים), והיו כעשרים רגעים בחדרו.

כ"ק אד"ש שאלם אם יודעים הם את כל השיחות, כי כ"ק אד"ש בעצמו אינגו זוכר מה הי' בהתועדות פורים אחרי ב' השיחות הראשונות והמאמר שאחריהם. (כנראה שהי' ע"ד שכינה מדברת מתוך גרונו. ושמעתי כי כבר הי' לעולמים דומה לזה אצל הנשיאים הקודמים).

הם חזרו לפניו קצת מהשיחות וספרו לו סדר הענינים בההתועדות ועל כמה דברים תמה בעצמו, וכאשר סיפרו לו שניגנו ניגון אדה"ז והבבא הד' רק פעם אחת שאל: מדוע? ואמר א"ש: כי כן צוה אדמו"ר, ואמר: איך האָב אַזוי געהייסן, נו. (כלומר בניחותא). וביקשם למסור לו את הראשי פרקים מהשיחות, והיום מסרום לכ"ק אד"ש.

יואל צלצל אלי ויספר לי כי כ"ק אד"ש החזיר את הרשימות ובכמה מקומות

הרה״ח ר׳ אברהם שם-טוב

הרה״ח ר׳ יואל כהן

הגיה את השיחות ובמקומות שדיבר עם אנשים פרטיים מחק את הכתוב. ואין יואל שי׳ יודע אם הכוונה היא לפרסמם, ואמרתי לו שדעתי היא שדוד ראַסקין ישאל ע״י הרב חודקוב, אם לפרסם את הרשימות בהתוכן שי״ל אי״ה ע״י צא״ח.

ביום הראשון הייתי בבית המדרש בעת שחזר יואל את המאמר וכן ביום ב׳ בחזרו כמה מהשיחות, עד שעה מאוחרת. יואל אמר שיש במאמר חידוש בענין פנימיות וחיצוניות הרצון, ובו יובנו כמה מקומות בתרס״ו ועוד.

כן עזרתי ביום ב׳ לדוד ראַסקין לסדר את רשימת השיעורים שע״י צא״ח על מנת לפרסמם בעיתון ביום ועש״ק.

ביום ג׳ היתה חתונת הת׳ ברוך בריקמאַן עם בתו של הרב חייקין ממאָנטריאַל. כ״ק אד״ש הי׳ מסדר הקידושין, ובאנו מהחתונה בשעה הראשונה אחר חצות. אתמול הי׳ אצלי יואל שי׳, ועזרתי לו בהכנת תוכן השיחות דהתועדות פורים, והי׳ יותר מג׳ שעות. ונקוה כי יודפסו בימים הקרובים אחרי אישורו של כ״ק אדמו״ר שליט״א.

השבוע ביקרה אצלנו מרת פרוס, חמותו של שלום לברטוב (קאבילאַקער) ומרדכי דובינסקי, וסיפרה דבר נפלא מכ"ק אד"ש.

אחד הבע"ב בבית הכנסת בו משמש שלום לברטוב בתור שמש, יש לו בת, ילדה כבת י"א, ול"ע נשרו שערות ראשה, באופן מבהיל עד שהיתה מתבוששת לצאת החוצה. היו אתה אצל הרבה רופאים, וגם אצל גוטע אידן, אבל ללא הועיל. ויעצם שלום לברטוב שילכו לכ"ק אד"ש, ושמעו לעצתו.

כ"ק אד"ש אמר להם, שבאם תקבל הילדה, אשר כשתגדל ותנשא לאיש תלבש פאה נכרית, יעזור השי"ת שיגדלו שערותי', וקבלה עלי' והבטיחה, וכעבור זמן קצת התחילו שערותי' לגדול, וכעת יש לה שערות גדולות ונאות.

ב"ה מוצש"ק פ' פרה, ויק"פ, כ"ג אדר.

(הוספות לפורים)

כפי שסיפר לי יעקב האָלצמאַן, קרא כ"ק אד"ש בעצמו את המגילה עבור הרבנית תחי', קרא במהירות גדולה.

בעת ההתועדות אמר לזלמן בליזובסקי ("המלאך", גיסו של הרמ"ז גרינגלאַז) (הלשון בערך): ער זאָל זיך אָננעמען אויף זיך מיר צו פאָלגן, אַפילו אויב עס וועט ביי אים אויסקומען אַז עס איז ניט ווי עס שטייט אין שולחן ערוך, ער קען זיך אויף מיר פאַרלאָזן, עס איז מתאים מיטן שו"ע. והיום בעת ההתועדות אמר: ער האָט שוין אָנגעהויבן צו פאָלגן, זאָל זיין אַ גוטע התחלה.

באשר ראה – היום – אַז דער עולם וואונדערט זיך אמר בשחוק: עס איז געווען אַן אַרמיאַנין אין ראָסטאָוו פלעגט ער זאָגן "מאָי טוואָיי פאנייאַיי".

גם קרא את שלום העכט, ואמר מען רופט אים סידני, זאָל אים די פרוי רופן שלום, וועט ביי זיי זיין שלום אין הויז און עס וועט זיין אַ בן זכר.

בסיום ההתועדות דש"ק העבר דבר אודות נחיצות הלימוד דא"ח קודם התפלה בש"ק, ואמר שיבואו לכה"פ 9 אַזייגער פאַרטאָג – בשחוק – ואמר הרש"ל מסתמא מיינט מען ניט די תלמידים, הכריז שוב, שאינו מדבר אודות התלמידים שיש להם סדרם הקבוע.

השבוע נפטר בנו של יהושע גודמאַן (גיסו של יודא קרינסקי) ילד בן 7, פתאום, זוהי טרגדי' איומה, כי לפני כשנה ומחצה נפטר אצלם ר"ל בן, ג"כ ילד בן 7 שנה פתאום. מחר מתכוננים כמה מחברנו לנסוע לניו הייוועו לנחמם, ינחמם השי"ת בתוך שאצו"י.

לייבל גרונער מספר, שהי' נראה מתשובתו של כ"ק אד"ש, כאשר הודיעוהו אודות מצבו של הילד, שמשהו אינו בסדר. וכן מספר שאצל הילד הקודם ר"ל, כאשר הודיע יהושע להרב חדקוב אודות מצב הילד ע"י הטלפון הי' כ"ק במשרדו של הרב חודקוב, והרב חודקוב מסר לכ"ק אד"ש אודות המצב ואמר, נו, וכאשר אמר יהושע להרב חודקוב בהטלפון שמבקש שיברכו ברפואה שלימה רפואה קרובה, אמר: אַז ער וועט זיצן אויף מיין אָרט וועט ער זאָגן וואָס צו זאָגן. והוא פלא.

היום היתה התועדות כב' שעות, היו ג' שיחות ומאמר ד"ה וידבר כו' זאת חוקת התורה. ניט געוועו, כנראה, שטאַרק אויפגעלייגט אבל דבר אודות שמחה דחודש אדר, וגם ציוה לנגן א פורים'דיקן ניגון. ולבסוף גם נראה הי' שפוזרו העננים ונראה שמחה בפניו.

תשובת כ"ק אד"ש כאשר נתנו לו את תוכן השיחות: איך האָב דאָך שוין געגעבן פאַר צעירי חב"ד (כוונתו לרשימת הראשי פרקים משיחת פורים ע"י יואל ואברהם שם טוב). וכאשר אמר לייבל גראָנער שאין אלו אלא ראשי פרקים. אמר, עס איז דאָך אויך דאָס זעלבע, ואמר להוסיף בהם את ב' השיחות הראשונות שלא היו בהר"פ.

אמנם יש בהם הרבה עיבוד כי לא נרשמו להפצה, והיום הי' אצלי יואל

ואברהם ועבדנו קצת ע״ז. אח״כ היתה חזרה בביה״מ ע״י יואל מהמאמר והשיחות. ואח״כ מלוה מלכה אצל ר׳ מרדכי גראָנער, לטובת מעמד. וכ״ק נתן לזה ב׳ מכתבים מכ״ק אדמו״ר (מהוריי״צ), אחד מהם לר׳ זלמן דוכמאַן אודות לימוד תניא, והב׳ למר יוסף פלאייער משיקאַגאָ משנת תש״ג, בו מתאונן שאין עוזרים לו בעבודתו, מכתב תוכני ומאד מעניין, ומסתמא יפורסם במשך הזמן.

מענדל בוימגאַרטן מספר: אחת מקרובותיו, אחר שנולד אצלם ולד הראשון, הרבה שנים לא היו אצלם ילדים, והלכו לכ״ק אד״ש ואמר שאם תשמור טהרת המשפחה יוָלד להם ילד, ובראשונה לא רצתה בשום אופן, ואחרי הפצרות הסכימה, ותיכף בפעם הראשונה נפקדה בע״ה.

אחד מדיטרויט לא היו לו בנים זמן רב, וציווה כ״ק אד״ש שיבדוק את תפיליו, ומצא פסול במלה ״בניכם״ שבפסוק למען ירבו ימיכם כו׳ וכאשר תקן התפילין נפקדה זוגתו בזרעא חייא וקיימא.

ב״ה ד, כ״ז אדר.

ביום הראשון נסעתי עם שלום בער גאָלדשמיד, לעת ערב, לניו הייווען לנחם את יהושע גודמאַן על פטירת ילדו. הדרך ארכה כשתי שעות ובאנו לשם לפני תפילת ערבית ושהינו שם כשעה, מצאנו שם את הורי׳, ר׳ שמעי׳ קרינסקי וזוגתו ובניהם, וועלוול, יוסף דובער, ושמואל פנחס, וכן הי׳ שם גיסו משה העכט (מנהל הישיבה דשם), זאב שילדקרויט והערשל פאָגעלמאַן.

סיפרנו כמה סיפורים מכ״ק אדמו״ר שליט״א, טוב הדבר שבאנו, כי עכ״פ הסיח דעתו לכמה רגעים מצערו הנורא.

יהושע סיפר, אשר בהיות כ״ק אדמו״ר בארה״ב בשנת תרפ״ט בא אליו איש אחד, אַן ערליכער, ואמר שבנו הוא אידיאָלאָג אצל הקומוניסטים (דומה להרבה צעירים יהודים בזמן ההוא), ועומד הוא להתחתן בקרוב ורצונו לקרבו ליהדות, ויאמר לו כ״ק אדמו״ר שידבר אתו אודות טהרת המשפחה, ויאמר לו, בהיות אשר אחת מטענותיהם היא שצריך לתת להנוער בחירה חפשית לבחור בדת, ובאם יולד ילד בלי טהרה אין בחירתו חפשית כ״כ. הלה מסר את הדברים לבנו והדברים נתקבלו אצלו וקיבל על עצמו להזהר בטהרת המשפחה.

חזרנו לניו יאָרק קרוב לשעה העשירית.

ביום ב' ביקרני יואל ועבדנו כמה שעות על ראשי הפרקים דשיחות פורים, כי הי' צורך לתווך את הר"פ עם התוכן שסודר בשבוע הקודם. היתה עבודה רבה ובעזבו את מעוננו שעה חצי הראשונה עוד לא גמרנו כמה שיחות. נחמן סודאק וב"ש כהן עוזרים עם ההעתקה.

אתמול ביום ג' למדו אצל יואל, למדו שו"ע ואח"כ חזר יואל על השיחות דש"ק. אחרי גמר הלימוד בשעה 10:30, נשארתי אצלו לעזור עם תוכן השיחות ועבדנו כשתי שעות.

תמול קבלנו מכתב מדודנו ר"נ שי' נעמאַנאָוו ותוכנו התעוררות לעבודה שבלב, ער איז פשוט אַ חסיד ווי עס איז געווען אַמאָל וכל הענינים נוגעים לו בנפשו, ניט גינאַרטערהייד.

בש"ק פ' תשא חזרתי בביה"כ של ר"מ טייטלבוים (ז.א. בבית כנסת זה הוא מכהן בתור שמש) את שיחת כ"ק אד"ש מפורים תשי"ז (תשט"ז?) ובש"ק העבר אחת השיחות של כ"ק אד"ש בשבת זו בענין ח"י ברכות התפלה כנגד ח"י פעמים כאשר צוה ה' את משה דמשכן שני, ובענין החיוב דקבלת המצוה דואהבת לרעך כמוך לפני התפילה.

היום גמרתי לסדר את המורה שיעור לתניא באידיש, שסודר ע"י ליב גראָנער לשנה פשוטה, ודומני כי כ"ק שליט"א יקחנו אתו מחר בביקורו על האהל.

בזמן האחרון נוסע כ"ק אד"ש על האהל במכוניתו והנהג הוא יהודה קרינסקי, מבלי שילוהו מישהו אחר כנהוג בזמן הקודם.

שכחתי להוסיף להתועדות דש"ק שאחר פורים:

אמר לאחד ממאָנטרעאָל שיאמר לחיים, און דער צלם אלקים זאָל זיין בגילוי (כוונתו להזקן).

בהתועדות ש"ק האחרון היתה שבע ברכות של ברוך בריקמאַן וציוה לנגן אַ

חתונה ניגון, וניגנו עוד ישמע (הירושלמי) כנהוג.

אמר שאלו הנוסעים לאה"ק יאמרו לחיים והזכיר את מינסקי וכמובן גם את הרב שניאור גאַרעליק. אח"כ אמר הרב ברוך נאה ג"כ לחיים ואמר שנוסע אי"ה בשבוע זה, ושאל כ"ק באיזה ספינה הוא נוסע ואמר, קווין עליזאַבעט, ונהנה כ"ק אד"ש, ואמר בקול רם שצריך להכריז אשר הנסיעה באניות היהודיות היא חילול שבת בפרהסיא.

הערב אסיפה כללית של נשי חב"ד למסור להן שיחת כ"ק אד"ש מפורים בהנוגע לנשים ביחוד.

ביום הראשון היו הקשורי תנאים של הת' יעקב ווינטער מפיטסבורג עם חסיא פולנער בשעטו"מ.

בש"ק זה, פ' פרה, בעת אמירת ההפטרה אמר: בהקדשי בכם לעיניכם וגם לעיניהם, כדעת המנחת שי.

ב"ה, א, ב' ניסן, יום הילולא של אדמנ"ע, שעה חצי השתים עשרה

כפי שסיפר לי דוד ראַסקין, הכינו הת' יחיו את תוכן השיחות במכונת כתיבה, ונשארו כמה עמודים חלק ושאלו אם להוסיף גם את מכתבו של כ"ק שליט"א לצא"ח מר"ח שבט ש.ז., ואמר כ"ק שליט"א שיתן מכתב מיוחד להדפיסו, ושוב (כעבור איזה זמן) כשבקשו ממנו את המכתב אמר שאחרי שיגיה את התוכן אז יתן גם את המכתב (מצד א' טוב הדבר מאד מאד שכ"ק שליט"א יגיה את התוכן, אמנם טוב הדבר שהדבר לא יִדָּחֶה עי"ז) נקוה כי בהקדם תודפס השיחה בצירוף המכתב.

יעקב ווינטער (החתן של חסיא פולנער) בהיותו על יחידות בשבוע זה שאל מכ"ק

הרה״ח ר׳ חייקל חאנין
עם חתנו הרה״ח ר׳ אייזיק שוויי

הרה״ח ר׳ דוד רסקין

אם תהי׳ התועדות בש״ק, ואמר כ״ק שליט״א שגם אצלו הדבר בספק עדיין.

העולם התכוננו כי תהי׳ התועדות בש״ק, וגם הכינו את הסוכה, כי ביום ה׳ ועש״ק ירד שלג רב, אמנם אחרי התפלה בשאול הרב חדקוב את כ״ק אד״ש ענה שלא יתועד.

בש״ק הי׳ האויפרופן של הת׳ אייזיק שוויי, המיועד להיות חתנו של ר׳ חייקל חאַנין מפאַריז שבא עם זוגתו במיוחד בשבוע העבר. היתה התועדות מאנ״ש, און דער עולם האָט אַ סאַך געטרונקען. אח״כ לקחתי את החתן למעוננו, ובאו כמה מהתמימים והתלמידים יחיו כארבעה מנינים כ״י בל״ע, שתו הרבה משקה, אָבער ס׳איז געווען תוהו׳דיק, ושברו כמה כלים כנהוג, ואח״כ הלכו לביתו של זעליג כצמאַן, חתנו הבכור של ר׳ חייקל הנ״ל, און אויך דאָרטן האָט מען געווילדעוועט.

במוצש״ק היתה ההתועדות החדשית של צא״ח בביתו של ר׳ יעקב ליפסקער, היו גם ר׳ זלמן דוכמאַן ורש״א קאַזאַרנאָווסקי וסיפרו הרבה סיפורים מעניינים:

ר׳ זלמן דוכמאַן מספר, ששמע בעצמו מכ״ק אדמו״ר (מהוריי״צ) באחת ההתועדויות שאמר: אַז עס טרעפט זיך עפעס זאָל מען זיך מצייר זיין דעם טאַטנס פנים, און ווער עס האָט אים ניט געקענט זאָל זיך מצייר זיין מיין פנים. איך בין שטאַרק פאַחאָזשע אויפן טאַטן. ואמר שוב: איך בין שטאַרק ענליך אויפן טאַטן.

הרב קאַזאַרנאָווסקי סיפר בארוכה אודות עמידתו להפריזיוו וכמה ענינים נפלאים אודות אדנ״ע אבל איני יודע את פרטי העיירות וכו׳, כן ספר בפרטיות אודות שידוכו עם זוגתו (היא בת הרה״ח ר׳ אשר שו״ב מניקאָלאַייעוו) אמנם פרט אחד הוא, שכאשר סיפר לכ״ק אדמו״ר (מהוריי״צ) אודות השידוך ואשר מבקש ההסכמה ראה (שנשתנו פניו?) און ער האָט זיך גערדרייט אויפן בענקל. וכאשר ראה זאת, מבלי לחכות למענה עזב את היכלו. וסיפר הדברים לאחד החסידים, והלה אמר לו, שכבר הי׳ מעשה דומה לזו, ואז ציוה כ״ק אדמו״ר לילך להאוהל (הדבר הי׳ בשנת תר״ף בראָסטאָוו). הרב קאַזאַרנאָווסקי הלך להאוהל וכתב בהפדיון שמבקש הסכמה על השידוך, ומבקש שהמענה יתן אדמו״ר ע״י בנו רבינו שליט״א. וכאשר נכנס שוב לכ״ק אדמו״ר, איז ער געווען זייער אויפגעלייגט, ונתן הסכמתו הק׳ והוסיף: דער טאַטע האָט פאַר דיר געלאָזן נדן. ונתן לו סכום של אלף רובל.

היו עוד הרבה סיפורים, אבל הרבה אינם מדוייקים וגם השעה מאוחרת והנני עיף ויגע מעבודת היום.

אצל מרדכי שי׳ דובינסקי נולדה בת למז״ט.

ב״ה, ב׳ ג ניסן.

כרגע סיימתי קריאת מכתבו של אחי יצחק שי׳ מיט גערעכטע טענות, ואקוה כי בקבלו שורות אלה, ששילוחם נדחה בכמה סיבות, יירגע. גם אראה לפעול על יואל שי׳.

תמול ערב ביקרה אצלנו לאה וישבה כחצי שעה. כן צלצל אלי יואל בערב והודיעני תוצאות האסיפה לטובת הישיבה שנקראה ע״י הרש״ג שי׳, היו רק אנשים ספורים, וזה מצער, כי הלא הישיבה היא צפור נפשנו וגם כ״ק אד״ש דבר אודותה בפורים. אני לא יכולתי להשתתף בה, כי נקראה לשעה 3 אחה״צ, בשעה שהנני עסוק בבית הדפוס.

כפי שאמר לי יואל הוחלט ליסד ועד מהתמימים לעניני הישיבה, וגם אני

נבחרתי לועד זה. אמנם איני יודע אם אוכל להשתתף כי זמני מוגבל מאד.

אבקשך יצחק להראות או לכה״פ לספר לחותנך שי׳ מהמסופר כאן אולי זה יביא לו עידוד.

קבלתי מכתב מחברי צבי צאלער מציריך, שויצרי׳, בו מודיעני כי שלח לאמנו תחי׳ 250 גלולות אליסאטין בדואר אויר ו-250 בדואר רגיל, ואקוה כי כבר קיבלתם. כן מודיע כי בקבלו את תוכן השיחות מיו״ד שבט חזרם בכמה התועדויות, וביחוד בעיר באַזעל בה יש לו חוג מסוים של צעירים שהשפיע עליהם מרוח החסידות, גם שלחו למען העתיקו לכמה ערים בשויצרי׳. הוא הנהו היחידי במדינה זו, המסור ונתון לכ״ק אד״ש, הנהו יר״ש גדול, תמים אמיתי ולמדן. בקי בשו״ע או״ח ויורה דעה. זה עתה גמרתי מכתב מיוחד אליו, להודות לו על שילוח הכדורים.

הננו מתכוננים ללכת לחתונתו של אייזיק, המחותן אומר שזוכר את אבא שי׳ עוד ממאָסקוואַ, וגם ראכם באה״ק בעת ביקורו. כ״ק אד״ש יהי׳ מסדר הקידושין בשטו״מ.

ביום ה׳ העבר נגמרה היחידות בשעה 6:30 בבקר, ביקרוהו ד״ר יעקב גריפל בראש משלחת לעניני אירופה ושהו כשעתיים ומחצה, כן ביקרוהו אנשים בנוגע להאסיפת מחאה הקשורה עם בריכת השחי׳, שנערכה אתמול, פרטים אינם ידועים לי עדיין.

ב״ה, ג, ד ניסן תשח״י, ברוקלין, שעה חצי השתים עשרה

תמול חתונת אייזיק שוויי, החופה בשעה העשירית בערך. כ״ק אד״ש מסדר הקידושין. בעת הנסיעה באוטובוס לאולם ״מילראז שאטא״ סיפר לי יואל (דברנו אודות ספרו של ר׳ חיים נאה) אשר בשנת האבילות ר״ל, כדרכו של כ״ק אד״ש בהתפללו בחדרו של כ״ק חותנו אדמו״ר הי׳ משוחח עם הנמצאים בחדר אחר התפלה. ופעם אחת שאלוהו בדבר השיעור של ט״ק, ואמר שישנו טלית קטן מכ״ק חותנו וצריך למודדו, כי שיעורו קטן מהשיעורים הגדולים (כמו של החת״ס ועוד) אמנם בדרך כלל יש לסמוך על שיעוריו של ר׳ חיים נאה, דער שוועור האט געהאַלטן פון זיין לערנען. ואמר יואל: עס איז דאָך עפעס דאָ דער שיעור פון עפעס איינעם דער חזון איש. ואמר כ״ק אד״ש בשחוק:

איינער דער חזון איש... זיי גיבן אים פדיונות און ער זאָגט "עפעס איינער". אח"כ אמר בביטול: דאָס איז גלאַט גאָרנישט, אַבי קריגן אויף חסידים.

ואני ספרתי כי העילוי ר' חיים צימערמאַן הראני לפני זמן קצר מכתבו של כ"ק אד"ש לר' חיים אורי ליפשיץ (מנהל איגוד הרבנים) שהדפיס מאמר ב"הכרם" אודות קו התאריך, ובו מבטל את ר' מנחם כשר (מחבר הספרים "תורה שלמה") וכותב עליו לשונות חריפים וע"ז כותב לו כ"ק אדמו"ר שליט"א שאין נאה לת"ח לכתוב ביטויים כאלה, כי מאחר שאצלם הוא נחשב לת"ח הרי זה ענין של בזיון ת"ח. ואם יאמרו שבזה רוצים להראות שאינו ת"ח, מדוע זה לקחו ענין שמבינים בו רק יחידי סגולה, הרי הי' להם להתריע על הנ"ל על מ"ש שצריך לשתות כוס חמישי שהוא ממש נגד הדין, והוא חושב שיודע יותר מהשו"ע והרמ"א וכל האחרונים.

בש"ק אמר את ההפטרה* בהוספת הפסוקים הראשונים: כל העם הארץ כו' ובסופה כה אמר . . . איש מאחוזתו, אשר רק הנשיאים אומרים אותם כידוע.

היום למדו אצל שלום בער בוטמאַן. דוד ראַסקין צלצל לשם אלי ואמר לי כי מחר תהי' אי"ה האסיפה של העוסקים בצא"ח. כן אמר שכ"ק אד"ש נתן כבר חלק מתוכן השיחות מוגה בהרבה הוספות, להעתיקו.

ליב גראָנער סיפר לי אתמול כי כ"ק אד"ש עוסק הרבה בהגהת התוכן, ואמר לו: אה, ווער האָט דאָס צוזאַמענגעשטעלט? ולא ענה ליב ע"ז, ואמר כ"ק: וואָס אַמאָל ווערט עס ערגער.

כי אני ויואל החלטנו שלא לשנות את הראשי פרקים שהוכנו על ידו וע"י אברהם שם טוב, כי כבר הוגהו ע"י כ"ק אד"ש (כמסופר לעיל), וכנראה שלא טוב עשינו, וכ"ק אד"ש מאד לא מרוצה מזה, וצריכים היינו לסדר הכל מחדש. וזו הוראה על להבא.

אודות אסיפת מחאה על בריכת השחי' בירושלים שמעתי כי כ"ק הורה

*) דפרשת החודש

שכמה תלמידים ישתתפו בה. את הפרטים עדיין לא אדע.

יודל קרינסקי סיפר לי, שכאשר היתה האסיפה וההפגנה לפני כמה שנים, בנוגע לגיוס בנות, באו שלשה אנשים, כנראה משלוחיו של הרב דסאַטמאַר, ואמרו להרב חדקוב שרוצים לדבר עם כ״ק אד״ש ולא הניחם להכנס (ביניהם הי׳ גם הרב דקראַסנע), וכאשר עמדו בתוקף ע״ז אמר להם: ואי׳ הייתם בעת החלטתכם ובעת התיישבתם בדבר סידור ההפגנה.

ביום הראשון היתה אסיפת המחנכים שע״י צא״ח, וגם הרב חודקוב הי׳ שם ונאם בפני הנאספים. אני לא נוכחתי בה.

היום ספר לי הרב שטערן, אב״ד דעברעצין (למדן מופלג) שכאשר עבר אחיו את אויסטראַליע, נהג בה ביום ש״ק וגם ביום הראשון בחומרת שבת קודש אלא שביום הראשון הניח תפילין אבל לא עשה שום עבודה. וביקר הוא אז אצל כ״ק אד״ש וסיפר לו אודות זה, ואמר אז כ״ק אד״ש שדעתו היא שאין מקור לחומרה זו, ואף שיכול להיות שעי״ז יהי׳ אצל הנוסע ממקום אחד הש״ק ביום הששי ואצל הנוסע ממקום אחר הש״ק ביום השמיני, ואף שהוא פלפל עמו הרבה בזה, אבל כ״ק אד״ש עמד על דעתו. ושהה אז אצל כ״ק שליט״א כשעה ורבע.

ה׳ ו ניסן, שעה עשירית ערב.

תמול ערב היתה אסיפת צא״ח ונוכחו בה: דוד ראַסקין, משה פסח גאָלדמאַן, מענדל בוימגאַרטן, חיים אשר גארפינקל, יואל כהן, יודל קרינסקי ואני. דנינו בדבר הכנת הנאומים לימות החג וכן שיבקרו את הרבנים בחול המועד, וגם לסדר התועדות עבור תלמידי ישיבות הלומדים דא״ח. אני וחיים אשר ממונים על ביקורי הרבנים.

היום נסעה מכונית עם חברים לדיטרויט, בה מכין בערל שם טוב התוועדות וכו׳. עלי עם יואל ועוד לנסוע במוצש״ק למאָנסי, כשעתיים מניו יורק.

צריך אני להפסיק כי הזמן קצר לחה״פ והמלאכה מרובה.

א, ט' ניסן, שעה 12 לילה.

בש"ק אמר כ"ק אד"ש הפטרת צו כמנהגנו בהשמטת הקטע מגזי נזרך, באמרו את המלים אבדה האמונה ונכרתה מפיהם, וכן כמה פסוקים לפני פסוק זה נשבר קולו ואמרם בקול נמוך, בקול בוכים.

בש"ק העבר סיפר לי מר ריינין שבהיותו אצל כ"ק אד"ש בפאַריז (כמדומה שזה הי' בשנת תרצ"ח), בהכנסו לחדרו הי' כ"ק אד"ש לומד באיזה ספר קטן. וביקש את מר ריינין לחכות עד גמרו הלימוד. ובגמרו הראהו שהי' ספרו של הרה"ק ר' אהרן מסטאַראַשעליע, וסיפר לו אז כ"ק אדמו"ר שליט"א כי כ"ק אדה"ז עמד פעם אצל החלון וראה את כ"ק אדהאמ"צ הולך עם חברו הרה"ק מסטאַראַשעליע ואמר: הנאהבים והנעימים בחייהם, הלואי – ובמותם לא נפרדו. (נוסח הידוע בינינו הוא שאמר: תרין רעין, הלוואי דלא מתפרשין, צ"ג).

כאשר גמר מר ריינין לספר לי ראיתי דמעות נושרות מעיניו. איש מוזר הוא מר ריינין, היו לו התקרבויות גדולות מכ"ק אדמו"ר וגם – להבדיל בין חלחה"ח – כ"ק אדמו"ר שליט"א מקרבו, ודבר טוב הוא אילו יכולתי לשמוע ממנו הרבה, כי בודאי הרבה יש לו לספר.

אתמול, במוצש"ק, נסענו למונסי. הנוסעים היו: מענדל בוימגאַרטן, יואל כהן, ישראל פרידמאַן, אלעזר (נכדו של הרב ר"ש גאַרעליק שבא ביום ה' מארה"ק), זלמן ליפסקר ואני.

ההתועדות היתה בביתו של ר' גרשון העלמאַן, היו רק אנשים אחדים (כי האנשים עסוקים לכבוד החג). יואל חזר כמה שיחות ואני סיפרתי כמה סיפורים.

מר העלמאַן הראה לנו ציור תמונתו של כ"ק אדמו"ר (מהוריי"צ) מעשה ידי הצייר התמים תנחום לוין. נזכרתי שכאשר גמר תנחום את התמונה הביאה לכ"ק אדמו"ר שליט"א, ואז קרא כ"ק שליט"א אותי ואת הת' אברהם ראָזענפעלד ועוד כמה תלמידים לחדרו, התמונה עמדה על שולחנו ושאלנו כ"ק אד"ש אם לדעתנו תמונה זו היא דומה לתואר פני קודש כ"ק חותנו

אדמו"ר. הדבר הי' בשנה הראשונה אחר ההסתלקות.

מר העלמאַן הוא מקושר לכ"ק אד"ש ולכל ש"ק מברכים הוא בא במיוחד לכאן להיות בההתועדות.

ה, יג ניסן. שעה שתים עשרה לילה.

במוצש"ק זכיתי לעמוד משמאלו של כ"ק אד"ש בעת קידוש הלבנה, ראיתי שבאמרו (כמדומה לי) כשם שאני רוקד כו' עשה באצבעותיו על שפמו (ז"א בגודל ובהסמוך לו). באמרו שלום עליכם פנה לר"ז דוכמאַן, ואח"כ אלי ואח"כ לשלום ישראל חודקוב (בנו של הרב חודקוב, לפני בר מצוה).

ביום ג' י"א ניסן יום הולדתו, לאוי"ט, נסע על האוהל אחרי הצהרים, ושהה שם כחמשה שעות.

אתמול בערב אור ליום י"ג ניסן, יאצ"ט כ"ק אדמו"ר הצ"צ, התועד ר' שמואל לויטין (כ"ק אד"ש לא נתן מעות על משקה כמנהגו בשנים הקודמות), וסיפר ר"ז דוכמאַן ששמע שפעם אחת הביא משרתו של כ"ק אדהצ"צ, ר' חיים בער, ככר לחם תיכף אחר הבדלה ביום אחרון ש"פ, ואמר שזה ממה שמכרו בחמץ, ואמר רח"ב: עס איז פשוט דער רבי איז אַ חלוש, אַ גאַנצן פסח גאָר ניט געגעסן, דאַרף ער עס האָבן.

יצחק גראָנער (אחי ליבל) סיפר שאמר פעם לכ"ק אד"ש (זה הי' לפני הסתלקות כ"ק חותנו אדמו"ר) ששמע אשר כ"ק אדמו"ר עושה הבדלה על בירה במוצאי חג הפסח, והבירה היא מכורה בחמץ, ואמר לו כ"ק אד"ש, שיודע הוא שהי' מבדיל על בירה, אבל כמדומה לו שהיו קונים את הבירה מנכרי, במוצאי החג.

יצחק גראָנער אמר, שאינו יודע איך משתמשים בחמץ תיכף אחר הפסח אחרי ששטר המכירה דעלמא אינו כפי המיוסד מאדמוה"ז בערב קבלן. ואמר ר"ש לויטין שלדעתו הדבר פשוט, אחרי שתיקונו של אדמוה"ז הוא רק על מכירות שיש בהם חשש דאורייתא שאין מועיל בזה הערמה, אבל חמץ לאחר הפסח הוא רק מדרבנן משום קנסא, וממילא מועיל גם שטר המכירה שנוהגים אחרים.

סיפר ר"ז דוכמאַן שפעם אחת בלענינגראַד הי' אצל כ"ק אדמו"ר (מהוריי"צ) יהודי ספרדי וקבל לפני כ"ק אדמו"ר שאין נותנים להם להתפלל (ז"א הבולשעוויקעס). וכ"ק אדמו"ר חזר כמה פעמים: אין נותנים לנו להתפלל, אנו מתפללים מתחת לארץ. וכעבור זמן אמר לו שילך לשמואל בצלאל אלטהויז ויתלמד אצלו ניגון (אחד הניגונים הידועים אצלנו) וינגן אצלם את הניגון וועט מען זיי לאָזן דאַוונען.

אור ליום י"א ניסן התועדו התלמידים אצל ברוך שלום שוויי, היו שם גם ר' חייקל חאַנין ור"מ טייטלבוים, גם אני ישבתי כמה שעות. יואל האָט גענומען אַ קאַפעטשקע, ואח"כ הלכו לבית המדרש והתועדו שם. בעת ההתועדות סיפר ר' מיכאל טייטעלבוים, שחותנו ר' לייזער טשיטשערסקער התאונן לפני כ"ק אדמו"ר שבעת תפלתו אם יכנס איש לבית הכנסת דאַוועגט זיך גישמאַקער ואמר לו כ"ק אדמו"ר: אַ נשמה איז אַ נר, נר אלקים נשמת אדם, אַז עס גייט אַריין נאָך אַ ליכט הויבט אָן די ליכט מער פלאַקערן. (הל' אינו מדויק).

שרהל'ה תחי' האָט געקראָגן מאגלען, אבל כנראה באופן קל והשי"ת ישלח דברו וירפאה, ביום י"א ניסן מסרתי אודותה ע"י ליב גראָנער לכ"ק אד"ש.

תמול ערב צלצל אלי ליב גראָנער ואמר שהגיע מברק אלי, אמרתי לו לפתחו, והנה הידיעה כי אצל ליבל שי' נולד בן למז"ט. אמרתי לו למסור זאת תיכף לכ"ק אדמו"ר שליט"א, אח"כ סיפר לי יודל קרינסקי שגם לכ"ק אד"ש הגיע מברק עם ידיעה זו.

מוצאי יום ב' דחה"פ, שעה אחת עשרה

ביום ו' ערב חה"פ בשעה חצי הי"א ביער כ"ק אדמו"ר את חמצו במרתף שב-770 בתנור האינסינירייטאָר (תנור מיוחד לשריפת אשפה), לפני השריפה נתן לליב גראָנער את כל העתונים שנתקבצו אצלו במשך השנה, וכאשר ירד להמרתף הביא אתו גם את הפדיונות מכל השנה ובעצמו השליך את הכל

להתנור ובמקל ערבב את החמץ והפדיונות שישלוט בהם האור ואז אמר את היהי רצון.

בשעה השלישית התפלל תפלת המנחה בצבור ואח״כ התחיל לחלק את המצות מצוה שנאפו לאחר חצות במאפית ר״י קאָרף. בהכנסי נתן עבורי ובקשתי עבור אבינו שי׳ ועבור האחים ודודנו שבא״י יחיו, ונתן לי כמה חתיכות עבורם ואמר: אַ כשרן און אַ פריילי‏כן פסח, ואח״כ ביקשתיו עבור גיסי יחי׳, ונתן לי ואמר שוב אַ כשר און אַ פריילי‏כן פסח.

ר״ז דוכמאַן סיפר לי מה שאמר לו ר״ש לויטין, שבהכנסו ביום י״ב לכ״ק אד״ש לקנות החמץ עם חתנו ר״ב גאָראָדעצקי שהי׳ הערב קבלן, אמר כ״ק אד״ש שכתוב בספרים אשר בשנה בה קוראים שמונה פעמים פ׳ שמיני תהי׳ שנה מבורכת, והוסיף כ״ק שליט״א, שתהי׳ שנה מבורכת וטובה.

הסדרים נערכו כמו בכל שנה בחדר האוכל של הרבנית תחי׳ וכ״ק אד״ש ישב על מקומו הקבוע לשמאלו של הכסא בו הי׳ יושב כ״ק חותנו, ולפני כסאו (של כ״ק חותנו) העמידו טס כסף עם מפית כפולה. לשמאלו של כ״ק אד״ש עמד כסא ועליו כרים אשר עליהם היסב כ״ק שליט״א. לשמאלו ישב הרש״ל ולידו ר״מ קונין ולידו התלמידים ליב ראַסקין, הערש ליב ביעגון (אגב איז ער געוואָרן אַ חתן לעצטע וואָך עם אחותו של משה הערסאָן. שניהם מבראַזיל), קלמן בריקמאַן ויעקב צבי האָלצמאַן, המשמש את כ״ק אדמו״ר שליט״א. מול כ״ק שליט״א יושב הרש״ג (גם לשמאלו הוכן כסא עם כרים, אבל לא היסב) לימינו יושב בנו רש״ב, לימינו ר׳ יעקב כץ (הממונה מאת כ״ק אדמו״ר מהוריי״צ לאמירת ההגדה). לימינו ר׳ הענדל ליבערמאַן ואח״כ יצחק חורגין.

בלילה הראשון באתי בעת אמירת ההלל ובשני לפני אכילת האפיקומן.

את ההלל עד גמר ההגדה אומר כ״ק אד״ש בקול רם קצת ובניגון דומה לאמירת הפסוקים שלפני התקיעות בר״ה, את המלים הוא אומר בדביקות רבה און מיט אַ שטאַרקע הטעמה אויף די נגינה. בכמה מקומות הי׳ נדמה, אַז אָט אָט ויפרוץ בבכי.

כפי הנדמה אמר במן המיצר: ה׳ לי <u>ו</u>לא אירא, בהוספת ואו. כן שמעתי שאמר יהללוך כו׳ <u>על</u> כל מעשיך, ובברכת ובכן ישתבח: ומעולם <u>ו</u>עד עולם.

בסדר הב׳ ראיתי באכלו את האפיקומן, ושמו לפיו חתיכות חתיכות (לא כולו ביחד, כפי שסיפרו לי), ושיעור האפיקומן הי׳ כחצי מצה (והוא פלא כי שיעורו של הרא״ח נאה הוא כזית – 1 אונץ, שהוא קצת יותר מחצי מצה,

והאפיקומן הוא שני זיתים. צ"ג). נחמן סודאַק אמר לי, כי גם את המרור לא שם כולו בפיו, אלא נשיכה נשיכה. לקח מעט חרוסת שמונח על השולחן ושם בקערת הכוס שלו, שהיו בה שיורי יין, ואח"כ הטביל המרור ביין וטפטף על החרוסת ואז הטביל את המרור בחרוסת. המרור הי' חריין מעוטף בסאַלאַט, ואחר כל נשיכה עטף את הפתוח בסאַלאַט.

את כוסו של אלי' מילא אחר ברכת המזון (בלילה הראשון איני יודע).

בעת אמירת ההגדה (בשתי הלילות) הרים עינו לר"י כץ והראה גם בידיו הק' שיאמר העכער. כן הי' איזה פעמים.

אחרי אמירת לשנה הבאה בירושלים שפך את כוסו של אלי' לבקבוקו שאחז בידיו יעקב האָלצמאַן (הנותן גם למילוי הכוסות את הבקבוק לידי ק' של כ"ק אד"ש השופך בעצמו להכוס). סדר השפיכה חזרה היא באופן נפלא ואין אתנו יודע את הסדר, הוא שופך מהבקבוק לכוסו, ומכוסו של אלי' לכוסו ומכוסו להבקבוק וחוזר חלילה כמה פעמים. גם שופך מהקערה להכוס, וקשה לדעת את המספר של השפיכות. ונחמן סודאק אומר כי בלילה הראשון הי' ז' שפיכות ובשני ט'. אבל אני מפקפק ע"ז.

בעת השפיכות מנגנים הנמצאים בחדר את הניגון א-לי אתה הידוע. כ"ק אד"ש בצאתו מראה שינגנו בשמחה יותר.

(היחידי הנוהג להסב בעת הסדר הוא רש"ב בהרש"ג, שיש לו גם כוס מיוחד אינו דומה להאחרים וגם יין מיוחד).

בלילה הראשון אחר הסדר ירד לחדרו וישב בו עד שעה השני' (הסדר נגמר בשעה 12 בערך), ובלילה השני (שנגמר בשעה 1 בערך) יצא מחדרו לבאר ההגדה בבית המדרש כדרכו בכל שנה.

התועדות זו ארכה משעה 1:15 עד שעה 4, וביאר את הפיסקאות: מגיד (ב' שיחות) הא לחמא, אמר ראב"ע הרי אני כו' (ב' שיחות), אחד חכם, ויאמר לאברהם כי גר כו', אילו קרע את הים, כמה מעלות טובות. כאן אמר את המאמר ד"ה כמה מעלות טובות, ואח"כ ביאר הפיסקא צפון.

בגמרו אחת השיחות בתחילת ההתועדות אמר לנגן ניגון שמח, וניגן ר' משה דובינסקי את הניגון והיא שעמדה, וכאשר גמרו ניגון זה אמר כ"ק שליט"א: אין תורה איז סדר אויך תורה. דער ניגון איז שייך צו שפעטער. אני ומענדל בוימגאַרטן התחלנו הניגון ממצרים גאלתנו. ואמר כ"ק שליט"א: דאָס איז נאָך שפעטער (כוונתו לנשמת).

בגמרו אחת השיחות אמר: עס איז דאָ דער וואָס דער שווער האָט אים אויסגעקליבן צו זאָגן די הגדה. עס שטייט אין סידור האריז"ל אַז די הגדה דאַרף מען זאָגן בשמחה ובקול רם. ער האָט געזאָגט ניט בשמחה און ניט בקול רם. (כוונתו לר' יעקב כץ). מסתמא איז ער דאָ, איז זאָל ער כאָטש יעצט זאָגן אַ פריילִיכן ניגון.

מר כץ לא הי' בעת ההתועדות ונראה הי' שכ"ק אדמו"ר שליט"א הצטער מזה. ויאמר: נו, איז זאָל דער עולם זאָגן אַ פריילִיכן ניגון.

כעבור איזה זמן חפשו שוב, ואז אמר: דער רבי נ"ע האָט אַמאָל פאַרבראַכט אין פיעטערבורג, – דאָס איז נאָך געווען ווען עס האָט זיך גערופן פיעטערבורג – און עס איז דאָרטן דאַן געווען אַ חסיד, אַ גביר, אַ איש מכובד (וכו'), ולא הי' בעת ההתועדות, ואמר אז כ"ק אדמו"ר נ"ע: מען דאַרף גיין און זאָגן אים אַז ער איז אַ . . און ברייִנגען צום פאַרברייִנגען. איז מען געגאַנגען און מען האָט אים געבראַכט.

כנראה שמישהו הלך להביא את ר"י כץ, וכשראהו כ"ק אד"ש שבא נהנה מזה.

כשהתחיל לבאר הפיסקא "אילו קרע לנו את הים" אמר: פאַר פסח האָט מען מיר געבראַכט אַ הגדה אויף וועלכע עס איז דאָ אַ הסכמה פון מיין פאָטער, וועל איך איבער זאָגן עפעס פון דאָרטן.

(מביא ההגדה הי' התלמיד שבתי האַלפערין, ומצאה בין השמות).

(אגב, סיפר לי משה גראָנער, -אחי ליבל הצעיר – שהרב ווייצמאַן ז"ל (שהי' רב בבראָרנזוויל בבית הכנסת בו אני חוזר דא"ח) הי' פעם אצל כ"ק אד"ש. ולפני הכנסו הראה למשה גראָנער גלוי' כתובה בכי"ק של אביו של כ"ק אדמו"ר שליט"א, שהביא במתנה לכ"ק אד"ש, אחרי כן סיפר שכאשר ראה כ"ק אד"ש גלוי' זו עמד מלוא קומתו).

ד, ג דחוהמ"פ, שעה תשיעית ערב

במוצאי יו"ט ראשון, ישבו תלמידי הישיבה בבית המדרש וגם אני ישבתי עמם עד שעה הרביעית בוקר. קראנו שיחה ושוחחנו קצת, אמנם בראותי אַז עס ווערט אַ ביסל ווילד, קמתי והלכתי. שתיתי הרבה יין, ולמחרת כמובן לא הרגשתי בטוב.

ספרתי את מה שסיפר לי הת' ישעי' טרייטל ממאָנטרעאַל, שבהיות אביו ר' מנשה פעם אצל כ"ק אד"ש, אמר לו שיחוסם משתלשל מהראי"ה מאפטא, ושאל אם כ"ק שליט"א שמע את שמעו. ואמר כ"ק אד"ש: ווער האָט עס ניט געהערט פון דעם גרויסן אוהב ישראל.

וסיפרו התלמידים, שפעם אמר כ"ק שליט"א (כמדומה שזה הי' בעת סעודה) בהנוגע להאפטער: בכלל בין איך אים ניט מחויב צו פאַרענטפערן, נאָר אין דעם איז ער גערעכט (דיברו אז בהנוגע לאיזה מנהג ומישהו הזכירו ושאל על הנהגתו, וע"ז הי' מענה כ"ק אד"ש).

י"מ גורארי' סיפר גם קצת אודות ביקורו של כ"ק אדמו"ר שליט"א אצל זקנו, הרבי מקופיטשניץ שליט"א כאשר בא לנחמו על פטירת אחותו הרבנית של ר' לייזערל מוויזניץ ז"ל. ועלי לשאול אותו שוב אודות הפרטים בזה.

ביום א דחוה"מ בערב קבץ הרב סימפסאָן את תלמידי הישיבה ומסר להם את תוכחתו של כ"ק אדמו"ר שליט"א אודות התועדות של תלמידי הישיבה לפני חה"פ שהי' זייער ווילד, ואמר שהיו צריכים אַריינרופן זיי ולהוכיח ע"ז.

אתמול אחר התפילה בבוקר קרב הרב יאָלעס מפילאַדעלפיא (כמנהגו בכל שנה) לכ"ק אד"ש (וכל הנמצאים בבית המדרש הצטופפו כמובן סביבם, ואני זכיתי לעמוד קרוב לכ"ק אד"ש) והזכירו אודות המאמר ד"ה בעצם היום הזה, שאמר כ"ק אדמו"ר (מהוריי"צ) בחוהמ"פ תש"א (לפני מנין מצומצם וכ"ק אדמו"ר בעצמו השלים המנין) ואמר הרב יאָלעס שבשנה זו מלאו טו"ב שנה לאמירת המאמר. ואמר לכ"ק אד"ש שמנהגו להביא בכל שנה מתנה לכ"ק אדמו"ר, ונתן לכ"ק אד"ש ה' שקלי כסף, ואמר שקבל אותם לפדיון בכור, שנולד בטהרה וכו' ואמר כ"ק אדמו"ר שליט"א (תוכן הדברים):

דער אויבערשטער זאָל העלפן עס זאָל זיין פדיון הבן. די גמרא זאָגט אין פסחים אַז אבי הבן מברך שתי ברכות. בכלל, פסח האָט אַ שייכות צו מילה. דאָס איז די איינציגע מצוה וואָס מילה מעכבת וגם מילת עבדיו מעכבת מלאכול בפסח (לבד מתרומה), און נאָך מילה דאַרף זיין פדיון הבן און אבי

הבן מברך שתים (ושאל הרב יאָלעס מהי הנפקותא אם אבי הבן מברך או לא מברך, ואמר כ״ק אדמו״ר שליט״א: דער חילוק איז, שהכהן אסור לנגוע בטומאה והאב מותר, כאמור כי אם לבנו גו׳. – וכפי הסברו של הרב יאָלעס היתה הכוונה בזה ע״ד השוכן אתם בתוך טומאותם).

זאָל דער אויבערשטער העלפן ס׳זאָל זיין פדיון הבן און אבי הבן מברך שתי ברכות, ברכת הפדיון וברכת שהחיינו. ובכדי לברך שהחיינו דאַרף זיין שמחה בגלוי, ויש דעות שמברכים שהחיינו רק על מצוה שיש בה הנאת הגוף, ומצוה שאין בה הנאת הגוף אין מברכים עלי׳ שהחיינו. עס זאָל זיין אַ גאולה שיש בה הנאת הגוף, אַז דער גוף זאָל אויסגעלייזט ווערן מהענינים המבלבלים אותו. דער אַלטער רבי פסק׳נט אין תניא, שהגאולה תלוי׳ בעבודתנו כל משך זמן הגלות, ומה שהקב״ה אומר לישראל לעשות טוט ער אַליין, איז במילא דאַרף שוין יעצט זיין די הכנה, אַ גילוי פון דער גאולה, עס זאָל זיין אַ גאולה שלימה, אַ אתחלתא דגאולה שלימה שוין, און דאַן אַ גאולה שלימה ואמיתית בקרוב ממש.

הרב יאָלעס אמר שרצונו להכנס כעת ליחידות והסכים כ״ק אד״ש. כעבור כמה רגעים נכנס ר׳ שלמה האָרנשטיין ליחידות ואחריו הרב יאָלעס.

תמול ערב הי׳ אצלי יואל לרשום תוכן השיחות מליל השני. וישב עד שעה 1 אחר חצות. זה עתה נכנס אלי שוב לגמור הרשימה, ועלי להפסיק את הכתיבה.

א, איסרו חג הפסח, שעה שתים עשרה לילה.

מה שסיפר לי הת׳ יצחק מאיר גורארי׳ אודות ביקורו של כ״ק אד״ש אצל הרבי מקופיטשניץ לנחמו על פטירת אחותו הרבנית דוויזניץ (לפני כמה שנים): דיברו אודות הרבי מוויזניץ, ואמר הקופיטשניצער שהוויזניצער הוסיף שמחה בא״י. ואח״כ דיבר אודות החזון איש, אבל הנוכחים לא שמעו מה ענה כ״ק אד״ש (ביניהם היו הרש״ל ור״ז גורארי׳). אמנם כשנכנסו להמכונית לחזור הביתה, העיר הרש״ל: איך זה שייך שהקופיטשניצער ידבר אודות החזון איש? ואמר ע״ז כ״ק אד״ש: אבל אני אמרתי לו: אָבער דער חזון איש האָט ניט מוסיף געווען קיין שמחה אין בני ברק.

כשנכנס כ"ק אדמו"ר שליט"א לחדר הספרים של הקופיטשניצער, ראה שו"ע של אדמו"ר הזקן ואמר: איצטער איז דאָך אַרויסגעגאַנגען די נייע שולחן ערוך'ס ושם יש גם צילום כתי"ק של אדמוה"ז ונראה שם שבכתבו, כתב ומחק כמה פעמים עד שכתבו כמו שהוא לפנינו.

סיפר לי שלום בער בוטמאַן, וכנראה שהדבר ידוע כאן בין התלמידים, שזמן קרוב לפני חג הפסח בהכנס הרב חודקוב לחדר כ"ק אד"ש, שאלו כ"ק אם ידוע לו (להרב חודקוב) משלומו של הרבי דוויזניץ, והלה לא ידע מה לענות. ואח"כ צלצל הרב חודקוב לר' אוריאל צימר, וגם הוא לא ידע דבר, ושאלו אצל כולם, ז"א, אצל חסידו וגם אצל הסקווערער והסטמאַרער, וגם הם לא ידעו מאומה. ואח"כ נודע שהי' חולה גדול ר"ל על קיבתו ואת הסדר של פסח סידר בעצמו כי הי' חלוש במאד. ולכן שאל כ"ק אדמו"ר שליט"א על שלומו.

ביום ד' ג' דחוה"מ נסעה חמותי תחי' למאָנטרעאַל על הימים האחרונים.

תמול קרוב לשעה הרביעית בוקר, בגמר ההתועדות דאחרון ש"פ, בבואי הביתה סיפרה ראשא תחי' שאחי' ליבע צלצל ממאָנטרעאַל והודיע שזו' ילדה בן למז"ט ביום הש"ק בבוקר. והודעתי זאת תיכף ע"י הרב חודקוב לכ"ק אד"ש.

גיסי יחי' ביקש מאד שאבוא להב"מ, אבל אינני בטוח שאסע, כי ביום ש"ק זה תהי' התועדות בקידושא רבא, כמנהגו של כ"ק אד"ש בשבתות שאחרי החגים פסח וסוכות, לקדש בעצמו, וההתועדות – לעילא ולעילא.

ביום שביעי ש"פ לעת ערב התקיימה התהלוכה של צא"ח לוויליאַמסבורג, כנהוג בכל שנה. בפעם הזאת הי' רב מספר המשתתפים על השנים הקודמות למרות הגשם והאויר הזועף. בבואנו לוויליאַמסבורג נתחלקנו לבתי הכנסיות שבשכונה לנאום בהם. נאמו בקרוב למאה בתי כנסיות כ"י, ובמקומות רבים נתקבלו החברים בחיבה. ואח"כ נתקבצנו כולנו בביתו של הרה"ח ר' אברהם זיסקינד (גיסו של הרה"ח ר' מרדכי מענטליק ורמ"פ כץ), ושם קידשנו, ויצאנו לרחובה של עיר בריקוד של שמחה.

המתפללים בבתי כנסיות שבסביבה שאך יצאו בגמרם את תפלתם נתאספו סביבותינו לחזות בהמראה, ובבואנו להככר הגדולה שממול בית הכנסת של הסאַטמערער (בשעה ההיא לא ידעתי עדיין ששם הוא בית תפלתו) ואחרי ריקוד בשירה אדירה, הגביהוני החבריא על כתפיהם ונאמתי בפני הקהל המצטופף. תוכן דיבורי: שיחת כ״ק אדמו״ר שליט״א במעלתו של משה רבינו ע״ה בלימוד זכות על בנ״י החוטאים בעגל אף שהי׳ חטא ע״ז במזיד, ומסר נפשו עליהם עד שאמר ואם אין מחני נא כו׳, וגמרתי שבהתמסרות למשה שבדורנו, כ״ק אד״ש, גם בכוחנו לזכות את בנ״י, להחזירם בתשובה ולקרב את הגאולה.

אם כי פה ושם נשמעו קריאות: דאָרטן גיסט זיך בלוט און זיי זיינען מלמד זכות וכדומה, אבל בדרך כלל הקשיבו המתאספים קשב רב.

בשירה ובריקודים חזרנו לבית המדרש של כ״ק אד״ש. והממונים מסרו דו״ח להרב חודקוב ע״מ למסור לכ״ק אד״ש, שבאותה שעה סעד סעודת החג בביתה של הרבנית שליט״א כנהוג.

ההתועדות דאחרון ש״פ, סעודת מלך המשיח, התקיימה בהחצר. התחילה קרוב להשקיעה, בשעת 6:30 בערך ונמשכה עד קרוב לשעה השלישית בוקר ובסיומה תפלת ערבית, וכ״ק שליט״א הבדיל בעצמו ואח״כ חלוקת כוס של ברכה.

היו הרבה שיחות, והשיחות ברובם אודות מלך המשיח. סיפר גם כמה סיפורים, וצוה לנגן את הניגונים של כל הנשיאים, גם את הניגון של הבעש״ט בן ג׳ תנועות שהם של הבעש״ט, הה״מ ואדמוה״ז.

המשתתפים בההתועדות היו רבים, ורבים באו גם ממקומות רחוקים ומערי השדה שבאו אחרי התפללם ערבית בבתיהם.

אחת השיחות היתה מיוחדת להתהלוכה בוויליאַמסבורג, ודיבר בענין והדריך בנעלים. וצוה את המשתתפים בתהלוכה לומר לחיים ולנגן ניגון שמח.

אמר להרש״ג שי׳ שיתן יין לארבע כוסות וצוה את הרב סימפסאָן להכריז אודות שתיית הד׳ כוסות, והוא הכריז אבל הכרזתו לא היתה כנראה די ברורה, וחזר הרב מענטליק על ההכרזה בפקודתו של כ״ק אד״ש, שכן צוה

כ"ק אדמו"ר נ"ע בליובאַוויטש להתלמידים של הישיבה. כ"ק אד"ש אמר, שיחזרו גם מה שאמר הוא שליט"א בשנים הקודמות ורמז ליואל, ויואל הכריז שכ"ק אד"ש אמר בשנים הקודמות שישתו לא רק התלמידים אלא שעל כולם לשתות הארבע כוסות. והי' נראה שכ"ק שליט"א נהנה מהכרזה זו. גם כ"ק אדמו"ר שליט"א בעצמו שתה כל הד' כוסות בהפסקים.

אחרי שתיית הכוס הראשון אמר: ס'איז דאָך שוין נאָכן ערשטן כוס קען מען שוין זינגען והיא שעמדה, ושרו את הניגון.

(רשימה זו היא שלא כסדר ההתועדות, כי עדיין לא שמעתי חזרה והנני רושם רק כפי זכרוני). הת' הספרדי אהרן טאַוויל מארגענטינאַ התחיל לנגן את הניגון "עזרני א-ל חי", ורמז כ"ק אד"ש להרב מענטליק שגם התלמיד יהושע חדד ממרוקו ינגן את הניגון. וניגן גם הוא, ובגמר הניגון צוה כ"ק אד"ש שינגן גם את הניגון "אין אדיר כבורא", יהושע חדד שר את החרוזים והקהל ענו אחריו את החרוז "מפי א-ל יבורך ישראל", ובגמר הניגון כפלו הרבה פעמים על חרוז זה, וכ"ק שליט"א הכה באגרופו על השולחן, וכפי מהירות ידיו מיהר הקהל את קצב הניגון. כ"ק שליט"א התחיל לספוק את ידיו במהירות גדולה והקהל בניגונו אחריו עד שכ"ק אד"ש עמד מלא קומתו ורקד על מקומו וכל הקהל אחריו בשמחה רבה.

כ"ק אדמו"ר שליט"א ראה שבא אברהם האָלדערמאַן מנואַרק (אברהם קאַליסקער, נקרא גם אברהם בעל עגלה, כי הי' נהגו של כ"ק אדמו"ר בהיותו בשנת תר"ץ בארה"ב ואודותו – סדרה מיוחדת) ורמז שישתה יין, הלה קרב בהולכו על השולחנות, וישב על השולחן סמוך לכ"ק אד"ש (מקומו של יצחק בהיותו כאן). אחרי שתותו את הכוס השלישי רצה לאכול מהמצה, ואמר כ"ק אד"ש: בין כוס השלישי והרביעי אסור לאכול, וצוהו לשתות עוד כוס, ובגמרו את הכוס הרביעי אמר כ"ק: שיתחיל את הכוסות מחדש, און פאַר קידוש טאָר מען ניט עסן.

לאיזה אנשים שבאו בלילה צוה שיטלו את ידיהם.

קרא לילד אחד תלמיד בהישיבה, קרובו של ישראל שמואל ענגל, יתום שבא מדיטרויט וחולה בידו וברגלו השמאלית, והוא קרוב להיות בר מצוה, וצוהו לגשת אליו, והי' קשה לו ללכת, ואמר שישראל שמואל יעזור לו, ובגשתו נתן לו ג' חתיכות מצה בג' פעמים ובכל פעם רמז שיקח בידו השמאלית דוקא.

אצל כמה מהמשתתפים שאל אם שתו כל הד' כוסות.

כנהוג בכל שנה חילק יין להנוסעים ולאלו הנמצאים בערי השדה. השנה היו בקבוקי יין קטנים חתומים מבית חרושת "קדם", ובכל זאת אמר בגמר החלוקה שהנוסעים למקומות רחוקים יבשלו היין שלא תשלוט בהם עין כו'.

קרוב לגמר ההתועדות מילא כוס מיינו המיוחד להרב גאָראָדעצקי ולהרב זיסקינד, ואח"כ הביט סביביו לראות למי יוכל למלאות את הכוס האחרון, ויעקב צבי האָלצמאַן שעמד לא רחוק מימינו רמז בידיו שיתן לו ואמר: דו טרייבסט היינט אַ טראק? (הוא נוהג מכונית משא), כ"ק שליט"א עשה תנועה בידיו ומילא גם את כוסו. ר"ז דוכמאַן רצה שיתן גם לו, אבל כ"ק עשה תנועת ביטול בידיו ולא נתן לו.

הרבה מהמתאספים היו קצת מבוסמים, ואחדים גם נתנו חזרה על השלחן וביניהם הי' גם הרמ"ד טעלעשעווסקי, וכאשר חילק כ"ק שליט"א את היין להנוסעים קרב גם הוא, ולא הי' יכול לעמוד על רגליו, וכ"ק אד"ש חייך לקראתו ובצחוק קל נתן לו ואמר: "ופרצת ימה וקדמה וצפונה ונגבה – נחלה בלי מצרים".

בחלוקת היין נתן להרב גאָראָדעצקי ראשונה ואחריו לר"י כץ עבור טשיקאַגו.

בכל ההתועדות ניגנו כמעט רק ניגוני שמחה, וכ"ק ספק בידיו ופניו הפיקו שמחה רבה. היתה שיחה מיוחדת גם לנשים.

בתוך ההתועדות באו האחים שולזינגר, הרב האָלאַנדער (מהסתדרות הרבנים) והקומפוזיטור נחמי' ווינאָוער וכ"ק אד"ש קירבם במאד.

בתוך ההתועדות אמר את המאמר ד"ה והחרים ה' את לשון ים מצרים ובתוכו ביאר את הכתוב למנצח אל תשחת מכתם לדוד, מקפיטל נ"ז למספר שנותיו, כמנהגו בכל שנה לאוי"ט.

ד' כ"ו ניסן תשח"י, שעה שמינית ערב

ר' חיים סערעבריאַנסקי שבא מאוסטרלי' בחול המועד שאל את כ"ק אדמו"ר שליט"א איך עליו להתנהג בענין ספירת העומר אחר שבאוסטרלי' הוא יום אחד מוקדם (למשל היום הוא שם כבר כ"ז ניסן) והוא התחיל לספור כמו שסופרים שם ובבואו לכאן התחיל לספור כמנהגנו. וזו היא תשובת כ"ק אדמו"ר שליט"א על הפיתקא ששאל ר"ח הנ"ל, ביום יו"ד לעומר כ"ד

אור ליום כ"ה ניסן תשח"י: (הסימנים: 1) 2) הן מה שהעיר כ"ק שליט"א על הפתק)

"הרי כתבתי לבא לחה"פ (ולא באמצע הספירה)

"1) בהנוגע להברכה – ישמע מאחר.

"2) יספור ע"פ מה שהתחיל (שלדעתי זוהי העיקרית אצלו, וליתר שאת) וגם כפי שסופרים כאן. ובהפסק ביניהם ולא בסמיכות (דמיחזי כשיקרא, וגם שזהו היפך לענין ספירה – היינו בירור ולא ספק, שלכן צ"ע אם הי' יכול לברך אפילו אם כל הימים הי' סופר ב' ספירות).

"יבקש הרבנים לפס"ד בהנוגע לחה"ש, כי ע"פ הנ"ל חה"ש (הנקבע רק ע"י ספירת כאו"א ולא דב"ד) צ"ל אצלו מוקדם יום א' (ש"ק ויום א') וחידוש גדול הדבר".

ביום השני חזר יואל על המאמר (אחרי שישבנו קצת על רשימת השיחות) ואתמול חזר על חלק מהשיחות. הוא השאיר לי כמה רשימות מהתוכן ועברתי עליהם, והיום עברתי על הרשימות הנוספות.

את הרשימות משיחת ליל ב' דפסח כבר מסרו לידיו של כ"ק אדמו"ר שליט"א עוד בחוה"מ.

בהיותנו על יחידות בחודש שבט בשנה העברה וכ"ק אד"ש שאל את מצבנו בפרנסה, אמר שעלי להתלמד אומנות האופסט (דפוס הליטאָגראַפיאַ). שאלתי אולי נכון הדבר לפתוח דפוס כזה לעצמי ואמר כ"ק אד"ש: צו וואָס עפענען אַ נייעם געשעפט, און ווייטער אַריינלייגן געלט, ס'איז בעסער צו פאַרגרעסערן דעם געשעפט. וכאשר אמרתי שאיני רואה שהבע"ב ירצוני בתור שותף אמר: ס'איז נאָך צו פרי, זאָלן זיי זיך צוגעוואוינען צום געדאַנק.

לפני כמה חדשים כתבתי לכ"ק אד"ש שדברתי עם הבע"ב, ואין הדבר זז ממקומו, וצוני לדבר עם הרב חודקוב. דברתי עמו אז ואמר לי שלדעתו עלי לקבל את חלק האפסעט, והוא בעצמו ידבר עמהם אודות זה.

במשך חדשים אלו שאלתי אותו כמה פעמים ואמר שלא דבר עמהם עדיין. בחשבי שאולי היתה כוונת כ"ק שליט"א שאודיע להם שזהו רצוני, דברתי בימים האחרונות אתם בעצמי וספרתי להם דברים כהווייתם. אמנם הם אמרו מפורש שאינם רוצים אותי בתור שותף, גם להאפסעט מאחר שאיני אומן בזה עדיין (כי המכונה עובדת לפרקים נדירים ביותר, ולא הי' סיפק בידי להתלמד, אף שיש לי מושג קל באומנות זו). ואמרו שכבר חשבו שאולי ידברו עם בערל יוניק שלמד את האומנות בבית ספר לדפוס (ושילם עבור זה כשש מאות שקלים).

אתמול ספרתי הדברים להרב חודקוב, ואמר שדעתו היא שימסרו, או נכון יותר, ימכרו את כל העסק של האפסעט אלי ואני אקח בתור שותף איש אומן (נראה הי' כי כוונתו היא לבערל יוניק הנ"ל, אשר כ"ק צוהו להתלמד אומנות זו, וגם רצה – עוד לפני בואי לכאן – שיכנס בתור שותף לעסק האפסעט, וגם בזה לא רצו הבע"ב). ואמרתי לו, שאין רצוי הדבר שאדבר שוב עמהם, מאחר שהנני רואה שאין דברי מתקבלים אצלם אפילו אם אציע להם הצעה נכונה. ואמר, שעלי לחכות עוד שבוע, וידבר עמהם בעצמו אודות זה (יכול להיות כי כ"ק אד"ש דבר עמו אודות זה). עכ"פ בשבועות הקרובות נראה איך יפול דבר.

מסיפורי כ"ק אד"ש בעת ההתועדות דאחש"פ:

כ"ק מו"ח אדמו"ר סיפר אשר אחד המשכילים בא לכ"ק אביו אדמו"ר נ"ע לליובאַוויטש ושאלו, איזו הוכחה ישנה למציאות מלאכים בעולם מאחר שאיש לא משש אותם ואיש לא ראם, כי הם מיסודות הדקים של אש ורוח, אשר אין חוש המישוש וחוש הראות שולטים בהם, ואיך יודעים להכריח מציאותם.

בראות כ"ק אדמו"ר נ"ע שבדברי שכל וועט ער זיך מיט אים ניט איינקערן, אמר לו משל ע"ז:

מקראסנאיע לליובאַוויטש נוסעים בעגלה.

(כ"ק אדמו"ר שליט"א הפסיק הסיפור ואמר: מאחר שהזכרתי את הדרך

מקראַסנאַיע לליובאַוויטש רוצה אני לספר סיפור):

כאשר התחילו לבנות ברוסיא כבישים ומסילות הברזל ברחבי המדינה, פקד הקיסר ניקאָלאַי כי יסללו מסילת ברזל שתעבור דרך ליובאַוויטש ואמר ע"ז כ"ק אדמו"ר הצ"צ: "אין מיינע ד' אמות בין איך בעל הבית". ולא רצה אדמו"ר הצ"צ שיסללו כביש בליובאַוויטש, כמארז"ל ישיבת כרכים קשה. בא איש יהודי לכ"ק אדמו"ר הצ"צ נ"ע ויספר לו כי מציעים לו לקבל בקבלנות את סלילת מסילת הברזל במחוז ליובאַוויטש שתעבור גם בסמוך להעיר, ושואל הוא את דעתו של כ"ק אדמו"ר הצמח צדק אם לקבל הצעה זו.

כ"ק אדמו"ר הצ"צ אמר לו, שיקבל ע"ע את סלילת המסילה בחלקה עד ליובאַוויטש מעבר מזה וכן את החלק השני שבעבר העיר מזה אמנם החלק העובר בסמוך להעיר לא יקבל.

וכן הי' אשר האיש קבל ע"ע רק את חלקי המסילה עד העיר וממנה והלאה והרוויח בזה הון רב ואת הקבלנות של סלילת המסילה קרוב לליובאַוויטש קיבל אינו יהודי. וכאשר התחיל הלה לבנות חלק זה ראה שהיסודות שבנו שקעו במקומות רבים. וכן הי' כאשר חזרו ובנו את היסודות מחדש, והפסיד ממון רב. כמאמר הצ"צ: אין מיינע ד"א בין איך בעה"ב. ולא עברה מסילה דרך ליובאַוויטש עד ימיו של כ"ק אדנ"ע.

(וסיים כ"ק אדמו"ר שליט"א את הסיפור הקודם:)

בעגלה ההולכת מקראַסנאָיע לליובאַוויטש יושבים חכמים החושבים אודות מלאכים.

הסוס המושך את העגלה חושב, שהנסיעה לליובאַוויטש היא לכבודו אשר בבואו להעיר יתנו לו תבן ומספוא למאכלו.

בעל העגלה המנהיג את הסוס חושב אשר הנסיעה היא לכבודו, שירויח בהנסיעה, ויוכל להביא לביתו צרכי השבת.

והחכמים היושבים בעגלה חושבים אודות מלאכים.

וסיים כ"ק אדמו"ר נ"ע להמשכיל: "צי דערפאַר וואָס דער פערד טראַכט וועגן האָבער זיינען די מלאכים קיין מלאכים ניט?"

א, אדר"ח אייר. שעה אחת עשרה לילה

זה עתה באתי מהאסיפה שקרא ועד המסדר אודות תיקון השאַלאַש בהחצר, ונצרך ע"ז סכום קרוב לב' אלפים, כי מחוקי העיר אסור לבנות בנין בחצר ולכן

הצורך הוא לכסות את הסוכה בכל ערב ש״ק ולהוריד את הכיסוי אחריו. היו לא יותר מאיזה מנינים שי׳ ונחלט כי כ״א מאנ״ש יתנדב 25 שקל וגם יתן כ״א 2 דולר לחודש לשלם לאיש שישגיח לעשות כל הדברים הנוגעים לבית המדרש בעתם ובזמנם. בנין מתאים חפשו עד הנה ולא מצאו.

אתמול התועד כ״ק אד״ש. יצא בשעה 1:30 (כפי שאמרו, מסר כ״ק אד״ש שבכל שבתות מבה״ח תתחיל ההתועדות בשעה 1:30 ולא בשעה 1.00 כפי שעד הנה) והתועד עד 4:15. התועדות קצרה בערך ההתועדויות שאחרי החגים.

היו ג׳ שיחות ומאמר ד״ה כימי צאתכם מא״מ שארך כשעה.

תוכן השיחות: להיות מסור לכ״ק אדמו״ר מבלי לשאול ולהתיישב, וסיפר ממ״ש בס׳ שבחי האריז״ל, שהאריז״ל יצא פעם עם תלמידיו בעש״ק לקבל שבת מלכתא לשדה אל מחוץ לעיר, כי עפ״י קבלה צריך לקבל שבת בשדה. ויאמר האריז״ל כי נכון הדבר שילכו למקום רחוק בירושלים עיה״ק ולקבל שבת שם, ואף כי מרחק רב הוא הלוקח זמן, אמנם אצל תלמידיו לא הי׳ זאת פלא. ויאמרו כמה תלמידים שילכו לבתיהם וימלכו בדביתהו, ודבר זה פעל נמיכות הרוח אצל האריז״ל. ואח״כ אמר, כי אילו היו מקבלים את השבת בירושלים היו מביאים את הגאולה.

וביאר כ״ק אד״ש, שאף כי דבר זה לילך לבתיהם ולשאול עצת האשה הוא עפ״י שו״ע ובפרט בענין ש״ק שיש בזה ענין של שלום בית נר שבת כו׳, אמנם מצד התקשרותם להמשפיע שלהם היו צריכים לדעת שמאמר רבם הי׳ מתאים לשו״ע, כי כתוב בטעמי המצות להרח״ו שהי׳ גאון גדול גם בנגלה, ובזה שאמרו שיזיל ואימליך בדביתהו עכבו את ביאת המשיח.

ואמר כ״ק אדמו״ר שליט״א אשר זה הי׳ דרכו של כ״ק מו״ח אדמו״ר שהי׳ שולח את התלמידים (בשנים הראשונות) ודוקא אחרי ימי החגים, וואָס דאַן פאַרשטייט מען מער וואָס מען האָט געוואָלט בלייבן כאן, ומ״מ שלחם כ״ק אדמו״ר לערי השדה און זיי האָבן געפאָלגט, והצליחו בהענינים וגם בעניניהם הפרטיים, ויצליחו כו׳ (וצוה לומר לחיים להתלמידים שנסעו אז, ביניהם יצחק גראָנער, שלום בער פאָפּאַק ועוד).

(כנראה שהדברים היו בעיקר קשורים עם הת׳ א. ש. שכפי הנשמע רצה

כ"ק אד"ש לשלחו למאַראָקאָ, ומשום איזה סיבות לא נסע, וע"ז היו מסובים הדברים).

צוה שהתלמידים שבאו מניו הייוען יאמרו לחיים, וצוה את יצחק גראָנער לסדרם. ואמר שיאמרו ניגון שיודעים, וניגנו ממצרים גאלתנו והנאספים אתם. כ"ק אד"ש גם הוא ניגן ובידיו מיהר ביותר את קצב הניגון בשמחה רבה.

אמר להתלמיד גדלי' צינאַמעס (הנוסע ללמוד לא"י) שיאמר לחיים ונתן לו לעקח, ואמר דו זאָלסט זיך אויפפירן ווי עס פאַסט פאַר אַ תמים. מען זאָל זיך אויף דיר פאַרקוקן.

קרא את הילד חיים ארי' הבר מצוה ונתן לו לעקאַח, והראה לו לקבל בידו השמאלית, וכן נתן לעקאַח לשני אחיו הצעירים, וצוה לנגן לכבודו ניגון שמח וגם הוא ניגן אותו בשמחה רבה.

אני אמרתי לחיים עבור גיסי, שהב"מ הי' בש"ק זה, וכ"ק ענה לחיים ולברכה.

כשהלכו לסדר את התלמידים מניו הייוען אמר: דערווײַלע זאָלן זאָגן לחיים די תלמידים פון מאָנטרעאַל, קאַנאַדאַ היא לצד צפון, מקום הקור, זיי זאָלן דאָרטן אויך אָנוואַרימען, ואמרו תלמידים אלו לחיים.

אמר למיכל ראַסקין שיאמר לחיים, ויקח כוס מלא, אַ פולן כוס, און ער זאָל האָבן אַ פולע קלייט (כי פתח חנות לפירות לפני החג).

אמר להרש"ז העכט משיקאַגו שישתה הד' כוסות והוסיף: ס'איז דאָך זמן המנחה, שהוא זמן שכרות כמ"ש בשו"ע.

במוצש"ק היתה התועדות מלוה מלכה אצל ר"מ דובינסקי וישבתי שם עד שעה הראשונה אחר חצות. יואל חזר את השיחות. וסיפר ר"ז דוכמאַן:

כשנפטר האדמו"ר מרעציצא נ"ע, רצה בנו הר"ר חיים שניאורסאָן לקבל את הרבנות ובא לפני כ"ק אדמו"ר (מהורש"ב) נ"ע, ואמר לו שיודע הוא כמה ענינים הצריכים לזה וגם את העצות שיתן, אבל באם תבא לפניו שאלה אודות ניתוח אינו יודע מה להשיב. ויענהו כ"ק אדמו"ר נ"ע, נו, אַז מען ווייסט ניט טויג טאָקע ניט.

ר"מ דובינסקי מספר מה ששמע שאחרי הסתלקות כ"ק אדמו"ר הצ"צ

ואדמו״ר מהרי״ל נ״ע בנו רצה לנסוע לקאָפּוסט, שאל אותו אחיו אדמו״ר מוהר״ש נ״ע אם לימדו אביו לעשות פדיון, ויאמר: כן, וישאלהו שוב אם לימדו גם לעשות את הפדיון בעודהו בדרך, ויאמר: לא. אח״כ אמר כ״ק אדמו״ר מהר״ש, עס האָט אים פאַרדראָסן, שהי׳ צריך לעכב את הנסיעה.

היום יש להבע״ב דבית הדפוס ראיון עם הרב חודקוב. וכפי הנראה ידבר הרב חודקוב אתם גם אודותי.

היום נסע הת׳ שלום-בער דרייזין לא״י. מסרתי לו את הסאכארין עבור אבינו שי׳. זה כמה שבועות לא קבלנו מכתב מהבית, גם לא אישור על המצות שמורה. נקוה כי הכל טוב בעזהשי״ת.

ב״ה, ה, יא אייר תשח״י, שעה אחת עשרה לילה

במשך השבועות האחרונות לא היו מאורעות מיוחדות, וגם הייתי קצת עסוק ולכן לא כתבתי.

ביום ג׳ היתה אסיפת נשים בביתה של זוג׳ של נתן גורארי׳, והרב דוד האָלאַנדער, שנסע בשנה העברה לארצות מזרח אירופה נאם בפניהן וגם הראה סרט צילומים מסיוריו, וגם צילום האהל שנבנה על קברו של כ״ק אדמו״ר נ״ע ברוסטוב.

חשבתי כי אוכל ללמוד או לכתוב מעט, אבל יואל בא לבקרני, ואחריו בא גם מרדכי דובינסקי וישבנו כמה שעות.

בשבוע העבר היתה אסיפה מטעם צא״ח ודנינו בדבר קנין בנין עבור צא״ח, כי כן היתה הוראה לפני חג הפסח ע״י הרב חודקוב. הכוונה היא בנין קטן בו יוכלו ללמוד ולהתפלל ולהתאסף. הצעות ממשיות אינן עדיין בדבר זה. היתה הצעה לקנות את הבנין של הספינקער שי׳ כי העתיק לבנין חדש, אבל אחרו את המועד, כי כבר מכרו.

כן דנו באסיפה זו לבקר בניו בריטאָן, בו גר הת׳ נעלסון, ויש לו גם השפעה בעיר. וכן לבקר את סאוט פאלסבוירג בו גר נפתלי נס. וכן לסדר התועדות בבייאָן.

נסיעת הת' לדיטרויט על שבת הגדול היתה בהצלחה מופלגה. כי חוץ מזה שבקרו בכמה בתי כנסיות, היתה התועדות מלוה מלכה נוכחו בה כמה מרבני העיר והתל' נאמו בפניהם וביחוד הצטיין בנאומו אברהם שם-טוב, שדבר גם בהלכה מה שעשה רושם טוב. בכלל השפעתו של בערל שם טוב בעיר גדולה היא. יש לו כבר היכרות גדולה, והביא גם כמה אנשים כבר לכ"ק אדמו"ר שליט"א.

אתמול למדו בביתו של ישראל דוכמאַן ובשבוע העבר בביתו של חיים הערש מאָסקאָוויטש. התחיל שוב את שו"ע אדמוה"ז. ולומדים את המאמר זכור-תרס"ה.

היום נגמרה הדפסת מורה שיעור ללימוד תניא באידיש, שנסדר ע"י ליב גראָנער.

שמעתי מיחזקאל לאַנגזאַם (גיסו של מרדכי שוסטערמאַן) שאחד הבע"ב בבית הכנסת (בו הוא משרת בתור שמש) הי' חולה, וציוהו כ"ק אדמו"ר שליט"א שילמוד תניא, ובאם קשה עליו ילמוד את השיעור באידיש.

ישנה הצעה שליב ראַסקין יקח ע"ע לעבוד כמה שעות במזכירות צא"ח, כי העבודה רבה, ובלי איש מיוחד קשה לסדר הענינים. דוד הציע זאת להרב חודקוב, והדבר נתקבל אצלו.

הרב חודקוב דיבר עם בעלי בית הדפוס אודות השותפות, אבל כנראה שהם מתנגדים לזה. בימים האחרונים הם קצת מבולבלים ונדמה לי שזה בסיבת השיחה עם הרב חדוקוב, כי כנראה שעליהם לתת תשובה, ואינם יודעים איך להחליט.

האמת היא, כי לי לעצמי קשה מאד כל הענין, ואיני רוצה שיחשוב מישהו שלקחתי ח"ו חלק מפרנסתו. איך שהוא השי"ת ינהיג בודאי בדרך הישרה עבור כולם ונשמע הוראתו של כ"ק אד"ש בזה. אבל בדרך כלל זה גוזל קצת את המנוחה, וגם בעת העבודה בדפוס האוירה מתוחה אף שאין מזכירים דבר וחצי דבר.

מרדכי דובינסקי הי׳ ביום ג׳ העבר ליום הולדתו אצל כ״ק אד״ש ביחידות. סיפר כי שאל אם לנסוע לנאות דשא לימי הקיץ. כ״ק שליט״א ענה בשלילה (כנראה לסיבת שינוי האויר עבור התינוקות).

ליב גראָנער סיפר לי, כי בשנה העברה שאל גם הוא אם לנסוע וגם לו ענה בשלילה (מצד אותה הסיבה), ואח״כ שאל אם לנסוע לפאַר ראַקאָוויי (לא רחוק מהעיר, על שפת הים), ואמר: וואָס איז דער חילוק, העיקר הוא שינוי האויר ומה לי פאַר ראַקאָוויי או מקום אחר. וסיים: מען קען דאָ אויך האָבן אַ פריילינכן זומער. ואמר לייבל, שב״ה, שבקיץ זה היו כולם בריאים ת״ל.

ביום ב׳ הייתי אצל ד״ר שפירא, בשכנות בית המדרש, ועקר אצלי את שן הבינה, שהטריד אותי במשך כמה שבועות.

סיפר לי כי ריפא גם את שניו של כ״ק אדמו״ר מהוריי״צ – ולהבדיל בין החיים – גם את כ״ק אד״ש וכל בני המשפחה. פעם בבואו לכ״ק אדמו״ר, ולא הי׳ מבין את לשונו וחנה תחי׳ היתה מבארת מה שאומר כ״ק אדמו״ר, אמר שהוא מגזע המתנגדים. ואמר כ״ק אדמו״ר: ס׳זיינען ניטאָ קיין מתנגדים, ס׳זיינען פאַראַן **אידן**. וכן הי׳ פעם אחרת שאמרה חנה עליו שהוא יהודי טוב, ואמר כ״ק אדמו״ר: ס׳זיינען ניטאָ קיין שלעכטע אידן, ס׳זיינען דאָ **אידן**.

א, יד אייר , פסח שני. שעה שתים עשרה לילה

בש״ק אמר כ״ק אד״ש קדיש יתום בכל הג׳ תפילות, כי הי׳ יאָרצייט של אחיו, ר׳ לייב ע״ה. בתפילות הלילה ושחרית עמדתי לא רחוק מכ״ק אד״ש וראיתי הנהגתו. העובר לפני התיבה ר׳ שמואל דער שניידער ובשחרית ר״א פאָפאַק.

לקבלת שבת ישב, ועמד למזמור לדוד. למזמור לכה דודי עמד ופניו לצפון כשהתחילו לומר והיו למשיסה פנה ופניו למזרח עד בואי בשלום שפנה לימינו ופניו למערב, ובסוף פנה שוב דרך ימינו למזרח.

אחרי מזמור שיר ליום השבת אמר את הקדיש. קידת ראשו באמירת הקדיש הוא: יתגדל, ויקרב משיחי׳, בחייכון, יהא שמי׳, שמי׳ דקודב״ה, דאמירן בעלמא.

כ"ק אד"ש אומר את הקדיש לבדו, ובגמרו – אומרים החיובים.

אחרי הקדיש יתום שאחר מזמור שיר ליום השבת ישב (בעת שכבר התחילו החיובים אמירתם) ועמד בעת אמירת השכיבנו. בעת שאמר הש"ץ את הקדיש שלפני ש"ע, ניגב את עיני קדשו, וכנראה שבכה, ובכלל הי' מאד אַנגעצויגן.

ליב גראָנער מספר, אשר הרבנית תחי' אמו של כ"ק אד"ש איננה יודעת מפטירת בנה ר"ל ע"ה, כי היא מקבלת ממנו מכתבים, אשר כ"ק אדמו"ר שליט"א כותבם. כן היא שולחת לו חבילות וחושבת אשר הוא מקבלם.

ומובן גודל העג"נ שיש לכ"ק אדמו"ר שליט"א, השי"ת ישמח לבבו.

בעת קריאת התורה עומד כ"ק אד"ש ופניו לצפון ומביט לתוך החומש (ע"פ תורה תמימה. גם כ"ק חותנו הי' מביט בחומש ע"פ זה). בתוך הקריאה לפעמים תכופות, וכן בעת חזרת הש"ץ, אוחז באצבעותיו את ד' ציציות טליתו.

בעת אמירת ברכו מרכין ראשו, כאשר הש"ץ מתחיל לאמרו ומרכין עוד יותר באמירת הקהל ומגביהו כאשר הקהל מסיים אמירתו.

כשצועד לאחוריו לפני תפלת שמו"ע מתחיל ברגל שמאל ובצעד הג' עוקר רגלו הימנית אבל אינו מעמידו יחד עם השמאלית אלא מעמידו שוב לפניו לפסוע הג' פסיעות להתפלה.

ב"ה, ה' ל"ג בעומר, שעה י"א לילה

בש"ק התועדו כמה מהתמימים בביתו של יוסף רייטשעס, יותר נכון היתה זו אסיפה ולא קידוש, ונושא הדיבורים בקשר עם התועדות כ"ק אדמו"ר שליט"א בש"ק מברכים העבר, והחלטנו אשר עלינו, ז.א. כל אחד מאתנו, להודיע לכ"ק שליט"א, כי הננו מוכנים לכל משרה וכל תפקיד אשר ישים עלינו כ"ק אדמו"ר שליט"א, הן בעיר והן מחוצה לה או מחוץ למדינה.

ביום הראשון מסרנו, אני וראשא, פתקא לכ"ק אדמו"ר שליט"א. למחרת נתן לי הרב חודקוב את הפתקא עם תשובת כ"ק אד"ש, ע"מ להעתיקה וזו לשון קדשו:

"בטח נכתב הנ"ל בהסכם מלא של זוג' תי'.

"ומגויסים לעבודה כאן כאו"א במסגרתו

"(צאגו"ח, נשי חב"ד)".

גם מענדל בוימגאַרטן אשר מסר פתקא דומה באותו יום קבל תשובה דומה אמנם בהוספת ברכה וזו הלשון בפתקתו (אם אין זכרוני מטעני):

"בטח נכתב הנ"ל בהסכם זוג' תי'

"עתה מגויסים לעבודה כאן בהפצת המעיינות כאו"א במסגרתו

"(צאגו"ח, נשי חב"ד) ויה"ר שי' בשטומ"צ."

בערל אלעניק סיפר לי שהוא כתב פתקא דומה לפני כמה חדשים אחרי התועדות כ"ק אדמו"ר שליט"א שדיבר בה במעלתם של בערל שם טוב ויוסף ראָזענפעלד הנוסעים בשליחותו, וכ"ק שליט"א אמר אז: "מען זאָל זיך אויף זיי פאַרקוקן. ומהם יראו וכן יעשו", וכ"ק ברכם אז בברכות מופלגות בהצלחה גדולה.

וכ"ק ענה על פתקתו של בערל אשר עבודתם היא בהפצת המעיינות בעיר ומזמן לזמן לנסוע מסביב לה.

בערל יוניק מספר, אשר הוא מסר פתקא דומה לכ"ק אדמו"ר שליט"א תיכף אחרי ההתועדות בש"ק מברכים וכ"ק שליט"א ענה בשאלה, אם הוא שילם כבר את כל חובותיו. בערל יוניק ענה שבע"ה ישלם החובות בעוד איזה חדשים. ושוב שאל בערל על הצעה שהציעו לו בעל בית הדפוס בו אני עובד, להשתתף עמם במסחר האופסט, וכ"ק ענה אותו: "צו וואָס דאַרפסטו דאָס". (לפני זמן רצה כ"ק שליט"א מאוד שישתתף עמהם, אלא שהם לא רצו, וכנראה שמשהו השתנה במשך הזמן).

אתמול הלכתי עם משה גאָלדמאַן לבית המדרש הגדול באיסט ניו יורק, להפיץ ספרי המל"ח, נאמתי כעשרים רגע, ואחרי תפלת ערבית התועדנו בקצרה עם המתפללים.

הננו מתכוננים לנסוע על ש"ק הבע"ל לניו הייוועו, אי"ה, בשליחות צאגו"ח, לנאום בבתי כנסיות ולהתועד, והשי"ת יצליחנו.

ביום א' היתה אסיפת צא"ח בביתו של בערל אלעניק, ודנינו בדבר הפצת הספרים בבתי כנסיות בל"ג בעומר, ובדבר הנסיעות להעיירות. ב"ה שנמצאים תמימים הרוצים לנסוע.

אגב, יואל לקח חלק גדול בהתעוררות לכתיבת הפתקאות האמורות לעיל.

ב"ה, מוצש"ק אחו"ק. כ"ז אייר

הנני מצטער מאד שאינני יכול להמשיך את הכתיבה בסדר, כי הנני עסוק מאד בשבועות האחרונים, עד שאני הנני ממעט אפילו בשינה, ובודאי יסלחו הקוראים.

בש"ק העבר היינו בניו הייוועו, הנוסעים משה פסח גאָלדמאַן, חיים סערעבראַנסקי, דובער אַלעניק, אני, שלום בער קיובמאַן והנהג יוסף רייטשעס. לפני הנסיעה בעש"ק מסר דוד ראַסקין את שמות הנוסעים לכ"ק אדמו"ר שליט"א, שמם ושם אמם, וכ"ק שליט"א רשם על הפתקא שנכון מאד מה שנסע חיים סערעבראַנסקי, וגם הוסיף, שצריך אויסניצן את אלעזר גאַרעליק (בודאי לא תפרסמו דברים אלה שהם שייכים רק להנהלת צא"ח, אלא שידעתי ש"מים גנובים ימתקו" ובודאי תתענגו על פרטים מעין אלה).

בש"ק נאמנו בבתי הכנסיות שבעיר הן בבקר, והן בערב בזמן המנחה, כן סדרנו קידושא רבא בביתו של הרב משה העכט, מנהל הישיבה דשם. קראנו מכתבו של כ"ק אדמו"ר נבג"מ בדבר קביעות עתים לתורה, הנדפס ב"בטאון" האחרון. והת' שד"ב קיובמאַן חזר דא"ח. היו כל האברכים שבעיר וגם כמה מהבע"ב החשובים. ובמוצש"ק היתה מלוה מלכה בביתו של זאב שילדקרויט.

ברור הדבר שהנסיעה הביאה תועלת רבה בהתעוררות התמימים שבשם

חוץ מהתועלת בדברי ההתעוררות בהבתי כנסיות.

עיר זו היא בת רבע מליון תושבים, אשר ביניהם דרים כעשרים וחמשה אלף יהודים. יש בה ישיבה אחי תמימים בת כ-ג׳ מאות תלמידים, העומדת כנראה על בסיס טוב, כי המנהל משה העכט עובד במרץ רב, והוא איש בעל רצון ותקיף.

זכורני: כשהתועד כ״ק אד״ש בי״ט כסלו בשנה העברה צוה למשה העכט, שעמד בריחוק מקום לומר לחיים, והכריז כ״ק אד״ש, וגם הראה באצבעותיו: ״ניט צוויי הונדערט, ניט דריי הונדערט, נאָר צעהן הונדערט״. כי כאשר עמדו לקנות את הבית החדש עבור הישיבה בעיר (אגב בזריזות רבה מצד המנהל הנ״ל בהשפעתו על אחד ממנהיגי הקהילה שממנה קנו את הבנין) בקש מכ״ק אד״ש שיברכם שיהי׳ בה לכה״פ כמאתים תלמידים, וכ״ק כנראה נתן ע״ז את ברכתו, ולזה רמזו דבריו הק׳ הנאמרים לעיל.

דוד דייטש, בנו של החסיד הישיש רמ״מ דייטש שיחי׳, העתיק דירתו לעיר כנראה בפקודתו של כ״ק אד״ש. הנהו עוסק במסחר הפלאַסטיק וב״ה שמצליח בעסקיו בלי ע״ה. מסור ונתון לכ״ק אד״ש בכל נפשו ומאודו, והשפעתו ניכרת בעיר, כי הנהו עסקן בעל מרץ, ניט קיין טיפש, אבל תמים, אַן ערענסטער, אם כי פשוט. וגם פעל הרבה בהשפעתו על המנהל בהנוגע להתקשרות, כי הי׳ קצת... וגם מנהיג את ב״ב בטוב, וכמדומה אַז דער רבי שליט״א איז פון אים צופרידן.

כשהייתי בביתו לפני המלוה מלכה עם חיים סערעברנסקי, ושוחחנו קצת, אַביסל וואַרים געשמועסט, סיפר לנו, שהי׳ לפני כשנה ומחצה, אצל כ״ק אד״ש ביחידות, ולא סיפר לנו מה דיבר אתו כ״ק אד״ש, אלא שכנראה שכ״ק אד״ש רצה דבר מה ממנו. ושאלו כ״ק שליט״א אם יציית לו (אויב ער וועט פאָלגן) ואמר בפשיטות, וואָס הייסט פאָלגן, אַוודאַי, מען איז דאָך אַ סאָלדאַט, ווי דער רבי וועט זאָגן וועט מען טאָן (וכנראה שהדברים נאמרו בתמימות). כ״ק אדמו״ר שליט״א נתרגש מתמימות מענה זה, ולא יכול להתאפק, ויבך מרוב שמחה. וגם הוא בכה עמו.

דער רבי האָט אמת׳ע סאָלדאַטן, ואנן לגבייהו כקליפת השום.

גם זוג׳ סיפרה לנו כמה ענינים ממופתי כ״ק אד״ש עמהם ועם אחרים אבל אין זמני אתי, ואולי בהזדמנות אחרת אכתוב עד״ז.

ב' ער"ח סיון, שעה 11 לילה

בש"ק מברכים התועד כ"ק אד"ש בהסוכה. יצא בשעה 1:30, בערך והתועד עד שעה 3:15 בערך. דיבר שתי שיחות בענין שמיטה והר סיני, אח"כ מאמר דא"ח ד"ה להבין ענין ספירת העומר, וביאר בפרטיות ענין כל הספירות הכלולות בספירת החסד, הי' מאמר קצר, ואח"כ עוד שתי שיחות בענין ירחא תליתאי ופ' במדבר.

על ש"ק באו כמה תלמידים מישיבת אחי תמימים בברונקס, עם הר"מ הרב פוטערמאַן ומשה לעווערטאָוו, וציוה כ"ק אד"ש שיאמרו לחיים וינגנו, וניגנו ממצרים גאלתנו, וגם כ"ק אד"ש עזרם וכל הקהל אחריו.

כן ציוה לנגון ניגון אני מאמין.

כן הזכיר את הכינוס של נשי חב"ד שיהי' אי"ה מחר, וברך שיהי' בהצלחה.

מתוכן השיחות של חג הפסח הגיה כ"ק אד"ש רק את השיחה הראשונה מליל ב' דחה"פ, ואמר להרב חודקוב וכן לליב גראָנער כי אין הסגנון טוב, ואם הלאה יהי' באותו האופן יפסיק את ההגהה. וכאשר שאלו ליב גראָנער שאין אנחנו יודעים איך לשפר את הכתיבה, אמר שיראו מה שהוסיף וע"פ זה יתקנו להבא. אנחנו עברנו על הוספותיו וראינו שבהסגנון לא הוסיף רק מלים בודדות אלא שהוסיף בכמה מקומות את הענינים גופא. אמנם מה שהוסיף הוא לא כפי שחזרו את השיחות, ובכמה מקומות גם לא כפי שאמר אותן. ומובן שאין אנחנו יכולים לשנות בעצמנו. וכן סיפר לי יואל שאח"כ אמר כ"ק אד"ש שזאת היא כוונתו, ז"א לא לסגנון המלים אלא להתוכן גופא.

עכ"פ מסרו את התוכן גם לר"ש זלמנוב שיעבור עליו, וגם הוסיף דבר מה אבל כמובן רק בהסגנון.

כנראה שלא יצא תוכן השיחות זה חוץ מלילה השני' דחה"פ שכבר ניתן להדפיס.

הרב חודקוב הציע שצאגו"ח יוציאו לאור חוברת חדשית ובה תוכן השיחות מכל חודש בהוספת רשימת פעולות, מאמרים ועוד. יכול להיות שזהו מה שאמר לו כ"ק אד"ש, אמנם עדיין לא מצאנו את האיש המתאים לזה, ונקוה כי בזמן הקרוב יצא הדבר לפועל.

היתה הצעה שידפיסו את התוכן בדפוס ככל הקונטרסים, אלא שכ"ק שליט"א אמר שיש לעיין שלא יובלט שזהו מכתב מצאגו"ח. עכ"פ לע"ע החלטנו שידפס כמו עד עתה עד שנתחיל להוציא את הירחון.

ביום ג' העבר הי' אצל כ"ק אדמו"ר שליט"א מר פורת, קונסול ישראל בניו יורק, אתו בא גם הרב הולנדר (אומרים שבזמן האחרון הוא שואל גם על עניניו הפרטיים אצל כ"ק אדמו"ר שליט"א. ובכלל הרב הולנדר הוא יוצא ונכנס אצל כ"ק אד"ש).

הם שהו אצל כ"ק אד"ש כשתי שעות בערך. על מה דיברו לא נודע. אח"כ דיבר עם התלמידים והראו לו את תוכני השיחות ואת הבטאון וביקש שירשמו את שמו על הרשימה וישלחו לו כל פעם שי"ל.

אתמול היתה אסיפה רבתי מטעם צא"ח, נוכחו כמה חברים ודיברו אודות התהלוכה דחג השבועות הבע"ל, שמסדרים שילכו לאיסט ניו יאָרק ולבאָראָ פאַרק. מקום רחוק כשעתיים מ-770. כן נרשמו חברים להנסיעות בערי השדה. על ש"ק שלאחר חה"ש מסדרים נסיעה לקליוולאַנד ולאָלבאני ואולי גם לפילאַדעלפיאַ.

כן מסרו דו"ח מפעולות צא"ח באה"ק – אלעזר גאַרעליק, ואוסטרלי' – חיים סערעבראַנסקי.

אני לא נוכחתי בהאסיפה וכשבאתי בשעה אחת עשרה כבר הי' אחרי האסיפה. הייתי עסוק בהגהה הבולעטין שי"ל להכינוס מחר אי"ה מנשי ובנות חב"ד. בחוברת זו ישנה השיחה של כ"ק אד"ש מיו"ד שבט העבר, מוגהת ממנו. כן כמה מכתבים מכ"ק אד"ש. והיום עובדים בבית הדפוס גם בלילה בכדי לגמרו לפני הכינוס. יש בחוברת זו גם מאמר מלאה תי', וכ"ק אד"ש שליט"א עבר גם על מאמר זה ותיקן באיזהו מקומן. המאמר הוא בעל תוכן רב בענין ספירת העומר.

לאה תי' עובדת בזמן האחרון במרץ רב לסידור הכינוס, כי היא מזכירת הקאונסיל, ז"א המוסד העליון של כל הסניפים. ראוי' היא לשבח על עבודתה זו.

עומדים לסדר קורסים לחשמלאות ע"י המרכז לעניני חינוך. העוסק בזה הוא משה קאַזאַרנובסקי, העובד בחברת החשמל הניו יורקית.

הננו מתפלאים שזה כשני חדשים שלא קבלנו מכתב מהבית. מדוע אין ההורים כותבים כלום? הננו בטוחים כי הכל בסדר בעה"ש אבל כאמור, שכמעט חדשיים לא קבלנו מהם אף מלה.

ביום א' בשבוע העבר היתה אסיפת צא"ח בביתנו, ודנו בענינים השוטפים. ב"ה שהפעולות נתרחבו בזמן האחרון, ורשימת המשתתפים הולכת וגדלה, גם קמה התעוררות לחזרת דא"ח בבתי כנסיות.

ליב ראַסקין נתקבל בתור מזכיר חלקי בסידור הרשימות ובדברים אחרים אבל הכל בחשאי ואין הקהל יודע מזה.

ביום ג' העבר למדו אצל יחזקאל לעווינטאָוו, ובשבוע שלפני זה אצל יעקב סיימאָן. מספר המשתתפים הולך וגדל בע"ה.

מענה כ"ק אד"ש לחיים אשר גאָרפינקל ולצבי אלימלך שפאַלטר על פתקאותיהם בדומה להמענה אלינו.

שד"ב בוטמאַן הי' ביחידות אצל כ"ק אד"ש, ואמר לו שמוכן הוא לנסוע בשליחות כ"ק אד"ש לכל מקום שהוא. אבל כ"ק אד"ש אמר לו שיהי' כאן ויתעסק באיזה ענין שיוכל אויסניצן זיינע כשרונות.

ב"ה. עש"ק במדבר, שעה ה' אחה"צ

הרב יאָלעס לא בא אתמול לכ"ק אד"ש וממילא לא שמענו סיום על מס' סוטה כמנהגו בכל שנה. אומרים שכ"ק שליט"א הבטיחו שיכתוב לו הסיום בכתב.

תוכן השיחות דליל ב׳ דחה״פ כבר נדפס. כן יצא בסטנסיל שיחה לנאום בחג השבועות וכ״ק שליט״א הגיהה.

חותנתי תי׳ באה אתמול בוקר ממאָנטרעאַל.

אנו מתכוננים לחג קבלת התורה בשמחה ובפנימיות.

ב״ה, ה׳ ט׳ סיון, שעה שתים עשרה

בש״ק פ׳ במדבר התועד כ״ק אד״ש. יצא בשעה 1:30 והתועד כשעה ורבע. היו כמה שיחות ובתוכם סיום על מסכת סוטה. (כאמור מקודם שכ״ק אומר סיום על מס׳ זו בכל ערב חה״ש לכבודו של הרב יאָלעס). כנראה שבתוך הדברים אמר גם מאמר מאדמה״ז.

באמירת ההפטורה, בהפסוקים קרוב לסיומה בכה מעט.

בליל א׳ דחה״ש אמר מאמר דא״ח ד״ה משכני בשעה השלישית לפנות בוקר.

בעת הסעודה שאלו כמה מזקני אנ״ש כמו הרב סימפסאָן להרש״ג, על איזה מאמר מיוסד מאמרו של כ״ק אד״ש, והרב סימפסאָן רצה לומר, שהוא על מאמר מתרס״ו, וכ״ק שליט״א אמר שבהמאמרים שלמד מתרס״ו, אין מאמר זה. ושוב רצו לומר שהוא מתרס״ח, שבו מבואר ענין התכללות המדות. ויאמר כ״ק אד״ש, שאמנם כן, מבואר שם ענין התכללות המדות, אלא שבמאמרו הוא אין מדובר מענין זה. וכנראה שבכלל לא הי׳ מרוצה משיחה זו ואמר, אַז אַלע רביים, דער שווער וכו׳ אמרו מאמרים ולא אמרו המקור לזה, ואף שהאומר דבר בשם אומרו מביא גאולה לעולם, אין ענין זה שייך באמירת המאמרים. (ואח״כ בהתועדות דיום ב׳ דיבר שיחה מיוחדת לבאר ענין זה).

בערב אחרי תפלת המנחה נערכו התהלוכות מטעם צאגו״ח, כ-ט׳ מנינים הלכו לבאָראָ פאַרק וכ-ו׳ מנינים לאיסט ניו יאָרק. ואף כי ירד גשם שוטף לא נתעכבו הצעירים בלכתם.

אחד מהמסובים בעת סעודת ליל ב׳ סיפר לי, שהרש״ג אמר: דאָס קענען

נאָר ליובאַוויטשער. וכ"ק שליט"א הי' בהתרגשות שמחה, וזה הי' נראה מתנועות ידיו, וגם ניגב את עיני קדשו.

ביום ב' דחג השבועות, לעת ערב בשעה 8 בערך יצא כ"ק אד"ש להתועד. נטל את ידיו בהכלי שהגיש לו דובער יוניק, ובצע על ב' חלות. אמר לחיים וצוה שגם הקהל יאמרו לחיים. אח"כ הכריז שכל אלו שלא נטלו עדיין יטלו ידיהם לסעודה, וצוה לנגן. ר"ש זלמנוב התחיל לנגן והכל אחריו, וכעבור כמה רגעים התחיל כ"ק שליט"א למהר את הניגון ובידיו ספק על השלחן וגם ספק את כפיו בשמחה.

במשך ההתועדות היו כי"ב-י"ג שיחות. ביניהם שיחה מיוחדת בהנוגע להתהלוכה, וביאר באריכות מעלת העבודה ברגלים ובפרט כשזה נעשה בלי חשבונות ע"ד פזר רגליך לעני ולמצות. וברך את המשתתפים בתהלוכה בברכת ברוך אתה בבואך כו' וצוה שכולם יאמרו לחיים וינגנו ניגון שמחה. וניגנו "נאַפּאָלעאָנ'ס מאַרש".

צוה שהילדים שנמצאו בעת ההתועדות יאמרו לחיים וינגנו. ונגנו "ממצרים גאלתנו", וכ"ק שליט"א נשתתף בהנגינה וגם רמז שהקהל ינגן. ודיבר שיחה מיוחדת בהנוגע אליהם.

כן דיבר שיחה מיוחדת (כנזכר לעיל) על שאין הנשיאים מראים מקורות המאמרים שלהם.

אמר מאמר דא"ח ד"ה קרוב ה' לכל קוראיו, בהמשך להמאמר הקודם.

בתוך המאמר כשהזכיר פתגמו של אדה"ז "איך וויל ניט דיין ג"ע" כו', נשבר קולו וניגב את עיניו, וכן הי' גם בהזכירו פתגם זה במאמר הקודם.

כן דיבר שיחה מיוחדת בהנוגע לנשי ישראל, בעמדו על זה שמגילת רות נקראת על שמה ולא על שמו של בועז.

בעת ההתועדות הי' בשמחה רבה, וכנראה שהי' להתועדות זו איזה המשך להתועדות דשמח"ת ושבת בראשית, שכידוע קיצר בהתועדות דשמח"ת האי שתא. וניגנו גם הרבה מניגוני שמח"ת.

בתוך הסעודה צוה לנגן את הניגון "אני מאמין" וכפלו אותו כמה פעמים.

כן צוה לנגן את ניגון הבינוני (ניגונו של כ"ק חותנו). כאשר גמרו לנגנו, הנה

ר' שמשון חאַריטאָנאָוו, שעמד על ספסל בקצה השלחנות ממול כ"ק אד"ש, התחיל לנגן ניגון זה שוב בעצמו (יש לו איזה שינויים בנוסח ניגון זה ששמע מאביו ר' שלום), וכל הקהל החריש, וכ"ק אד"ש הקשיב קשב רב לניגונו, ובגמרו חייך כ"ק אד"ש ואמר: "אַז חאַריטאָנאָוו זאָל מסכים זיין צו זינגען, איז עס נאָר בזמן מתן תורתנו, דער אויבערשטער זאָל העלפן עס זיין אַ התחלה טובה על כל השנים כולן".

אח"כ בתוך הסעודה צוה לנגן ניגון אדנ"ע, וניגנו ניגון ראָסטאָוו, אח"כ צוה לנגן לנגן ניגון אדמו"ר מוהר"ש, אדמו"ר הצ"צ ואדמו"ר האמצעי וניגון בן ג' תנועות של הבעש"ט, הה"מ ואדה"ז. ואח"כ ניגון צמאה לך נפשי לאדה"ז, לאחריו ניגון אבינו מלכנו וניגון בן ד' בבות ובבא הרביעית פעם אחת.

כמה מהאורחים כמו: דובער בוימגאַרטן מארגנטינה, צבי חיטריק מבראַזיל, וגם כמה אנשים מניו יורק העמידו יי"ש על יד כ"ק אד"ש, וכן ר' נחמן קובאַלסקי הנוהג להביא "ביכורים" בכל חג השבועות הביא טאָרט גדול, סל פירות ובקבוק יי"ש, וכ"ק אד"ש צוה לפתוח את הבקבוקים ושפך בעצמו לכוסו מכל אחד מהם ושתה מהכוס. וצוה לחלק את כל היי"ש בין הנאספים.

דיבר במיוחד על אלו הנמצאים במקומות שונים להפצת דא"ח ורוצים לעזוב אותם, ודבר אשר עליהם להשאר במקומם ולעבוד עבודתם, ולעשות מקומות אלו מקומות תורה ולגדור פרצותיהם.

בתוך הסעודה צוה לנגון גם ניגון אין אדיר כבורא.

ר' דובער בוימגאַרטן התקרר בתהלוכה, והי' לו חום גבוה, וסיפרו זאת לכ"ק אד"ש וצוה שיבוא לההתועדות, וגם נתן לו מהחלה שלו.

כשבא הרב יאָלעס מפילאַדעלפיא, חתך כ"ק שליט"א מהטאָרט ונתן לו.

אחרי ניגון בן ד' בבות צוה לנגן, "ניע זשוריטיע חלאָפצי", והי' בשמחה רבה ועמד מלוא קומתו ורקד על מקומו משך זמן, וכמובן גם כל הקהל עמדו על רגליהם ורקדו.

מסל הפירות שהביא ר"נ קובאַלסקי, לקח ענב אחד וברך עליו, וביקש מען זאָל ניט חאַפן, אבל לא הועיל, והזקנים התחילו לחטוף, וגם חטפו מהטאָרט, שטעם כ"ק ממנו, והי' נראה שהי' מאד לא מרוצה מזה.

ובשנה העברה צוה לנגן בהזדמנות דומה את הניגון "עסן עסט מען".

ההתועדות נגמרה קרוב לשעה 3. כ"ק ברך על הכוס, התפללו מעריב והוא

הבדיל בעצמו ואח"כ חלוקת כוס של ברכה, שנמשכה כמה שעות.

דובער בוימגאַרטן שבא מארגנטינה, בה הוא נמצא בתור שליח מיוחד של כ"ק אד"ש, וכבר הביא תלמידים לישיבה מהספרדים אשר בבואנוס איירעס, סיפר לי דבר נפלא שקרא לו ביום י"ב תמוז העבר.

ביום זה הי' צריך לעבור את הגבול מברזיל לארגנטינה. גבול זה מסומן בנהר או אגם, ואת הנהר עוברים בפערי (פאַראָם) ז.א. ספינה גדולה שלתוכה נכנסים גם מכוניות על משאם ואנשיהם.

ביום זה בבוקר, לקח קצת יי"ש עם יהודי אחד יליד פולין, שבצעירותו למד בישיבת חכמי לובלין, אמנם במשך הזמן נתפקר וחי חיי הפקר הן בכשרות ושבת והן בהנחת תפילין.

בערל דיבר אתו ועוררו ע"ד שמירת המצוות, אמנם האיש לא היטה אוזן, ונוסף ע"ז גם דבר דברי שטות ועזות כלפי כו' בטענות הידועות בהשמדת ששת המיליון וכדומה. בראות בערל שדיבוריו אין פועלים הפסיק מלדבר, והאיש המשיך בשטויותיו כו'.

לעת ערב נכנס בערל במכוניתו להפערי על כל מטענה של בגדים וחפצים נוסף על הסכום של אלפיים שקל שהי' לו במזודה.

כעבור משך זמן של נסיעה בהספינה התנגשה באנית מטען של בננות ולא עברו רגעים אחדים והאני' בה נסע בערל עם כל מטענה והמכוניות והאנשים ירדו תהומה, וגם הוא במכוניתו נטבע בנהר. המכונית היתה סגורה, ודקות מספר חשב שח"ו לא יהי' בין החיים, וחשב אם עליו לחשוב מלות הוידוי, אמנם החליט שבי"ב תמוז אין אומרים תחנון.

בכוחות על-אנושיים התגבר על אחת הדלתות וצף על פני המים. שמונים איש נטבעו, ובחמלת ה' עליו אחז אחת הקורות, ואם כי המים זרמו בחזקה, עד שהאנשים שרצו לבוא לעזרתו מהחוף לא יכלו לשחות, והוא איננו יודע לשחות ובכל זאת בנפלאות הבורא נתקרב להחוף וניצל.

באותו יום בבוקר הרגיש איזה הרגשה משונה, והבריק לכ"ק אד"ש להזכירו לטובה. וכפי חשבונו הזמן בו טבע הי' באותו זמן שכ"ק הי' נמצא על ציון כ"ק חותנו.

בהיותו על החוף שהי׳ כולו רווי מים, ורצו לקחתו לבית חולים אבל לא רצה בשום אופן, כי תפיליו נמצאו במכונית שנטבעה, ורצה למהר לעיר אחרת בה נמצאים יהודים שומרי דת.

לראשונה הובילום לתחנת המשטרה בעיירה למסור דו״ח על המאורע, וירא כי היהודי הפולני גם הוא בא לשם, כי כנראה שרצה לדעת משלומו.

בראותו שלא יוכל להועיל בהרבה להשוטרים, כי דבורו אז בהשפה הספרדית לא הי׳ אז כל כך טוב, הלך לפינה מרוחקת, ויעמוד להתפלל ערבית. אויף האַרצן איז אים געווען כמובן גוט ביטער, ובהתפללו התחיל להכיר את הנס הגדול שעשה אתו השי״ת. ובדברי התפלה באמת ואמונה, המעביר בניו בין גזרי יום סוף כו׳ וכו׳ נתעורר במאד ויבך בכי רב, והתפלה ארכה זמן רב. ובגמרו תפלה נרגשת זו ניגש שוב אל מקום מעמד האנשים לראות מה עליו לעשות הלאה.

להפתעתו ראה את היהודי הנזכר והנה עיניו נפוחות מבכי, ויאמר: אה, האָב איך יעצט געדאַוונט אַ מעריב, איך געדענק שוין ניט ווען איך האָב אַזוי געדאַוונט. ויספר כי בראותו את בערל מתפלל נשבר לבו בקרבו ויעמוד להתפלל מעריב. ויבטיח באותו מעמד, שיעבור עליו מה, הוא יניח תפילין בכל יום.

כעבור כמה חדשים פגש שוב את האיש הזה. ואם כי לא שינה את דרכיו בשמירת שבת וכשרות אבל תפילין מניח בכל יום, ויראהו את התפילין שנושא אותו בכל מקום היותו.

ישנם עוד כמה פרטים בדבר זה ואולי בהזדמנות אחרת אכתוב אי״ה.

א׳ י״ג סיון, שעה שביעית ערב

הרשימה הנזכרת כתבתי בכמה הפסקות כי לא הי׳ לי זמן פנוי לזה.

הנני כותב את האמת כי הנני מאוכזב קצת מכל הענין. כי כאשר כתב לי יצחק בדברים תקיפים, כי באמת רצה להתקשר עם אחד התלמידים אלא, עס האָט אים ניט געפאַסט, חשבתי שבאם אכתוב כפי יכולתי יכתוב גם הוא אלי מפרטי חייהם, כי בודאי שום תלמיד לא ירצה להסכם חד צדדי. ולפועל: אם כי הנני מתאמץ לכתוב כפי יכולתי על אף זמני המצומצם. כמעט לא קבלתי תשובה חוץ משני מכתבים קצרים באישור קבלת מכתבי, אינו כותב כלום

על חייהם, אף כי בודאי במשך זמן של שלשה חדשים וחצי היו כמה דברים מעניינים בשבילנו, ועוד זאת ששמעתי מתלמידים דברים מעניינים מהנעשה בארץ ומכם אף מלה.

עוד זאת, זה קרוב ל-ג' חדשים שלא קבלתי מכתב מההורים וגם לא מליבל וזהבה, אם כי כתבתי להם. ולולי הד"ש שקבלתי מר' אברהם מאַיאָר, ובנימין האַלפרין, המבקר על אחת האוניות הישראליות וביקר בחנותו של אבא לפני הפליגו, לא הייתי יודע מה הי' להם.

על חג השבועות נמצא אצלנו הת' ניסן מאַנגל ממאָנטרעאַל, והיום הוא חוזר להתם. הוא הנהו אחד הילדים שנצלו מכבשני האש בגרמני', וכשבע שנים ויותר שהוא לומד בתו"ת במאָנטרעאַל, אַ חסידישער בחור, בעל כשרונות ובעל מעלות. כפי ששמעתי שכ"ק צוה עליו ללמוד באוניברסיטה אף כי בעצמו מאד לא רצה. הוא בעל השפעה, וידעתי מאנשים שכ"ק שליט"א שלחם אליו לדבר אתו וללמוד אצלו. כעת הוא מורה חלקי בישיבה הנזכרת.

ב, י"ד סיון, שעה שתים עשרה לילה

בשבוע העבר היום ה' למדו אצל משה קאַזאַרנאָווסקי, והתחילו ללמוד קונט' י"ב תמוז תש"ט, והיום למדו אצל חיים אשר גאָרפינקל.

על שבת קדש נסעו בשליחות צא"ח לקליוולאַנד, מענדל בוימגאַרטן יהושע דובראַווסקי, לייב מאָצקין, דובער אַלעניק, נחמן סודאַק ושמרי' פרוס. ביום עש"ק ביקרו את הישיבה דטעלז, ובש"ק בקרו בבתי כנסיות ונאמו בהם, באחד הבתי כנסיות קבעו אמירת תהלים ובשני קביעות לימוד, והיתה גם התועדות קידושא רבא.

ניסן מאַנגל סיפר לי שהת' משה, בנו של ר' אלי' נחום שקליאַר הי' ביחידות אצל כ"ק אד"ש, ושאלו: כשבאים לבית הכנסת בעת אמירת הלל, אם לומר עם הצבור או לאמרו אחרי גמר התפילה ביחידות. ויאמר לו: הרביים היו נוהגים לומר הלל כסדרו אחר התפלה, וישאלהו שוב ובאם מאחרים תפלת הצבור? ויאמר: פאַרשפעטיגט מען ניט. וישאל שוב, און ווי איז אויב מען האָט פאָרט פאַרשפעטיגט? ויאמר: אם אומרים הלל שלם, אומרים אותו אחר התפלה, ואם חצי הלל שצריך לצאת בברכה, יאמרהו עם הצבור.

אתמול הי' יואל אצלי לרשום את תוכן השיחות דחה"ש. רשמנו אתמול רק חלק מהתוכן, ואי"ה מחר נקוה לגמרו.

כבוד קדושת אד"ש, הגיה ביום ה' את קטע השיחה די' שבט תשי"ג, בכדי לחזור אותה בבתי כנסיות בש"ק, וזו היא כבר השיחה השני' היוצאת ע"י צא"ח, בתור חומר לנאומים בבתי כנסיות. הרב חודקוב כשמסרה לכ"ק אד"ש, אמר כ"ק שליט"א: עס זיינען דאָך שוין דאָ כמה שיחות בקובץ ליובאַוויטש וכו', ויאמר לו הרב חודקוב שרוצים להוציא שיחה זו בתור חומר מיוחד לש"ק זה, ויאמר כ"ק אד"ש: טוב, אגיה אותה. נדפסה במימיוגראַף (סטענסיל).

רשימת החוזרים בבתי כנסיות ב"ה מתרבה, וכנראה שישנם יותר על מאה חוזרים כ"י.

אתמול מסר כ"ק אד"ש מכתביו על דבר האניות הישראליות, על מנת להדפיסם בחוברת ה"פרדס" לחודש הבא. ע"פ בקשתו של העורך הרב עלבערג. ירחון זה נדפס בבית דפוסנו.

ב"ה, ה' י"ז סיון, שעה שביעית ערב.

(המשך לרשימת חה"ש)

בתוך הסעודה דיבר כ"ק אד"ש שיחה מיוחדת בקשר עם כינוס התורה שתוכנן למחר, איסרו חג. הוא הזמין להכינוס את אלו שהוזמנו כבר, וגם את אלו שלא הוזמנו עדיין, אם שלא הוזמנו בלי כוונה או אפילו בכוונה (דבר זה אמר פעמיים, בשחוק).

בקשר עם שיחה זו אמר שינגנו ניגון אחד מי יודע, אחד החופר בור. כשהתחיל יואל לנגנו עם ניגון "מתנגדי" משונה, אמר כ"ק שלא ע"ז כוונתו, אז התחיל ר' אברהם מאַיאָר לנגנו מהתחלתו "תנו, תנו רבנן, רבנן בתרייתא". אמנם, לא ידע כנראה את כל בבות הניגון, וגם כנראה שהתבייש, וכ"ק רמז שינגנו, והתחילו הקהל לעזור לו, אמנם כמובן שלא את כל הבבות ידע, ובאחדות עזר כ"ק אד"ש בעצמו עד שעזר גם בבא האחרונה: י"ג שערים היו

במקדש. בגמר הניגון אמר כ"ק שליט"א: דער אויבערשטער זאָל העלפן אַז די וואָס לערנען ביי די בחורים חסידות זאָלן זיך בעסער אויסלערנען.

יואל לא גמר עדיין את רשימת התוכן, ולא אדע מתי נוכל לעבור עליו כי כמעט עברו שבועיים מחה"ש.

היום אסיפת צא"ח בביתו של משה גאָלדמאַן.

אתמול הייתי אצל יואל, כי חשבתי שאוכל לעשות משהו בנוגע להתוכן, אמנם עסוק הוא עם רשימות החידושי תורה שנאמרו בעת הכינוס של תורה, שכ"ק אד"ש רוצה שיודפסו.

הכינוס הי' ביום ג', אסרו חג השבועות, ואני לא נוכחתי בו, כי הי' יום עבודה אצלי, אלא שבאתי בערב, להתועדות ר"ש לויטין, והעיקר לחזרת המאמר דחה"ש.

כפי שאמרו לי הי' זה כינוס של כמה מרבני ליובאַוויטש, כי כ"ק שליט"א אמר להרב מענטליק, שיזמינו רק רבני אנ"ש, ואמרו בו חידושי תורה, בין המחדשים היו: ר"מ גרינברג, רב דפטרסון, נ. דזש., רמ"מ פעלדמאַן, צבי חיטריק מבראַזיל, דובער שמטוב מדיטרויט, חיים סערעבראַנסקי מאוסטראַליע, אָזדאַבע מטאָראָנטאָ, ועוד. ובסוף הכינוס הי' התועדות וגם חזרת המאמר. הדברים בפרטיותם – לא אדע. וכנראה שההצעה היתה של הרב מענטליק וכ"ק שליט"א לא רק שקיבלה, אלא שרצה בפרוש שתצא לפועל.

יצחק קורן, ראש תנועת המושבים של פא"י בארץ, ביקר אצל כ"ק אדמו"ר שליט"א ביום ג' העבר. נכנס בשעה 8:10 ויצא בשעה 11:50 ורק אז יצא כ"ק אדמו"ר שליט"א להתפלל ערבית עם הציבור, לעומת כל הימים שהוא מתפלל עם הציבור משעה 9:30.

ב"ה, א, כ"ז סיון.

אחרי הפסקה אשתדל שוב לרשום על המתרחש ואתכם הסליחה.

אתמול ש"ק מברכים שלח התוועד כ"ק אד"ש כדרכו. היו מקודם כמה

שיחות בענין המרגלים ואמר מאמר דא״ח ד״ה שלח לך אנשים, ותוכנו במעלת מדת היסוד, ויוסף הוא המשביר, אשר נתן מלחמו לדל. והוא בהמשך להמאמרים דחה״ש. וכנראה שקשור עם חודש תמוז, חודש הגאולה. בדברו במעלת יוסף הצדיק רעד קולו, ובכה מעט.

אמר גם שיחה בענין חלה, ושיחה מיוחדת במעלתו של יוסף הצדיק וגם כאן רעד קולו. וצוה לנגן ניגון אני מאמין. ובשיחה אחרונה נתן ברכתו הק׳ להמוסדות בהם מתחנכים ילדים וילדות, וכנראה שזה קשור בהבאַנקעט שעושים מוסדות בית רבקה.

על שאלת צעאגו״ח בענין הנגינה, נראה מהמענה שהכוונה היא, שינגנו כל הקהל וגם כמה מהבחורים ואברכים יכינו עצמם להנגינה, ויסדרו הניגונים מקודם, וגם תהי׳ מקהלה שתנוצח ע״י איש יודע נגן, בעל מקצוע.

ביום ה׳ העבר סדרנו כמה ניגונים לש״ק, והי׳ קצת יותר טוב בעת ההתועדות, אָבער נאָך ניט כראוי.

נמצא כאן דודו של כ״ק אד״ש וגיסו של כ״ק אדמו״ר נ״ע*. בא ביום ב׳ לפני שבועיים בבוקר, וכ״ק אד״ש, אחרי גמרו את היחידות דיום א׳ נסע לשדה התעופה לקבל פניו.

הוא מסר גם לי ד״ש מאבינו שי׳.

בעת ההתועדות סדרו לו מקום מיוחד ע״י שולחן כ״ק שליט״א משמאלו, ממול הרש״ג שי׳.

כאמור לעיל מסר כ״ק אדמו״ר שליט״א מכתביו ע״ד האניות הישראליות להדפיסם בקובץ הפרדס, ונדפסו בהחוברת לחודש זה. מכתבים אלו הם ליקוטים ממכתביו להר״ש זוין ולמר וילהלם בירושלים.

ב, ה׳ תמוז, שעה 11 לילה.

כ״ק אדמו״ר שליט״א התועד בש״ק ג׳ תמוז כרגיל. יצא בשעה 1:30 והתועד כשעה ומחצה.

*) ר׳ בן ציון שניאורסאהן.

הרה"ח ר' גרשון מענדל גרליק

הרה"ח ר' מרדכי שוסטרמאן

בש"ק עלו לתורה ג' חתנים: גרשון מענדל גאַרעליק (הכלה היא בתו של ר' שלום פאָזנער מפיטסבורג; שמואל דוד גורקאָוו; ושמואל העבער (אביו דודנו של ר' חיים אליעזר הבר וגיסו של הרב מ"ד ריווקין). וגם בר מצוה של זלמן בן ר' מענדל מאַראָזאָוו.

כ"ק אדמו"ר שליט"א הי' בשמחה רבה. דיבר ה' שיחות וביניהם מאמר דא"ח ד"ה השם נפשנו בחיים ביאור על מ"ש בספר נועם אלימלך בענין ואתפלג קורח הו"ע ויבדל בין מים למים וביאור הצ"צ ע"ז. המאמר לא נאמר בניגון מיוחד וגם הקהל ישבו במקומותיהם.

תוכן השיחות בביאור החג דג' תמוז שהוא עוד נעלה – אצל החסידים – מהחג די"ב תמוז. גם הביא מ"ש בסדר עולם דהנס של יהושע, שמש בגבעון דום הי' בג' תמוז. ואשר הנס דג' תמוז הוא נוגע ביחוד לכ"ק אדמו"ר.

צוה לנגן ניגוני שמחה. ובאחת השיחות צוה גם לנגן ניגון חתונה. המחותנים נתנו יי"ש. וכ"ק אדמו"ר שליט"א מסר היי"ש לכ"א מהמחותנים ע"מ לחלקם להמתאספים.

אתמול היתה החתונה של גרשון מענדל וכ"ק אד"ש הי' מסדר הקידושין.

ואח״כ נסעו החתן-כלה והמחותנים באוירון לפיטסבורג להסעודה. גם כמה מהבחורים נסעו לשם.

בערב היתה הבר מצוה אצל זלמן מאַראָזאָוו.

הת׳ יהושע ווילנסקי מברידזפאָרט הביא לכ״ק אדמו״ר את אחותה של מרת גאָלדאַ מאיר. היא אחת המתעסקות בהקהלה דשם בפרט בעניני חינוך. חלק מהזמן הי׳ גם יהושע אתה אצל כ״ק אד״ש, ואח״כ רמז לו שיצא. ודבר איתה בעניני חינוך והעיקר שיהי׳ החינוך כדבעי.

(אם תשתדלו לכתוב יותר גם אני אשתדל, כי הנני עסוק מאוד ועליכם להשפיע עלי שאעשה את המאמץ לכתיבה מפורטת).

ב״ה, ד׳ יד תמוז, שעה שתים עשרה לילה.

ההתועדות דחג הגאולה ביום ב, יב תמוז הותחלה אחרי תפלת ערבית בשעה חצי העשירית, ונמשכה עד קרוב לשעה 3.

התועדו בהסוכה, ולקראת חג הגאולה הגביהו התלמידים את הגג ועשאוהו בשיפוע, בכדי שירדו הגשמים מעליו. מתכנן הבנין הוא הת׳ מענדל פוטערפאַס, ובזה גם נכנס יותר אויר להסוכה ונראה יותר מרווח.

בהכנס כ״ק אדמו״ר שליט״א וישב על מקומו, כנראה אַז ער איז געווען פון דעם זייער צופרידן, ויאמר: ס׳איז נאָר אַ התחלה, עס זאָל זיין אַ גוטע התחלה אויף הרחבה. ושמחה נראתה על פניו.

ר״ש זלמנוב התחיל את הניגון די״ב תמוז, וכ״ק ניגנו בשמחה, ובגמר ניגון זה התחיל כ״ק בעצמו ניגון אחד שמח החביב עליו (אחד הניגונים שניגן ר״מ דוואָרקין ע״ה), וניגנו בשמחה רבה.

ודיבר שיחה אודות י״ב תמוז אשר הוא המשך הגאולה דיציאת מצרים והסביר החילוק של הגאולות עד הגאולה העתידה ע״י משיח צדקנו. והתחלתי לנגן ״ממצרים גאלתנו״.

ואח״ז עוד כמה שיחות, וביניהן ניגונים שמחים. ופ״א התחיל כ״ק אד״ש

בעצמו ניגון שמח"ת (הרכין ראשו לקראת יואל שי' והתחיל את הניגון) וניגנו בשמחה גדולה ובחזקה, וגם טפף בידיו.

אמר מאמר דא"ח ד"ה מי מנה עפר יעקב, בביאור השמות יעקב וישראל. ויצא יעקב מבאר שבע, חרון גרון, וגם החילוקים דבאר שבע (בקמץ ובסגל).

באחת השיחות שאחרי המאמר ביאר הפסוק והשב לשכננו שבעתיים מקאַפיטל ע"ט. וביום ג' קרא את יואל ואמר לו כמה דברים וביניהם גם ששיחה זו יכניסו בהמאמר.

גם דיבר בהמאמר ענין ופרצת ימה וקדמה כו' וסיימו: יעלה הפורץ לפנינו שהוא משיח צדקנו שהוא מבני פרץ במהרה בימינו.

אחר המאמר דיבר אודות הבנין בכפר חב"ד, שהוא בנין ביהכ"נ ובהמ"ד, ונתן ברכה גדולה לזה. ואחרי שיחה זו צוה שכל אלה שקנו או שקונים בנינים עבור המוסדות יאמרו לחיים, והזכיר: הישיבה דבוסטון (שבאותו יום גמרו את הקנין), בית רבקה במאָנטרעאַל שקנו בנין חדש, מוסד אהלי תורה (של ר"מ טייטלבוים שקנו בנין באיסטערן פאַרקוויי), וגם את גן ישראל, וצוה שיאמרו לחיים גם עבור גן ישראל בכפר חב"ד, ועוד.

ר"ז דוכמאַן שהי' מבוסם, ביקש גם ברכה עבור ועד המסדר לבנין בית המדרש וכ"ק שליט"א תמה ע"ז ואמר: זיי האָבן דען אַ בנין? ועוד כמה פעמים שדיבר שלא כענין וכ"ק השתיקו.

באחת השיחות סיפר מה שסיפר כ"ק חותנו אשר בהיותו בן ט"ו בי"ב תמוז והיו אז בנאות דשא, אמר לו אז כ"ק אביו שיבוא אליו בהשכמה ובא אליו בשעה הרביעית, ואמר שיסעו לליובאַוויטש (אף שכפי הסדר היו נוסעים לליובאַוויטש ביום ב' כנהוג, וזה הי' כנראה ביום ד'). הנסיעה ארכה כמה שעות. בעת הנסיעה אמר כ"ק אדמו"ר לאביו שא"ז הרבנית (אם כ"ק אדנ"ע) הלא אינה יודעת שבאים ותפחד מהביאה הפתאומית ויענהו: די באָבע ווייסט שוין.

בבואם לליובאַוויטש הלכו להרבנית, וכ"ק אדנ"ע נכנס אליה ושהה משך זמן ובצאתו האָט זי אים באַגלייט מיט אַ ליכטיקן פנים און מיט האַרציקע ברכות. ואז נסעו להאוהל.

בין הענינים שהיו על האוהל, שמסר לו שם ענין הנשיאות, ושם את שתי ידיו עליו ויברכהו. ודיבר אודות ענין העקדה, ענין המסירות נפש, (היו הרבה

פרטים בזה ואיני זוכרם כרגע, ואקצר) וסיים: אַזוי און ניט אַנדערש. ואמר לפניו ד״ה פותחין בברכה בענין מתניים המעמידים את הגוף, ענין מס״נ (מאגרת הקודש).

כ״ק אד״ש הסביר את הענינים איך שהם שייכים לכאו״א, אַזוי און ניט אַנדערש.

במשך ההתועדות צוה לנגן ניגוני האדמורי״ם מהבעש״ט עד ניגון הבינוני, שהי׳ חביב אצל כ״ק חותנו.

בודאי ידוע לכם מההפגנה שהיתה בוואַשינגטון ע״י הבית הלבן, מחברי נטורי קרתא. ביום ה׳ העבר היתה משלחת של ז׳ או ח׳ רבנים, כנראה מחסידי הסטמר אצל כ״ק אד״ש, גם הרב חודקוב נכנס עמהם, ושהו כשעה וחצי. תוכן הדברים אינו ידוע לנו, וכפי הנשמע ביקשו שכ״ק אד״ש יצא בגלוי יחד אתם, ומסתמא לא הסכים כ״ק שליט״א לזה.

בשיחה מיוחדת דיבר כ״ק שליט״א בענין זה, וקשה לי לרשום גם תוכן שיחה זו אמנם אשתדל לכתוב כפי הבנתי.

סיפר שאצל כ״ק חותנו היו בשלחן הכתיבה כמה כתבים ישנים, בכוונה שאם יבואו לחפש יוכל לערב בין כתבים אלה את המכתבים והענינים הדורשים הסתר שלא יוכלו המחפשים להשים עיניהם בהם. וכן הי׳ שבהחיפוש שהי׳ בעת המאסר לא יכלו למצוא את הדברים שרצו כי עירבם בין הכתבים הישנים.

גם סיפר בשחוק, שהי׳ יהודי בעיירה קטנה שבראותו שוטר, פאָליצייסקי פחד במאד. וישאלוהו למה מפחד? ויאמר, שכתב מכתב למישהו, וידבק עליו בול דואר שהיתה עליו תמונת הקיסר, אלא שהפך את הבול ופני הקיסר למטה, ובמילא הוא בזיון להקיסר ומפחד הוא, שהדבר נודע להקיסר, והשוטר הוא בא כוחו ובטח יאסרהו.

עס איז דאָ אַ ענין וואָס אַלע האָבן געלייענט, וכולם כותבים אודות זה. יש בדבר זה האשמה, וכולם צועקים שהדביקו את הבול פאַרקערט ועצם הדבר צריך בירור, אם ההאשמה אינה נכונה, איז דאָך די זאַך אַ סאַך ערגער מזה שהדביקו את הבול הפוך, או ששלחו את המכתב לכתובת בלתי נכונה. ואם ההאשמה נכונה היא, וואָס איז נוגע שהפכו את הבול, הלא צריכים לברר את עצם הדבר, אלא שרוצים להבליע את עצם ההאשמה בתוך הטענות אַז מען זאָל ניט ריידן וועגן דעם עצם ענין.

דיבר הרבה מזה שאין שומעים את דעת הרבנים אלא דעת בעלי בתים, שגם שומרי תורה שביניהם אינם ראויים לשבת בדין עם רבנים. וצריכים להושיב שלשה או שני רבנים לברר את הדבר.

אמר גם שצריך להתלמד מהקאָנסערוואַטיווע והריפאָרמער את הדברים הטובים (אמר: דינם כבר נפסק בש"ע, אָבער אָן זייער שאדן דאַרף מען זיך פון זיי לערנען): א) שלא לדבר בקריאת התורה וחזרת הש"ץ. ב) החלטתם שלא לאסוף כספים באופן בלתי נאות כמו ממשחק הבינגו, פינג-פונג ומשחק קלפים.ג) בשכל עניני דת רק הרב הוא המכריע, ואין לשום אחד מהבע"ב להתערב בזה, ובאם יתערב יענש.

גם אמר שבענין הקודם, מתערבים גם אלה שצריכים לשבת רק על התורה והעבודה, ומנתקים אותם מהלימוד בטענה שהוא דבר גדול וצריכים הם להתעסק בזה על קדושת שמו ית'.

(הרשום לעיל אינו מדויק, וכאמור שרשמתי הדברים כפי שהבנתים וכ"ק אד"ש כשקרא את יואל אמר לו שירשום את המאמר והשיחות בהקדם האפשרי, אַלע שרייבן אין די בלעטער וכו').

כאשר דיבר כ"ק אודות כפר חב"ד אמר בנימין אַלטהויז לחיים, וכנראה שכ"ק יאמר לו דבר מה, אמנם השיב לו רק לחיים ולברכה, ודודו של כ"ק שליט"א שישב לשמאלו אמר: זיין טאַטע טוט דאָך אין דעם, ואמר כ"ק: באַ עם איז פאַראַן דער ימה וקדמה כו' אָבער עס פעלט דער ופרצת.

הרש"ג שי' לקח הרבה משקה (ואחר ההתועדות נתן גם חזרה) והיו איזה דין ודברים בינו ובין כ"ק אד"ש. מה היו הדברים לא שמעתי, אמנם שמעתי מה שכ"ק אמר בקול רם: דאָ זיינען דאָך פאַראַן די תלמידים פון תומכי תמימים, איז ביז די הנהלה וועט זיך מתבונן זיין זאָל אַלע תלמידים שרייען ופרצת ימה כו' ויאמרו ניגון שמח.

התלמידים עם כל המתאספים התחילו לצעוק בקול רם: ופרצת ימה וקדמה וצפונה ונגבה, ואני התחלתי ניגון שמח מאד. כ"ק שליט"א עמד מלוא קומתו וניגן בקול את הניגון והי' בשמחה גדולה ובתוך הניגון אמר שוב: זאָלן אַלע שרייען ופרצת כו'. ושוב צעק כל הקהל בקול וגם כ"ק צעק בקול ובהדגשה: **ופרצת ימה וקדמה וצפונה ונגבה**, ושוב את הניגון בקול ובשמחה רבה עד שישב על כסא קדשו.

היתה שיחה מיוחדת אודות ההנהלה אַז עס קומט צו די קינדער און צו די

אייניקלאַך זוכט מען אַלע וועגן און אַז עס קומט צו דער ישיבה ישנם מניעות כו׳ (כנראה שבעיקר התכוון להרב . . . שקירב את נכדיו סמוך לכ״ק אד״ש לומר לחיים).

כן היתה שיחה מיוחדת לנשים.

בניגון אדמו״ר הזקן ציוה לנגן את הבבא הרביעית ג׳ פעמים.

השעה מאוחרת, ועלי לקום בבוקר לעבודה.

אומרים שכ״ק יסע מחר לגן ישראל. שאלתי את הרב חודקוב ואמר שאינו יודע מזה כלום. וכבר הי׳ כן לפני שנתיים שלא ידעו מהנסיעה עד שעתיים לפניה.

א, ח״י תמוז, צום שבעה עשר יהפך לשמחה, שעה 12 לילה

הנני מצטער מאד כי איני כותב רשימתי בסדר. זמני מצומצם מאד לאחרונה. קיבלתי עלי הגהת חלק מחידושי הר״ן ע״מ נדה מהרב שטערן, והוא משלם לי בספרים (כמובן שכסף לקנין ספרים אין לי עדיין). אתמול הכינותי יחד עם יואל את תוכן השיחות די״ב תמוז, וישבנו עד שעה שלישית אחר חצות.

בש״ק זה נכנס כ״ק אדמו״ר שליט״א לבית המדרש בשעה 7:05, והיו אז כעשרה תלמידים בכל ביהמ״ד, ויאמר לדוד ראַסקין: גרייט צו די בחורים איך וועל חזר'ן חסידות.

בשעה 8 בדיוק נכנסו התלמידים לחדר קדשו ויאמר מאמר דא״ח זה: והי׳ שארית יעקב וגו׳ שארך כארבעים רגעים. החוזרים יואל ואברהם שם טוב לא היו בעת אמירת המאמר. וכ״ק אד״ש צוה לסגור את הדלת לפני אמירתו. בתוך המאמר אמר עוד הפעם את החלק ע״פ והשב לשכנינו שבעתיים, דקפי׳ ע״ט. התלמידים אומרים כי פניו היו נוהרים (לעומת הרצינות בעת האמירה דש״פ זכור. כנזכר לעיל ברשימתי).

הת׳ ישראל פרידמאַן חזר על המאמר. וכנראה שחזרו בטוב.

מרת גייסינסקי (זוג׳ של ר׳ משה אהרן) סיפרה לי ביום ועש״ק, שלפני זמן, בהיותה מעוברת, אמרו לה הרופאים שצריכים לנתחה, וכנראה שמצבה הי׳ רציני, ותודיע בכתב לכ״ק אד״ש אודות זה. בערב צלצל אלי׳ הרב חודקוב

ויאמר בשם כ"ק אד"ש: איר מיט אייער מאַן וועט דערלעבן צו פירן אייערע קינדער צו דער חופה.

כעבור כמה ימים ומצבה לא הוטב, והרופאים אמרו שוב שצריך לנתח, נכנסה לכ"ק אד"ש, ותשפוך לפניו את מר לבבה. כ"ק שליט"א הפסיק את שטף דיבורה ויאמר: איך האָב ניט וואָס צו מוסיף אויף דעם וואָס איך האָב איבערגעגעבן בשם הרב חודקוב.

וב"ה שהכל עבר כשורה והולידה בת בריאה לאוי"ט.

חותנתי מתכוננת לנסוע ביום השלישי הבא לנאות דשא לגיסי בקאַנאַדאַ על משך כמה שבועות. גם שרה'לה תחי' תסע אתה אי"ה. שאלתי את כ"ק אד"ש אם נכון הדבר שתסע אתה. ויענה: עס זאָל זיין בשעה טובה ומוצלחת.

על ש"ק פ' חוקת נסעתי לברונקס בשליחות צא"ח והייתי עם הת' שמרי' פרוס אצל גיסו מרדכי דובינסקי, ובעלר יוניק עם חיים סערעבראַנסקי היו אצל משה לעבערטאָוו. נאמנו בהרבה בתי כנסיות וגם היתה קידושא רבא אצל מרדכי דובינסקי.

באותו ש"ק הי' מספר נכון של תלמידים בברייטאָן (גם זה חלק מהעיר ניו יורק) וגם הם נאמו בהרבה בתי כנסיות וסדרו התועדות.

ביום הראשון י"א תמוז נסע רא"א ליס עם מענדל בוימגאַרטן לאָלבאַני וסידרו שם התועדות מפוארה.

ענין הנסיעות כבר נכנס בסדר העבודה של צא"ח וב"ה שמספר נכון של חברים משתתף בזה.

כן, חזרת דא"ח בבתי כנסיות נתחזקה, ביחוד אחרי שמו"ל מדי שבוע בשבוע את קטעי שיחותיו של כ"ק אד"ש, שהם חומר טוב להחזרה.

בנוסף על הלימוד של שו"ע ודא"ח ביום השלישי או השני בשבוע, התחלנו ללמוד גם גמרא מס' נדה ביום החמישי. בערל יוניק גבאי החבורה. הודיע ע"ז

בפתקא לכ"ק אד"ש וירשום כ"ק שליט"א את המענה: אזכירם על האוהל להצלחה בכל הנ"ל ועי"ז גם לתוספות הצלחה בכל עניניהם.

ד.

תש"כ

זכרונות מ"בית חיינו"

תש"כ

ביום ב', כ"ז אלול, ימלאו לי ל"ב שנים לאוי"ט, ומכיון שאין יחידות באופן רשמי בכל חודש אלול וכן בחודש תשרי, בקשתי את הרב חמ"א שי' חודקוב אשר באם מישהו יכנס ביום א' לכ"ק אדמו"ר שליט"א יתן גם לי רשות להכנס ליחידות והסכים.

וביום א', י"ט אלול אמר לי שאוכל להכנס בין השעות 8-10. כשבאתי לבית המדרש לפני שעה שמינית הי' כל הפרוזדור מלא והנשים צדקניות חברות הבית רבקה והישיבה תו"ת אשר כמו בכל שנה נכנסות לקבל אצל כ"ק אד"ש את ברכתו לפני ר"ה. הן נכנסו בשעה התשיעית בלוית ר' יצחק גולדין ורא"י קורנבליט שרשמו את שמותיהן ושם אמותיהן. גם חמותו תי' נכנסה לכ"ק שליט"א.

הן נכנסו כולן יחד ומחמת מספרן הגדול לא יכלו להכנס כולן להיכל הקודש והרבה נשארו בחדר המדרגות. הי' בלתי סדר. וכשכילה כ"ק לשוחח ולברך הגישו הרבה מהן פתקאות עם בקשות ובשום אופן לא יכול ר"ל גראָנער להוציאן.

עוד אלו יוצאות – אלו באין: הרב קזרנובסקי עם משלחת מביהכ"נ בברייטאָן וחבריה, הרב מאיר ישר, שמואל שולזינגר (בעל הדפוס), נשיא ביהכ"נ ובע"ב אחדים. הם אספו סכום של אלפיים ומחצה שקלים עבור בתי ספר למלאכה בכפר חב"ד ונכנסו לכ"ק. אחר שיצאו נשאר עוד בהיכל הקדש מר שמואל שולזינגר וכפי שסיפר אח"כ דרש כ"ק מאתו כי יוציאו לאור את התלמוד

הרה״ח ר׳ שלמה אהרן קזרנובסקי

ירושלמי, (זה כבר זמן רב אשר כ״ק אד״ש דורש מהאחים שולזינגר להו״ל את הירושלמי, ובפורים (תשי״ז?) דיבר שיחה מיוחדת אודות ענין ההדפסה אשר כנראה היתה מיועדת להם). כן אמר לו הרב רש״א קזרנובסקי (הוא בעצמו אינו זוכר זאת) אשר בעת שהיו חברי המשלחת בחדר ק׳ שאל הפרז. את כ״ק אד״ש: מה זה חסיד ליובאוויטש? וכ״ק אחז את שולזינגר בידיו ואמר: אָט דאָס איז אַ ליובאַוויטשער חסיד!

לאחרי שיצאו הם נכנסו ועוד כמה אנשים לפני, ואחרי נכנס הרב מלצר בהגאון רא״ז ז״ל.

כ״ק אד״ש יצא להתפלל ערבית בביהמ״ד, ואחרי כן נמשכה היחידות ואני נכנסתי בשעה 11 בערך.

מסרתי פתקא וז״ל:

״ביום ב, כ״ז אלול ימלאו לי אי״ה ל״ב שנה ואבקש את כ״ק אד״ש לברכני. צבי הירש בן דאבא.״

פני קדשו היו מאירים ושאל: ״וואָס מאַכט די טאָכטער?״ (כי לפני ימים אחדים מסרתי לכ״ק על דבר ה״הייווס״ והן כתמים אדומים שנראו על כל בשרה של בתנו שרה תחי׳, וב״ה שכעבוד ימים אחדים ירדו). ואמרתי שהוטב לה אלא שבכלל איז זי אַ צעקיאָכענע, וגם הקיאה במוצש״ק. ושאל: ״ווי איז ביי אייך אין שטוב, הייס צי קאַלט?״ ואמרתי: געוויינטלעך. ואמר: ״מסתמא איז עס פון דער היץ״.

ואמר: האָסט מסתמא געהאַט שבת אַן עלי׳. ועוד לא גמר דבריו, והביט בהצעטל, ואמר: ״ס׳איז דאָך כ״ז אלול, נו, וועסטו שבת בעטן אַן עליה, וביום ההולדת וועסטו געבן צדקה פאַרן דאַוונען און פאַר מנחה און זאָלסט האָבן אַ שנת הצלחה און דער אויבערשטער זאָל דיר געבן, דיר מיט דער בעל-הבית׳טע מיט די קינדער אַ כתיבה וחתימה טובה, לשנה טובה ומתוקה

התוועדות בשנות הכ"פים

בגשמיות וברוחניות גם יחד". ושאל: וועסט פאָרן ערב ר"ה אויפן ציון? ואמרתי: "אי"ה", ואמר "נו, וועסטו לאָזן אַ צעטל און וועסט אויך דערמאָנען וועגן דיין יום הולדת. ס'איז דאָך אויף איבערמאָרגן". והשי"ת ימלא ברכתו הקדושה לטוב לנו.

ביום ה', כ"ג אלול, אמר כ"ק שליט"א כל הקדישים בכל התפילות. בשחרית עברתי לפני התיבה*. כ"ק עלה לתורה, ולקח אתו את הסידור תורה אור ואמר קדיש אחר הקריאה. סדר הברכה: אוחז את הס"ת בעצי חיים ולפני אמרו ברכו מגביה את הספר קצת וכן מגביה בסוף הברכה, וכן בברכה האחרונה.

בעת הקדיש שאמר בהסידור אחז ביד ימינו בעץ החיים. סדר הקדיש: . . . [נחתך הכת"י קצת] ויצמח פורקניה... בעגלא... יהא ש"ר – ומגביה – יתברך וישתבח ויתפאר ויתרומם ויתנשא (בכל מילה מרכין יותר עמוק) ומגביה בויתהדר... שמי' דקוב"ה... – דאמירן בעלמא. באמרו: וחיים טובים עלינו מנענע בראשו. בעושה שלום ג' פסיעות מלאות לאחוריו: עושה – לימינו; שלום – לשמאלו; במרומיו – לפניו; הוא – זוקף. ועל כו' ואמרו אמן –

*) בהיותו בשנת האבילות על פטירת אביו, ר' משה דובער ע"ה בניסן שנה זו (תש"כ).

מגביה עקביו. (באמרו תתקבל כאשר עובר לפני התיבה מרכין ראשו מעט מאוד.) אמר עם הציבור לדוד אורי וכמדומה גם אר״א א׳ ר׳ חנינא ותנא דבי אלי׳. ועלינו.

החיובים אומרים קדיש אחרי גמרו הוא את הקדיש. בעת שאמרנו קדיש וכן באמירת יתר המזמורים אחר משניות, ואחרי התפילה גמר את משניות ובקול רם בע״פ: מחט שהיא נתונה על מעלת המערה... ר׳ חנניא ב״ע אומר... ובאמרו שורות תניא בלחש מעביר יד שמאלו על עיניו.

כן אמר קדיש היום בש״ק (כמדומה יא״צ דודתו הרבנית מרת חי׳ מושקא ז״ל). אמר גם את הקדישים אחרי אמירת כל ספר התהלים לפני התפילה. אחרי אמירת כל התהלים ראיתי שפתח על הדף שבו נדפס היהי רצון שאחר תהלים. בעת שאמרנו הקדישים עמד וישב אחר אמירת דאמירן בעלמא ואמרו אמן. תהלים אומר בספר יהל אור הוא תהלים אהל י״י השלם.

בשעה 1.30 התועד, היו ג׳ שיחות שתים לפני המאמר ואחד לאחריו. ותוכן: אתם נצבים היום כולכם ראשיכם כו׳, גם המאמר פתח אתם נצבים. בהשיחה האחרונה בכה הרבה ודיבר בקול נמוך ודיבר מענין התשובה אַז ס׳מאַכט איבער די שנה העברה, ועל ידי זה גם אילני סרק מוציאים פירות והם אלה מבנ״י שאין בהם תורה ומצוות ועי״ז גם יהי׳ כן בגשמיות.

הצלחה אם עושים מסחר ומרויחים. כי מתחלה דיבר אודות תשובה אַז מ׳שטעלט זיך איבער מן הקצה, אבל מה יהי׳ עם המצות הלא הכל הוא מסדר השתל׳. וצריך שהי׳ ט׳ חדשים עד הלידה וכן בכל הענינים וועט דאָך עס זיין איך ווייס ווען, ועל כן אמר האזינו השמים שאמר זה משה, לא כישעי׳, כי משה הי׳ העכער פון וועלט ומצד זה יכול להיות שתלד אשה בכל יום וכן בשאר הענינים, וזהו ענין ההצלחה שעושים מסחר שע״פ טבע, קען מען גאָר ניט פאַרדינען ואדרבה ובכל זאת מרוויחים הרבה מאד אַז מ׳ווערט אַן עשיר גדול בכל הדברים, אלא שצריך להיות ענין התשובה, ואמר הרבה ברכות לשנה הבאה בכתיבה וחתימה טובה. והשי״ת ימלא ברכותיו בכל הפרטים.

התחלתי את הניגון של ר״א מניקאָלאַיעוו (כ״ק אדנ״ע), והיתה התעוררות וכ״ק צוה לחזור אותו פעמיים.

כשהזכיר ענין הפצת המעיינות וקאתי מר התחלתי את הניגון במלים אלו.

בש״ק זה קידש על היין, ואמר גם לחיים. אחרי ההתועדות ברך מעין ג׳, ופתח בעצמו כי בשמחה תצאו.

הת' משולם רוזנפלד שחתונתו הי' השבוע רצה לסדר ז"ב, אבל כנראה שהרב חודקוב לא הי' יכול למסור זאת לכ"ק אד"ש, כי הי' כל הזמן בדבקות.

מוצש"ק שעה 2.30 אחרי סליחות

אמירת סליחות אחרי חצות בשעה 1.10 בערך, וגמרו 1.50, בביה"כ החדש שבנו בחצר בית המדרש. בעזרת נשים עשו מחיצה גבוה מאד למעלה מקומת איש, כי כן צוה הרב חודקוב כנראה בפקודת אד"ש, ואמר שבאם לאו לא יצא כ"ק שליט"א לסליחות. עבר לפני התיבה הר"ש זלמנוב.

אחרי סליחות פנה כ"ק שליט"א להעומדים סביבו והתחיל את הבבא השני' של הניגון רחמנא, ויצא לחדרו והקהל שרו את הניגון ורקדו זמן רב. אני עמדתי בעת האמירה בחדר צא"ח שחלונו יוצאת לבית הכנסת החדש.

על פרשת תרומה

מאת: הרב צבי הירש גאנזבורג

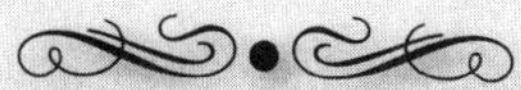

דרשה

פ׳ תרומה

די הייַנטיקע פּרשה, ווי אויך די ווייַטערדיקע סדרות תצוה, ויקהל פקודי, ריידן וועגן בויען דעם משכן און די כלי המשכן מיט אַלע זייערע פּרטים. מיר ווייסן וואָס דער אַלטער רבי זאָגט "והתורה היא נצחיית", אַז די תורה איז אַן אייביקע, און חסידות טייַטש דאָס אויס אַז אויסער דעם וואָס די דיני התורה בייַטן זיך ניט אין קיין שום צייַט און אָרט, זייַנען **אַלע** מצוות התורה אַן אָנווייַזונג ווי מיר זאָלן זיך אויפפירן אין אונזער שטענדיקן לעבן.

די מצוות פון בויען דעם משכן און זייַנע כלים, זייַנען אין פּלוג געזאָגט געוואָרן, ווי צו טאָן זיי אין מדבר ווען די אידן זייַנען אַרויס פון מצרים. פרעגט זיך די שאלה: וואָס האָבן די אַלע מצוות פאַר אַ שייכות צו אונז צו אין אונזער צייַט.

אויף פּסוק ח׳ אין אונזער פּרשה, "ועשו לי מקדש ושכנתי בתוכם", "זיי זאָלן מיר מאַכן אַ הייליקטום" און איך וועל רוען אין זיי, פרעגן די חז"ל: עס האָט דאָך געדאַרפט שטיין, "איך וועל רוען אין **אים**", בתוכו, אין משכן, און זיי ענטפערן: "בתוך כל אחד ואחד מישראל", אַז דער אויבערשטער וועט רוען אין יעדן אייַנציקן אידן. דאָס מיינט, אַז פּונקט ווי כלל ישראל איז מחוייב צו מאַכן אַ מקדש וואו השי"ת זאָל זיך כביכול געפינען, אַזוי איז יעדער יחיד מחוייב צו מאַכן ביי זיך אין האַרצן אַ הייליקן אָרט וואו השי"ת זאָל זייַן. און אָט די מצוה פון מאַכן אַ פּערזענלעכן משכן, איז פאַרשטייט זיך אויך שייך צו יעדערן פון אונז אין אונזער צייַט.

ווי קען עס אַ איד מאַכן אַז ער אַליין זאָל ווערן אַ משכן פאַר דעם אויבערשטן? דאָס וועלן מיר פאַרשטיין פון די ווייַטערדיקע פּסוקים, וואָס זאָגן אָן ווי דער משכן און די כלים זאָלן געבויט ווערן.

די ערשטע מצוה איז צו מאַכן דעם ארון וואו עס זאָלן זיך געפינען די לוחות. דאָס איז געווען דער הייליקסטער אָרט אין משכן און בית המקדש, אַן אָרט וואָס האָט קיינמאָל ניט געטאָרט געריירט ווערן, ווייל עס האָט זיך דאָרט געפונען די טייערסטע זאַך – די תורה וואָס פאַרבינדט אידן מיט דעם אויבערשטער. אויך אין דער אידישער האַרץ איז פאַראַן אַן אָרט וואָס טאָר קיינמאָל ניט באַרירט ווערן, און ווערט טאַקע קיינמאָל ניט אָנגערירט. דאָס איז דאָס פינטעלע איד, די נקודה פון דער אידישער נשמה, וואָס איז גאַנץ אין אַלע צייטן און אין אַלע אומשטענדן. ווייל דאָס איז די אידישע ג-טלעכע געשטאַלט וואָס קען בשום אופן ניט געענדערט ווערן. ווי דער זוהר זאָגט, כאָטש אַ איד באַוועגט זיך אין פאַרשיידענע ריכטונגען – און צוליב אומשטענדן קען ער זיך אַמאָל בייטן – ווערט אָבער זיין אינערלעכע געשטאַלט זיין אַלעמאָל גאַנץ.

דאָס איז נאָך אָבער פאַר אונז ניט גענוג. דאָס אינערלעכע פון האַרצן מוז אויך ווירקן אויף דער מענטשלעכע אויפפירונג, און וואָס איז ספעציעל שייך פרויען זאל זיך דאָס אָנזעען אין דער הנהגה פון שטוב און דער חינוך פון די קינדער. האָט מען אונז אויך געהייסן מאַכן אַ שולחן, אַ טיש.

די גמרא זאָגט, אַז דער אידישער טיש ווערט גערופן דער "שולחן אשר לפני ה'", דער הייליקער ג-טלעכער שולחן, און ער האָט דעם כח צו מכפר זיין אויף די זינד ווי דאָס איז געווען מיט די קרבנות אין בית המקדש. ווי אַזוי? דערמיט וואָס ער באַווירקט דאָס הויז מיטן הויזגעזינט. אויב צום טיש ווערן געלאַדן אָרעמעלייט ווען מ'גיט אָפּצועסן – ווערט ביי די קינדער טייער די מצוה פון צדקה און הכנסת אורחים; אויב מ'האָט דעם זכות צו געבן ביים טיש עסן צו אידן תלמידי חכמים לערנט מען זיך פון זיי תורה און מדות טובות. דאָס איז דאָך געווען אַמאָל דער מנהג פון געבן ישיבה בחורים צו עסן "טעג", וואָס דורך דעם זיינען ביי די בני בית געוואָרן טייער די לומדי תורה. זיי האָבן געזען ווי מ'איז מכבד די תורה לערנען, האָבן דורך דעם די אינגלעך באַקומען אַ דראַנג צו לערנען תורה און די מיידלעך – זיי זאָלן זיך פאַרבינדן מיט בני תורה אויפן גאַנצן לעבן.

באַזונדער אין אונזער צייט, ווען דער רבי שליט"א האָט איינגעפירט, מ'זאָל אַרייננעמען צו זיך אויך אַזעלכע אידישע קינדער וועלכע זיינען נאָך דערווייל

ווייט פון תורה און מצוות און מיר דאַרפן זיי באַווירקן מיט **אונזער** אויפפירונג, מיר זאָלן זיי מקרב זיין צום אויבערשטן – איז גמר גוט פאַרשטאַנדיק ווי דער שולחן איז אויף אונז מכפר. ווייל די מצוות פון יענע אידן ווערן אויך פאַררעכנט אויף אונזער חשבון, און **זייערע** מצוות און גוטע מעשים זיינען ביי השי"ת גאָר גאָר טייער, עס ווערן דאָך דערנעענטערט זיינען קינדער וועלכע זיינען פון אים געווען אָפגעפרעמדט.

אויך האָט מען אונז געהייסן מאַכן אַ מנורה אין דעם משכן און בית המקדש. די גמרא פרעגט: "וכי לאורה הוא צריך?" פעלט דען ליכטיקייט ביים אויבערשטן? היינט צו וואָס דאַרף מען באַלייכטן דעם בית השם? און די גמרא ענטפערט: בכדי די **גאַנצע וועלט** זאָל וויסן, אַז די שכינה רוט צווישן אידן. די פענצטער אין בית המקדש זיינען געווען געבויט אַזוי, אַז אין אינעווייניק זיינען זיי געווען שמאָל און אין דרויסן ברייט. ניט ווי אין מענטשלעכער הויז, וואו די פענסטער ווערן געמאַכט בכדי צו באַלייכטן דאָס הויז, נאָר פאַרקערט, בכדי דאָס ליכט פון בית המקדש זאָל באַלייכטן די גאַס.

פאַרשטייען מיר שוין אַליין דעם מיין פון דער מנורה אין דעם אידישן הארץ-משכן: מיר דאַרפן טאַקע אַריינברענגען קדושה צו אונז, מיר מוזן אָבער אויך באַלייכטן די אידישע גאַס, אַז אויך אַנדערע אידן זאָל ווערן ליכטיק מיט דער ליכט פון תורה, קדושה און חסידות. דאָס איז דאָך וואָס דער רבי שליט"א פאָדערט פון אונז צו פאַרשפרייטן אידישקייט און די קוואַלן פון חסידות אויך אין "דרויסן", די אַרבעט פון "ופרצת".

אַזוי ווערן אויך אויסגעטייטשט די איבעריקע כלי המשכן מיט אַלע זייער פרטים.

דאַן ווערט אונז אָנגעזאָגט, אַז די ראם פון משכן זאָל ווערן געבויט פון עצי שטים, דאָס איז אַ האָלץ פון אַ געוויסן בוים וואָס ווערט גערופן שיטים, טענענבוים. דער וואָרט שיטים האָט אָבער אין לשון קודש נאָך אַ טייטש: שיטה, הטי', אָפגעקערט. דאָס איז אויך די סיבה, וואָס אַ נאַרישן מענטשן רופן מיר מיטן נאָמען, שוטה, ווייל ער קערט זיך אָפּ פון דעם נאָרמאַלן

מענטשלעכן אויפפיר.

די גמרא זאָגט: א מענטש טוט ניט קיין עבירה ביז אים באַפאַלט אַ רוח שטות, ער באגייט אַ נאַרישקייט. אויב אַ מענטש וואָלט געפילט אַז מיט טאָן אַן עבירה ווערט ער אָפּגעריסן פון דעם אויבערשטן, וואָלט ער זי בשום אופן ניט געקענט טאָן. נאָר די נאַרישקייט פאַרבלענדט אים די אויגן און אים דוכט זיך אַז ער בלייבט נאָך אַלץ דער זעלבער איד.

דערפאַר ווייסן מיר, אַז ווען עס קומט צו אַ זאַך וואו דער מענטש קען זיך ניט נאַרן, ווי למשל, ווען מ'צווינגט אַ אידן צו שמד, ח"ו, איז יעדער איד גרייט צו אַוועקגעבן זיין לעבן, אין בוכשטעבלעכן זין און ניט ווערן אָפּגעריסן. דאָס האָט מען אויך געזעען ביי אידן וועלכע זיינען געווען גאָר ווייט פון אידישקייט ווי דער אַלטער רבי האָט געזאָגט: "אַ איד ניט ער וויל און ניט ער קען זיין אָפּגעריסן פון דעם אויבערשטן". נאָר אין אַנדערע, קלענער עבירות פילט מען ניט אַזוי פיל ווי מ'ווערט דערווייטערט און אָפּגעריסן צוליב דער נאַרישקייט וואָס פאַרבלענדט די אויגן און פאַרטעמפּט די געפילן.

בכדי צו אַריבערוועגן אָט דעם שטות פון דער אַנדער זייט, האָט מען אונז געהייסן בויען דעם אינערלעכן משכן פון הייליקע עצי שטים, דעם הייליקן "שטות", דאָס מיינט זיך פירן אין דעם וועג פון חסידות און קדושה ניט אויפן דורכשניטלעכן וועגן. אַפילו לויטן שולחן ערוך קען מען געפינען גענוג וועגן אויף צו מאַכן זיך גרינגער. מיר מוזן אָבער טאָן אונזער דינסט צום אויבערשטן אַפילו מיט זאַכן וואָס זיינען אונז ניט פאַרשטענדלעך אין נאָרמאַלן שכל, אַ זאַך וואָס מענטשן קענען אַמאָל באטראַכטן ווי נאַריש, ניט מענטשלעך.

די גמרא דערציילט וועגן איינעם פון די אמוראים, וואָס פלעגט פריילעך מאַכן חתן כלה אין אַ וועג וואָס האָט פאַר די אַנדערע מענטשן אויסגעקוקט ווילד. אָבער ווען ער איז נסתלק געוואָרן, האָט אַ זייל פון פייער אָפּגעטיילט אים פון די אַנדערע מענטשן. דאָס איז דער ריכטיקער מיין פון שטות דקדושה. דאָס איז די ראם אין וועלכער מיר דאַרפן בויען דעם משכן פון אונזער האַרץ, און דאַן זיינען מיר זיכער אַז דער אויבערשטער רוט צווישן אונז – ושכנתי בתוכם.

מכתבים

מכתבים שקיבל ר' צבי הירש מחבריו

מ"בית חיינו" 770

ר' צבי הירש (עומד מאחרי הרב יוסף וויינברג) עומד סמוך לרבי בחתונת הרשד"ב גולדשמידט

ראש השנה תשי"ב

ב"ה, יום ד' ה' תשרי תשי"ב, ברוקלין.

ידידי מחותני מר צבי הירש שי' גנזבורג

שלום וברכה!

אחדשה"ט, אתפלא שאינך עונה לי על מכתבי, בטח קבלת הרשימה דתוכן השיחות דח"י אלול, גם קטע השיחה שיצאה לאור. עדיין לא גמרתי לרשום סיום תוכן השיחות דח"י אלול, כמו"כ המאמר והשיחה דפ' נצבים וילך ובימים אלו אי"ה אסדר זה, ואשלח לך. אך לפלא שאינך כותב כלום.

לעת אתה אני ישלח לך רשימה קצרה (זהו לא בכלל רשימות הקצרות שאחרי כל התועדות, רשימה זו אסדר לחוד, אף שלא יהי' בה יותר מברשימה זו, אך למען הסדר אסדר כך מיום ב' דר"ה.

תשליך הי' ביום ב' דר"ה כמובן, ולהיות שכ"ק אדמו"ר שליט"א רצה שגמר הסעודה יהי' קודם השקיעה, כדי שיוכל לחלק הכוס של ברכה, לכן הלכו במהירות גדולה (בדיוק יותר – מ'איז פשוט געלאָפען) לתשליך. כשגמרו לומר התשליך, צוה כ"ק אדמו"ר שליט"א לרקוד שם, כמו בכל שנה, אבל הרקוד הי' בקיצור. ומיד שבאו, כעבור חמשה רגעים לערך, מיד הופיע כ"ק אדמו"ר שליט"א לביהמ"ד, מקום ההתועדות. וגם בעת הסעודה לא דיבר כלום, לבד מה שצוה לומר לחיים, ולנגן ב' הנגונים, כמבואר בהרשימה.

ביום א' דר"ה עלה לתורה למפטיר והי' הרבה בכיות, גם ביום ב' בכה במפטיר, ובהפסוקים שקודם התקיעות.

בניגון של הפסוקים, הי' שינויים קלים, מכמו דשנה העברה. א' השינויים הוא, שתי' עלה שבפסוק עלה אלקים, לא ניגן כלל, רק כמו בשאר הפסוקים.

כמו"כ, אמר תי' במרחב, עם חי"ת קמוצה, כמ"ש בסידור. (בא' המאמרים דשנת תרצ"ז, אי' שמקובל שצריך לומר עם חי"ת פתוחה, אף שעפ"י דקדוק הוא חי"ת קמוצה) – בשנה העברה אמר עם חי"ת פתוחה – כ"ה בזכרוני

ובזכרון הרבה בחורים (מסתמא גם אתה זוכר זה).

אבקשך לכתוב לי ומה לכתוב, הרי תוכל בעצמך לשער מה שמעניין לי.

ידידך הפורש בשלומך, ומברכך בכוח"ט בתוך כלל ישראל.

יואל

שכחתי לכתוב, שתקיעה הראשונה תקע כ"ק אדמו"ר שליט"א בעצמו.

הגיע לך ברכת שנה טובה, איני ידוע ממי, ואפשר שזה מעניין לך לכן אני שולח לך המצורף.

עזריאל שי' חייקין יש לו כל השיחה דיום ב' דר"ה ותוכל לראותה אצלו.

יואל

שבט תשי"ד

ב"ה, ב' שבט תשי"ד ברוקלין

כבוד חברי היקר מר צבי הירש שי'

שלום וברכה!

זה זמן מה שהנני מחכה למכתב ממך לשמוע משלומך הטוב ומהנשמע אצלך בפרנסתך ועדיין מחכה אני על זה, וכנראה אַז מ'קען נאָך וואַרטען.

בודאי שמעת אודות החדשות אצלי, התנאים לא התקיים עדיין ומקוים אשר תיכף אחר היאָרצייט יהי' זה. לע"ע הנני לומד עדיין (איך מיין אַז איך דאַרף) ואחר שאקבל הסמיכה נראה מה שיהי'.

כן בודאי שמעת אודות הקישורי-תנאים של הת' מרדכי שאַרפשטיין שהתקיים במוצש"ק העבר עם בת הרב ישראל זובער ע"ה, והתנאים של משה יעקב טעלעשעווסקי עם בת ר' חיים מינקאָוויץ של טאָראָנטאָ, ובמחנכם התקיים התנאים של שלום דובער שניאורסאָהן עס איז געווען אַ פריילּיכע וואָך, פיר חתנים. כן מקוים אשר תתפשט עוד בשבוע זו או בשבוע הבע"ל, כן ירבו.

לבד מזה אין חדשות בהישיבה הכל כרגיל. אצל . . . שי׳ (הידוע) אין חדשות גם כן, אשר זה אינו דבר המשמח. כי כפי שאתה יודע טבעו, הנה הוא חשב אשר יכול לקנות פסוק ח״י פעמים ח״י און ער וועט פייפין אויף אַלע גבירים, ולדאבון אשר עדיין אינו עושה שום דבר, ובאמת אינו יודע במה להתחיל, כי כנראה רצון כ״ק אדמו״ר שליט״א שהוא יקבל משרת רבנות, דבר שהוא נגד רצונו, און ווי וועט ער אויסקומען מיט בעלי-בתים, ער קען נאָך אָפּ זידלען פון קאָפּ ביז אונטען. ומקוים שבמשך איזה ימים יתברר הדבר איך יעשה. ולע״ע איז פריילעך מיט אים, הוא נערוויז במאד און זייער ווילד, והשי״ת יעזרהו בכל עניניו.

בש״ק העבר, כמו בכל שבת מברכים הי׳ התועדות ואמר מאמר ד״ה וארא אל אברהם וגו׳, ושמי הוי׳ לא נודעתי להם, והקשה הקושיא הידוע הלא כבר התודע בשם זה אל האבות וכן אל בנ״י שהיו במצרים, וכן אל פרעה שאמר מי הוי׳, אשר אשמע בקולו, היינו שלא רצה לקבל משם הוי׳ אלא אלקים יענה שלום פרעה, הלא ידע משם זה, וביאר אשר יש שם הוי׳ דלתתא ושם הוי׳ דלעילא, כעת מה שגלוי בעולם הוא ממכ״ע וסוכ״ע שהוא עיקר החיות הוא נמצא בעולם אבל בהעלם, וזהו עבודת האדם לעשות לו ית׳ דירה בתחתונים אשר שם דר בכל עצמותו ולא רק הארה, וכן הוא בגילוי זה אשר ע״י תומ״צ, שזהו תכלית כוונת בריאת העולם, וזה התחיל ביציאת מצרים, כמ״ש בהוציאך את העם וגו׳ תעבדון וגו׳ על ההר הזה, הרי יציאת מצרים הוא התחלה להר סיני אשר זהו תכלית כוונת הבריאה, ועי״ז עושים לו דירה אשר יומשך בכל עצמותו היינו בחי׳ סוכ״ע, וזהו הענין דשם הוי׳ דלעילא, אשר יתגלה בביאת המשיח, ולע״ע הוא גילוי שם הוי׳ דלתתא אשר משם זה ידעו האבות וכן בנ״י. החיזוק והכח על זה, היינו שיוכל לעבוד עבודתו ניתן ע״י משה רבינו, וכן הוא בכל דור ודור אשר אתפשטותא דמשה בכל דרא, אשר הם הנותנים כח לכל או״א, און דער אויבערשטער זאָל העלפין אַז דער רבי זאָל אונז ברייננגען אל ארץ זבת חלב ודבש פריער ברוחניות (באמרו זה בכה הרבה) און נאָכער אל ארץ זבת חלב ודבש בגשמיות, אונז פירען אל ארצנו הקדושה בביאת משיח צדקנו במהרה בימינו.

כמובן שזהו רק מילים אחדים ממה שנאמר והיות שאין הזמן גרמא להאריך וועל איך יוצא זיין מיט דעם. כן הי׳ רק רייד א׳ ותוכנו, בסדרה וארא מתחיל הגאולה דאי׳ במדרש אשר כשהביא הקב״ה המכות על מצרים בטלו עבודה מאבותינו. וזהו התשובה על מה שמסיים בהסדרה הקודם אשר משה בחזרו

ממצרים טען להקב"ה הצל לא הצלת ולמה הרעות לעם הזה, והיינו אשר החשך הי' כל כך כפול ומכופל אשר לא רק האנשים פשוטים לא ראו שום הצלה מגלות זה ולא רק הזקנים אלא אפילו משה רבינו, מנהיג הדור לא ראה, היינו שהגלות הי' כל כך מר ורע. וע"ז בא תיכף התשובה אשר דוקא מזה יבוא ההצלה, וזהו אשר תיכף התחיל להביא המכות עליהם, וזהו הוראה לכל אחד אשר גם אם בעבודתו בא זמן כזה שאינו רואה שום אויסוועג און דער גלות איז אַ חשך כפול ומכופל ואינו יודע איך יפטר מזה, און אויב מיתתן של צדיקים גדולה מחורבן ביהמ"ק הי' גם זה אשר מנהיג הדור נסתלק ועלה למדרי' יותר עליונה אשר וואָס קען זיין אַ גרעסער גלות פאַר דעם, דאַרף מען וויסען אַז עס איז די התחלה פון דער גאולה, וואָס דער גאולה איז אַ גאולה אשר אין אחרי' גלות, ובפרט אשר זהו החודש אשר בו הי' עליית מנהיג הדור למדרי' יותר עליונה וממילא הוא מעלה עמו כל הענינים, צריכים לעשות כל מה שאשר ביכולתינו לעזור לו בזה.

הרייד הי' קצר לפי ערך היינו רק איזה מינוט, וזהו בערך תוכן הרייד, לא הי' אויפגעלייגט כל כך.

מעולם הדפוס, הנני יכול לבשרך אשר לבד התניא החדש אשר יצא לאור ליום י"ט כסלו, אשר בו נדפס החוברת "מפתחות" מכ"ק אדמו"ר שליט"א, הנה עתה יצא לאור אותו התניא עם המורה השיעור ועם המפתחות בפורמט כיס, יפה עד מאד. כל הרואה את ההוצאה הזו מתפלא על יפי' הן בגידול האותיות הן בהכריכה, ונוח לשאתו בכיס. עס איז זייער שיין! כן יצא לאור המאמר באתי לגני שאמרו כ"ק אדמו"ר שליט"א ביו"ד שבט תשי"ג, ויצא לאור ליום יו"ד שבט הבע"ל. המאמר רצוף פה.

יותר אין לי מה לחדש והנני לבקשך עוד פעם לכתוב איזה שורות ולהודיע מצבך.

פ"ש לכל ידידינו ומכירנו

לייבל

גנזבורג-ח"א

RABBI MENACHEM M. SCHNEERSON
Lubavitch
770 Eastern Parkway
Brooklyn 13, N. Y.
HYacinth 3-9250

מנחם מענדל שניאורסאהן
ליובאוויטש
770 איסטערן פארקוויי
ברוקלין, נ. י.

ב"ה, כז' אייר תש"כ
ברוקלין

הרה"ח אי"א נו"נ מלאכתו מלאכת
שמים מוה' יצחק שי'

שלום וברכה!

מאשר הנני קבלת מכתבו מכ"א אייר.

ובעת רצון אזכיר את הענינים אודותם כותב-על הציון הק' של כ"ק מו"ח אדמו"ר זצוקללה"ה נבג"מ זי"ע, שעל שמו נקראת הרשת וכל עניני', ובודאי שזה יוסיף עוד בהתעוררות ר"ר שיהי' הכל בהצלחה בכל הפרטים. ותקותי חזקה שלמרות שהוא כתוך יב' חדש ל"ע ול"ע, הרי יעבוד בעבודתו במנוחת הנפש ובטוב לבב ובטחון חזק, אשר חפץ ה' בידו יצליח לפעול להפיץ היהדות ועניני' ובנקודה הפנימית חינוך עטה"ק. [ובן זוגתו תחי'-בעניני' היא], ולא עוד אלא שכיון שעבודת ה' צ"ל לא רק בטוב לבב אלא גם בשמחה, הרי ע"כ צ"ל שאין בזה סתירה. ושמחה פורצת גדר, כוונתי שאף שמוכרחת השערה ותכניה מראש, ככתוב כ"פ, הנה לאחרי שנכנסו בעובי הענין ופועלים במסירה ונתינה ובאופן מסודר, משפיעים מלמעלה הצלחה ותוספת ברכה, שיהי' הס"ה טוב ועוד הרבה יותר מאשר שיערו מראש-הן בענינים הרוחנים והן בענינים הגשמים, ובפרט שבכהנ"ל-גם הגשמיות רוחניות הוא.

מצו"פ ב' מכתבים כללים משבועות האחרונים, שבודאי ינצלום לעניניהם.

בברכה לבשו"ט בכל האמור ולקבלת התורה בשמחה ובפנימיות

מכתב רבינו לר' יצחק גנזבורג לאחר פטירת אביהם, ר' משה דובער ע"ה

RABBI MENACHEM M. SCHNEERSON
Lubavitch
770 Eastern Parkway
Brooklyn 13, N. Y.

HYacinth 3-9250

מנחם מענדל שניאורסאהן
ליובאוויטש

770 איסטערן פּאַרקוויי
ברוקלין, נ. י.

ב"ה, י"ד שבט, ה'תשל"ל
ברוקלין, נ.י.

מרת שרה תחי' גנזבורג

ברכה ושלום:

בעתו קבלתי מכתבה, ומפני סיבות נתעכב המענה עד עתה, בו כותבת אודות פטירת אמה ע"ה, תבדל היא וכל הילדים ואבי' שיחיו לחיים טובים ארוכים, וההרגשים והמחשבות בקשר עם זה.

והנה באמת אין אתנו יודע עד מה הנהגת השם יתברך ויתעלה, אשר הוא בורא האדם ומנהיגו ומשגיח עליו בהשגחה פרטית. אבל בודאי ובודאי אשר הוא עצם הטוב, וכמבנון הידוע – מטבע הטוב להיטיב, ומה שלפעמים הנהגות השי"ת אינן מובנות כלל וכלל בשכל האדם, הרי אין זה פלא כלל, כי מה ערך ליצור מוגבל ומדוד וסופי לגבי בלי-גבול וסוף בכלל ולבלי-גבול ולאין-סוף האמתי. אבל זה הרי רצה השי"ת וגילה מקצת מחכמתו לבני אדם בשר ודם בתורתו הקדושה הנקראת תורה אור ותורת חיים, זאת אומרת אשר היא המאירה דרך האדם בחייו באופן שיהי' אור מושג גם לפי ערך כוחות המוגבלים של האדם. ועל פי המבואר בתורתנו שבכתב ושבעל פה, יש למצוא ביאור והבנה גם במאורע הנ"ל וכיוצא בו.

והביאור הוא בעצם שני פסקי-דינים בהלכה למעשה, אשר לכאורה בסתירה עומדים זה לזה, ולא עוד אלא ששניהם באו באותו הסימן בשולחן ערוך (יו"ד שצ"ד) ובתחלתו: אין מתקשין (בענייני אבלות וכו') יותר מדי (כפי הוראות חכמינו ז"ל) וכל המתקשה כו' עיי"ש. ובסוף סימן זה מובא שמי שאינו מתאבל כמו שציוו חכמים הרי זה אכזרי. והנה, ממה נפשך, באם מאורע מסוג זה טבעי להתאבל, מהו הרעש על המרבה להתאבל, ועד כדי כך שעונשו חמור על זה, כמבואר בשו"ע שם. ואם ענשו חמור עד כדי כך, הרי לכאורה אין זו אכזריות אם האבלות פחותה ממה שציוו חכמים.

וההסברה בזה – מסיום הסימן ממבאר ענין האבלות, ובלשון השו"ע הועתק מהרמב"ם: "יפחד וידאג ויפשפש במעשיו ויחזור בתשובה".

מובן וגם פשוט שהנשמה נצחית היא, שהרי אין כל סבה לומר שבשביל חולי הבשר והדם וכו' יוגרע חיות הנפש או שתתבטל חיות הנפש והנשמה. ואין קלקול זה נוגע אלא רק להבשר והדם עצמם ולהקשר שביניהם לבין הנפש והנשמה. זאת אומרת, שיכול לבוא הפסק הקשר – מיתה, ר"ל – ובהפסק הקשר של הנפש עם הבשר הרי עולה הנפש ומשתחררת מכבלי הגוף והמדידה וההגבלה שלו, ועל ידי המעשים טובים שעשתה במשך היותה בגוף עלי' אדמות נתעלית למצב נעלה עוד יותר מאשר היתה לפני ירידתה בגוף, ובלשון הידוע, שירידת הנפש (בתוך הגוף) היא ירידה צורך עלי', עלי' למעלה מכפי שהיתה קודם הירידה.

מזה מובן שכל הקרוב לנפש זו וכל מי שהיתה יקרה לו צריך להכיר אשר הנפש עלתה למעלה אפילו ממדרגתה שהיתה לפני זה, אלא שבשביל החיים בעולמנו זה הרי זו אבידה. וכמו שכל הקרוב קרוב יותר ויקר בעיניו עלית הנפש מדרגה לדרגה, הרי גם בפרט השני גדול הכאב, כיון שגדול החסרון על ידי היפרדה מהגוף ומהחיים בעולם הזה.

ונוסף לזה גם כן, שלכאורה יכולה היתה הנפש לעלות למעלה עוד יותר דוקא בעולם הזה, ובלשון חכמינו ז"ל במשנתם יפה שעה אחת בתשובה ומעשים טובים בעולם הזה מכל חיי העולם הבא.

כיון ~~מממממממ~~ שבמאורע כהאמור ישנם שני צדדים המכים האמורים – שחרור הנפש מכבלי הגוף ועליתה לעולם נעלה עולם האמת, ולאידך גם גרעון

מכתב תנחומין לשרה תחי' ליבערמאן לאחרי פטירת אמהם, מרת ראשא ע"ה

\- ב -

וחסרון האמורים, מזה התוצאות בשני פסקי-דינים האמורים: שמשך זמן הקצוב על ידי חכמינו ז"ל על פי תורת אמת צריכה להיות אבלות, וביחד עם זה אסור להתקשות יותר מדי (לבטא [illegible]יסים ובכיים אלו עצמם-בתוכן האבלות). ולא עוד אלא שתוכן האבלות הוא-שזקוק החי להסברה למה מגיע לו החסרון והגרעון, שזהו עיקר הטעם שמאורע כהאמור הוא מסוג שמתאבלים עליו - שלכן יפחד וידאג ויפשפש במעשיו ויחזור בתשובה.

ונתוסף עוד על ידי זה-שאז הרי קיים קשר בין החיים בעלמא דין עם הנשמה שעלתה למעלה, שהרי קיימת ונצחית היא ורואה ומתבוננת בהנעשה עם הקשורים והקרובים אלי׳, וכל מעשה טוב הנעשה על ידם מוסיף לה נחת רוח, ובפרט הנעשה על ידי אלה שחינכה וגידלה אותם חינוך המביא לידי מעשים טובים האמורים, זאת אומרת שחלק לה במעשים אלה הנעשים על ידי החינוך שנתנה לילדי׳ ומושפעי׳.

כיון שכל האמור הם הוראות תורתנו, שהיא חכמתו ורצונו של הקב"ה, הרי קיום הוראות אלו עבודת ה׳ היא, עלי׳ נאמר עבדו את הוי׳ בשמחה. וכיון שהתורה ציוותה את כל אחד ואחת על זה, אשר ציווי התורה גם נתינת כח הוא, בודאי ובודאי יש בכח כל אחד ואחת לקיים זה, ולא עוד אלא ככתוב האמור, עבדו את ה׳ בשמחה.

כל האמור הרי הוא בנוגע לכל אחד ואחת מבני המשפחה, ובמדה יתרה ובנתינת כח גדול יותר וגם באחריות גדולה יותר הוא בנוגע לאלה שהם יכולים להשפיע על שאר בני המשפחה, שמהם ומהנהגתם יראו וכן יעשו ויתנהגו. שלכן לכל לראש ההכרח לקיים את האמור לעיל במילואו הוא על ראש המשפחה ועל הגדול שבילדים, כוונתי במקרה זה אלי׳ ולאבי׳ שיחי׳. וגם בזה הרי ההבטחה-יגעת ומצאת.

בהאמור ג"כ מענה על שאלתה במה תוכל להקל וכו׳. והמענה מובן מהאמור - על ידי הנהגה מתאימה לתוכן הכתוב לעיל, ומתוך בטחון חזק בה׳ שתצליח בזה.

ויהי רצון שתבשר טוב בכל האמור, בטוב הנראה והנגלה.

בברכה להצלחה בכל ענינו ולבשו"ט

ב"ה, י"ד טבת, היתש"ל
ברוקלין, נ.י.

הוו"ח אי"א נו"נ מו"ה צבי הירש שי׳

שלום וברכה!

בודאי תראה לו בתו תחי׳ מכתבי מענה על מכתבה היא. וכמפורש שם הדברים מופנים גם אליו, ויתרה מזו, אולי ביותר אליו, שהרי הוא ראש המשפחה, ובפרט שזכה ולמד בישיבת תומכי תמימים, אשר להם ניתן התואר נרות להאיר.

ותקותי חזקה אשר יראה את הדרך ויאיר את הדרך בשביל עצמו ולכל בני ביתו שיחיו, מתאים לתוכן הכתוב, הלקוח מתורתנו הנקראת תורת חיים.

ויהי רצון שיגדל את כל יוצאי חלציו לתורה ולחופה ולמעשים טובים, בטוב הנראה והנגלה.

בברכה.

מכתב לר׳ צבי הירש בהמשך להנ"ל

חב"ד עסקן ר' העשקע גאַנזבורג נפטר געוואָרן

אין ליובאַוויטש שילדערט מען נאָך ווי דער נפטר, אַלס יונגער אלמן, האָט זיך צעזונגען ביים רבי'ן "מי וואַדיאַם ניאַ פאַטאָניעם"

פון יוסף יצחק יעקבסאָן

מאָנטיק ביינאַכט, כ"ג חשון תשס"ו, איז אָנגעקומען די טרויעריקע ידיעה אַז דער באַוואוסטער חב"ד חסיד און עסקן, הרב צבי הירש (העשקע) גאַנזבורג, איז נפטר געוואָרן אין באָקאַ ריטאָן, פלאָרידע, וואו ער האָט געוואוינט אין די לעצטע יאָרן.

הרב גאַנזבורג, 78, איז געווען נישט געזונט במשך די לעצטע פאָר יאָר. מאָנטיק אָוונט האָט ער געהאַט שוועריקייטן אָטעמען. מען האָט גערופן אַן אַמבולאַנס, און מ'האָט אים אַוועקגעפירט אין שפיטאָל, וואו ער האָט אויסגעהויכט זיין נשמה, האָט זיין טאָכטער שיינע יעקבסאָן געזאָגט.

ר' העשקע גאַנזבורג ז"ל

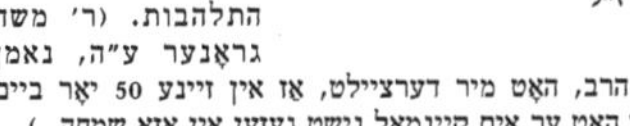

ר' העשקע גאַנזבורג איז געבוירן געוואָרן כ"ז אלול תרפ"ח (1928) אין מאָסקווע צו זיין פאָטער הרב משה דובער און דאָבע. האָט געהאַט צוויי ברידער, לייבל און איטשקע. מען האָט דעם אינגל אַ נאָמען געגעבן נאָך זיין עלטער זיידן, ר' צבי הירש, וועלכער האָט מאריך ימים געווען ביז 113 יאָר (אויף זיין לויה האָט מען געזאָגט אַז ער האָט געלייגט תפילין 100 יאָר...).

די פאַמיליע האָט עולה געווען קיין ארץ ישראל אין 1935, און זיך באַזעצט אין תל אביב. אין 1947 איז העשקע געקומען קיין ברוקלין, לערנען אין דער ליובאַוויטשער ישיבה תומכי תמימים נעבן דעם פריערדיקן ליובאַוויטשער רבי'ן, אדמו"ר ר' יוסף יצחק זצ"ל. אין 1948 האָט ער געפרעגט ביים רבי'ן צי ער זאָל צוריקפאָרן קיין ארץ ישראל כדי צו אָנטיילנעמען אין דער מלחמה. דער רבי האָט געזאָגט, אַז אַ דיזערטיר איז נישט דער וועלכער גייט נישט אויפן פראָנט, נאָר דער וועלכער פאַרלאָזט זיין פאָזיציע אין אַ צייט פון מלחמה. דיין פאָזיציע איז צו זיצן דאָ און לערנען תורה...

אין 1952 האָט העשקע חתונה געהאַט אין מאָנטרעאָל מיט ראַשע דענבערג ע"ה. מיט עטלעכע יאָר שפעטער האָט ער זיך באַזעצט אין ניו יאָרק, וואו ער האָט געאַרבעט אין דער דרוק פאַבריק פון די שולזינגער ברידער, אין "בלשן" דרוק, ביז ער האָט געגרינדעט "עמפייער פרעס" (בשותפות מיט יבלחט"א ר' מאָטל חן). דער נפטר איז געווען אַ מיטגליד פון דער הנהלה פון צעירי אגודת חב"ד, און זייער אַקטיוו אין די "מבצעים" פון דעם ליובאַוויטשער רבי'ן. ער האָט אָפט באַזוכט טורמעס און מיליטערישע אַנשטאַלטן כדי צו מזכה זיין די אידן דאָרט מיט מצוות. ער האָט אויך פיל געאַרבעט אין צוגרייטן די שיחות פון ליובאַוויטשער רבי'ן צום דרוק און איז געווען דער אָפיציעלער "בעל מנגן" ביי די פאַרברענגענישן פון דעם רבי'ן, דער וועלכער פלעגט אָנהויבן די ניגונים נאָך דעם רבינ'ס שיחות.

דער נפטר איז געווען אַ גוט באַוואוסטער חסידישער טיפ, אַ איד אַ פיקח, מיט אַ זעלטענעם הומאַריסטישן חוש, אַ האַרציקע גוטמוטיקייט און אַ טיפן הרגש פאַר אהבת ישראל.

סוכות תש"ל, 1969, האָט ער פאַרלוירן זיין יונגע פרוי, מרת ראַשאַ לבית דענבורג ע"ה. זי איז געשטאָרבן פון לוקימיאַ אין עלטער פון 37 און איבערגעלאָזט פינף יונגע קינדער, וועלכע דער נפטר האָט געהאָדעוועט. צווישן חב"ד חסידים דערציילט מען נאָך אַלץ וועגן יענעם שמחת תורה 1969, ווען בעת דעם פאַרברענגען פון דעם ליובאַוויטשער רבי'ן, האָט ר' העשקע, אַ פרישער אַלמן, אָנגעהויבן זינגען דעם רוסישן-חסידישן ניגון "מי וואדיאָם ניאַ פאַטאָניעם"... ("אין וואַסער וועלן מיר נישט דערטרונקען ווערן און אין פייער וועלן מיר נישט פאַרברענט ווערן"). ווען דער רבי האָט געזען ווער עס האָט אָנגעהויבן דעם ניגון – און וואָס פאַראַ ניגון עס איז געווען! – איז ער ממש ווי אויפגעשפרונגען פון זיין אָרט און אָנגעהויבן טאַנצן מיט אַ מוראדיקע און אומבאַשרייבלעכע התלהבות. (ר' משה גראָנער ע"ה, נאמן בית הרב, האָט מיר דערציילט, אַז אין זיינע 50 יאָר ביים רבי'ן האָט ער אים קיינמאָל נישט געזען אין אַזאַ שמחה...)

מיט עטלעכע יאָרן שפעטער האָט ר' צבי הירש געהייראַט מרת הענטשאַ לבית סטאָון, די טאָכטער פון דעם באַוואוסטן אידישן פילאַנטראָפּ, אוירווינג (יצחק) סטאָון ע"ה.

ר' העשקע האָט איבערגעלאָזט אַ פרוי, הענטשאַ; צוויי זין, ר' ישעי' און ר' בערל, דריי טעכטער, שרה און איר מאַן הרב חיים מאיר ליבערמאַן, רייכל און איר מאַן הרב אהרן מאיר מאַרגאָלין און שיינע חי' און איר מאַן הרב סימון יעקבסאָן, ווי אויך מערערע אייניקלעך און אור אייניקלעך. זיין ברודער, ר' איטשקע גאַנזבורג ז"ל, איז נפטר געוואָרן פאַראַיאָרן.

דינסטיק נאָכמיטאָג איז די לויה אַרויס פון דעם שומרי הדת טשאַפּעל אין באָראָ פּאַרק, אַדורכגעגאַנגען דעם גרויסן ליובאַוויטשן בית מדרש אויף 770 איסטערן פאַרקוויי, וואו אַ גרויסער עולם האָט באַגלייט דעם נפטר אויף זיין לעצטן וועג. דער נפטר איז באַערדיקט געוואָרן אין דעם מאָנטיפיאָרי בית החיים, אין קווינס, נישט ווייט פון דעם אוהל פון די ליובאַוויטשער רביים זצ"ל.

און ביי סתימת הגולל האָט איינער פון די אָנוועזנדע שטילערהייט אַראָפּגעלאָזט אַ טרער און זיך אונטערגעזונגען "מי וואַדיאָם ניאַ פאַטאָניעם"...

כתבה הספד באלגעמיינער דזשורנאל על ר' צבי הירש ע"ה